AF518650

Indigenous Markets in India
(A Study in Tribal Areas)

Indigenous Markets in India

(A Study in Tribal Areas)

Dr. K. Mohan Reddy

SERIALS PUBLICATIONS
NEW DELHI (INDIA)

© Dr. K. Mohan Reddy

First Published – 2010

ISBN: 978-81-8387-311-6

All rights reserved with the Publisher, including the right to translate or reproduce this book or parts there of except for brief quotations in critical articles or reviews.

Published by

SERIALS PUBLICATIONS
4830/24, 1st Floor, Ansari Road
Darya Ganj, New Delhi-110002 (India)
Phone : 23245225. Fax : 91-11-23272135
E-mail: serials@satyam.net.in

CONTENTS

FOREWORD

From times immemorial, markets had a crucial role as the conduit for the flow of goods and services from producers to consumers. A simple mechanism of earlier times had become a very complex mechanism as many layers had engulfed this marketisation process. Today we find many interjecting parties between the producer and consumer often at a loss to both the original parties. In the course of time there emerged a classificatory scheme for markets where the minute segmentation had led to markets being labelled as perfect or imperfect, regulated or unregulated, organized or unorganized and even as formal or informal markets. As many features that separate one form or the other are blended in the present market structure, the author of the book rightly employed the word "Indigenous Markets" that combines the characteristics of an imperfect, unregulated and unorganized markets as well as informal markets. He further had chosen to study the nature of indigenous markets in tribal areas as their survival persists even in the era of globalisation. A novel technique employed by the author to unravel the subtleties in the operation of these indigenous markets in tribal areas is to include both tribal and non-tribal farmers in the sample of respondents.

Though many studies had reported the imperfections in the purchase of products from tribals, a regularisation of the marketing process to a certain extent is being monitored by an institution like Girijan Co-operative Corporation and this study undertakes an analysis of the operations of GCC in its entirety. Contrary to the usually held hypothesis that income differences among tribal households is not as stark as the differences among non-tribal households, it had been revealed in this study that at least in the case of agricultural income, the inequalities are more marked among tribal households than the inequalities among non-tribal households. Further, even after their peasantisation, incomes from minor forest produce are substantial additions to the agricultural incomes of the tribal households in the villages chosen for the study in the districts of Adilabad, Khammam and Warangal in the Telangana region of Andhra Pradesh.

Researchers using econometric methods for analyzing data gathered from tribal areas are a rare tribe but the present author joins that group as he meticulously employs statistical techniques like ANOVA, multiple regression, logistic regression analysis and discriminant analysis to draw better inferences from the data collected by him from eight villages in the study area. Findings that he reports from the data so anlaysed also lend support to the sound decision taken by the author to go beyond analyzing the data through two-way and three-way breakups and utilizing simple statistical tools like averages and measures of dispersion. For instance one observation that emerges from this study by applying logit model is that by merely having the institutional lending agencies in the tribal areas do not guarantee and protect the interests of the tribal households as well as the marginal farmers among non-tribal peasants in the tribal areas has its validity as evident from the government's recent debt redemption scheme. Indirectly this study validates Karla Hoff and Joseph Stigler's observation that institutional intervention in the credit market in the form of subsidies may perversely result in increased costs of credit.

The author has drawn inferences that throw new light on the variables influencing marketed surplus. He found that regressors like percentage of produce consumed, percentage of area under commercial crops to be statistically significant in the total sample as well as the sub-samples comprising of tribal households. Thus, non-price variables have a significant role in determining the marketed surplus.

The widely discussed concept of marketable surplus had also been anlaysed in this study and one observation is that the percentage of produce as marketable surplus is relatively higher than the percentage of produce as marketed surplus in the study area and in the case of tribals the percentage of produce as marketed surplus is higher than the percentage of marketable surplus indicating the presence of forced sales.

An observation in this study that should be taken cognizance by literacy missions is that an improvement in literacy status of the respondents, especially in the case of non-tribals has an overall negative influence on linkages. Another observation that needs further probe is that in the case of tribals an improvement in literacy levels, a rise in agricultural income as well as earnings from agricultural labour leads to an increase in linkages rather than reducing it. But a rise in incomes accruing from exchange of minor forest produce (MFP), incomes from non-casual labour would reduce these linkages lending support to observations made in earlier studies. For the sub-sample of tribals the author's finding that the important variables for the discriminant function are agricultural incomes, incomes from wage labour, MFP incomes and proportion of male workers to total workers in that hierarchical order reveals that in spite of various sub-plans for tribal areas, agrarian transition has not yet taken place in the tribal economy.

The author makes an observation that there had been a lot of differences not only among the districts in the marketing process but they also persist between the tribal and non-tribal households. The only variable which was found to be common for all regression equations is the percentage of produce consumed. This work also brings out the divergence in the two broad channels in the tribal markets, namely the institutional and the non-institutional one. The maladies afflicting tribal markets in either of the channels such as under-weighment, excessive driages, underrating of the quality of the products are the common grouses of all producers. Further the tribals outpourings against credit-cum-procurement assistants of GCC showcases the persistence of the deficiencies in the institutional marketing. The study also throws more light on the predominant role of the private traders and merchants in preserving the linkages between credit and product markets. The study also contains suggestions made by tribals to eliminate exploitation at the shandy points. Taking the cue from this work, the policy makers can make a feasibility report based on the suggestions made by tribal peasants for improving the functioning of markets in tribal areas.

I found this work to be a signal contribution in the realm of issue based economic science. To my knowledge, till recently most of the research work on topics such as marketed surplus or linkages between markets had been carried out in respect of well developed markets in non-tribal areas. But this seminal work focuses on the functioning of indigenous markets opening up new vistas of knowledge on hitherto less researched topics in tribal areas such as linkages among different markets and the marketable potential of the produce in these areas. Though doing research in tribal areas poses certain hurdles, the author had succeeded in bringing out a study with great rigour. My comments may be partisan, as I happened to be his research supervisor. But my research experience leads me to applaud my scholar for bringing out this stupendous work in a book form. I have great appreciation for such a thought provoking and critically oriented multi-observation laden work. I have a fond hope that many more utilitarian studies of this nature will flow from the pen of the author.

Prof. C. Siva Rama Krishna Rao
Former Dean, Faculty of Social Sciences
Kakatkya University, Warangal,
Andhra Pradesh

LIST OF ABBREVIATIONS

AC	:	Agricultural Consultant
AO	:	Agricultural Officer
AP	:	Agricultural Produce
CCI	:	Cotton Corporation of India
CCPA	:	Credit-Cum-Procurement Assistant
D.R. Depot	:	Daily Requirements Depot
GCC	:	Girijan Co-operative Corporation
ITDA	:	Integrated Tribal Development Agency
MFP	:	Minor Forest Produce
NABARD	:	National Bank of Agriculture and RuralDevelopment
SAO Loans	:	Loans for Seasonal Agricultural Operations
TRICOR	:	Scheduled Tribes Co-operative Finance Corporation
TRIFED	:	Tribal Co-operative Marketing Federation /Corporation.
VDSS	:	Village Development Support System
VLW	:	Village Liaison Worker
VTDA	:	Village Tribal Development Association

ACKNOWLEDGEMENTS

My acknowledgements here may look long but it is imperative on my part to express my debt to many *individuals* and *institutions* who have helped me untiringly from time to time during my work which leads me to complete both enviable and unenviable tasks of this nature.

The present book is the outcome of my doctoral thesis submitted to Kakatiya University.

This work is the offspring under the able and scholarly guidance of my beloved teacher. Thus, at the outset, I feel that it has been my unique privilege to pursue my work under the able and generous supervision of *Prof. C. Siva Rama Krishna Rao, Former Dean, Faculty of Social Sciences.* I express my profound sense of gratitude and intrinsic affection to him for the valuable guidance, critical remarks on the work from time and again, unending benevolence and co-operation and unstinted encouragement and inspiration while bringing out research study into this shape. Despite the multifarious duties, he always made himself available for frequent consultations and had taken a lot of time with patience in going through every line of the draft and seeing it to reach the present standard. Therefore, I feel that it is too difficult to redeem his debt just by saying these few words. Further, I am also indebted to him for accepting to write the foreword to this book.

I have immense pleasure in expressing my gratefulness to *Prof. V. Gopal Reddy, Former Vice-Chancellor of Kakatiya University, Warangal and Present Vice-Chancellor of Palamoor University, Mahabubnagar and to my teachers, Prof. N. Linga Murthy, Vice-Chancellor of Kakatiya University, Warangal and Prof. Mohd. Iqbal Ali, Vice-Chancellor of Satavahana University, Karimnagar* who have constantly encouraged and provided a congenial atmosphere while carrying out my research work into this form.

I am greatly indebted to *Prof. P. Ramaiah,* Professor of Emeritus, Department of Economics, Osmania University, Hyderabad and *Prof. K. Murali Manohar,* Former Director, School of Distance Learning and Continuing Education, Kakatiya University, Warangal who have been the sources of encouragement for pursuing this work smoothly.

I am very much beholden to *Prof. T. Papi Reddy,* Chairperson, Board of Studies and Controller of Examinations, *Dr. B. Ramulu and Dr. S. Kanakachary* who constantly prodded me to work swiftly and encouraged me from time and again during the period of my study. My thanks are also due to *Prof. B. Janardhan Rao (late) and Dr.(Mrs.) E. Revathi,* who read some of the drafts and made the constructive suggestions.

I am also greatly indebted to the Faculty members in the Department *Prof. (Mrs.) N. Vijaya, Dean, Faculty of Social Sciences, Prof. (Mrs). T. Jyothi Rani, Prof. (Mrs.) B.R.Shayamala Devi, Prof. A. Sadanandam, Prof. G. Rajaiah, Prof. K. Venkat Narayana, Prof. M. Ashok Kumar, Prof. G. Sudershan* and other faculty members who encouraged me during my study.

In particular, I am very much beholden to *Prof. G. Parthasarathy,* Former Director, Institute of Development and Planning Studies, Visakhapatnam, *Prof. D.N. Reddy,* University of Hyderabad, *Prof. S. Kishan Rao,* Osmania University, Hyderabad, for making the critical remarks over my research proposal.

I am highly thankful to my friends *Dr. M. Venkat Reddy, Dr. D. Ravinder, Dr. K. Ramanuja Rao, Dr. G. Laxma Reddy, Dr. S. Radha Krishna, Dr. P. Ravinder, Sri. K. Rambabu, Dr. V. Keshava Rao (Scientist), Dr. K. Ramesh Babu, Dr. K. Ramchandraiah, Dr. S. Vidya Sagar and Sri. V. Sampath Kumar,* who encouraged and helped me at various stages of this work. My thanks are also due to my co-scholar friends, *Dr. M. Ramesh Reddy, Sri. N. Ramgopal Reddy, Dr. Gulam Rabbani, Sri. J. Sreedhar Rao,* who had been of great help during my intensive field investigation. My thanks are also due to other co-scholars, friends and well-wishers, who helped me at various stages of my work.

In particular, I am greatly indebted to *Sri. R.D. Naik,* Incharge Computer Centre, *Dr.(Mrs.)V. Gowri,* Department of Research Methodology, *Dr. D.P. Singh* (Statistical Analyist), *Sri. P.M. Salvi,* Systems Incharge, *Mrs. S. Devdhar,* Hostel Superintendent, *Sri. P.D. Pawar, Sri. S.M. Mahale, Sri. V.K. Sindhe, Sri. Padhke* and other supporting staff of EDP Unit, Tata Institute of Social Sciences, Bombay, for their kind and generous co-operation and benevolent attitude during my stay at their prestigious institute for the data processing.

At this juncture, I deem it a privilege to express my gratitude to all the *sample households* and *other elderly persons* in the villages for their enthusiastic attitude and co-operation extended to me and attention bestowed on me during my field study and investigation.

I place on record my sincere thanks for the co-operation and help rendered by the *officials* and *other personnel of the Eturnagaram, Palwancha and Utnoor Divisions* of GCC who gave access to their innumerable secondary data and further my special thanks are also due to the *CCPAs, AOs, liaison workers and other staff* concerned who actively provided the factual information regarding the villages and the households. Further, my thanks are also due to all the *MROs* concerned who provided me the latest census figures pertaining to the study villages.

I also thank *the authorities* of Kakatiya University for providing me all necessary facilities for publishing this book. I also thank the personnel of various academic and research institutions which I visited for their kind co-operation during my visits from time to time.

I have immense pleasure to acknowledge my debt to *all the family members* of my esteemed supervisor, who extended their kind hospitality towards me during my frequent visits.

Finally, I am heavily indebted to *all my family members.* I acknowledge my gratitude to my better-half *Smt. K. Anitha* and my daughter *Snigdhashree* for their co-operation extended and sparing time to me while bringing out my research work for publication. My special thanks are also due to my younger brothers, *Mr. K. Krishna Reddy, Mr. K. Ravinder Reddy and Mr. K. Venkat Reddy* for making all this possible through their timely and sustained encouragement and for bearing with tolerance, all the domestic problems silently, while I was busy with my research work. I specially owe my debt of gratitude to my grandmother *Smt. M. Susheelamma* and my mother *Smt. K. Venkatamma* for their unstinted encouragement and sustained co-operation to me. It would not have been possible to complete this work successfully but for their selfless manner in which they toiled at home and in fields. At this moment, I pay my tributes to the memories of my late grandfather *Sri. M. Ramchandra Reddy,* late father *Sri. K. Chandra Reddy* and late sister *Smt. K. Vimala* who persistently inspired me to pursue my studies and in the meanwhile they laid down their lives just for the cause of academic development of their offspring. I also thank another sister *Smt. K. Hymavathi* and my brother-in-law *Sri. K. Indra Reddy* for their encouragement to publish my work in a book form.

My thanks are also due to *Mr. M. Bhaskar, Sri. V.V. Nagabhushanam and Sri. D. Devender* for their neat and meticulous typing.

My special thanks are also due to Serials Publications, New Delhi for taking up the publishing work and brining out the book neatly within a short span of time. I also take this opportunity to thank all my friends and well-wishers who inspired me for doing research work on tribals and it is their encouragement that propelled me to publish this work.

K. Mohan Reddy

1

INTRODUCTION

The taxonomy of markets includes many distinctions such as perfect, imperfect markets, regulated and unregulated markets; organised and unorganised markets; formal and informal markets. But markets operating in indigenous communities are not specifically distinguished, though they may be loosely called imperfect market that operates in indigenous communities. In a sense, they are imperfect, unregulated and also unorganised. The above three terms connote different meanings; the word *'imperfect competition"* had been used by *Joan Robinson* to delineate the monopolistic tendencies that prevail in the market structure and in a sense this may represent one aspect of the markets; namely, whether the number of sellers are more or a few in the markets. Imperfections may also mean lack of perfect knowledge about what goes on in the market or rather it may signify lack of perfect information. These aspects have gained importance in the current literature and with the growth of communications and technology, atleast to a certain extent; marketing information is instantaneously available in certain quarters like share-markets. Viewed from this angle, the markets that operate in areas predominantly inhabited by aboriginals are to be labelled as imperfect markets. But a caveat here. In the case of imperfect markets in the literature, certain exploitative practices like underweighment, collection of different types of charges and other practices are not strictly considered as imperfections, since the imperfections reflect only the monopolistic tendencies in the market. Hence, especially in developing countries, government intervention is needed and the distinction we often make from this angle is whether the market is regulated one or an unregulated one.

Regulated markets are often distinguished from unregulated markets in the light of the regulations that are stipulated in the market yards mainly meant for purchases of various commodities on a wholesale basis. For instance, in India the activities in the market are often regulated by Government decrees and this institutionalised system is often guided by constituting marketing committees. In this type of marketing an aspect of prominence is to mitigate the evils of the marketing system through standardisation of commission rates and weighing procedures. Hence, if we call a market as an unregulated one, we can refer only to those aspects but it would not encompass the whole gamut of marketing relations.

A third distinction often made in the literature is with reference to organised and unorganised markets. This distinction highlights the value of inter-personal and social relationships that often play a crucial role in the unorganised markets. The organised markets are supposed to be impersonal in nature, and in the Hicksian sense they can be often regarded as fix price markets or markets where fixed prices prevail. Inspite of the strides made in marketing in the developing economies, markets in these countries do not fit into smoothly operating institutions often assumed in the literature on markets. Information among transactors in both factor and product markets is usually scarce and often incomplete because many institutions are either partially developed or underdeveloped. Various implicit or informal contracts through personalized inter-changes become methods of circumventing the problem of perfect information during production or exchange[1]. The laws and rules are often unable to monitor and organise economic transactions and assure equality of access to every one. Insurance against risks is at best partial, if not restricted to a privileged few. For a vast majority of transactors in the market economy, therefore, regular behavioural relations become necessary methods of defining the *'rules of business'*. As long as these relational contracts are stable over periods of time, they can be expected to generate private and often social wealth[2].

The unorganised market in a different parlance is also called as *'informal sector'*, though the current ILO definition of informal sector is different from one adopted by many writers on the marketing literature. ILO develops this idea mainly with reference to urban areas and its definition of urban informal sector is as follows:

'The informal sector consists of small-scale units engaged in production and distribution of goods and services with the primary objective of generating employment and incomes to their participants not withstanding the constraints on capital, both physical and human know how'[3].

Even if this definition is extended to rural areas, the nature of unorganised markets will be different from the urban informal markets because these informal markets deal with petty trade and business, where the producers are often self-employed, while the unorganised markets not only deal with commodity markets but also deal with factor markets. In this regard various markets are to be reckoned with often, interlinked transactions. *Pranab K. Bardhan* makes a distinction between *'inadequately formed'* markets and *'imperfect'* markets. In an incomplete market, according to him, it may sometimes be possible to conceptually construct price analogs, but they are often far-fetched to be meaningful. For instance, in many loan transactions in the village, particularly when they are inter-twined with transactions with labour or land-lease, it may be very difficult to get an idea of the implicit interest rate charged, taking all the transactions together; the parties involved are themselves unaware or vague about it, not to speak of the question of equality of this implicit rate as between different loan transactions in the same village[4].

'Indigenous communities' have their own special characteristic features. Often we use this term to connote tribal communities or aboriginal societies. A broad view of these

communities will make us understand why the markets operating in these areas are distinct from other markets. According to one view, 'Indigenous communities, peoples and Nations are those which, having a historical continuity with pre-invasion and pre-colonial societies that developed on their territories, consider themselves distinct from other sectors of the societies now prevailing in these territories or parts of them. They form at present non-dominant sectors of society and are determined to preserve, develop and transmit to future generations their ancestral territories and their ethnic identity as the basis of their constrained existence as peoples, in accordance with their cultural patterns, social institutions and legal systems[5].

With the above definition, one will be able to say that the indigenous communities engage in economic activities that range from shifting cultivation in or near forests to wage labour or even small-scale market oriented activities.

Hence, the above version of Indigenous communities engulfs the multi-stranded nature of relationships in small face-to-face communities. *Gluckman* in his studies of tribal Africa has called such societies '*multiplex*' with each individual claiming not one, but a variety of roles in interacting with fellow members of his community. According to *Bailey*, 'the watershed between the traditional and modern society is exactly this distinction between single-interest and multiplex relationships'[6].

Multiplex relationships between the same economic agents in a poor agrarian community are often described as interlinked contracts encompassing several markets, particularly those of land, labour and credit. Besides the interlinkages among factor markets, there can be linkages also between factor markets and commodity markets. In this context, the terms 'market' and 'contract' need to be interpreted somewhat loosely as interlinked factor markets here do not necessarily refer to formal or organized or monetized markets.

Any transaction in the service of these factors based primarily on economic principles is deemed as a 'market' relationship, even though the transactors do not always bid their prices or offer their services in the impersonal atmosphere of an open market place. Similarly a 'contract' does not necessarily refer to explicit contracts with legal sanctions, but more often to implicit agreements enforced by nothing more than the prevailing custom, social interaction, and goodwill in a small closed community and the enlightened self-interest of the individual in a situation of limited alternative opportunities.

The market form of organisation as an ubiquitous one, had been questioned by anthropologists like *Karl Polanyi*. To him, the transactional mode of non-market economies is primarily one of the obligatory payments and some commitment to sharing - what Polanyi calls the principle of reciprocity and re-distribution. But the non-market economies are slowly being converted into market economies and a generation of social anthropologists and empirical economists have shown us how over the years the traditional system of obligatory payments, custom-determined laws and communal sharing and insurance has been eroded by the steady penetration of market forces. This erosion process is slower in some societies than in others, but even in those former cases the evolving transitional patterns show a remarkable degree of sensitivity to market stimuli, and transactions can hardly be described as mere expressions of social obligations. Hence, the simple economic propositions regarding transactions in these societies made on the basis of a market principle may make sense, eventhough different historical categories of markets still coexist, interact, and evolve under the same social formation[7].

But even when the market principle is active, the domain of its operations is quite often rather narrow. Here, one should make a distinction between the expression 'market principle', and 'organised and explicit' market mechanism. For instance, the moral boundaries of the village community tend to have a strong, though not overriding influence on the economic boundaries of the market. The resultant fragmentation is particularly acute in the rural credit market. As agriculture is a business with slow turnover of capital and since extreme poverty leaves little scope for 'internal financing' by peasants, credit plays a crucial role in a poor agrarian economy, and market fragmentation here inexorably leads to a splintering of all the other markets involved in such an economy.

Therefore, markets operating in indigenous communities, especially in tribal economies, can be labelled as indigenous markets as they blend contractual systems with personalised relations. The crucial test of a transition from an insular, subsistence type of life to productive activities in unorganised markets comes about when perceived economic opportunities are seized upon and utilized by negotiating and executing contracts that are stable over a period of time. It is to be mentioned here that in a subsistence-oriented community, most of the agreements may be involuntary in nature based on status. It should also be noted that these behavioural relations may also be seized by certain groups for executing complex business contracts. For instance, ethnic and tribal groups in Asia and Africa sometimes utilized social norms for the execution of business contracts. An example would suffice how this can happen. Early inthiscentury in Ghana some individuals perceived economic opportunities in cocoa cultivation without having the suitable land[8]. Other tribal groups controlled access to such lands 'owned' as communal property. There were no institutions that could facilitate a market transaction between the two groups and two responses emerged. Some of these entrepreneurs utilized their existing kinship relations to negotiate collectively for land. Others, who did not have extended family connections informally contracted with strangers to form 'companies' and again collectively negotiated for lands. Such instances can also be observed in a country like India, where non-tribals though not owners of land enter into contracts with tribals to gain access to their lands and latter control the lives of the tribals also.

Many early writers have shown how these contractual relations play a decisive role in the interlocking of various markets in plain areas but very few studies had been conducted to analyse the interlinkages among various markets in tribal areas. These markets can be considered as imperfect, unregulated, unorganised, and informal in nature. Since no specific term had been used in the literature to explain all these connotations of the markets in tribal areas, an attempt is made here to designate them as 'Indigenous Markets', where they are simultaneously imperfect, unregulated, unorganised, and informal - all rolled into one. These markets contain various types of imperfections either in product markets or in factor markets, and governmental intervention is minimum and their unorganised nature often gives scope for a lot of exploitation. As contracts are informal in these markets, and as also the stability of these contracts is endangered by outside market forces, they do not have a continuity and this gives rise to the indigenous nature of the markets.

In the tribal areas of Andhra Pradesh, there is only one institutional marketing channel that is operating with Governmental support namely, Girijan Cooperative Corporation (GCC). Though this is institutionalised in nature, a few studies on the functioning of GCC highlighted the leakages in its functioning and at times its unsystematic way of conducting marketing transactions. Since it is monopolistic in nature, especially as far as the purchase of minor forest produce (MFP) is concerned from the tribals, they face an imperfect market structure and all the attendant evils of monopoly also surfaced at times in the functioning of this organisation. The other market forms, though may be following the marketing principle, cannot be strictly called as regular markets and their irregularity coupled with the prescribed nature of transactions is a crucial feature of the indigenous markets. As the economy is subjected to more marketing forces, there is an opening of those areas and transitional modes of transactions are taking place in the tribal areas. In order to capture these marketing transactions and marketing principles involved in the indigenous markets operating in the tribal areas, it had been felt that there is a need to study such relations that define the development process in those areas and hence this study had been undertaken. As indigenous markets still flourish among indigenous communities, the study had been undertaken in the tribal areas of Andhra Pradesh, a state which has a concentration of tribal areas among different states in India next only to Madhya Pradesh.

As against this background, the present study is designed with the following objectives and hypotheses.

OBJECTIVES

The objectives of the study are as follows:

(1) To analyse the interlinkages between the credit and product markets in the tribal areas with a view to examine the role of markets in the tribal economy;

(2) to describe the institutional and non-institutional marketing channels in the tribal areas;

(3) to examine the functioning of Girijan Cooperative Corpo-ration, an institutional marketing system in providing marketing facilities for the products grown in tribal areas;

(4) to find out the factors that influence marketable surplus and marketed surplus of the products in tribal areas;

(5) to examine the accessibility of formal and informal credit institutions in the tribal areas; and

(6) to analyse the impact of infrastructural facilities on indigenous markets.

HYPOTHESES

The hypotheses of the study are as follows:

(1) The barter system in the tribal areas is slowly being replaced by a monetised economy, albeit slowly, and this is leading to the tardy growth of rural organised markets in tribal areas.

(2) While the markets are slowly developing for commodities as well as the inputs, the interlinkages between the factor markets, of which credit market has prominence, and product markets are still quite strong in tribal areas which is mainly due to the migration of non-tribals, with an adverse affect on the tribals.

(3) Monetisation of transactions in tribal areas is leading to changes in cropping pattern in such a manner that the tribals are also generating marketable surplus of agricultural produce with the benefits more in favour of non-tribals.

(4) The monopoly of GCC is leading to the decline of the imperfections in the unorganised markets.

METHODOLOGY

The methodology adopted for the study is as given hereunder.

RESEARCH DESIGN

The research design adopted for the study is to examine the functioning of indigenous markets in relation to the institutional and non-institutional marketing process in the tribal areas. For this, the research design adopted in the study is an analytical one where both data from primary as well as secondary sources had been collected. The substantiation part of the analysis had been derived from the sources of the historical data. Further, the collection of the data over the details of the economic history of the tribal formation in the specific region had also been taken up as a preparatory requirement for fundamental theoretical categorisation over the phenomenon of the market and its economic relation with the tribals. This demands an understanding over the origin and penetration of the markets into these regions in the initial stages of the post-colonial and as well during the colonial context. The data on this particular aspect had also been collated from various sources namely the primary sources (interviews with the tribal and non-tribal elders) and the secondary sources. Thus, the data collected through this historical method had been logically linked to the overall contemporary economic transition of the tribal system.

SAMPLE DESIGN

In view of the research design adopted for the study, a sample design had been worked out for the present study. A hierarchical or nested random sampling frame had been

Table 1
A Bird's – Eye View of the Study Area

Name of the District/ Mandal Covered	*Name of the District/ Branch Covered*	*Name of the Shandy/ Day*	*Name of the Village*	*Distance from the Shandy Point*	*No. of Households in the Villages*	*No. of Sample Households in the Village*	*Percentage of Sample units Surveyed**
Khammam/	Palwancha/	Dammapet	1. Anakampalam	17 Kms.	372	40	11.0
Dammapet	Dammapet	on Tuesday	2. Patwarigudem	14 Kms	622	60	10.0
Warangal/	Eturnagaram/	Katapur	1. Pambapur	3 kms	125	50	4.0
Tadvai	Eturnagaram	on Sunday	2. Narsapur	2 kms	125	40	32.0
Adilabad/	Utnoor/	Indravelli	3. katapur	Local	509	10	02.0**
Indravelli	Utnoor	on Monday	1. Wadagon	8 kms	319	40	13.0
			2. Angi	4 kms	100	40	40.0
			3. Indravelli (B)	Local	1090	20	02.0**

* The decimals are rounded upto the nearest number

** The percentage of sample units is less due to the designed sample non-tribal households had been taken up from the undesigned sample villages owing to the non-availability of the non-tribal households in the designed villages.

adopted while selecting the sample households in the study area. At the first stage, three districts in Andhra Pradesh, representing the three different tribal concentrations of the state had been chosen. Among these three districts Khammam is popularly known for Hill Reddies, Warangal is known for Koyas and Adilabad is prominent for Gonds. At the second stage from each of these districts, the area under one divisional office of GCC had also been chosen. At the third stage from each divisional office, the area under one branch office had been chosen. The coverage had been such that at least one Mandal and one Shandy point had also been selected, where the marketing centre is available. At the fourth stage, two and in some cases three villages from each mandal have been chosen at random, where they are located within a radius of 20 Kms. from the Shandy points. Finally, at the fifth stage, from each one of these villages, forty tribal households, and ten non-tribal households have been selected at random. Thus, altogether 240 tribal households have been drawn for the sample from the different tribal groups like Koyas, Gonds, Kolams, Pardhans, Andhs and further, 60 non-tribal households have also been drawn for the sample from different categories - SCs, BCs and OCs. Therefore, on the whole 300 households have been selected for the study from the two different strata - tribals and non-tribals.

In the sample design, further it is to be noted that one branch office out of five in Khammam; one branch office out of four each in Warangal and Adilabad had been selected for the present study. While selecting the jurisdiction under these branches, the number of shandy points under each branch, the procurement made by the branches during the last four and five years and the distance criteria from the shandy point were also taken into account in order to assess the functioning of GCC in the sample villages in the realm of tribal development especially in relation to its credit and marketing objectives. Among branches of GCC, Eturnagaram branch in Warangal division, Dammapet branch in the Palwancha division and the Utnoor branch in the Utnoor division had been selected. The rationale behind in the selection of these branches had been ascribed to the highest procurement than all other branches in the concerned divisional offices[9].

By and large, three villages from the Tadvai Mandal of Eturnagaram branch in Warangal, two villages from the Dammapet Mandal of Dammapet branch in Khammam and finally three villages from the Indravelli mandal of Utnoor branch in Adilabad have been selected for the present study.

Table 2
Village-wise Distribution of Sample Households

Name of the Village	*Region*			
	Khammam	*Warangal*	*Adilabad*	*Row Total*
Ankampalem	40 (100.0) (40.0)	–	–	40 (13.3)
Patwarigudem	60 (100.0) (60.0)	–	–	60 (20.0)
Pambapur	–	50 (100.0) (50.0)	–	50 (16.7)
Narsapur	–	40 (100.0) (40.0)	–	40 (13.3)
Katapur	–	10 (100.0) (10.0)	–	10 (3.3)
Wadagaon	–	–	40 (100.0) (40.0)	40 (13.3)
Anji	–	–	40 (100.0) (40.0)	40 (13.3)
Indravelli(B)	–	–	20 (100.0) (20.0)	20 (6.7)
Col.total	100 (33.3)	100 (33.3)	100 (33.3)	300 (100.0)

Source: Field study and hereafter refers to the same.
Note: Figures in parentheses indicate row-wise and column-wise percentages and hereafter refers to the same.

The panorama of the study area had been depicted in Table -1. The village-wise sample chosen in the three sample districts had also been presented in Table-2, and Table-3 depicts the configuration of the sample tribal and non-tribal households in the selected sample districts.

Here for the non-uniformity of the sample drawn for the study, it should be noted that in the process of selection, the designed sample non-tribal households were not available in the designed sample villages. Hence, the researcher had administered the schedules for the sample non-tribal households in the adjacent villages too. Therefore, though the designed sample villages are only six but for the aforesaid reason, two more villages were added to the originally designed sample villages. Thus altogether it became a study of eight villages.

Table 3

Region-wise and Group-wise Distribution of Sample Households

Group-wise Category	*Region*			
	Khammam	*Warangal*	*Adilabad*	*Row Total*
Tribal	80(33.3) (80.0)	80(33.3) (80.0)	80(33.3) (80.0)	240 (80.0)
Non-tribal	20(33.3) (20.0)	20(33.3) (20.0)	20(33.3) (20.0)	60 (20.0)
Col. Total	100 (33.3)	100 (33.3)	100 (33.3)	300 (100.0)

DATA BASE

The data for the study had been collected from the primary as well as secondary sources. The primary data have been collected through administering the structured interview schedules to the designed sample households to obtain the required information. To obtain the necessary information from the sample households, different types of interview schedules were prepared for the collection of primary data. The village schedule was also designed and served to the key persons in the villages to give an overall picture of the sample villages and the interview schedules were designed and administered to the designed sample respondents to have the intended information. Besides, the researcher had also conducted personal interviews. He also held discussions with private traders, money-lenders, shandy inspectors (credit-cum-procurement assistants), branch managers, measurers, weighing boys and other officials whose involvement is greater on the marketing side. The researcher has gathered necessary information on the basis of field observations. Further, discussions were also made with the old and enlightened people and the concerned village patwaries and the respective village sarpanches in order to have the information as a backdrop for the analysis as in relation to the general village background, *'modus operandi'* of different marketing channels in the villages among the different tribal and non-tribal groups, changing roles of institutional and non-institutional credit agencies as in relation to the charging of different rates of interest, linkages of credit with product markets and the other related oral history of almost all of the aspects peculiar to the designed sample villages of the study area.

In addition to the primary data, the secondary data had also been collected to corroborate with the empirical findings from the various Government Reports on tribals and also the research studies conducted by academicians. The articles published in various journals and the various books published in this area of specialisation had also been referred. In view of the collection of secondary data, the researcher had extensively toured and visited most of the libraries[10] in the State of Andhra Pradesh.

TIME SPAN OF ANALYSIS

The field investigation had been taken-up during the 1994-95 and the data relate to the 1993-94 reference year. Further, the field work had also been carried out at two terminal periods in a year. Prior to the undertaking of the field investigation, the researcher visited the designed sample villages to make a reconnaissance with the help of the local people and at this visit the village schedules were properly filled-in with the help of the old inhabitants and some literate, knowledgeable and other key persons in the villages.

The first phase of investigation had been undertaken in March 1994, where most of the rabi agricultural activities were coming to an end and the tribal households used to begin the collection of minor forest produce (MFP) and this was continued till the end of July 1994, where most of the Khariff agricultural activities had just begun. The second phase of field investigation had also been taken-up in the beginning of

November, 1994 and it was continued upto the end of December 1994, where most of the Khariff agricultural operations were coming to an end and the preparations for the next season (Rabi) were not ready. Therefore, the first phase of investigation had been taken up from the end of March to the end of July 1994 and the second phase of field work had been taken up from the beginning of November to the end of December, 1994. Therefore, altogether, six months had been utilised for the field investigation including the journey days of the researcher. By and large, in each sample village the researcher had stayed for about 20 days for the field investigation. However, the researcher felt that the time spent for field work in the villages was inadequate to have a deeper analysis over the interlinkages in factor and product markets and it had been felt that to understand the multi-farious activities involved in the 'modus operandi' of institutional and non-institutional marketing channels that have been existing since many years requires a much longer stay. But keeping in view of the time and financial constraints, the researcher had documented the information with the help of different interview schedules on the basis of the information provided by the households and the researcher took notes from the field observations and analysed the field notes in the thesis wherever required. Thus, this part of the survey was based on both observational and measurement techniques.

PRELIMINARY SURVEY AND PRE-TESTING

Prior to the field investigation, a preliminary survey and pre-testing was also conducted to decide on the questions to be deleted and to be added to the structured interview schedule. Of the total sample size that had been taken-up at the field investigation, the ten per cent of the interview schedules for both the tribals and non-tribals were served and pre-tested in Damaravai village of Tadvai Mandal during the month of December, 1993. Thus, only after the preliminary survey and pre-testing, a decision was made on the variables to be deleted and to be added and then the structured interview schedule was designed and formulated to obtain the required information from the sample tribal and non-tribal households of the aforesaid sample villages.

PLAN OF DATA ANALYSIS AND TOOLS USED

The data of complex nature had been tabulated in the form of two-way and three-way tables and computed in a suitable form for statistical analysis with the help of the computer software statistical package of SPSS/PC+.

Here, it is to be noted that wherever the tribal and non-tribal group-wise analysis required, only that had been taken-up and wherever the regional analysis required that had also been taken up without making the distinction between the sample tribal and non-tribal households. And finally analysis along regional lines as well as based on tribal-nontribal distinction is sine-qua-non that had also been taken up with the help of three-way cross-breaks.

The tools used for processing the data are, two-way and three-way cross-breaks. Thus, the presentation is often self-explanatory. In addition to the use of measures of central tendency, measures of dispersion and the simple column-wise and row-wise percentages, certain non-parametric and the parametric tests and the other suitable quantitative techniques had also been adopted to find the inter-dependability and the strength of the association between the variables used in the analysis and further to find out the relationships between the parameters used in the analysis. The statistical techniques like, Chi-square and other measures based on chi-square, Karl Pearson correlation co-efficient, analysis of variance, multiple regression analysis, logistic regression analysis and the discriminant analysis had been taken-up and some of them have been explained hereunder.

CHI-SQUARE

The Chi-square test is a test of the independence hypothesis. A statistic often used to test the hypothesis that the row and column variables are independent is the 'Pearson Chi-Square'. For calculating the χ^2 test, the following formula is used:

$$\chi^2 = \Sigma\left(\frac{(f_o - f_e)^2}{f_e}\right) \sim \chi^2 \text{ dist. with (r-1) (c-1) degrees of}$$

freedom.

where fe is expected frequency, while fo is observed frequency.

Likelihood Ratio

It is an alternative measure to the commonly used pearson chi-square and this test is based on maximum likelihood theory and is often used in the analysis of categorical data. For large samples, the pearson and likelihood ratio chi-square statistics give very similar results.

Mantel-Haenszel Test for Linear Association

This is another measure of linear association between the row and column variables in cross-breaks. It is computed by multiplying the squared pearson correlation co-efficient by the number of cases minus 1.

Phi-Co-efficient

The Pearson chi-square is not, strictly speaking, a measure of association. Therefore, the phi-co-efficient modifies the pearson chi-square by dividing it by the sample size and taking the square root of the result:

$$\delta = \sqrt{\frac{X^2}{N}}$$

Cramer's V

Cramer introduced the following variant:

$$V = \sqrt{\frac{X^2}{N(k-1)}}$$

Where 'k' is the smaller of the number of rows and columns. It can attain the maximum of 1 for tables of any dimension. If one of the table dimensions is 2, V and O are identical.

LOGISTIC REGRESSION ANALYSIS

It is popularly known as 'logit model'. The logistic model[11] in the study had been used for both the linked and non-linked borrowers and as well for the formal and informal sources of borrowers in order to identify the effect of a unit change in the explanatory variables on the given probability is simply in terms of the odds ratio.

In the logit model one can directly estimate the probability of an event occuring. The model is written as:

$$P_i = \frac{1}{1+e^{-zi}}$$

Where $Z_i = B_1 + B_2 X_i$

Z_i ranges from -α to + α; P_i ranges between 0 and 1 and that P_i is non-linearly related to Z_i. Under the OLS procedure, it has to satisfy the two requirements, i.e., as $Zi \rightarrow +\alpha, e^{-zi}$ tends to zero and as $Zi \rightarrow -\alpha, e^{-zi}$ increases indefinitely, where e is the familiar base of the natural logarithm, approximately e = 2.71828.

Thus, while satisfying the above conditions, there is an estimation problem as Pi is not only non-linear in X but in the B's as well. Therefore, one cannot use the familiar OLS procedure to estimate the parameters because these estimates are not efficient. Moreover there is no guarantee that the predicted probability will be in the range of 0-1[12]. Keeping this in view, the researcher had taken-up the logit model for both the linked and non-linked borrowers as well as formal and informal sources of borrowers.

For estimation purposes, the model can be written as follows:

$L_i = In\left(\frac{(P_i)}{1-P_i}\right)$ $= B_1 + B_2 x_i + U_i$ and the estimated

$$L_i = In\left(\frac{\left(\hat{P}_i\right)}{1-\hat{P}_i}\right) = B_1 + B_2\, x_i + \mu;$$

In the binary logit model, the probability P that a borrower with a given set of characteristics, i.e., given X is will go for formal credit sources is given by

$P = e^{\Sigma Bk}\ x_{ik}/1{+}e\ \ \Sigma B_k\ X_{ik}$ and the probability of the sample households going for other than formal credit source is given by

$$1-p=\frac{1}{\left(1+e\sum^{Bk\,Xik}\right)}$$

Given the data on individual sample borrowers, the parameters of the model Bkxis can be estimated by the maximum likelihood method. In MLS of estimation[13], the value among all the possible values of a parameters is so selected that it makes the probability of obtaining a particular value of the parameter that has been observed as great as possible.

$$L = \prod_{i=1}^{N_1} e\ \Sigma^{Bk}\ X_{ik} /\ (1 + e\ \Sigma Bk\ Xik)j;\pi_i{}^{N}{=}N_1{+}1\ ^{1(1\ +\ e\Sigma Bk\ Xik)}$$

Where N_1 is the number of borrowers who had the credit from formal sources and $N\text{-}N_1$ is the number of borrowers who had the credit from other than formal sources Y=0. The co-efficients of the logit model do not represent marginal probabilities but measure the change in the log of the odds (P/1-P), of borrowers going for formal credit sources as a result of a unit change in the explanatory variables. The effect of unit change in the explanatory variables on the probability is given by

$$\delta P/\ \delta X_k = P(1\text{-}P)B_k$$

The similar logit estimation procedure had also been adopted for the borrowers with linked and non-linked transactions. Therefore, it is to be noted that in the model or procedure, one is to make use of the borrowers with linked transactions in the case of the number of borrowers who had the credit from formal sources and simultaneously make use of borrowers with non-linked transactions in the case of the number of borrowers who had the credit from other than the formal sources.

THE DISCRIMINANT ANALYSIS

It is a stastistical technique that allows the researcher to study the differences between two or more groups of objects with respect to several variables simultaneously. The function maximally discriminates the members of the group. It tells us to which group each member probably belongs. When dealing with two groups, it is nothing more than a multiple regression equation with the dependent variable a nominal variable (Coded 0, 1) representing group membership. With three or more groups, however, it goes beyond multiple regression methods. In the present study, a sub-set of variables measuring different characteristics of the linked borrowers and others are used to construct the function[14]. With the help of this model, one will be able to know the relative importance of the variables with respect to their power to discriminate between groups of the linked borrowers with the non-linked borrowers in the present study. In discriminant analysis, the weights are estimated so that they result in the "best" separation between the groups. The linear discriminant equation is as follows:

$$D = B_0 + B_1X_1 + B_2X_2 + \ldots\ldots + B_kX_k$$

Where X's are the values of the independent variables and B's are co-efficients estimated from the data.

Eigen Value

It is the ratio of the between-groups to within groups sums of squares. Thus,

$$\text{Eigen Value} = \frac{\text{between groups SS}}{\text{within groups SS}}$$

Large eigen values are associated with "good" functions.

The Canonical Correlation

It is a measure of the degree of association between the discriminant scores and the groups. This is related to the eigen value by the following formula:

$$r_i^* = \sqrt{\frac{\lambda_i}{1+\lambda_i}}$$

Where i = the relevant discriminant function

l = is a constant called the "eigen value".

Wilk's Lambda

It is a multivariate measure of group differences over several variables (the discriminating variables). The following formula may be used:

$$\wedge = \pi^{q}_{i=k+1} \frac{1}{1+\lambda_i}$$

Where k denotes the number of functions already derived, means that the individuals terms are to be multiplied to yield the final product.

It is an "inverse" measure. Values of it which are near zero denote high discrimination. As it increases towards its maximum value of 1, it is reporting progressively less discrimination and the group centroids are identical (no group differences).

LIMITATIONS

As usual, the study is embedded with all the limitations of the area and time specific studies. The study is circumscribed by the following limitations: They are:

(i) The duration of the field investigation was confined to a limited period.

(ii) The sample households have expressed the quantity of agricultural produce and MFP in terms of local measurement. But in the processing of data, it was converted into common unit of measurement, i.e., quintals and kilograms. In the process, the figures have been approximated to the nearest number; but the details furnished at the time of interview were cross-checked by the researcher to ensure accuracy of the data.

(iii) As it is a sample study it is not free from the sampling errors since it covers the fraction of the tribal and non-tribal households.

CHAPTERISATION

The chapterisation scheme of the study is as given hereunder:

The present study is organised into *Ten Chapters* including the present *introductory one*. The methodology adopted in this study besides a brief introduction had been discussed in this chapter. In the *Second Chapter*, an attempt is made to review the existing literature on the indigenous markets in tribals areas. The *Third Chapter* traces out the historical genesis of the tribal markets. The *Fourth Chapter* makes an analysis of the Girijan Co-operative Corporation of Andhra Pradesh. Some of the salient features of the study area and the socio-economic profile of the sample households had been presented in the *Fifth Chapter*.

The *Sixth Chapter* examined the nature of the credit market with a specific purpose to analyse the interlinking of the various agrarian markets in the tribal areas with special reference to the linkages of credit with inputs and product markets. Further, an analysis of the access to credit from the formal and informal agencies that existed in the study area had also been undertaken in this chapter.

The *Seventh Chapter* throws light on the marketable surplus and marketed surplus of various products of the tribal and non-tribal sample households that had been randomly chosen for the study. This Chapter intends to analyse the influence of various other factors' over the marketable surplus and marketed surplus.

The *Eighth Chapter* had been devoted for examining the various facets involved in the indigenous marketing pattern in tribal areas based on the field findings and it also throws light on the 'modus operandi' of the Girijan Co-operative Corporation.

The views and opinions of the tribal and non-tribal farmers in the selected villages in the form of case studies had been presented in the *Ninth chapter.* The *last and final chapter* is *summary and conclusions.*

NOTES & REFERENCES

1. Geertz, Clifford: (1978), 'The Bazar Economy, Information and Change in Peasant Marketing', American Economic Review, Vol.68, No.2, May, pp.28-31.
2. Jagannathan, N. Vijay: (1987), Informal Markets in Developing Countries, Oxford University Press, Inc., New York, p.3.
3. Sethuraman, S.V., (1981), The Urban Informal Sector in Developing Countries, Geneva: International Labour Office, p.17.
4. Bardhan, Pranab, K., Land, (1986), Labour and Rural Poverty : Essays in Development Economics, Oxford University Press, New Delhi, p.159.
5. Heintz, Hans-Joachn, C.F., (1992), 'International Law and Indigenous Peoples', Law and State, Vol.45, pp.41-42.
6. Bailey, F.G., (1971), 'The Peasant View of Bad Life', In T. Shanin (Ed.), Peasants and Peasant Societies, Middlesex; Penguin Books.
7. Bardhan, Pranab, K.: Op.cit.,p.158.
8. Hill, Poly, (1970), Migrant Cocoa Farmers of Southern Ghana, Cambridge University Press, New York.
9. This had been discussed at length in Chapter - IV.
10. They include: University Library of his research place, Osmania University Library, State Archives, Government of Andhra Pradesh, University of Hyderabad Library, Centre for Economic and Social Studies Library, National Institute of Rural Development (NIRD) Library, International Crop Research Institute of Semi-Arid Tropics (ICRISAT) Library, State Tribal Cultural Research and Training Institute (TCR & TI, Hyderabad) library and finally visited the Library of Tata Institute of Social Sciences, Bombay.

11. The specification of the variables had been explained in the Chapter-VI, where the analysis had been used. Therefore, here as such the logit model had been explained to have an idea over it.

12. For Proofs, see the following references. They are:

    (a) Kmenta, J., Elements of Econometrics, Macmillan, New York, 1971, pp.425-428.

    (b) Theil, H., Principles of Econometrics, Amsterdam, North-Holland, 1971, pp.628-633.

13. In logistic regression, the parameters of the model are estimated using the maximum likelihood method. That is, the co-efficients that make our observed results mostly "likely" are selected. Since the logistic regression model is non-linear, an interactive algorithm is necessary for parameter estimation.

14. The specification of the variables used in the analysis had been dealt clearly in the chapter-VI.

2

CURRENT STATUS OF EXISTING LITERATURE ON MARKETS IN TRIBAL AREAS

A review of research literature provides insights of historical importance to use them as founding foot-prints for further march[1]. An attempt is made here to review a few apparently relevant books and articles that had been published by numerous authors. The available literature had been grouped into three categories. They are: i) research works on tribal economy as a backdrop for the marketing structure; ii) tribal markets (periodic markets); and iii) the research works done on the realm of interlinkages of factor markets.

I

Distinguished Indian sociologists and anthropologists have made extensive works on socio-cultural pattern of the tribes.

For instance, Guha[2] discussed how the correct policies of administration were a means to safeguard the tribal integrity and organisations. Further, he also examined the racial affinities of the Indian aborigines.

In the pre-Independence period, a renowned anthropologist Prof. Haimendorf[3] was a pioneer on studies in tribal Telangana who published four separate volumes on the four dominant tribal groups of the regions known as *Chenchus* of

Mahabubnagar, the *Koyas* of Warangal, the Hill *Reddies* of the Bison Hills (Khammam-East Godavari), and the *Raj Gonds* of Adilabad.

Aiyappan (1948)[4] was the first scholar administrator who attempted to portray a vivid picture of the economic and social conditions in the Agency area.Besides Aiyappan's study, Malayappan Committee[5] also (1952) focused on the basic problems that beset the tribal community, viz., exploitation; illiteracy; disease and lack of communication. The reports submitted by both these officers pointed out the exploitative nature of the production, trade and exchange relations in the agency area. Further, they confessed that the interaction between the tribals and non-tribals had worked against the well-being of the tribal households in the agency area.

Mamoria[6] in his book on 'Tribal Demography in India', analysed the major demographic structure of tribal India and he made an observation that the demographic structure of the tribes never documented any marked dynamism. And in one of his papers he also made an attempt to classify the tribal households on the basis of spatial distribution, linguistic affiliation, economic organisations, cultural heritage and social customs.

Vidyarthi[7] has done many valuable and excellent studies on socio-cultural-economic organisation of the tribals of India and he evaluated the welfare schemes with regard to the tribals in the modern times. He conducted a stupendous work on the Maler economy which centres round hill cultivation. He also collected some of the research papers from outstanding scholars and arranged them in chronological order in the light of anthropological development in India.

Surajit Sinha[8] in his three perceptive essays examined the positions of the tribals of contemporary India in historical perspectives and analysed their extent of integration with the cultural, social, political and economic systems of India.

Ghurye[9] analysed the historic development of the Indian tribes including the effect of the British occupation and he has also made a survey of the tribal development since Independence.

Gouranga Chattopadhyay and Barun De[10], in their paper pointed out that the tribals as part of the *'fringe'* community are making and will continue to make efforts to be a part of the urban industrial system with a view to minimise the resistance of the *'core'*. Further, they also opined that the research is also needed to test the tentative hypothesis, i.e., the values and behavioural norms of the tribals may be more in conformity with the values and norms of industrial organisation than those of the non-tribal Indians.

V. Raghavaiah[11] in his works made an attempt to present the chronological picturesque of the tribal revolts since 1778 and further he had also presented an overview of the problems of the tribals that they had been facing from times immemorial. Further, the author also gave an excellent analysis with regard to the ethnological structure of the important tribes of India.

N.Y. Naidu[12] in his paper analysed the panorama of tribal exploitation. To him, lack of sound administration at the grass-roots and social infrastructure, lack of implementation of constitutional safeguards by the State and Central Governments, police indifference and exploitative behaviour of the officials, non-protection of tribal land rights, illegitimate and exorbitant collection of land revenue, illegal occupation of tribal land, and exploitation of agricultural and forest produce by the landlords-cum-traders as well as political exploitation by non-tribal leaders in the tribal villages, are some of the important factors contributing to the unrest and tension among the tribals.

M.L. Patel's[13] work is a pioneering attempt in relation to the land problems in the districts of Madhya Pradesh. He also made an attempt to examine the existing agrarian situation of the tribals.

Mamata Chaudhari[14], in her essay on 'Ancient Indian Tribes and their Integration into the Hindu Society', raised the question about the definition of tribe though, since her main objective was to examine the process of integration, she didn't pursue the point any further. Her analysis presents a tribe as a distinct socio-cultural entity devoid of having any sense of hierarchy.

The development and contents of land policies in Andhra Pradesh, Maharashtra, Orissa, Bihar, Madhya Pradesh, Rajasthan and Gujarat which affect the tribals had been critically examined in a book edited by S.N. Dubey and Ratna Murdia[15]. The presenters had also identified the reasons - loopholes in the tenancy legislation, slackness in the implementation of legislative provisions and socio-economic conditions of the tribals - of land alienation and examined the measures taken by the respective State Governments to prevent alienation and restore the alienated land.

In a book edited by Ranjit Gupta[16] the papers broadly discussed the tribal issues under the following heads:

(i) Problems of tribal development;

(ii) Approach to tribal development; and

(iii) Administrative and organisational framework for tribal development.

B.D. Sharma[17] in his book on 'Tribal Development : Concept and Frame', presented an objective assessment of tribal problems and he gave a clear cut picture of the political and administrative dimensions of tribal development. Further, his practical but perceptive insights make a contribution of unique significance.

Pradip Kumar Bose[18], in his paper examined the stratification among the tribals in Gujarat. He found that four distinct peasant classes have emerged among the tribal households. They are: rich peasant, middle peasant, poor peasant and agricultural labourers. As a logical consequence of this stratification, to him, instead of tribal solidarity, class interest has been gaining momentum. Finally he concluded that there is no clear manifestation of class consciousness on the part of the tribal agricultural labourers, and they are often duped by the upper class tribals in the name of 'tribal development', 'tribal backwardness', etc., which in effect serve the latter.

Ghanshyam Shah[19] in his paper highlighted the economic differentiations within a caste with special reference to the Chaudhri tribe. He concluded that the differentiations have taken place owing to the wealth and occupation. In pursuance of their interests, the better-off vocal sections of the tribals often clash with similar strata of the non-tribal society. It is not a caste clash. But it is a conflict for economic interests between two ethnic groups belonging to the same class.

S.D. Kulkarni[20] in his paper examined the origin and development of the Bhil movement in Shahada tahsil in Dhule district of Maharashtra, which started initially as a movement of the tribals against various kinds of oppressive practices by the non-tribals and later evolved into a peasant movement.

Ramaiah[21] in his book, made an attempt to examine the socio-economic conditions of the Koya tribals of Andhra Pradesh in Warangal district based on the 408 Koya tribal families from 51 villages. In another book on 'Issues in Tribal Development', he had thrown much light on various aspects and the major issues involved in the tribal development such as socio-economic conditions in tribal areas, land alienation, agriculture, forestry, co-operation and industrial development and the whole process of planning that has been launched in these areas.

K.S. Singh[22] in his paper examined the recent changes that had been taking place in tribal society in India with respect to social, economic and political changes. A. Somasekar[23] in his work, made an attempt to assess the economic conditions of scheduled tribes at micro level with specific reference to Koyas of Bhadrachalam Taluk of Khammam district in Godavari valley.

S. Jaganmohan Rao[24] in his work, made an attempt to examine the functional role of Girijan Co-operative Corporation of the Warangal district in view of its pivotal role in the tribal upliftment and awakenment. To him, it is reported to have *'fallen sick'*. This finding is based on the analysis of secondary data.

Murali Manohar, Ramaiah and Siva Rama Krishna Rao[25] edited a book on 'Political Economy of Tribal Development' which touched upon the aspects like tribal indebtedness, tribal polity, land alienation and tribal movements.

H.V. Trivedi[26] in his book on 'Economic Development of Tribes in India', examined the situation of tribal economy's of development from the regional perspective. For this study, he has taken the tribal region of Southern Rajasthan. In his analysis he argues that development plans have neither been able to uplift the economic lot of the tribal society in particular nor that of the masses in general.

B. Janardhan Rao[27] in his book, a pioneering attempt, had analysed the land alienation in tribal areas based on the empirical data and data also collected from the land records of the three tribal villages over a period of eighty years, from1900 to 1980. He observed that the state policy of the land restoration had not helped the tribals, but in a way protected the interests of the rich classes of the non-tribals.

P.C. Mohapatro[28] dealt with multi-dimensional aspects of tribals of India, viz: socio-cultural aspects, agricultural practices (both settled and shifting cultivation), forest policy, non-agricultural practices including the problems of development of cottage and small-scale industries. His study is an admixture of sectoral analyses with regional approach. This study urged for the three types of broad development strategies for the tribal development. They are:

(i) Socio-economic development strategies;

(ii) Spatial development strategies; and

(iii) Administrative development strategies.

K. Balagopal[29] in his article on 'Pitting the Tribals against the non-tribal poor' expressed that the expropriation of the lands of the non-tribal landlords and a rationalisation of the State's monopoly over forest land and forest produce will go a wrong way towards solving the problems of the tribals and the non-tribal poor in the tribal areas of the East Godavari district.

Srivastava and Chaturvedi[30] in their study on 'Dependency and common property resources of Tribal and Rural Poor', rejected the outmoded anthropological craze of keeping the aborigines as *'museum pieces'* of civilisations. With common property resources as the core of an enclave social formation in India today, the authors have shown its functionality and linkage with the modern macro-economic system. The authors felt that the working of the trio-tenancy, usury and marketing has kept the tribals dependent on a historically rooted system.

Prabhakar Reddy[31] in his paper on 'Tribal Land Alienation in Andhra Pradesh' stated that in spite of laws prohibiting the transfer of land from the tribals to non-tribals, tribal households in Andhra Pradesh have been losing their lands. He concluded that there has been a sharp decline in land ownership of tribal households and a corresponding increase in that of non-tribal households. Thus, most of the tribal households have become landless and survive only as agricultural labourers and tenants.

Malabilnas Das Gupta[32] in his paper examined the cause and mode of tribal land alienation in Tripura. This study had shown that the outright sale of land has been the most prevalent mode of alienation of tribal lands. Therefore, it is to be stated that this study is in sharp contrast to the conventional wisdom and the findings* of the earlier studies on the subject matter.

Ramaiah and Murali Manohar[33] examined the extent and magnitude of tribal indebtedness in relation to the other variables like size of household, land holdings, incomes and consumption expenditure and the role of different credit agencies among 5 out of 33 tribal communities of Andhra Pradesh based on 504 sample tribal households from the four Telangana districts - Khammam, Warangal, Adilabad and Mahabubnagar of Andhra Pradesh.

Gopu Sudhakar[34] in his study made an attempt to understand and analyse the impact of the institutional performance over the very question of tribal survival and the relevance of preservative strategies of the forest resource which has been adopted in the post-independence period in the country. Further, it is observed that a large chunk of Minor Forest Produce collected by the tribes remain uncovered by the State marketing mechanism.

D.S. Nag[35] an economist endeavours to trace out the operational aspects of economic forces like competition, exchange economy and factor mobility in the economic life of

Baiga Tribe living in the four districts of Madhya Pradesh by making an exhaustive survey of the various economic activities ranging from cultivation, handicrafts and forests to magic and disease cure. His incisive analysis covering all facets of Tribal economy enables him to suggest a concrete plan of action to transform the economy**.

Another economist Saxena[36] had chosen 500 tribal families of Western hills in Madhya Pradesh as his sample and presented economy of five tribes, namely Bhils, Bhilalas, Sahariyas, Korkus and Gonds of erstwhile Central India.

In addition to the above mentioned studies conducted on tribal economy, many surveys and studies had been conducted by the Tribal Research Institutes in the country. Academicians, administrators and institutions located in States having high concentration of tribal population, have shown interest in the problems of tribal development. While a few of these believe that the basic problems of tribal society is its exploitation[37], others feel that land alienation constitutes the chief villain to be handled[38]. Another set of literature consists of reports made by various Commissions and Committees[39]. Most of these reports spot out the problems, as of tribal development and not that of developing the region inhabited by tribals. However, most of the reports are directed to highlight the problems of tribal society and the apparent lacunae in the programme initiated by various state governments.

Thus, the foregoing review of the entire range of literature reveals that most of the scholastic works have viewed the problem from a macro perspective rather than from a micro perspective. In view of all the limitations, the researcher felt that the studies could have highlighted the linkages of tribal economy with the outside market economy. However certain studies had been undertaken on marketing problems in tribal areas and a review of that literature is undertaken in the next section.

II

Bromley[40] through his bibliography has established that a vast extent of literature is available on periodic markets from all parts of the world. However, he observed that there are only eight such studies on periodic markets in South Asia and they are mainly confined to the periodic markets in urban centres. Going through the bibliography and finding the dearth of literature on periodic markets in South Asia, Harriss[41] wondered if such a neglect cropped from the belief that periodic markets are unimportant, or was it because of the field work difficulties that one has to encounter by going into the tribal and other interior belts. Despite the data being very old, one of the reports[42] dealt with all the aspects of rural markets in the Indian context.

The origin of shandies (periodic markets) and the periodic marketing system has been studied by geographers and anthropo-logists. In India also a few studies have been conducted by geographers and anthropologists on shandies. While the geographers' studies emphasised the spatio-temporal aspects of these markets, the anthropologists analysed the ethnic origin and the culture of the people participating in the periodic market activities. Thus, it is clear from the above, that literature on the role of shandies in the tribal economy is too limited and incomprehensive.

Stine[43] in his study on 'Temporal Aspects of Teritiary production elements in Korea', pointed out that periodic markets and mobile trading are developed on economic principles, but at the same time they are also influenced by the social and cultural factors of the people.

Mintz[44] and Piault[45] examined the social functions of market, trade, and the role of local authorities and privileged trading groups. Mangal Singh[46] observed that rural periodic markets frequently operate along with the urban daily markets. Surajit Sinha[47] explained how the physical and ethnic environment help in the formation of a weekly market. To him, the market is principally a result of selective exploitation of the environment by the different communities with consequent inter-change of goods.

Hutton[48] in his study examined the market intervals of the periodic markets. To him, periodic market gatherings are related to socio-cultural concepts of time, the length of the accepted week or month, and the existence of days set aside for rest, religious ceremonies, or public gatherings and festivals.

Deshpande[49] in his paper explained how the market villages and periodic fairs play a fundamental role in a rural economy. He observed that they have played a significant role in the national economy of many countries when human contact was purely local, means of communications inadequate and the rural economy was simple.

Elwin[50] in his study examined that the agricultural produce movement can be seen in weekly markets where traders strike a profitable bargain. As in relation to the marketing practices in Bastar district of Madhya Pradesh, Grigson[51] identified that the tribal weekly markets are socio-economic activities with cultural interactions.

Tamaskar[52] in his study discussed the settlement pattern, topography, the location of the market and organisational pattern adopted by the sellers in establishing the shops according to the commodities sold. Some of the relative conceptual bases of periodic marketing system have also been examined.

Karl Polanyi, et. al[53] edited a book on 'Trade and Market in the Early Empires', which is an anthology of a well-known collection of essays, drew upon both ancient and contemporary developing societies for illustrations of market and non-market distributive systems. Greater emphasis was laid on the extent to which exchange and the allocation of output may rest upon reciprocity, obligation, and other grounds outside the neo-classical price-market mechanism. In their attempt, they made a distinction between the 'self regulating market', and the 'market place'.

J.N. Chaturvedi[54] made an attempt to develop a theory of marketing for under developed countries, in which he held that middlemen are an undesirable luxury, instead of forming a socially useful institution as in the developed economies.

Bohannan-Dalton[55] edited a book on 'Markets in Africa', which underscores the nature of markets with regard to the different types of indigenous economic systems in various sub-

Saharan Africa. Their work is considered as a well-known anthology, which brought together a considerable body of eclectic information on tribal and regional marketing patterns which has both substantive and theoretical value. Keeping in view of the categorisation of primitive African economies based on market and marketless communities, it dealt with the form rather than functions of the markets.

G. William Skinner[56] in his paper, drew mainly upon the central place theory as it is an anthropological and geographical study. His study primarily focused upon the concept of 'Standard marketing towns', i.e., the lowest level markets capable of supplying all of the peasantry's normal trade needs. Further, his study brought out the application of economic location theory to explain the periodic markets.

Thusu[57] conducted a study as in relation to the functioning of weekly market at 'Leda' in South Bastar, wherein he described the caste and trade relationships in the district. A similar study had also been conducted by Naik and Bhourkar[58] on the tribal markets in Jabua districts of Western Madhya Pradesh. They also discussed the economic organisation of the tribals of Bastar district.

Raymond Firth[59] in his book gave a detailed description of the marketing institutions, credit system, income distribution system, and many recent developments within the Malay fishing communities.

Tarasish Mukhopadhyaya[60] in his paper on 'Ecology and Markets in Eastern Midnapur', made an attempt to show how far ecological and environmental factors play in determining certain structural aspects of the village, caste composition, occupation and weekly markets. In his study, he compared the villages, markets and castes in two ecologically distinct regions of West Bengal - one being the new delta region in Eastern Midnapur and the other in the moribund deltaic portion of Murshidabad district. There are significant differences in the economic pursuits of various castes in these two regions which can ultimately be traced to ecological differences.

D.P. Sinha[61] in his pioneering work presented an analysis with regard to the culture change in the Banari inter-tribal market. In his study, he not only traced out the activities of one tribal unit in relation to the Banari market, but also examined some of the ways by which agents of change from the outside may tend to disrupt the balance of a traditionally self-sustaining economy. His study is concerned not with a community as such, but rather with the institution of a weekly market, which serves to bring together members of a number of communities from a well-defined territory to participate in activities signifying inter-dependence rather than independence, and extension rather than isolation, of the people who take part. Finally, he concluded that the little fair, both market and ceremony, maintains a network of socio-cultural ties among the peoples of its 'hinter-land' and gives them 'a common base for their regional ethnology'.

Jay[62] conducted a detailed study on the nature of weekly markets, which are socio-economic activities with cultural interactions and produce movement in the 'Orchha' region, which is the most backward area in the district, wherein he examined the tribal market, where most of their farm produce is sold in the weekly markets.

Raghava Rao[63] in his report has made an attempt to throw light on the systems of marketing of produce and money-lending, the incidence and magnitude of indebtedness, various causes for indebtedness, and the state policy on these issues.

Ramesh Chandra[64] in his paper made an attempt to review the present structure of the market as a system in operation and also made an attempt to analyse the socio-economic implications of the market on the Bhil Tribals held in the village-Khera of the district, Dhar, Madhya Pradesh. While summing-up his study, he stated that Bhil economy is greatly affected by the market due to the exorbitant rates charged by the selling traders. His market under study - Badnawar weekly market is a source of reinforcement of kinship ties and socio-economic obligations, reciprocity and exchange for the Bhil.

Subba Rao's[65] study is related to the examination of economic efficiency of paddy marketing system at village level in West Godavari district of Andhra Pradesh. According to the author, there were many imperfections in marketing of paddy at village level. It was found that primary-secondary market price integration was weak particularly in less developed villages.

S.D. Kulkarni[66] in his paper examined the monopoly trade in tribal areas with special reference to the politics in Maharashtra and suggested that monopoly trading can be replaced by the Tribal Development Corporation (TDC) undertaking such trading on a very large-scale in tribal areas together with restricted private trade.

R.G. Bansod[67] in his paper on 'Shandies or the village Weekly Markets' made an attempt to give the characteristics, and the importance of the shandies in social, economic and cultural life of the tribals of Seethampetta and Polla shandies in the Seethampetta tribal block of the Srikakulam district of Andhra Pradesh.

M.M. Jana[68] in her paper examined the hierarchy of market centres in lower Silabti Basin which is situated in the north-eastern part of Midnapur district in West Bengal. And she stated that in lower silabati Basin, the markets are periodic rather than permanent and continuous like any other peasant society and there are a number of markets which are not located at the minimum aggregate travel distance. Further, she concluded that proper location of periodic markets is an important factor for ensuring good accessibility and low cost of transport.

Punalekar[69] made an elaborate study of the weekly markets in tribal areas of Surat-Valsad region of Gujarat. His study was mainly concentrated on the variety range of commodities brought for exchange, social composition of the traders, behav-iour of tribals as sellers or buyers of commodities and the market participation of tribals belonging to different socio-economic background. Further, he classified the tribals into small and middle farmers and the landless. He observed that the private merchants were making huge profits as there was no restriction on them for purchasing the minor forest produce from the tribals. Kaplan[70] gave an idea of how actively the trading is done at the market places.

Jain, H.C. and Sarawgi[71] pointed out the structural and operational changes in farm business of the selected tribal farmers after their utilisation of credit obtained from the co-operatives. They examined some of the important aspects of farm credit that are having important bearing on the pace of agricultural production in tribal areas. The study also investigated the impact of farm loans given by the co-operative organisations on farm income, production and employment of selected tribal farmers.

An evaluation study of 60 LAMP societies[72] was conducted by the Bihar State Planning Board through constitution of four teams, one each for administrative structure, credit, marketing, and consumer goods. After a critical review of the LAMPS in the State, the Planning Board made various invaluable suggestions for the development of above societies into unified credit-cum-marketing centres.

Hans-Georg Bohle[73] in his paper made an attempt to examine the spatio-temporal organisation of a rural periodic market system from a behaviouristic point of view. The basic assumption is that, spatial structures and spatial processes as observed in a weekly market system are the logical outcomes of the interaction between environment and cognitive processes of the human actors involved. Starting from this assumption, the Paper focuses on the relevant decision-making process of both traders and consumers in a South Indian weekly market system.

Kamal Nayan Kabra[74] highlights the role of periodic market structure and marketing practices adopted by tribals while selling lac in three districts of Bihar, marketing system of lac and the relationship between lac market structure and pricing and bargaining methods in periodic markets.

E. Gormsen[75] in his papers examined the changing role of periodic market places within the central place systems in the Puebla region of Mexico. To him, although it is certainly true that in the Third World countries the market places are very important elements in the spatial organisation of economic and social activities, their changing role for wholesale and retail trade, in rural and urban environments, and for different strata of the population should be evaluated in the context of the general stage of development in any particular country or region, in order to determine how they could be used for the benefit of the population.

Sudhir Wanmali[76] in his Paper attempts to describe and critically examine the functioning of government, private sector, and periodic market networks with empirical evidence from Singhbhum district, Bihar, India, obtained during the period 1972 to 1978. He suggests a spatial model that will incorporate the strengths of these networks for future provision of services in rural India. According to him, these markets are significant from social, economic, and ethnic points of view, and the rural life in the district tends to revolve around them. Almost all rural produce of all types, and many of the urban-based consumer goods, get exchanged at these markets. The marketing system as a whole, however, has emerged as a consequence of an urban demand for rural products, as well as rural demand for urban products.

M.L. Patel[77] made a detailed analysis of working of periodic markets in Mandala district in Madhya Pradesh by introducing the concept of rebound effect as an effective tool to prove the practical utility of central place theory.

Pawar and Others[78] dealt with the borrowing pattern of tribals from various sources, together with utilisation of loans, repayment of loans and impact of borrowings on farm income, expenditure, savings, etc. According to this study, the extent of availability of credit from institutional sources was relatively very low in case of the tribal farms.

Raja Gopal[79] through his study examined the socio-economic dynamics of marketing of agricultural produce, in the Bastar district of Madhya Pradesh. This study primarily concentrated on the crops like paddy and maize among cereals; mustard and til among oil seeds; Arhar (Cajanus indicus) and Urad (Phaseolus mungo), among the pulses. Further, the study analysed the salient organisational and operational feature of marketing of agricultural commodities in the wake of weekly markets. Further the author[80] in his study on 'Marketing in Peasant Economy-History and Trends', made an attempt to understand the marketing system on foodgrains in the rural and urban settlements.

Balgovind[81] in his study made an attempt to understand the nature of economic organisation in a tribal non-irrigated village of Sambalpur district in Orissa. In his Report, he dealt with the co-operative and exploitative economic exchanges in a tribal village.

Murali Krishna Rao[82] in his study made an elaborate attempt to examine the various facets of trading aspects. They are - travel pattern of buyers and sellers, the goods offered for sale, the total value of sales and purchases at different shandies, amount spent by buyers, opinion on deficiencies and reasons for female making the purchases, etc. The author collected data from 20 shandies in the tribal belt of Srikakulam district in Andhra Pradesh.

Saxena[83] in his study on 'Rural Markets and Development: A Case Study of Rajasthan State', examined the diversified pattern of rural marketing in Rajasthan. The study discussed about the periodic (weekly) markets as a spatial and functional unit and examined their periodicity and behavioural pattern of rural consumers and traders.

Krishna Murthy[84] in his study examined the performance of rural markets with respect to cattle. In this connection, he analysed the organisational aspects of rural cattle market, phenomenon of pricing behaviour and the phenomenon of dalari and his role in the shandy. He examined the role of dalaries in rural cattle market on the basis of perception and image of farmers.

S. Mahalingan[85] in his Paper, made an attempt to trace the tribal scene, marketable products of tribals, structure of tribal markets together with an analysis of its basic weakness and examination of some of the policy implications for the development of viable marketing structure in the tribal belts. His analysis is primarily based on the secondary data.

A Seminar was organised by G. Parthasarathy[86] wherein 22 Papers had been presented by the participants on the aspects like: share of marketed surplus, factors accounting for low share of market arrivals in market yards, and regulated markets and public policy. At the end, he rightly emphasised the need for repeating the market surveys, the earlier surveys being done, some three decades ago. And further, he categorically stated about the inadequacies and limitations of official data on market arrivals and prices and the need for review of methodology for collection and compilation of information.

In sum, the weaknesses of indigenous rural marketing literature are as follows[87]:

(i) In terms of participants, it almost ignores the majority of rural population, the rural poor;

(ii) In terms of products, it concentrates on tangible and ignores some of the basic need satisfying 'products' like health, education, drinking water, housing and other products like transportation, labour, land, money, etc. Even in tangibles, the focus seems to be exclusively on economic goods.

In general it can be said that a few researchers in India had made an attempt to study exclusively the role of shandies in the tribal economy, and their impact on the socio-economic development of the tribals. But all the above studies have highlighted the exploitation that takes place in these markets and how actively the business is transacted. But, they failed to examine as to how the periodic markets contribute to improve the standard of living of the rural masses, especially downtrodden like tribals. Besides, all the studies under review touched upon the geographical and anthropological aspects only and hardly made an attempt to focus on the commercial and trading activities such as the nature of weights and measures used, mode of exchange, volume of trade, etc. Albeit, only a few of them are related to rural markets.

Most of the above studies had explored the essential aspects pertaining to marketing of final products, but the interlinkages among different markets, that is land, labour and credit markets had not been analysed. Hence a review of the studies dealing with these aspects will be attempted to throw more light on markets in rural areas.

III

Amit Bhaduri[88] attempted to examine the influence exerted by the relations of production on the introduction of improved technology into the agriculture of Birbhum district in West Bengal. The study was based on survey data from 26 villages in 1970. Bhaduri observed the following features of Birbhum agriculture:

(i) Share cropping as the dominant form of tenancy;

(ii) The perpetual indebtedness of the small tenants;

(iii) Convergence of two modes of exploitation, viz., usury and land ownership in the hands of the same land owner; and

iv) Lack of accessibility of the market to the small tenants.

P.H. Prasad[89] in his studies on production relations in three districts of Bihar-Purnea, Saharsa and Monghyr, supported the view of Bhaduri regarding the semi-feudal relations of production in agriculture. He concluded that, "usurer's capital plays a historically reactionary role which is not only responsible for low use of means of production and inimical to net investment in the agricultural sector, but is also responsible for wide-spread poverty, debt and semi-feudal bondage".

Krishna Bharadwaj and P.K. Das[90] in their Article on 'Tenurial Conditions and Mode of Exploitation: A Study of some villages in Orissa', analysed the prevalence of a mode of exploitation that operates through a tie-up between land and labour. In their analysis, important differences among the irrigated, unirrigated, cash crop in tribal areas were also considered.

Pranab Bardhan and Ashok Rudra[91] in their Paper gave primary emphasis on the terms and conditions of land, labour and credit contracts and their findings primarily emanated from the large-scale survey of 275 randomly chosen villages in West Bengal, Bihar and some of the Eastern Districts of Uttar Pradesh. The landlord of the employer is an important source of credit to the tenant or wage labourer. But, they observed that the evidence in Eastern India, suggests the incidence of usury as the main mode of exploitation or of bonded labour is very rare. Further, they also observed that the consumption loans to tenants and wage labourers are occasionally interest free and some times interest is charged in the form of wage-cut for the casual labourer. But loans taken by the labourers, usually repaid in harvest time in the form of grains and in labour do not in general lead to long-term bondage relationships. Where the casual labourer takes advances from his employer against future commitment of labour for which he works at lower than market wage rate at the time of repayment. Apart from credit,some times homestead provided by the employer ties a labourer to him.

Pranab K. Bardhan[92] in his Paper, made an attempt to review the three specific questions, which are raised and answered to varying degrees by the theoretical concern with rural interlinked markets. They are:

(i) how the interlinkages of markets reinforces the impact of imperfections in each market;

(ii) how different transactions are some times personalised in an interlocking system of (unequal) exchange among the same participants in order to get around the problem of non-existence of a complete set of markets; and

(iii) how differential price mechanisms operate in different factor markets (For instance, price mechanism in one market and quantity rationing in a related market).

Pranab Bardhan and Ashok Rudra[93] in their Papers analysed the detailed terms and conditions of agricultural labour contracts and emphasised the heterogeneity of employer-employee relationships. They observed that the interlinked contracts ensure a guaranteed supply of labour just when employer needs it and also act as a kind of barrier to entry for other employers or creditors who operate in the labour market or in the credit market. Further, they said that the attachment relations with labourers and their careful interlocking with personalized transactions in credit or land allotment enable the employer to increase his social control over them.

Khasnabis Ratan & Jyoti Prakash Chakravarthi[94] undertook a survey on tenurial arrangements in Nadia district of West Bengal. In the study they concluded that the typical landlord did not enter into usury practices with his tenants who nevertheless needed both production and consumption loans. They also have found that, there is no strong interlinkage between tenancy contracts and credit contracts. Further, they also observed that the credit market was dominated by the non-landlord loan-givers, i.e., traders, professional money-lenders, school teachers, village doctors, etc. which refuted the idea proposed by Amit Bhaduri that the credit market was found to be dominated by the landlords. But their findings seem to be consistent with the findings of a large-scale survey undertaken by Bardhan and Rudra.

Desai et. al.[95] in their pioneering book made an attempt to examine the nature of interlocking of transactions. They differ according to the relative power of the contracting parties and the strategies adopted by different parties involved in the exchange process.

M. Chattopadhyay, and R. Bhattacharyya[96] in their Paper, made an attempt to examine the interlinkage approach in terms of a comprehensive framework of land, labour and credit relations, which is based on a socio-economic survey in a frontier region of Siliguri, Sub-Division.

Likewise Pulapre Balakrishna[97] in his Paper 'On the Significance of Interlinked Factor Markets in Agrarian Economics', makes a purposive evaluation of the notion of market-interlinkage as applied to poor agrarian economies. Firstly, his Paper commences with an overview of the issues that become relevant due to interlocking of factor markets. And consequently, his paper critically addresses the framework within which this phenomenon has recently been analysed. Finally, it provides a comprehensive approach to the study of agrarian development which yields market-interlinkage as a special case.

T.V.S. Rao and E.V.R.S. Subrahmanyam[98] wrote a paper on 'Inter-locking of credit and product markets and its impact on Agricultural Productivity', wherein they examined the different types of contracts and for this purpose, they selected product and money-markets and the credit and output sale transactions are analysed separately and together. They made an observation that the cultivators with interlocking did try to achieve higher productivity and observed that they succeeded in the case of groundnut, but failed in the case of sugarcane, inspite of higher fertilizer doses, because, they did not adopt HYVs to the same extent as farmers without tied sales.

Shubhashis Gangaopadhyay and Kunal Sengupta[99] in their paper made an attempt to analyse two aspects. They are:

(i) decision of the tenant about the amount of loan to be taken, and

(ii) the existence of two distinguishable types of loans for production and for consumption purposes.

They observed that, when both production and consumption loans are interlinked with the land market, rate of interest on consumption loans does not deviate from the market rate of interest, but the interest on production loans is less than (equal to) the market rate if tenants are risk averse (neutral).

Rao[100] in his paper, clearly pointed out that the dominant party dictates the terms of exchange, while the weaker party is obliged to accept it. It is due to the fact that the poorer the farm households in general, the more acute the need for consumption and other loans, the easier for the lender to extract a higher proportion of their income by more exploitative terms and conditions of lending through interlinked transactions.

Clive Bell and T.N. Srinivasan[101] in their paper on 'Interlinked Transactions in Rural Markets : An Empirical study of Andhra Pradesh, Bihar and Punjab', observed more informal credit linkages with marketing in more commercialised areas. Further, they found that the interlinked credit transactions observed in the developed and commercialised village are advantageous to both the parties concerned. And, further they concluded that interlinkages between credit and tenancy and labour are certainly evident in the more backward areas. But they discarded the claim of

Amit Bhaduri that usury is the dominant form of exploitation in a *'Semi-feudal'* mode of production.

Ravi Srivastava[102] in his article examined the nature of interlinked modes of exploitation on the basis of evidence from three villages in Uttar Pradesh. It is argued that the interlocked relationships arise out of a prior set of production relationships and the strategies of subsistence and accumulation of different classes, which may themselves change under certain conditions. He observed that the interlinkages facilitate the appropriation of surplus in more than one market by surplus appropriators, and may restrict mobility (once 'choices' have been made) for the weaker classes, but given that labourers can and do reproduce themselves in a limited number of alternative ways and that this is not always incompatible with the interests of the dominant landlords, the restrictions on the functioning of the labour market are of a relative nature.

Rakesh Hooja[103] in his book examined the phenomenon of interlocked factor markets in rural India. An attempt is also made to show how the planning and administrative system responds to interlocked factor markets and the resulting relationships in village India.

Kailas Sarap[104] in his book on 'Interlinked Agrarian Markets in Rural India', made a pioneering attempt to understand the implications of interlinked agrarian markets and the factors affecting the distribution of formal credit among different classes of borrowers-small and marginal farmers, tenant cultivators and landless labourers based on his empirical data drawn from the six villages of Sambalpur district in Orissa. The author analysed the nature and extent of different types of interlinked credit transactions among various sections of borrowers and identified the household characteristics associated with these linkages. He observed that interlinked credit transactions are found to be the highest among the tenants and landless labourers, followed by the small farmers. No medium or large farmers entered into interlinked credit transactions in the study region of the author. Therefore, he confessed that the phenomenon of linkage appears to be essentially a manifestation of the survival strategies adopted by collateral poor households with a low bargaining power. Further, he observed that the interlinked credit transactions seem to be confined to households with a low operated area, tenant households, and/or households with low educational and caste status.

M.V. Narayana Reddy[105] in his paper examined the interlinkages of credit with factor and product markets. He observed that the extent of interlinked credit transactions is less in the developed villages, while such interlinked credit transactions are highly prevalent in the backward villages. Further, the credit relations observed in the developed village are concerned with only labour market and found to be beneficial to agricultural labourers because, there are no wage cuts, besides provision of interest free loans. On the other hand, the input and output market linked credit transactions are dominant in the backward village, which are found to be exploitative to the weaker parties due to the hidden costs collected by the monopolist traders by over-valuing the prices of agricultural inputs supplied for the cotton crop and under-pricing the cotton output purchased by them. Finally, he concluded that the type of linkage which influences the positive or negative effect may be dependent on the relative bargaining power of the parties involved, the relative urgency of transaction to the concerned parties and the availability of formal credit which inturn is dependent on the state of development of the region in which the transaction takes place.

By and large, while most of the studies are limited to analysing the existence of interlocking *perse,* they do find these associated with very different production and accumulation conditions. The overall evidence is consistent with the view that certain aspects of such relationships change systematically with the penetration of capitalism, eventhough the outward form of interlocking may appear to be similar. Moreover all the above studies that had been conducted so far on the interlinkages of markets primarily concentrated on plain and non-tribal areas in different parts of the country. But no serious attempt had been made to examine the nature of interlinkages in the tribal areas. In view of this, in addition to the tribal marketing pattern, the researcher also made an attempt to examine the interlinkages in the tribal areas of Telangana region of Warangal, Khammam and Adilabad districts.

Finally in the light of this background, the present study attempts to analyse the tribal problem in general and their marketing pattern in particular. Besides, the present study makes an attempt even to examine the nature of interlinkages in factor and product markets in the tribal areas. Hence, the researcher feels that it would fill the gap in the development of existing literature both on the tribal marketing pattern and the interlinkages of markets.

NOTES & REFERENCES

1. *Thomas Edison* (1975), once said, "when I want to discover something, I begin by reading that has been done in the past ... I gather the data of many thousands of experiments as a starting point...". Quoted by Young and Schmid, *Principles and Techniques of Social Studies,*Prentice Hall India, p. 139.
2. (a) Guha, B.S.(1939), 'The Aboriginal Races of India', *Science and Culture,* Calcutta, Vol. IV, No. 12, pp.677-683.

   (b) Guha,B.S.(1951), 'The Indian Aborigines and their Administration', *Journal of the Asiatic Science,* Calcutta, Vol. 17, No. 1, pp. 19-44.
3. (a) Haimendorf, C.V.F.(1943), *Tribal Hyderabad* (Four Reports), H.E.H. Nizam Dominions, Hyderabad.

   (b) ——— (1945), *The Reddies of the Bison Hills - A Study in Acculturation,* Vol. 2., The Aboriginal Tribes of Hyderabad, London.

   (c) ——— (1945), *Tribal Population of Hyderabad : Yesterday and Today,* Census of India, 1941, Vol. 21, Hyderabad.

   (d) ——— (1945), *Progress and Problems of Aboriginal Rehabilitation in Adilabad District,* Hyderabad.

   (e) ——— (1948), *The Raj Gonds of Adilabad,* Vol. 3, The Aboriginal Tribes of Hyderabad, London.

   (f) ——— *The Gonds of Andhra Pradesh, Tradition and Change in an Indian Tribe,* London/Delhi (Vikas), 1979.

   (g) ——— (1982), *Tribes of India - The Struggle for Survival,* Oxford University Press, Delhi.

4. *Aiyappan Committee Report*, 1948.

5. *Malayappan Committee Report*, 1952.

6. (a) Mamoria, C.B. 1957), *Tribal Demography in India*, Kitab Mahal, Allahabad.

   (b) ——— (1957), Tribes in India - Their Classification', *The Modern Review*, Vol.150, No. 4, pp.278-283.

7. (a) Vidyarthi, L.P. (Ed.) (1959), *Anthropology and Tribal Welfa-re in India*, Council of Social and Cultural Research, Bihar.

   (b) ——— (1963), *The Maler - A Case Study in Nature - Man Spirit Complex of a Hill Tribe in Bihar*, Book Land, Calcutta.

   (c) ——— (1978), *Rise of Anthropology in India: The Tribal Dimensions* (Vol.I), Concept Publishing Company, New Delhi.

8. (a) Sinha, Surajit (1958), 'Tribal Cultures of Peninsular India as a Dimension of Little Tradition in the Study of Indian Civilisation: A Preliminary Statement', *Journal of American Folklore*, Vol.71, No.279, pp.504-518.

   (b) ——— (1962), 'State Formation and Rajput Myth in Tribal Central India', *Man in India*, Vol. 42, No.1, January-March, pp.35-80.

   (c) ——— (1965), 'Tribe-Caste and Tribe-Peasant Continua in Cultural India', *Man in India*, Vol.45, No.1, January-March, pp.57-83.

9. Ghurye, G.S. (1963), *The Scheduled Tribes*, Popular Prakashan, Bombay.

10. Chattopadhyay, Gouranga & Barun De (1969), 'Problem of Tribal Integration to Urban Industrial Society : A Theoretical Approach', *Economic and Political Weekly*, Vol.IV, No.52, December 27, pp.1985-1994.

11. (a) Raghavaiah, V. (1969.), *Tribes of India*, Bharatiya Adima Jati Sevak Sangh, New Delhi.

    (b) ——— (1971), *Tribal Revolts*, Andhra Rashtra Adima Jati Sevak Sangh, Nellore.

12. Naidu, N.Y. (1972), 'Tribal Revolt in Parvatipuram Agency', *Economic and Political Weekly*, Vol.III, No.48, November 25, pp.2337-2344.

13. (a) Patel, M.L.(1969), *Agro-Economic Survey of Tribal Mandla*, People's Publishing House Pvt., Ltd., New Delhi.

(b) ——— (1972), *Agro-Economic Problems of Tribal India,* Progress Publishers, Bhopal.

(c) ——— (1985), *Economic Dimension of Land Distribution of Tribal India,* Books Emporium, New Delhi.

14. Chaudhuri, Mamata (1976), 'Ancient Indian Tribes and their Integration into the Hindu Society', *Journal of the Indian Anthropological Society,* Vol.II, No.2, pp.125-145.
15. Dubey, S.N., & Ratna Murdia (Ed.) (1977), *Land Alienation and Restoration in Tribal Communities in India,* Himalaya Publishing House, Bombay.
16. Gupta, Ranjit, (Ed.) (1977), *Planning for Tribal Development,* Ankur Publishing House, New Delhi.
17. Sharma, B.D. (1978), *Tribal Development : The Concept and the Frame,* Prachi Prakashan, New Delhi.
18. Bose, P.K. (1981), 'Stratification among Tribals in Gujarat', *Economic and Political Weekly,* Vol.XVI, No.6, February 7. pp.191-196.
19. Shah, Ghanshyam, (1979), 'Tribal Identity and Class Differentiations: A Case Study of the Chaudhri Tribe', *Economic and Political Weekly,* Vol.XIV, Nos. 7 & 8, Annual Number, pp.459-464.
20. Kulkarni, S.D. (1979), 'Class and Caste in a Tribal Movement', *Economic and Political Weekly,* Vol.XIV, Nos. 7 & 8, Annual Number, pp.465-468.
21. (a) Ramaiah, P. (1981), *Tribal Economy of India - A Case Study of Koyas of Andhra Pradesh,* Light and Life Publishers, New Delhi.

    (b) ———(1988), *Issues in Tribal Development,* Chugh Publications, Allahabad.
22. Singh, K.S. (1982), 'Transformation of Tribal Society : Integration Vs. Assimilation', *Economic and Political Weekly,* Vol.XVII, No.33 & 34, August 14 & 21, pp.1318-1325 & 1376-1384.
23. Somasekar, A. (1983), *Economic Conditions of Tribals - A Case Study of Koyas of Godavari Valley,* Unpublished Ph.D. Thesis, submitted to the Department of Economics, Osmania University, Hyderabad.
24. Rao, S. Jaganmohan (1984), *The Girijan Co-operative Corporation and Tribal Development with special references to Warangal District,*

Unpublished Ph.D. Thesis, submitted to the Department of Economics, Kakatiya University, Warangal.

25. Manohar, K., Murali, Ramaiah, P., & C. Siva Rama Krishna Rao (1985), *Political Economy of Tribal Development*, Indian Institute of Public Administration, Local Branch, Department of Public Administration, Kakatiya University, Warangal.
26. Trivedi, H.V., (1985), *Economic Development of Tribes in India*, Himanshu Publications, Udaipur.
27. Rao, B. Janardhan (1987), *Land Alienation in Tribal Areas*, Kakatiya School of Public Administration, Warangal.
28. Mohapatro, Prafullo Chandrao ((1987), *Economic Development of Tribal India*, Ashish Publishing House, New Delhi.
29. Balagopal, K. (1989), 'Pitting the Tribals against the non-tribal poor', *Economic and Political Weekly*, Vol.XXIV, No.21, May 27, pp.1149-1154.
30. Srivastava, H.C. and M.K. Chaturvedi (1989), *Dependency and Common Property Resources of Tribal and Rural Poor*, Commonwealth Publishers, New Delhi.
31. Reddy, Prabhakar, T. (1989), 'Tribal Land Alienation in Andhra Pradesh', *Economic and Political Weekly*, Vol.XXIV, No.28, July 15, pp.1571-1573.
32. Das Gupta, Malabilnas (1991), 'Land Alienation among Tripura Tribals', *Economic and Political Weekly*, Vol.XXVI, No.36, September 7, pp.2113-2118.
33. Ramaiah, P., & K. Murali Manohar (1992), *Tribal Indebtedness*, Himalaya Publishing House, New Delhi.

* Land alienation had been taking place through the money-lending and seizure of mortgaged land.

34. Sudhakar, Gopu (1992), *Public Policy and Development - A Study of Forest Policy and Tribal Development*, Unpublished Ph.D. Thesis submitted to the Department of Public Administration, Kakatiya University, Warangal.
35. Nag, D.S. (1958), *Tribal Economy - An Economic Study of the Baiga*, Bhartiya Adim Jati Seva Sangh, Kingsway, New Delhi.
36. Saxena, R.P. (1964), *The Tribal Economy in Central India*, Firma, K.L. Mukhoyadhyan, Calcutta.

** Notable among them are: Controlled exploitation of forest wealth, Minor Irrigation works, reorganisation of tribal industries, and improved cattle breed, etc.

37. Shrikanth, L.M. (1952), *Commissioners for Scheduled Castes and Scheduled Tribes*, Indian Conference of Social Work, Souvenir, Chandigarh, 1960. And also Scheduled Tribes and Scheduled Areas Conference, New Delhi.

38. (a) Patel, M.L. (1974), *Changing Land Problems of Tribal India*, National Publishing House, New Delhi.

(b) Dubey, S.N. & Murdia, R. (1976), *Administration of Policy and Programmes for Backward Classes in India*, Somaiya, Bombay.

(c) Janardhan Rao, B. *Land Alienation in Tribal Areas*, Op.cit. 1987.

39. (a) Report of the *Scheduled Areas and Scheduled Tribes Commission*, Government of India, Vol.I & II, 1960-61.

(b) Report of the *Study Team on Tribal Development Programmes and Committee on Plan Projects*, Rajasthan, Planning Commission, 1969.

(c) Interim Report of *Working Group on Tribal Development for Medium Term Plan*, 1978-83.

40. Bromley, R.J. (1974), *Periodic Markets, Daily Markets and Fairs: A Bibliography*, Monash University Publications in Geography, Clayton, No.10.

41. Harriss Barbara, (1975), 'Poverty, Caste, Rurality of Transactions: A Speculative Explanation for Periodic Marketing in Northern Tamil Nadu, *2nd Indo-British Seminar*, Cambridge.

42. Report on *Fairs*, (1943), *Markets and Produce Exchanges in India*, Published by Government of India.

43. Stine, James, H. (1962), 'Temporal Aspects of Teritiary Production Elements in Korea', *Urban Systems and Economic Development*, Oregon, pp.68-88.

44. Mintz, S.W. (1961), 'Partik: Haitian Personal Economic Relations, in Viola E. Gar field', *American Ethnological Society Proceedings*, Annual Spring Meeting, Seattle, pp.54-63.

45. Marc Piault (1971), 'Cycle de Marches et 'Espaces' Socio-Politigues' in Calude Meillassoux, *The Development of Indigenous Trade and Market in West Africa*, Oxford University Press, London, pp.285-302.

46. Singh Shiw Mangal (1965), 'The Stability Theory of Rural Central Place Development', *National Geographical Journal of India*, Vol.II, pp.13-21.

47. Sinha Surajit (1951), 'The Weekly Market at Bannri, a village in South Manbhum', *Geographical Review of India,* 13(4), p.20.

48. Hutton, Webster, (1916), *Rent Ways : A Study in Early Law of Morality,* Macmillan, New York, pp. 101-123.

49. Deshpande, C.D. (1941), 'Market Villages and Periodic Fairs of Bombay and Karnataka', *The IndianGeographical Journal,* Madras, Vol.XVI, No.4, October-December, p.327.

50. Elwin, Verrier (1947), *Mariya and Their Ghotal,* Oxford University Press, London.

51. Grigson, W.Y. (1947), *Mariya Gonds of Bastar,* Part-III, Oxford University Press, London.

52. (a) Tamaskar, B.G. (1955), 'Patharia - A Study of the Settlement Pattern and Weekly Market', *Geographical Review of India,* Vol.XVII, No.4, December, p.1-12.

    (b) ——— (1978), 'Geographic Perspective on Periodic Marketing System and Network in the Chhattisgarh Plain', *Geographical Review of India,* Vol. 40, No.1, March, pp.15-24.

53. Polanyi, Karl, Arensberg, C.M., and Pearson, H.W. (Ed.) (1957), *Trade and Market in the Early Empires,* Free Press, Glencoe, Ill.

54. Chaturvedi, J.N. (1959), *Theory of Marketing in Underdeveloped Countries,* Kitab Mahal, Allahabad.

55. Bohannan, Paul and George Dalton (Ed.) (1962), *Markets in Africa,* Evanston, North-Western University Press.

56. Skinner, G. William (1964 & 65), 'Marketing and Social Structure in Rural China', *Journal of Asian Studies,* Vol.XXIV, pp. 3-44, 195-228 & 263-99.

57. Thusu, K.N. (1965), 'The Weekly Market at Leda - A Village in South-East Bastar', *Vanyajati,* Vol.XIII, No.4, OCtober pp.149-160.

58. Naik, T.B., & Bhourskar, K.M. (1964), *Tribal Economic Organisation and Market,* Trisul Research & Training Institute, Chindwarg, Madhya Pradesh.

59. Firth, Raymond (1966), *Malay Fishermen : Their Peasant Economy,* Archow Books, Hamden, Conn.

60. Mukhopadhyaya, Tarasish (1967), 'Ecology and Markets in Eastern Midnapur', *Man in India,* Vol.47, No.1, January-March, pp.61-73.

61. Sinha, D.P. (1968), *Culture Change in an Inter-Tribal Market*, Asia Publishing House, New Delhi.

62. Jay, Edward, J. (1968), *Tribal Village of Middle India*, Anthropological Survey of India, Memoi, No.21.

63. Rao, Raghava, D.V. (1973), *Marketing of Produce and Indebtedness among Tribals - Report on a Study in Chintalapalli Block*, Agro Economic Research Centre, Andhra University, Waltair.

64. Chandra Ramesh (1973), 'Market in a Tribal Village : Its Socio-Economic Implications among the Bhils', *Vanyajati*, Vol.XXI, No.2, April, pp.52-59.

65. Subba Rao, K. (1978), *Rice Marketing System and Compulsory Levies in Andhra Pradesh*, Allied Publishers, Private Limited, Bombay.

66. Kulkarni, S.D. (1977), 'Monopoly Trade in Tribal Areas and Its Politics in Maharashtra', *Economic and Political Weekly*, Vol.XII, No.51, December 17, pp.2085-2087.

67. Bansod, R.G. (1977), 'Shandies or the Village Weekly Markets', *The Administrator*, Vol.XXII, No.1, Spring, pp.399-402.

68. Jana, M.M. (1978), 'Hierarchy of Market Centres in Lower Silabati Basin', *Geographical Review of India*, Vol.40, No.2, June pp.164-174.

69. Punalekar, S.P. (1980), 'Weekly Markets in Tribal Areas', *Centre for Social Studies*, Surat, Gujarat.

70. Kaplan, D. (1965), 'The Mexican Market Place : Then and Now', Proceedings, *American & Ethnological Society*, Seattle.

71. Jain, H.C., & Sarawgi, A.K. (1982), 'A Study on the Impact of Farm Credit on Farm Income - Production and Employment in Selected Tribal Areas of Madhya Pradesh', *Land Bank Journal*, Vol.XX, No.1, 1981, pp.53-59. Also see his paper on 'A Comparative Study into the Impact of Farm Credit provided by the Co-operative and Commercial Banks in Tribal Areas of Madhya Pradesh', *Co-operative Perspective*, Vol.17, No.1, pp.61-69.

72. Singh Bhupinder (1983), 'Co-operatives in Tribal Areas', *Occasional Paper on Tribal Development-32*, Ministry of Home Affairs, Government of India.

73. Bohle, Hans-Georg (1981), 'Spatio-Temporal Decision Making in South Indian Weekly Markets: An Investigation into Consumer/Trade Perceptions and Preferences', *The National Geographical Journal of India*, Vol. XXVII, Parts-1 & 2, March-June, pp.1-13.

74. Kabra, K.N. (1983), *Dependence and Dominance : Political Economy of a Tribal Commodity,* Indian Institute of Public Administration, New Delhi.

75. (a) Gormsen, E. (1972), 'Considerations on the Formation of Central Place systems in Developing Countries', A Paper submitted to the *22nd International Geographical Congress,* Toronto, Canada, pp.1293-1295.

(b) ——— 'Weekly Markets in the Puebla Region of Mexico', in R.H.T. Smith, (Ed.) *Market Place Trade,* Vancouver, Canada, University of British Columbia, pp.240-253.

(c) ———(1983), 'The Role of Market Place in Developing Countries', A Paper presented at the International Workshop on *Agricultural Markets in the Semi-Arid Tropics,* pp.121-129.

76. Wanmali, Sudhir (1980), *Periodic Markets and Rural Development in India,* B.R. Publishing Corporation, New Delhi.

77. Patel, M.L. (1984), *Planning Strategy for Tribal Development,*Inter India Publications, New Delhi.

78. Pawar, J.R., et. al. (1984), 'Pattern of Borrowing and Repayment of Loans of the Farms in the Tribal Sub-Plan Areas of Western Maharashtra', *Tribal Research Bulletin,* Vol.VI, No.1, pp.10-12.

79. Gopal Raja (1986), *Dynamics of Agricultural Marketing in Tribal India,* Rainbow Publications, Coimbatore.

80. ——— (1988), *Marketing in Peasant Economy - History and Trends,* Manas Publications, Delhi.

81. Baboo Balgovind (1986), 'Economic Exchanges in a Tribal Village', *Man in India,* Vol.66, No.2, June pp.151-165.

82. Rao, M.K.I. (1988), *Marketing in Tribal Economy,* Inter-India Publications, New Delhi.

83. Saxena, H.M. (1988), *Rural Markets and Development - A Case Study of Rajasthan State,* Rawat Publications, Jaipur.

84. Murthy, Krishna, T. (1989), *Organisation and Working of Rural Markets in Telangana Region,* (Unpublished) Ph.D. Thesis, submitted to the Department of Commerce & Business Management, Kakatiya University, Warangal.

85. Mahalingam, S. (1989), 'Tribal Groups and Market Development in India', *Journal of Rural Development,* Vol.8, No.2, pp.135-145.

86. A Seminar on *Regulated Markets and Public Policy in Andhra Pradesh,* organised by the Institute of Development and Planning

Studies in collaboration with the Directorate of Marketing, Government of Andhra Pradesh and the Indian Society of Agricultural Marketing, Muvvalavanipalem, Visakhapatnam during 22-23, August 1993.

87. Jha, Mithileshwar (1988), 'Rural Marketing : Some Conceptual Issues' *Economic and Political Weekly*, Vol.XXII, No.9, February 27, pp.M.8 & M.9.

88. (a) Bhaduri, Amit (1973), 'A Study in Agricultural Backwardness under Semi-Feudalism', *The Economic Journal*, Vol.83, No.329, March , pp.120-137.

(b)————(1986), *Economic Power, Organisational Form and the Commercialisation of Backward Agriculture*, Mimeo, Delhi.

89. (a) Prasad, P.H.(1973), 'Production Relations : Achilles Heel of Indian Planning', *Economic and Political Weekly*, Vol.VIII, No.19, May 12, pp.869-872.

(b) ———— (1974), 'Reactionary Role of Usurers' Capital in Rural India', *Economic and Political Weekly*, Vol.9, Special Number, August, pp. 1305-1308.

90. Bharadwaj Krishna, & P.K. Das (1975), 'Tenurial Conditions and Mode of Exploitation - A Study of Some Villages in Orissa', *Economic and Political Weekly*, Vol.X, Nos.5, 6 & 7 (Annual Number), February pp.221-240.

91. Bardhan Pranab & Ashok Rudra (1978), 'Interinkage of Land, Labour and Credit Relations: An Analysis of Village Survey Data in East India', *Economic and Political Weekly*, Vol.XIII, No.6 & 7, February, pp.367-384.

92. Bardhan, K.P. (1980), 'Interlocking Factor Markets and Agrarian Development: A Review of Issues', *Oxford Economic Papers*, Vol.32, No.1, March, pp.82-98.

93. (a) Bardhan Pranab and Ashok Rudra (1981), 'Terms and Conditions of Labour Contracts in Agriculture : Results of a Survey in West Bengal, 1979', *Oxford Bulletin of Economics and Statistics*, Vol.43, NO.1, February, pp.89-111.

(b) ———(1980), 'Types of Labour Attachment in Agriculture : Results of a Survey in West Bengal, 1979', *Economic and Political Weekly*, Vol.XV, NO.35, August 30, pp.1477-1484.

94. Khasnabis Ratan & Jyoti Prakash Chakravarty (1982), 'Tenancy, Credit and Agrarian Backwardness: Results of a Field Survey', *Economic and Political Weekly*, Vol.XVII, No.13, 27th March, pp. A.21-A.32.

95. Desai, B.M., et. al., (1984), *Agrarian Power and Agricultural Productivity in South Asia*, Oxford University Press, Delhi.

96. Chattopadhyay, M. and Bhattacharyya, R. (1984), 'Land Labour and Credit Relations in a Peasant Movement Belt', *Social Scientist*, Vol.12, No.3, March pp.36-51.

97. Balakrishna, Pulapre (1984), 'On the Significance of Interlinked Factor Markets in Agrarian Economies', *The Indian Economic Journal*, Vol.31, No.4, April-June, pp.62-72.

98. Rao, T.V.S., & E.V.R.S. Subrahmanyam (1985), 'Interlocking of Credit and Product Markets and its Impact on Agricultural Productivity', in S. Mazoor, Alm (Ed.), *Agricultural Markets in the Semi-Arid Tropics*, ICRISAT, Hyderabad, pp.169-176.

99. Gangopadhyay, S. & Sengupta, K.(1986)'Interlinkages in Rural Markets', *Oxford Economic Papers*, Vol.38, No.1, March, pp.112-121.

100. Rao, J.M. (1988), 'Interest Rates in Backward Agriculture', *Cambridge Journal of Economics*, Vol.4, No.2, January, pp.159-167.

101. Bell Clive and T.N. Srinivasan (1989), 'Interlinked Transactions in Rural Markets: An Empirical Study of Andhra Pradesh, Bihar and Punjab', *Oxford Bulletin of Economics and Statistics*, Vol.51, No.1, February, pp.73-83.

102. Srivastava, Ravi (1989), 'Interlinked Modes of Exploitation in Indian Agriculture during Transition: A Case Study', *The Journal of Peasant Studies*, Vol.16, No.4, July pp.493-522.

103. Hooja, Rakesh (1990), *Planning, Interlocked Markets and Rural Development*, Rawat Publications, Jaipur.

104 (a) Sarap, Kailas (1991), *Interlinked Agrarian Markets in Rural India*, Sage Publications, New Delhi.

(b) —— (1991), 'Collateral and Other forms of Guarantee in Rural Credit Markets: Evidence from Eastern India', *Indian Economic Review*, Vol.XXVI, No.2, pp.167-168.

(c) ——— (1991), 'Changing Contractual Arrangement in Agriculture Labour Market: Evidence from Orissa', *Economic and Political Weekly*, Vol.XXVI, No.52, December 28, pp.A.167-A.176.

105. Reddy, Narayana, M.V. (1992), 'Interlinkages of Credit with Factor and Product Markets - A Study in Andhra Pradesh', *Indian Journal of Agricultural Economics*, Vol.47, October-December, pp.618-630.

3

GENESIS OF INDIGENOUS MARKETS- A HISTORICAL PERSPECTIVE

As the economy is an adaptive subsystem[1], according to the version of Kenneth Boulding, it focuses on exchange[2&3], Therefore, economic growth (a sustained increase in per capita income or wealth) is based upon institutional changes, of which the growing complexity and sophistication of the exchange system is to be considered as a major index[4]. Thus, Markets essentially involve exchanges. In light of this background, the present chapter had been devoted to examine the historical background of the tribal markets.

The exchange system is merely one aspect of the regulations of social relationships[5]. There are as many exchange systems as there are types of society which are co-terminus in nature. But here the market system is one form of exchange. Therefore, the so-called market principle is not just one principle, but a compendium of principles and hereunder the characteristics of exchange systems[6] are given. They are:

(i) the impersonality or otherwise of the interaction of buyers and sellers;

(ii) the systematization of exchange values, i.e., prices;

(iii) the degree to which buying and selling of specific goods and services are specialised functions;

(iv) the range of goods and services for which buying and selling are conventionally valid;

(v) the degree to which exchange transactions enter into the stages of production from raw-resources to consumable product or service;

(vi) the degree and nature of competition in buying and selling;

(vii) the degree to which buying and selling may be differentiated through the interposition of a medium of exchange.

Exchange is a surface phenomenon of economic life, which reflects the underlying socio-economic organisation of production. Consequently, exchange relations are not general, but specific to the different modes of economic organisation that shapes there. The concept of market, therefore emerges as a socio-economic device to facilitate the needs of people.

The concept of market may be understood in several ways. Broadly speaking, market may be taken as a place where people come to sell, purchase or even exchange their goods - soon after disposing of their selling articles in return of cash money if immediate exchange, barter is not in practice. It may just mean a business place, a specific site, where a group of buyers and a group of sellers meet[7]. In other sense, market is an assemblage of traders at a certain place and at a definite time. The market in practice, is the principal medium for the distribution of economic goods, affording a channel through which the products of farmers, artisans and craftsmen flow to the ultimate consumer; some times may be through middleman and through which the price is returned to the producer. Socially, a market can be viewed, as a more or less structured group of individuals whose bids and offers reflect the supply and demand situation and thereby establish the price[8].

Hence, the concept of market is a central concept in economics. It is however, an elusive concept as it may mean merely the geographical place where exchange takes place[9&10]. But the concept of market as economists use it also embraces the whole set of circumstances that surround the process of exchange. Therefore, market relates to the entire web of inter-relationships between buyers, sellers and products that are involved in exchange.

Economists use the word *"market"* in two substantially different senses. While they have etymological precedent for this - the Latin root *"mercatus"* means either the place of or the method of contact between buyers and sellers. The first sense in which economists use the word is concerned with the general conditions[11] under which buyers and sellers exchange goods and services. The second sense in which the word is used is to delineate the boundaries (usually geographic) that identify specific groups of buyers, sellers and commodities. This concept of the market is designated to the extent of the market process of moving goods from the producer to the user[12].

To the anthropologist, however, a market has more than economic, geographic, or social significance. For understanding the full cultural dimensions of a market, the social, religious, political, and other cultural factors are also important[13]. Recognition of these factors becomes more significant as we move from a highly complex economy to the economy of simple societies. In such societies, the economic behaviour is conditioned more directly by social and other cultural patterns of the people than is true of complex societies[14].

Markets in the most literal and immediate sense are places in which things are bought and sold. In the modern industrial system, however, the market is not a place; it has expanded to include the whole geographical area in which sellers compete with each other for customers[15]. *Alfred Marshall*, based his definition of the market on that of the French Economist A. Cournot:

"Economists understand by the term 'Market', not only particular market place in which things are bought and sold, but the whole of any region in which buyers and sellers are in such free intercourse with one another that the prices of the same goods tend to equality easily and quickly"[16].

To this, Marshall added:

"The more nearly perfect a market is, the stronger is the tendency for the same price to be paid for the same thing at the same time in all parts of the market"[17].

Marketing systems play a dual role in economic development. On the one hand they perform an allocative role and on the other they perform an extractive role. As such they act as resource allocater and resource extractor. Therefore, they continually bring about the inter-sectoral reallocation of resources. Hence, the form and direction, the size and the pace of this transfer of resources can be highly varied. The net effect of an exchange system upon a society depends very much on the relationships of people to the system of production[18]. It, therefore, determines the distribution or the consumption. Therefore, in its relational context, there is a need to study the origin and development of market centres and marketing and its various types as exist today.

The origin and development of marketing and market places are closely associated with development of man's activity or with the history of civilization. Simple unorganized and rudimentary trade or exchange of commodities is as old as man's society. Although, the earliest man believed in self-sufficiency and had no idea either of exchange or trade, his very limited wants were satisfied either by his immediate environment or by the place he used to move in search of food, water, favourable climate, etc., otherwise remained unfulfilled. This nomadic culture too had occasional free exchange of gifts or reciprocal exchange of needed items. With the growth of social contact and when man started living in groups, he began the practice of exchange of commodities[19]. The earliest system of marketing was no doubt barter - i.e., exchange of commodities. It's first form was *silent barter*. Later on, barter system became common and was in practice even after the development of coins as medium of exchange. In fact, there are some common characteristics in the sequence of market development throughout the world. This system of barter is still prevalent in many parts of India as well as in Andhra Pradesh.

Markets as centres of commerce seem to have had three separate points of origin[20]. The first was in rural fairs. The second point was in service to the landlords. The third, and most influential, origin of markets was in international trade.

The evolution of marketing in most societies has characteristically gone through the following four phases:[21]

(i) The complementary phase, where marketing is used essentially as a social tool;

(ii) The integrating phase, where marketing functions assume command of all of the company's activities;

(iii) The strategic phase, where marketing activity becomes the unifying guidance for all company activities;

(iv) The metaphysical phase, which is characterised by the transition of marketing from a strictly entre-preneurial tool to one where it assumes the dimensions of a social science. Objectives include the promotion of social interests far beyond those of the individual company or industrial sector[22].

The marketing literature provides sufficient evidence that the present position of the channels of distribution in less developed countries is at a natural stage of the evolution of the economy. Baker and El-Haddad emphasized that, "marketing in a society passes through a number of stages assuming a variety of roles corresponding with the level of development of the economy"[23]. One can, therefore, relate the present position of the distribution channels in the emerging nations to the evolutionary process of a non-monetary subsistence economy to a monetary one, and later from an economy of scarcity, where demand exceeds supply, to one of abundance, where supply of goods and services far exceeds the demand[24].

The evolution of marketing institutions in LDCs is a complex process that can be understood only by an analysis of the cultural, economic and legal institutions that are presently at play. Unfortunately, very little is known about the evolution of marketing institutions in LDCs[25].

The rise of the market has undergone a transformation process that had been there in the development of economics, wherein markets might be more or less *'perfect'*; it was the business of the economist to look for ways of making them as perfect as possible[26]. Since then there has been a great change. For instance, 'customary' economies or primitive non-market economies were known to historians and (especially) to anthropologists. The economy of a neolithic or early medieval village, as well as of the tribal communities which have survived until lately in many parts of the world, was not organised by its Ruler (if such existed); it was based upon a corpus of tradition. By that tradition, individual function was prescribed, and continued to be prescribed. It is important to emphasize that, the 'head' of the organisation (King or Chief or High Priest or Council of Elders)would himself be a part of the traditional structure. He also would have prescribed functions, together with appropriate rights that would go with them[27].

The exchange system of all economies, whether modern or not, derives from two sets of conditions[28]. They are: (i) on the demand side, there are at the moment of individual actions, specific unsatiated wants which define the goals of activity; (ii) on the supply side, all exchange is based on differentiation of role.

The process of exchange of agricultural commodities dates long back with the beginning of human civilisation. It has developed gradually with the span of changing behavioural dimensions of the settled and nomadic habitants, through various stages-*gift exchange, barter deed, early coinage and monetized exchanges*. The last stage may be defined as the stage of *commercialisation*. An analytical experience of this can be well understood from 19th Century onwards as considerable historical documentation is available there on[29]. It is evidenced that the commercialisation began with the rule of property by making land as an individual asset under civil law during the British colonialism in India which instilled the seeds of capitalist entrepeneurship in agriculture[30].

The marketing structure in agriculture has also an indirect bearing on the sociological dimensions in rural areas apart from the relation with economic factors[31]. As such, in peasant oriented society, social power configuration, the pattern of land holding, the tenancy system and credit linkages governs the marketing functions to a large extent and this sort of picturesque can also be found in the tribal society.

Where money is used in primitive economy, it is not all - purpose money; each kind can be used only for a special range of transactions[32], such as the use of cattle as a money object for acquiring a bride or wealth, but not for acquiring food or craft products. In primitive economy a given money object sometimes serves one use only, as when debts are calculated in terms of brass-rods but actually paid in strips of cloth[33]. Thus, the disposition[34] of natural resources, material outputs, and labour is often compartmentalized separately in primitive economy.

Market exchange as a principle compels its participants to seek material self-grain[35]; each must sell something of market value to acquire the material means of existence[36]. Market exchange refers not only to the existence of market places[37], but also the organisational process of purchase and sale at money price which is the mechanism of transacting material products, labour and natural resources. Land and labour use become re-arranged in response to such price changes because, the land owners and labourers depend for their livelihood on the money price of their land and labour, which in turn, depends on the sales price of the material product - land and labour produce[38]. Thus, one has to surmise that a market economy is a highly decentralised network[39], which reinforces the atomistic view of society.

Polanyi and his associates show that economy-made market networks and state that monetised internal and external trade do not exist as integrative transactions in most band and tribal economies. In these societies, production and distribution involve little of the profit motive[40]. ... The process of distribution, in many tribes, is set in a non-economic (non-economising) matrix, which takes the form of gift and ceremonial exchange[41].

From the 16th Century onwards, markets were both numerous and important. To comprehend the sudden change over to an utterly new type of economy in the 19th Century[42], we must now turn to the history of the market as an institution. The earlier view that primitive tribes lived without trade in private domestic economy must be described as incorrect[43].

The forms of trade have in some cases been employed as designations of entire economies, and the resulting types have been used in setting-up hypothetical developmental series supposedly making off the evolution of economic life[44]. Thus, while Gras has suggested[45] that *Hildebrandt's "stages"* of the development of economic systems-*barter, money, and credit economies*-must be revised into the progression of *gift economy, gift barter economy, pure barter, and money barter*, he nevertheless envisages them as primarily useful as marketing off the stages of a sequence of growth[46].

The market is also the focus of a network of kinship, social, economic, and ceremonial ties and obligations. These cut across ethnic, cultural, linguistic, class, caste, and geographic boundaries. The market is the centre of an economic redistribution system involving barter, ceremonial exchange, money and credit.

The process of distribution, in many tribes, is set in a non-economic matrix which takes the form of gift and ceremonial exchange[47]. Whereas, gift and ceremonial exchange usually accompany the scaling of some friendly part, as in cases of exchange incident upon marriage, trade is often consummated with an underlying sense of hostility, nonetheless real for the conventionalised expressions of friendship which frequently accompany it[48].

The practice of gift giving[49]- the intimate and magnanimous impulses which prompted gift giving among the primitive people everywhere demonstrated the advantages to be gained from the multiple uses of possessions. It was the first form of transfer of property rights to emerge, however, ephemeral it may have been[50].

Silent trading is reported from various parts of the world. *Grierson*[51] treated silent trade as an early stage in the evolution of inter-societal trade, with historical survivals in a variety of forms, that seemed to be modifications of an original form. To him, the silent trade has stood as the classical record of early trading contacts where exchange took place without the face-to-face meeting of the parties to the exchange[52].

Two major varieties of silent trade are discernible[53]:

(i) a long-distance type between traders from state societies and peoples from primitive "tribes" (not primitive "states", "chiefdoms", or "bands") (Carthaginian-West African: Egyptian Somali: Nuba and Habasha-Zanj tribes; Abyssinians - southern tribes; ancient Arabs-tribes in Nigeria, Guinea and Sierra Leone: Malay-Kubu: and Chinese and Indonesian-Phillippine, Moluccan, and New Guinea tribes); and

(ii) a short-distance type between traders from chiefdoms and tribes with people from band-organized societies (Bantu-Pygmy: early Malya-Semang: and Phillippine traders - Luzon Negritos).

Peasant societies[54] habitually use money for a wide range of transactions, many of which take place in market place situations. To this we may add the notion that peasant societies retain a high degree of subsistence production which does not find its way into the market. In this context, peasant societies may be defined as ways of life which are traditionally oriented, linked but separate from urban centres, combining market activity with subsistence production[55]. In peasant societies of this kind, the market place is the focus and distinctive feature of the network of exchange which binds the economy together, but the peasant system wherein the marketplace is already a part and parcel of it is wider in its ramifications. In this connection, it would be better to probe into its character. As such, a large proportion of produce does not find its way into the market place at all. The market place frequently exists alongside peasant systems, and may be interlinked with them[56&57]. Much of the production for domestic, and some for pre-statory consumption belongs to the subsistence sector. Another factor is that, market place systems are today normally part of national systems which contain industrial and sophisticated commercial sectors which impinge upon the market place; but yet are separated from it. Thus, market place systems do not exist in isolation but are flanked on the one hand by pre-station and subsistence, and on the other by a fully modern sector[58]. As in relation to this the barter system had acquired vital importance both in peasant and tribal economies. Owing to this reason, the barter system and the money economy had been discussed hereunder.

Barter include trading services for services[59]. Barter has been known to take place even where the trading parties are feuding or at war. If a symbiotic relationship exists between two societies but warfare prevents their meeting face-to-face, a procedure known as dumb or silent barter may be brought into play[60]. And, further in the direction of a market distribution economy is the phenomenon of money barter[61].

The literature on trade in non-literate societies makes clear that barter is by far the most prevalent mode of exchange, and that it is carried on by means of giving one commodity for another, either according to established ratios or by actual bargaining. It is important that, both these methods be recognised as co-existent, since bargaining by no means always accompanies barter. Therefore an extension or refinement upon the system of pairing transactions was evolved later as a step towards a barter transaction[62].

Even though barter may be considered primitive and crude as a method of exchange, it can actually be the most effective means of securing vital necessities where there is an acute scarcity of goods[63].

The *coercive barter* transaction is clearly illustrated in another type of primitive exchange[64]. "While the land people grow the betel nut and the pepper leaf, the sea people burn and refine the coral lime with which the betel and pepper leaf are chewed. In the market the same sized fish will command ten taro or forty betel nut. But a cup of lime commands eighty betel nut, but only four taro. Betel chewing need is matched against betel chewing need to coerce the sea people into providing enough lime for the land people"[65].

By and large, it is to be stated that, the traditional economic transactions are carried on through barter; commodities are measured by volume rather than by weight; production is small in scale; concern is with consumer goods rather than trade goods; competition is absent, prices being fixed by traditionally determined relative values rather than as a result of the interplay of demand and supply of commodities[66].

The presence or absence of markets or money does not necessarily affect the economic system of a primitive society. This refutes the 19th century myth that money was an invention, the appearance of which inevitably transformed a society by creating markets, forcing the pace of the division of labour and releasing man's natural propensity to barter, truck and exchange[67].

Trade does not arise within a community; it is an external affair involving different communities. 'In its beginnings commerce is a transaction between ethnic groups; it does not take place between members of the same tribe or of the same community, but it is, in the oldest social communities an external phenomenon, being directed only towards foreign tribes[68]. 'Strange though it may seem, medieval commerce developed from the beginnings under the influence, not of local, but of export trade[69]. 'In any case, the oldest commerce is an exchange relation between alien tribes'[70]. Thus, in the passage of time, significant developments occured in the pattern of trade in early medieval centuries in the expansion of maritime activity.

Medieval accounts of the traditional trade of Asia lay stress upon exotic luxuries and upon the spice trade in its diversity. In bulk, spices could represent a considerable portion of a ship's cargo. Thus, Marco Polo appears to reckon the cargo a Chinese junk could carry in terms of the number of bags or baskets of pepper, in addition to the crew and passengers and their personal effects. Apart from foreign luxuries and 'toys', the principal commodities in demand in China were spices, for which there was a greater market than in the westward trade[71].

The basis of the trade practised was destroyed by the Salt Policy of the British Indian Government introduced in the early 19th Century besides the introduction of railways, metalled roads, repeated famines and the forest policy of the government[72]. For tribals in the northern central provinces, the outcome of government policy, particularly the attempt to impose a market economy was little short of tragic. Between 1818-1920 they became deeply indebted, and lost much of their land to moneylenders turned malguzars. Others remained locked into traditional poverty[73]. As a result many in the administration dismissed the tribal community, though some like W.V. Grigson, Deputy Commissioner of Mandla in the thirties, were more sympathetic towards them. Grigson accounted tribal decline to the results of state policy and by implication, to the market economy developed by British administrators over the previous decades[74].

The transition from tribal to peasant economy, while shaped by particular historical conditions, implies fundamental structural and cognitive changes, not least the transformation of social relationships primarily involving gift exchanges into those based principally on the transaction of commodities[75]. Therefore, one significant implication of the change is that the unity of person and thing characteristic of tribal life gradually breaks down as people increasingly assume a peasant mode of existence. It is thus part of a *'process of commoditization'* which involves the *'progressive abstraction of social labour'*[76].

Contemporary markets represent survival forms of organisation that have withstood all the corroding influences of time. Various discoveries by research workers in the different branches of the social sciences have shed new light on the evolutionary nature of markets revealing significant changes in their character and functions through the ages[77]. Therefore, from these findings, one learns that, the market institution was a relatively mature socio-economic invention centuries before the Christian era. The prevalence of business partnerships, kinds of goods offered for exchange, legal agreements and contracts, and formal trade customs prevailing among middlemen five thousand years before our time have been found to be the indispensable means and services they have provided.

Market organisations can be found in all stages of development today owing to the uneven degrees of social and economic advancement in the nations of the world[78]. This general cross-section view of markets showing progressive gradations of development as they have come down to us from the past, range from a system of ceremonial gift-giving which prevails among certain primitive tribes in the south-western pacific to the highly formalized modern produce exchanges dealing exclusively in future contracts[79].

Another important dimension of the new situation is the extension of market mechanism and money economy in the tribal areas. The introduction of money and linkage of the local economy with distant markets make qualitative change in the situation. The surplus with some individuals, which in the closed system could only be socially enjoyed, can now provide the individual a base for more wealth, which can be stored in the form of money to any extent. The individual owner can now weigh the pros and cons of sharing the fruits with the fellow members of his community and acquiring new wealth in the form of money by giving away the surplus for consumption elsewhere. Money inflow into the tribal economy is matched by outflow of valuable commodities. This has no adverse implications so long as the export commodity is not essential for the well being of the community or when it is surplus over and above their limited requirements. In fact, at this stage the individual owners may have no incentive to sell. It is like a natural outflow of surplus, though with some notional exchange. But once a stage is reached where the local production and the local consumption needs just balance, the market mechanism, with insidious introduction of money, begins to play havoc with the socio-economic system as a whole[80&81]. There is a natural upper limit to personal consumption in a self-contained and closed economy. An individual may aspire for greater cattle wealth as a symbol of prestige; but the enjoyment of riches has to be shared in the community. The statistical computation of wealth and incomes of individuals in primitive societies on the basis of the cattle owned and income generation in modern terms may yield phenomenal figures. But in actual practice, there is no difference between him and the one who does not own any. Similar is the case with other commodities. Even when an individual may get money-value for his assets, it may not mean anything to him except some cash figures in a Pass Book, the significance of which he may not realise[82].

The modern role of the market is characterized by the growing use of money, measurement by weight, the introduction of mass-produced and manufactured commodities, price fixing by demand and supply of commodities, and other typical characteristics of a self-regulating market economy[83].

The structure of the marketing system of farm products in rural areas is unorganised. Markets and middlemen are frequently encountered in non-literate societies as aids to business enterprises of various sorts. They do not by any means always go together, although stated markets of any size are rarely without professional traders. Markets for inter-tribal dealing are not found except among populous groups, while, similarly, merchants whose primary means of earning a livelihood comes from trade within their own group are found only in societies where a sufficiently large economic surplus is produced to support them[84]. However, it is to be stated that, the large number of intermediaries seasonally evident in rural petty commodity markets, and appearing to satisfy structural conditions for perfect competition, gives us little indication of the process underlying the pattern. They detract attention from monopoly at another level and from the accumulation of physical and financial surpluses by inter-regional traders. Even Berg finds price differences substantially in excess of transport costs[85]. Therefore, the typical small merchant operated within a limited area and their functions were often, but not always, specialised, nor were their activities always confined to a particular locality.

Keeping in view of the aforesaid discussion, one can easily surmise that commercialisation had been penetrating at rapid strides in the realm of exchange system in general and tribal areas in particular. Therefore, commercialisation involves increasing market exchange for a number of purposes[86]. They are as follows:

(i) in order to purchase goods not produced by the household, food may be sold for cattle, salt, mill cloth, kerosene and jewellery. Food may be purchased when food production has failed;

(ii) in order to purchase goods produced but not owned by the household, food will be purchased by landless labourers paid in cash for their work in the production of food. Their labour power is commercialised. Food will be purchased or bartered in rural areas by labour paid in cash or in kind for their work in the production of non-staples (fruit and vegetables, spices, etc.) and agro-industrial crops (cotton, jute, rubber, etc.). These first two purposes may also be effected by exchange in kind, or barter, though commercialisation is characterised by increasing use of money in exchange; and

(iii) in order to obtain cash, food may be sold for cash in order to pay taxes, rent and to repay debts.

The domestic economy, may be regional or state, the marketing hierarchy may be of three-tiers[87]: financial and commercial centres; the market towns; and rural periodical markets, which serves the domestic economy and also connects the forward markets. The forward markets are to some extent meant for export agencies of rural products of farm and rural industrial sector. The markets were the regulated trade centres locally known as *'Mandi'*. These were the points at which primary produce was assembled for onward transmission to the main distributing centres or exporting centres. They were also the points at which goods were sent-up from main distributing centres for wholesaling and retailing. Down to this urban network of financial centres and 'Mandies', the vast hinterland was served by periodic markets and seasonal fairs, dispersed widely over the country side[88]. In this way, the rural and urban markets were functioning in the 19th century. This hierarchy is prevailing till to date as an unchanged phenomenon in rural areas in the country. More number of rural markets known as *'Shandies'* in South Indian States, *'paiths'* in Maharashtra and Western States, *'haats'* in North Indian States assembled once or twice a week for retail transactions in agricultural, forest and manufactured products. The weekly markets[89] in their typical traditional style assemble on the road side of the hamlet or village, or in the groove where buyers and sellers transact in their goods[90]. The traders and middlemen form a central level in the mechanism of the rural markets.

The periodic markets[91], on the other hand, whether it was located in an urban centre or in the open country side, was a purely rural institution labelled "panegyreis" by the Greeks and "nundinae" by the Romans[92]. Its defining characteristics were the opposite of those of the urban market place: a crucial separation from town structures and institutions, an autonomy from formally imposed controls, a lack of permanency, and a predominance of non-formalist functions[93]. They were much more than mere forums for the exchange of commodities and services; they were integral to the very social structure of the country side. They were centres of communication where a local man might become famed or from which he might shrink lest he incurs irreparable shame[94].

The various economic functions of the rural periodic market have long been the object of detailed investigation by numerous anthropologists, who have established its significance as one of the principal institutionalmechanisms of social integration in pre-modern societies[95]. Since the beginning of written history this same institution is recorded as being at the epic centre of the various social formations which have dominated the country side of the ancient Maghrib, that is, the fertile zone of North Africa between Libya in the east and Morocco in the west[96].

Some of the features of a rural market[97] are as follows:

(i) the same person is the seller as well as a buyer;

(ii) local productions are the selling items in the market; and

(iii) market covers a small area and population to feed.

The rural market was very much a feature of the inter-local trade of the period. A major feature of the inter-local trade was the predominantly one-way flow of commodities from the village to towns, a corollary of rural self-sufficiency. Such self-sufficiency was, of course, not total, and it is now recognized that the individual village was probably part of a narrow circuit of exchange which encompassed several villages, with the pedlar, the bats and the mandis mediating the distribution of commodities. Direct evidence for such inter-village trade for the period prior to the late eighteenth century is, however, extremely scarce. The commodities mentioned available in rural markets also include items like: salt, spices and metal ware which were either products of distant places or made of raw material which was not locally available. Still, almost certainly the economic needs of the pre-colonial village in India were met mostly from its own produce distributed through customary arrangements rather than through exchange. Incidentally, this pattern of economic organisation was peculiar to Indian rather than the whole of Asia, contrary to a still widely-held belief. In China, about 900 and 1,200 informal markets became the focal points of peasant life and 'Chinese peasants from this time on used commercial means to satisfy their needs for the exchange of many of the most basic services[98].

In the articulation of simple peasant marketing at the haat level with the superior market-places, crucial roles were played by the itinerant trade (phiriwala), the village-based trader who might also have been a wealthy farmer (bepari), and the buyer-up and merchants' agent (paikar). In the haat, the peasant sold his product directly to the consumer as well as to middlemen. Marketing system was designed for buying and selling in small lots, where the bulk of purchases were being made not with a view to re-sale but for consumption by poor peasants or artisans. This offers limited scope for role differentiation or specialization[99]. However, the itinerant trader went about within a limited area making small purchases and sales; his profit margin, arising out of small price differentials. The beparis' deal in cattle, poultry and grain, and not only bring the produce of their own farms for sale, but in the dry season, when the labour of their fields is at a stop, they make large purchases from the farmers'; the rich farmer also made large advances to poorer ones between June and November for which an interest was paid until the delivery of the grain at the harvest-time market price. The bepari thus had a considerable profit margin, could hold large stock waiting for a favourable market, and they would carry the grain to whatever warehouse (goals) gives the best price[100]. Though Buchanan-Hamilton describe them as men of small capital, in some trades, such as silk, they commanded sizeable capital, and served as a channel for the bigger merchant capitalists' advances to primary producers. Thus, despite the restricted opportunities in the framework of peasant marketing at the hat there developed the bepari reaching out to the entrepot merchant and the paikar penetrating into the country-side[101].

In the process of the evolution of specialized trading one phase is the rise of regular trading. The simplest way in which regular trading may grow up is probably as the following:

Any kind of social gathering provides an opportunity for trading; trading which begins as casual, but becomes habitual. The articles may have been brought for exchange. But if the participants do not bring just the same thing, they will be tempted to barter with one another some of the goods they have brought and it turns out to be a fair[102&103].

Tribal markets are characterized by their close knit socio-politico-economic relationships. Many of the earliest local traders were producers seeking an outlet for their goods or the means to obtain other commodities, and their customers were usually also producers. As a result, early markets had to be adopted to the requirements of producers trading on part-time rather than to the needs of full-time traders. Periodicity was an advantage for most market participants because, their economic roles were diverse[104]. The majority of traders, even in many contemporary markets are part-time having two or more different occupations, and engage in some form of primary or secondary production[105].

Thus, the rural markets are significant from social, economic and ethnic points of view and so the rural life tends to revolve around them. Almost all rural produce of all types, and many of the urban-based consumer goods, get exchanged at these markets[106]. As a result, the marketing system as a whole has been emerging owing to the urban demand for rural products and rural demand for urban products as well. Viewed from the angle of the village, the periodic markets appear to be the base of a system of provision of goods and services in rural India upon which other systems are built[107].

An interesting feature of the development has been the way the traditional market institutions have been acquiring new meaning among the tribals. It is well known that, traditionally tribes possessed little value on surplus accommodation and a market trading[108], since the market serves as the contact point between tribal peoples, peasant groups and agents from the national government and the industrialized world. Besides, while observing an experiment in culture change the institution of market may also be regarded as an ideal natural *'laboratory'*[109].

The transformation of rural markets in the country has developed well with the growing monetisation and techniques of exchange. High risks and low-profit margin - these were the two conditions of Indian trade in rural areas during the colonial and pre-colonial period which has gradually developed after the second world war period. The growing awareness of the importance of cost benefit ratios on the part of the rural producers and state intervention in farm and non-farm trade has resulted in several sophisticated changes[110]. They are: regulation of trade, government procurement, price support, speculation control, backward and forward linkages and extensive producer oriented approach. The major outcome of the change of the rural market structure was that it was engaged as regulation of agricultural markets, which has eliminated the influence of middlemen to some extent.

As a result, the first attempt to regulate agricultural markets in India was made in 1897. An Act passed in that year authorised the then British Resident in Hyderabad Assigned District to declare any place within his jurisdiction as a market place for sale and purchase of agricultural produce and to constitute a Committee to supervise and regulate the markets[111]. The Law did help to improve the buying and selling of cotton. Therefore, in practice the Law was applied only to cotton, the main cash crop of the region, and despite its title, did not include grain. Thirty years later, with the passage of the "Cotton Markets Act" (1927) in Bombay once again the Law was concerned only with a single crop.

The Royal Commission on Agriculture, reporting in 1928urged that all provinces should establish regulated markets to help orderly marketing of all agricultural produce. Hyderabad, Central Provinces and Madras promptly acted on the Commission's recommendations and passed appropriate legislation. Others followed with longer intervals - Punjab in 1939, also Mysore in the same year, though its Act was not operative until 1948, Madhya Pradesh in 1952, Kerala and Orissa in 1957. At the beginning of the Third Plan, Legislation for establishing regulated markets was in force in nine States. Four more states enacted the Agricultural Produce Markets Act by 1968 and the remaining states-Assam, Nagaland, Kerala and Jammu & Kashmir-are expected to do so during the Fourth Plan period[112]. And, in the same manner, similar directions and steps had also been taken to regulate the marketing systems and its evil machinations of the moneylender-cum-trader in tribal areas and recommended setting-up of an institutional agency, sponsored by the state, to put an end to exploitation. Therefore, in order to put an end to the abysmal process of exploitation and to free the tribals from the private traders and to ensure reasonable price to the MFP, the State Government had set-up the Andhra Pradesh Scheduled Tribes Finance and Development Corporation in 1956, as recommended by the Malayappan committee. This institution with its headquarters at Visakhapatnam started functioning from 1957 and in 1970, its name has been changed as *'The Girijan Co-operative Corporation'*. In view of this background, the entire gamut of this sort of institutional set-up had been analysed in the next chapter.

NOTES & REFERENCES

1. See Appendix-I.
2. Exchange becomes that aspect of behaviour which provides interconnection between individual acts of choice, and the possibility of institutionalized mechanisms of adjustment, such as price reactions. The actions of an isolated man can be subjected to economic analysis; but an economy is a system which gains reality through the social phenomenon of exchange. For detailed discussion, see Robbins, Lionel: An Essay on the *Nature of Significance of Economic Science,* Macmillan & Co., Ltd., London, 1937, and also see Firth, Raymond: *Malay Fishermen: Their Peasant Economy* Opt.cit., 1966.
3. Boulding, Kenneth (1941), *Economic Analysis,* Harper & Row Publishers, New York, pp.3-8.
4. Belshaw, Cyril, S. (1965), *Traditional Exchange and Modern Markets,* Prentice-Hall, Inc., London, p.6.
5. Compare the approach of George Homans, (1962), 'Social Behaviour as Exchange', *Sentiments and Activities,* Free Press, Inc., New York.
6. Belshaw, S.: Op.cit., pp.8-9.
7. Sinha, D.P. : Op.cit., 1968, p.9.
8. (a) Ibid., p.9.

   (b) *Encyclopedia of the Social Sciences,* Vol.10, 1933, p.131.
9. Sills, David, L.(1968), *International Encyclopedia of the Social Sciences,* The Macmillan Company & The Free Press, U.S.A., Vol.IX, p.575.
10. A nodal point where buyers and sellers meet to exchange the goods and services.
11. The conditions may be summarized in a series of alternative theoretical market structures, such as *"perfect competition"*, *"monopoly"*, *"oligopoly"* and *"monopolistic competition"*. These theoretical structures or models make assumptions about such things as the number of sellers and buyers and their perceptions of each other and yield predictions about market behaviour. In turn this predicted behaviour leads to predictions about market results: what will be the prices, quantities and qualities of outputs that emerge from the market. Market structure is not one-dimensional, but it is often convenient to think of different market

structures as differing from one another in terms of the kind and degree of competition that they lead to.

12. *The Encyclopedia of Americana,* Vol.18, American Corporation, New York, 1973, pp.299-300.
13. Sinha, D.P.: *Culture Change in Inter-Tribal Market,* Op.cit., P.9.
14. Ibid., p.9.
15. *Encyclopedia Britannica,* 'Marketing and Merchandising', Vol.XI, William, Benton Publisher, Chicago, (1943-1973), p.511.
16. Ibid., p. 511.
17. Ibid., p. 511.
18. Harriss, Barbara(1982), *Tropics of West Africa,* Occasional Paper on Development Studies, No.17, England, March p.1.
19. Saxena, H.M.(1988), *Rural Markets and Development - A Case Study of Rajasthan State,* Rawat Publications, Jaipur, p.11 & 12.
20. *Encyclopedia Britannica,* Vol.XI, William, Benton Publishers (1943-1973), Chicago, p.513.
21. Rao, R.(1976), 'Marketing and Economic Development', *Marketing and Management,* January, p.19 & 20.
22. Scherb, Otto, H.(1980), 'Brazel Pursues Industrial Eminence', *Advertising Age,* May 12, p.58.
23. Baker, Michael & A. El-Hadded(1981), 'Marketing and Economic Development', in *Proceedings of the European Academy for Advanced Research in Marketing,* X Annual Work-Shop, Copenhagen, 25-27, March Edited by H.H. Larsen and S. Heede, pp.1249-1282.
24. Kaynak, Edward (1986), *Marketing and Economic Development,* Praeger Publishers, New York, pp.77-78.
25. (a) Kaynak, Edward (1979), A Refined Approach to the wheel of Retailing, *European Journal of Marketing,* Vol.13, No.7, pp.237-245.

    (b) Anderson, Dole, A.(1970), *Marketing Development- The Tribal Experience,* MSU International Business and Economic Studies, East Lansing, pp.69-73.
26. Hicks, J.R. (1969), *A Theory of Economic History,* Oxford University Press, London, p.9.
27. Ibid..., p.13 & 14.
28. For further details see Belshaw,C.S.: Op.cit; p.110 & 111.

29. The historical documentation evidences the changing agrarian competitions in different regions of the country, recessional and raising terms of trade and technical relations in agriculture for the period of over a century from 1857 to 1980. For details see Choudary, B.B.: *Growth of Commercial Agriculture in Bengal,* Calcutta, 1964; Siddiqui Agra: *Agrarian Change in a Northern State-Uttar Pradesh (1819-1833),* Oxford, 1973; Whitecombe, E.: *Agrarian Conditions in Northern India - The United Provinces under British Rule 1860-1900,* California, 1971; Dandekar, V.M.: *Peasants-Labour Relationship,* Gokhale Institute of Politics and Economics, Pune, India, 1979; Bhardwaj, K.: *Technical Relations in Agricultural Development of India : Policy and Problems,* ed., C.H. Shah, C.M. Vakil, Orient Longman, 1979. Bhaduri, A.: 'A Study in Agricultural Backwardness under Semi-Feudalism', *Economic Journal,* March, 1973.

30. For details see Guha, R.: *A Rule of Property for Bengal,* Paris, 1973.

31. Gopal Raja: *Rural Marketing in India,* Op.cit., p.113.

32. A primitive transaction is termed *'spheres of exchange'*. There are various groups of goods and services and exchange of one item can only take place with another item in the same group. In South-Eastern New Guinea, for instance, a very important series of exchanges takes place between the possessors of shell arm-rings and of necklaces of shell discs, while other important exchanges are of fish for vegetables. But the food items can only be exchanged against each other, and so also the shell valuables. It would be unthinkable for a man who wished a shell valuable to offer in return Yams or fish or other property not of a shell kind. There is no free market, no final measure of the value of individual things, and no common medium whereby every type of goods and services can be translated into terms of every other. A primitive economy, thus, presents a strong contract to our money economy - See, Firth: 'Work and Wealth of Primitive Communities', in *Human Types,* by him, Mentor Books, New York, 1958, p.68.

33. Bohannan, Paul (1959), 'The Impact of money on an African Subsistence Economy', *Journal of Economic History,* 19; pp.491-503.

34. For the detailed discussion on it, See Dalton, George: Op.cit., pp.130-134.

35. Dalton, George, Op.cit., p.45.

36. For instance, labourers must sell their labour; land owners must sell the use of their land and natural resources; farm and factory owners must sell end products. The same market network transacts factor ingredients of production - labour, land, natural resources, finance, transportation - as well as finished goods and services of all varieties.
37. Indicates sites wherein buyers and sellers congregate.
38. Dalton, George, Op.cit., p.45.
39. It consists of a multitude of related but nonetheless individual purchase and sale transactions. The operational units are individual business firms buying resources and selling outputs and individual families buying household goods and selling labour and other resources.
40. Herskovits,M.J. (1952), *Economic Anthropology*, Knopf, New York, p.11.
41. Ibid., p. 155.
42. Polanyi, Karl (1957), *The Great Transformation*, Rinehart & Company, New York, p.55.
43. Although there are very few pure subsistence economies (economies in which commercial transactions are entirely absent), there are a good many primitive economies (especially in Africa) in which half or more of total income comes from subsistence production, and peasant economies in which, smaller, but significant, amounts of subsistence production are the rule. In the early 1950s, a U.N. Agency reported that, "... between 65 per cent and 75 per cent of the total cultivated land area of tropical Africa is devoted to subsistence production" - United Nations: *Enlargement of the Exchange in Tropical Africa*, United Nations, New York, 1954, p.13. In the 1960s, the problem of transforming subsistence agriculture in Africa was still very much a matter of concern. Harvard University Press, Cambridge, 1964. Clower, R., G. Dalton, M. Harwitz and A.A. Walters: *Growth Without Development : An Economic Survey of Liberia*, North-Western University Press, Evanston, 1966. Adelman, Irma & Cynthia Taft Morris: *Society, Politics, and Economic Development*, Johns Hopkins Press, Baltimore, 1967.
44. Herskovits, Melville, J.(1965), *Economic Anthropology: The Economic Life of Primitive Peoples*, W.W. Norton and Company, Inc., New York, p.183.

45. Gras, N.S.B.(1930), "Barter", *Encyclopedia of the Social Sciences*, Vol.II, pp.468-469.
46. Herskovits, Melville, J.: Op.cit., 1965, p.184.
47. Herskovits, Melville, J.: Op.Cit., 1965, p. 155.
48. Ibid., p.180.
49. Gradually, the savages extended the practice of gift giving to a wider circle of friendly persons, even exceeding the metes and bounds of their own tribal territories. When this occurred, the attitude of the recipient was generally characterised by an air of utter indifference: for it was considered indecorous to manifest any interest in the gift or to covet possession.
50. Bakken, Henry, H.(1953), *Theory of Markets and Marketing*, Mimir Publishers, Inc. p.265.
51. Grierson, P.J., Hamilton (1903), *The Silent Trade : A Contribution to the Early History of Human Intercourse*, Edinburgh : Wm. Green & Sons.
52. For a certain period of time, on the fringes of civilization in Africa, South-East Asia, and in some occasional cases in Northern Europe and Asia, one minor form of inter-societal or exterior economic exchange was *"silent trade"*. This was an impersonal form of trade without oral communication or close face-to-face contact. Divergence in both time and place raise the possibility that these regional occurences are not historically related. They might be cases of the independent development of similar institutions under similar conditions with some regional diffusion and some tenacity as a tradition over time.
53. Price John, A. (1980), 'On Silent Trade', in George Dalton (Ed.), *Research in Economic Anthropology - A Research Annual*, Vol.III, Jai Press Inc., p.76.
54. It may also be argued that most formerly primitive societies have been transformed into peasant societies through the introduction of money and markets.
55. Belshaw, Cyril, S.: Op.cit., p.8 & 9.
56. Ibid., p.75.
57. This is to be the case in Meso-America. In Fiji it is common for a man to earn money through marketing and spread it in stores on the purchase of whales' teeth, kerosene and cloth (items not found in the market place) for ceremonial purposes. In Africa the

markets co-exist with traditional systems in which lineage and age-set interests govern principles of exchange.

58. Belshaw, Cyril, S; Op.Cit., p.76.
59. Holmes, Lowell, D.: *Anthropology : An Introduction,* The Ronald Press Company, New York, 1971, p. 261.
60. Ibid., p.262.
61. Wherein a useful consumption commodity serves as a standard value for all goods exchanged.
62. For a long time, the act of bartering was incidental to the meeting of primitives wherever their paths crossed. The acquisition of goods through barter resulted in an increasing demand on the part of the primitive for more goods, not only from fellow tribes men but from neighbouring peoples, both friendly and hostile. Their contacts were not left to chance. They were pre-arranged as to time and place. Eventually, the gods of the primitive peoples were given a definite function in making hallow the grounds on which exchanges took place. It was their duty to protect and to sanctify the grounds, transforming it into a neutral territory free from conflict. For further details, see Bakken, Henry, H: *Theory of Markets and Marketing,* Op.cit., pp.267-269.
63. Bakken, Henry, H.: Op.cit. p.271.
64. Ibid., p.272.
65. Mead, Margaret: 'Melanesian Middlemen', Op.cit., p.127.
66. Sinha, D.P.(1968), Op.cit., p.59.
67. Polanyi, Karl (1957), Op.cit., p.58.
68. Weber, Max (1923), *General Economic History,* The Free Press, Glencoe, p.195.
69. Pirenne (1936), *Economic and Social History of Medieval Europe,* Routledge, London, p.142.
70. Weber, M.(1923), Op.cit., p.195.
71. For the detailed discussion See Raychaudhuri, Tapan and Irfan Habib (1982), *The Cambridge Economic History of India,* Vol.I, Orient Longman, Hyderabad, pp.136-139.
72. Radhakrishna,Meena (1989), 'From Tribal Community to Working Class Consciousness'- Case of Yerukula Women', *Economic and Political Weekly,* April 29, Vol. XXIV, No.17, p. WS-2.

73. Baker David, (1991), 'State Policy, the Market Economy, and Tribal Decline : The Central Province, 1861-1920', *The Indian Economic and Social History Review*, October-December, Vol.XXVIII, No.4, p.341.
74. Ibid., p.341.
75. Caplan, Lionel (1991), 'From Tribe to Peasant? The Limbus and the Nepalese State', *The Journal of Peasant Studies*, January, Vol.18, No.2, p.319.
76. Hart, K. (1982), 'On Commoditization', in E. Goody (Ed.), *From Craft to Industry : The Ethnography of Proto-Industrial Cloth Production*, Cambridge University Press, Cambridge, p.40.
77. Bakken, Henry, H.(1953), Op. Cit., p. 3.
78. Ibid., p.3.
79. Ibid., p.3.
80. As a result, deprivation sets in for a section of the people who would come to appreciate for the first time the meaning of economic power being concentrated with certain individuals. The surplus and the want could co-exist. The programme of economic development generally presumes free operation of market forces. Development is computed in terms of money incomes. This may give a completely distorted picture of the actual situation in the tribal area. The indices of development may move-up, but the real condition of the people may deteriorate. See Sharma, B.D., Op.Cit., pp. 18-26.
81. Sharma, B.D.: *Tribal Development : The Concept and Frame*, Op.cit., p.19.
82. Ibid., p. 18 & 19.
83. Ibid., p.59 & 60.
84. Herskovits, Melville, J.(1965), Op.Cit., p.216.
85. Berg, E.: 'Country Studies : Upper Volta', *Marketing Price Policy and Storage of Foodgrains in the Sahel : A Survey*, in CILSS, 1977, Vol.II, pp.25-27.
86. Harriss,Barbara: *Exchange Relations and Poverty in Dry-land Agriculture*, Concept Publishing Company, New Delhi, 1983, p.3.
87. Gopal Raja: *Rural Marketing in India*, Op.cit., p.113 & 114.
88. For more details on 'fairs and markets, 'see *Agricultural Marketing in India* : Marketing Series, No.45, Report on *Fairs, Markets and Produce Exchanges in India*, Delhi, 1943.

89. In the weekly market, a farmer is really a buyer not a seller. His main aim is to procure certain commodities which he cannot produce such as salt, kerosene, cloths and the like. For buying these commodities he has to part with certain portion of his produce either home-grown or collected from forest. In case of normal crop, the producers are paid low prices by the traders to benefit themselves, unless government makes procurement in a large way.

90. Gopal Raja (1986), *Dynamics of Agricultural Marketing in Tribal India,* Rainbow Publications, Coimbatore, pp.36-37.

91. The periodic markets may be explained as the agglomeration of buyers and sellers in villages, semi-urban and some parts of urban areas for marketing of the produce grown in the hinter-land at a given place, time and day. The periodic markets are held weekly, bi-weekly and fort-nightly according to local traditions. Weekly market is the main channel of distribution of local products and goods brought from outside the area. In the wekly markets, the farm, non-farm and manufactured goods brought from the areas of its hinter-land and urban areas are sold and purchased. The transactions in the markets are predominantly in cash, though barter system also exists in case of sale and purchase of local products like pottery, ironware, forest products, etc. The main unifying feature of these markets is, that they are attended by common group of professional traders, mainly coming from urban places.

92. Dalton, George(1979), (Ed.), *Research in Economic Anthropology-A Research Annual,* Jai Press, Inc., Greenwich, Vol.2, p.92.

93. Ibid., p.92.

94. Ibid., p.93.

95. (a) Bohannan, P., & Dalton, G., (Ed.): *Markets in Africa,* Op.cit., pp.36-52.

    (b) Benet, F.: 'Weekly Markets (1957), Their Importance for Research and Action', in *Contribution to Mediterranean Sociology* (Ed . J. Peristiany), Paris; Mouton, 1968, pp.163-166. K. Polanyi, c.M. Arensberg, and H.W. Pearson, Glencoe, III : Free Press, pp.188-217.

    (c) Fogg, W.(1938), 'A Tribal Market in the Spanish Zone of Morocco', *Africa,* 11: pp.428-458.

(d) ——(1939), 'The Importance of Tribal markets in the Commercial Life of the Countrywide of North-West Morocco, *Africa*, 12: pp.445-449.

(e) ————(1939), 'Tribal Markets in Spanish Morocco', *Journal of the Royal African Society*, 38: pp.322-336.

96. Bohannan, Paul (1963), *Social Anthropology*, Rinehart and Winston, Inc. New York; p.212. For further details, also see Bohannan, Op.cit., pp.212-219.

97. Chandra, Ramesh (1973), 'Market in a Tribal Village : Its Socio-Economic Implications among the Bhills', *Vanyajathi*, Vol.XXI, No.2, April, p.52.

98. Raychaudhuri, Tapan & Irfan Habib, Op.cit., (Vol.I), pp. 325-327.

99. Kumar Dharma & Tapan Ray Chaudhuri (Ed.) (1984), *The Cambridge Economic History of India*, (Vol. II), Orient Longman, Hyderabad, p.273.

100. Ibid., p.273 & 274.

101. Ibid., p.274.

102. Hicks, John: *A Theory of Economic History*, Op.cit., p.26 & 27.

103. A fair is mostly held with a religious background wherein people gather at regular intervals not for business purpose, but for holiday-making, while gathering in a market is purely for sale and purchase of commodities. The interval after which a fair is held is much longer, usually a year or a month, than a market which is held either weekly, bi-weekly or daily. Further, gathering in a fair is many times more than a market. Thus, every fair is a market, while every market is not a fair.

104. Bromley, R.J.: Richard Symanski & Charles M. Good (1975), 'The Rationale of periodic Markets', *Annals ofthe Association of American Geographers*, December, Vol. 65, No.4. p.531.

105. For example, John Whiteman, (1956), "The Kolkhoz Market", *Saiet Studies*, Vol.7, p.384; and Chimgkun Yang, A.(1944), *North China Local Market Economy: A Summary of a Study of Periodic Markets in Chowping, Hsien, Shantung*, Institute of Pacific Relations, Mimeo, New York, p.10; and R.J. Bromley, (1975), "Periodic and Daily Markets in High-Land Ecuador", Unpublished doctoral dissertation, Cambridge University, pp.298-323, and it was re-quoted from Bromley, R.J.,. Richard Symanski & Charles M. Good: Op.cit., p.531.

106. An observation has been made during the field investigation of the researcher.
107. Wanmali, Sudhir (1985), 'Net Works of Distribution of Goods and Services in rural India : Some Spatial Considerations', in *Agricultural Markets in the Semi-Arid Tropics* (Ed.), by D.R. Mohan Raj, Urindra Kumble and P. Sudhir, ICRISAT, Patancheru, Hyderabad, p.137.
108. Sinha Surajit: "Tribal Cultures of Peninsular India as a Dimension of Little Tradition in the Study of Indian Civilisation : A Preliminary Statement", *Journal of American Folklore*, Vol.71, 1958, pp.504-518.
109. An observation has been made during the field investi-gation of the researcher.
110. Gopal, Raja: *Rural Marketing in India*, Op.cit., p.115.
111. "Cotton and Grain Markets Act of Hyderabad", 1897, or the so-called Berar Law.
112. Government of India, *Fourth Five Year Plan*, 1969-71, p.143.

4

ORIGIN AND PERFORMANCE OF GIRIJAN CO-OPERATIVE CORPORATION

Indigenous markets are inclusive of the markets functioning in tribal areas. As it had been adumbrated in the last chapter, an important characteristic of these markets is selling and buying which will be often combined at the same time as in the case of shandies. State intervention became an imperative when these non-institutionalised markets have become centres of exploitation of illiterate and ignorant tribals. Theoretically state intervention in the field of marketing has its own merits. When a state owned corporation undertakes both buying and selling functions, the seller is expected to be paid a remunerative price for his products and likewise the commodities which he will be purchasing will be sold to him at reasonable prices. Besides these benefits, it will make a dent into the monopolistic character of the indigenous markets, though it may often acquire such a characteristic in its operations in practice. One such corporation which is performing the marketing role in tribal areas is the Girijan Cooperative Corporation. In Andhra Pradesh this Corporation is functioning under the above name. This chapter had been devoted for examining the entire gamut of GCC of Andhra Pradesh with the help of secondary data provided by the concerned Divisional Offices in the study area as in relation to its overall performance in fulfilling its twin objectives of credit and marketing in particular and other related aspects in general.

Without fear of contradiction it can be said that in India all the tribal groups are embedded with some unending problems like poverty, exploitation and underdevelopment. Besides, marketing and credit are the twin problems that had been persisting with them.

Another problem of the tribal areas is indebtedness which is the bane of the tribal economy and is a chronic and endemic malady[1] attributed to the peculiar set of economic and social customs of the adivasi tribes. The rate of indebtedness is very high owing to the peculiar characteristic features of the tribal economy[2]. The extent of indebtedness among the tribals varies from State to State. The average debt per family was Rs.50 in Andhra Pradesh; Rs.100 to Rs. 150 in West Bengal; Rs. 2,000 to Rs.2,500 in Tamil Nadu[3]. The agencies of rural finance are grossly inadequate to the everlasting demands of the tribals and hence they have no alternative except the moneylender. Therefore, the tribals are very often exposed to the traditional money-lending system, which is the worst form of exploitation rampant in tribal areas[4].

Added to the problem of indebtedness, land alienation[5] process affected by the people from the plains is also considered as one form of exploitation. In recent years, many of the fertile lands in the tribal belt gradually got transferred to the self-styled landlords[6] whose average holdings vary from 5 to 90 acres[7], while the average land holding of the tribals was as low as 0.66 acres[8]. Due to the persistence of above problems, State intervention to retrieve the tribals had many forms, of which undertaking of marketing activity is one.

STATE MARKETING OF FOREST PRODUCE IN INDIA

The constitution of India gave a special emphasis to the protection of the tribals' rights over their resources. Hence the Government of India has evolved an institutional approach towards the collection of minor and major forest produce from the tribals. Therefore, it is to be stated that, the need for co-operative marketing in India arose from a number of factors. Of these, the first factor was to discourage the malpractices involved in the existing marketing system.[9] The co-operative movement towards marketing activities was accorded considerable importance in the First Five Year Plan but activities remained at a low level of progress[10].The stress has been given to re-organise the marketing co-operatives to make them more viable during the Fourth Five Year Plan. During the Fifth Plan period, the policy on co-operation was formed with the objective to organise the marketing co-operative on the lines of Bawa Committee's recommendation (1972). This Committee on co-operative structure recommended that a tribal should be served in respect of his various needs under one roof instead of having to visit numerous agencies. The large-scale multipurpose co-operative societies (LAMPS) were organised in Bastar district to this effect[11].

Therefore, it is to be stated that the development of marketing facilities in the tribal economy is not only important in ensuring a reasonable price for the products sold by the tribals, but also for providing the domestic requirements of the tribals. In the absence of these facilities, the primitive people would have to walk for over several miles to purchase the basic necessities of rice, salt and kerosene.

Further, development of marketing system in tribal areas is of fundamental urgency to bring about the necessary agricultural revolution[12]. It is apt to say that proper incentives should exist for a tribal farmer to produce more. The most basic incentive is his access to the national/regional market. Marketing technology can play a significant role in enabling this phase of institutional development[13]. Due to lack of a well developed marketing system in the tribal economy, whatever may be the production capacity of the small and marginal farmers, all their produce is usurped by the middlemen. The absence of proper marketing and timely financial help make the tribals depend on the middlemen, who prevent them from leading even a hand to mouth existence. As a result, the tribal economy is ruined and they are mercilessly entangled in the cruel network of exploitation[14].

One important step to help tribals is to provide marketing facilities through shandies. In the initial stages, the tribals viewed with suspicion the steps taken by the Government to open shandies at interior places, as they were of the opinion that these were meant for their exploitation, but later these shandies were welcomed by the tribals as they brought a positive change in their way of life. The market centres in the tribal economy are not only important for business but are also centres of social conglomeration as they provide occasions for social get-to-gether to discuss varied topics of mutual interests ranging from enquiries about crops, market trends, political issues and last but not the least, matrimonial affairs which are usually settled at these places[15].

The issues like money-lending at exorbitant rates of interest, the exploitation of the tribes by the traders and the agricultural situation bracketed the need for the extension of the fair price return to the tribals altogether strengthened the establishment of GCC in the State of Andhra Pradesh. Nearly twenty five years of experience of GCC in the field of marketing in the tribal areas needs to be re-understood in the light of its performance over these years. The discussion made in the following pages focusses on this aspect.

THE ORIGIN AND PERFORMANCE OF G.C.C

Andhra Pradesh forests have a large variety of minor forest produce derived from a number of species of plants. Besides, a large number of animals and minerals, most of the agency areas (i.e., areas predominantly inhabited by tribal population) in the State are rich in forest produce. Forests have been the main source of living for the tribals[16].

The collection and trade of the MFP are done by two agencies: a) Forest Department - Beedi leaf and other than those not included in GCC; b) Girijan Co-operative Corporation - select MFP items. In this connection, the present chapter primarily throws light on the latter.

Some of the minor forest products available in Andhra Pradesh forests have good commercial value. These are: tamarind, gum, adda leaf, myrobalans, mohwa seed, mohwa flower, nuxvomic, soapnuts, honey and hill-brooms. Because of the absence of a semblance of marketing facilities in the tribal areas, they had no choice but to receive the brunt of the inequitable exchange system extended to them by the petty-traders. By taking stock of the prevailing situation and visualising the trade practices adopted by the plain people, the Government felt the need to effectively organise the marketing activities in the agency areas.

The Malayappan Committee was appointed to study the problem and the report highlighted the evil machinations of the moneylender-cum-trader in tribal areas and recommended the setting-up of an institutional agency, sponsored by the State, to put an end to the evil of exploitation. The Committee concluded that, "without this any number of development and ameliorative schemes will not benefit them in any way"[17]. Regulating the market system is also one such attempt in that direction[18]. Consequently, the pioneering attempt has been taken to avert the scourge of tribals especially in the field of marketing by the creation of GCC[19].

In order to put an end to the abysmal process of exploitation and to free the tribals from the private traders and to ensure reasonable prices to the MFP, the State Government set-up the Andhra Pradesh Scheduled Tribes Finance and Development Corporation in 1956, as recommended by the *Malayappan Committee*. This institution with its headquarters at Visakhapatnam started functioning from 1957 and in 1970 it has been renamed as the *'Girijan Co-operative Corporation'*.

The GCC is not paying any interest as in relation to the marketing of agricultural produce. It is significant to note that the purchase of MFP also declined in recent years[20]. Inspite of it's (GCC) edge over other institutions, it could not compete with the private traders in the marketing of agricultural produce. This is mainly due to the sellers' ignorance of market conditions, the long-standing contacts between the traders and sellers and the facility of timely credit given by the traders. Despite statutory monopoly of the Corporation regarding the purchase of minor forest produce[21] a part of it is invariably sold by the tribals to private traders.

Weekly shandies play a major role in tribal market as a large number of people gather there from the adjoining village to get their domestic requirements and to dispose-off their products. Usually, the merchants purchase the tribal products at a lower rate than the prevailing market rate and at the same time they demand high price for their domestic goods. Now, with the advent of the GCC, the Government has regulated the weekly shandies in the scheduled areas. A Shandy Inspector[22] is appointed by the GCC to regulate the market and to purchase the MFP brought by the tribals. But owing to the scant attention paid by the Shandy Inspectors to the problem, the exploitation of non-tribal traders has not been reduced.

In the purchase of MFP, the Corporation is a monopolistic agency. It aims at providing a remunerative price to the tribal for his produce collected from the forest, thus, putting an end to the underhand dealings of the petty-traders operating in tribal areas[23].

The main marketing activities of GCC can be identified as purchase of MFP and agricultural produce and sale of domestic requirements to the tribals at fair prices. The following are the main objectives:

(1) To purchase MFP on outright monopoly basis from the tribals by paying them fair prices;

(2) to supply all daily requirements to the tribals through D.R. depots at cheaper rates;

(3) to meet their credit requirements for agricultural development;

(4) to diversify the earning of the tribals and to supplement their income, the GCC is running some industrial units; and finally

(5) to take-up welfare schemes for the economic uplift of the tribals.

With the advent of the Corporation, the trading activities of the private traders and moneylenders have definitely shown a declining trend, if not totally disappeared. Since the Corporation has got a total monopoly with respect to the purchase of the MFP, it has also got the right to prosecute any private trader indulging in the purchase of MFP from the tribals. This power and also the Corporation's opening of D.R. Depots in the most interior places of the Agency Area have provided some relief to the tribals from the gruesome clutches of the private traders and moneylenders.

The produce brought by the tribals is generally purchased at Shandies, domestic requirement depots[24] and other purchasing points, especially established by the Corporation itself. In view of this, the Corporation adopted a specific purchase and sale price policy to ensure remunerative prices to the tribals and simultaneously to avert from the scourage of tribals especially in the field of marketing.

PURCHASE PRICE POLICY[25]

The Corporation fixes the purchase price of MFP on the basis of price, prevailing in the nearest wholesale market after deducting for items like -

(i) Forest rentals,

(ii) Establishment charges,

(iii) Transport charges,

(iv) Estimated loss in driage, and

(v) 10% allowance for price-fluctuations

Albeit, this practice has encountered sharp criticism for, it resulted in the failure on the part of the Corporation to pay remunerative price to the tribals. In view of this, the Government announced a modified purchase price policy of MFP[26].

In pursuance of the *'New Policy'*, the Corporation would fix the purchase of MFP without deducting forest rentals and establishment charges. The incidental charges are restricted to 15 per cent plus permissible percentage of driage. The 15 per cent incidental charges cover-trader charges, cost of transport and allowances of minor items like interest on working capital, etc. This is considered as a major break through in the purchase policy of the Corporation from a *'Fair Price'* to that of *'support price'*.

SALE PRICE POLICY[27]

The Corporation sells MFP procured from the tribals by various methods like-

(i) by direct negotiations,
(ii) by calling for tenders,
(iii) by conducting auctions,
(iv) on forward-contract basis,
(v) through urban sales depots, and
(vi) through mobile sales

In respect of items like wild-brooms, nuxvomica, the practice is to sell on a *'Forward Contract Basis'*, where the interested merchants will be asked to bid and enter into contract with the Corporation for the sale of procurable commodities in the ensuing season.

In respect of Gum-Karaya, etc., auctions and tenders are called for and the sale will be confirmed against the highest bidder or the tenderer, as the case may be, provided the rate obtained is favourable to the Corporation.

In respect of some of the major items, adda-leaf, tamarind, etc., which do not move for want of proper market rate, direct negotiations are held with the merchants to sell them. For easy disposal, they are pooled-up at a market place with a concentration to attract a better price. The procurement of products at all the societies will be gathered periodically and they will be put to sale by the Managing Director or the Commercial Manager of the Corporation.

GCC has been given monopoly rights over certain items of MFP to purchase from the tribal procurers and trade them. But the MFP items like Seethaphal, Grass Kanchas, etc., are not collected by GCC and are sold by the Department of Public Auction. The revenue per annum from each sale is in the order of Rs.80 lakhs[28].

The sale of minor items is left to the discretion of the Depot Managers of the Societies, in consultation with the Managing Director or the Commercial Manager.

Table - 1 gives the details of the purchase and sale price of different items of MFP and the difference between the purchase price and the sale price. It clearly shows that the cost price or purchase price is lower than the sale price of MFP items. In this connection it is opined that, "the Corporation being a business institution, should also be in a position to confidently take the risk of market fluctuations"[29]. But with the help of the Table, one can easily surmise that the State is also acting as a exploitative instrument with respect to the tribal households. By adopting the practice of maintaining large differences between purchase and sale prices, the activities of the GCC are no less nefarious than the private and petty traders and at the same time it is also running against its welfare objective.

The favourable trend in the marketing activity of the GCC was mainly due to the all-out efforts put in by the officials to motivate the hill people to sell their produce to the Corporation. From 1971 onwards, the procurement of minor forest produce had definitely shown an encouraging trend. However, it was observed that the private merchants were offering a higher price than the Corporation for the purchase of minor forest produce and they were smuggling it out of the tribal area[30]. Taking stock of the smuggling activity by the private merchants, the officials of the Girijan Corporation empowered the Shandy Inspectors to confiscate the minor forest produce purchased by the private merchants at the Shandy. This step of the Corporation has yielded results, but the Shandy Inspectors were unable to undertake the vigilance activity effectively as they were busy visiting the Shandies from dawn to dusk[31].

The main reasons for the Corporation to incur losses in its operations were the exorbitant overhead expenses and the corruption and malpractices adopted by the employees in the field units[32]. The existing practice adopted by the Corporation for the procurement of minor forest produce is that each Shandy Inspector is given a weekly advance of a certain amount of money depending upon the potential of the Shandy for the procurement of different items of minor forest produce. The Shandy Inspectors settle the account for the advance taken at the end of the week.

Table 1
Sale and Purchase Price of Some of the Important Minor Forest Produce Items

Name of the Commodity	*Sale* Price per Kg. (In Rs.)*	*Purchase Price per Kg. (In Rs.)*	*Difference*
1.	2.	3.	4.(col.3-4)
Adda Leaf	1.65	1.00	0.65 (39.40)
Apiary Honey	49.25	35.00	14.25 (28.94)
Bee-Wax	72.75	55.00	17.75 (24.40)
Cleaning nuts	11.70	8.00	3.70 (31.62)
De-Seeded Tamarind	8.45	6.00	2.45 (29.00)
Gum Karaya - I	106.00	80.00	26.00 (24.53)
Gum Karaya - II	64.00	48.00	16.00 (25.00)
Gum Karaya - III	35.00	26.00	9.00 (25.72)
Gum Tiruman - I	40.00	30.00	10.00 (25.00)
Gum Tiruman - II	27.00	20.00	7.00 (25.93)
Hill brooms	5.30	4.00	1.30 (24.53)
K.T. Bundles	8.50	6.00	2.50 (29.41)
Mohwa Flower	3.10	2.00	1.10 (35.50)
Mohwa Seed	8.80	6.00	2.80 (31.82)
Myrobalans	2.20	1.50	0.70 (31.82)
Nuxvomica	15.00	10.00	5.00 (33.34)
Pungam Seed	5.90	4.00	1.90 (32.20)
Rella Bark	0.70	0.50	0.20 (28.57)

Contd.

Name of the Commodity	*Sale* Price per Kg. (In Rs.)*	*Purchase Price per Kg. (In Rs.)*	*Difference*
R.S. Roots	110.20	30.00	80.20 (72.77)
Seeded Tamarind	4.85	3.25	1.60 (33.00)
Tamarind Seed	1.20	0.80	0.40 (33.34)
Rock Bee Honey	42.25	30.00	12.25 (29.00)
Wild Brooms	8.00	6.00	2.00 (25.00)

Source: *Compiled from the various records of Girijan Co-operative Corporation Ltd., Visakhapatnam of* different divisional offices of the researcher's study area - Utnoor, Eturnagaram and Palwancha, 1993-94.
* *Researcher had calculated the sale price as per the procedure for arriving at the sale price of the commodity which was given in the* ***Dairy****, 1994 of Girijan Co-operative Corporation Employees Union, p.37.*

Note:
1. The calculation of sale price is exclusive of sales tax, market cess and cost of gunny.
2. Figures in parantheses are percentage of difference in terms of sale price and here on should note that if the items mentioned under note-1 is included in the calculation, the percentage of difference would be much higher than the percentages in parantheses.

In order to stop such practice being adopted by the Shandy Inspectors, it is time that, they should be insisted upon settling the account every evening, so that the total quantity purchased and the price paid is submitted to the Manager of the Primary Marketing Society on the same day. This policy would go a long way in eliminating the embezzlement of funds by the Shandy Inspectors[33].

Besides MFP, the Corporation also purchases agricultural produce from the tribals. However, it may be mentioned that the Corporation does not enjoy any monopoly rights in the purchase of agricultural produce as in the case of MFP in open competition with the private merchants at the Shandy[34]. The basic objective of the Corporation in purchasing the agricultural produce is to maintain price stability and to eliminate the distress sales by the tribals, as far as possible. This in fact is only a trap and private merchants make use of spurious weights and measures and take more produce from the tribals than the marginal increase in price offered to them.

As specified in the above objectives, one of the main functions of the GCC is to sell domestic requirements to the tribals at fair prices. To attain the above objective, the Corporation has set-up a number of domestic requirement depots at various shandies and also at strategic centres which are in proximity to the tribal dwellings and in the remote places of the tribal areas. Thus, it paves the way for the tribals to be relieved from the evil practices of nefarious private traders, moneylenders and petty traders.

Inspite of a large network of domestic requirement depots in the tribal areas, the competition from the private and petty traders cannot be undermined[35]. The tribals still purchase some goods from the private merchants who come to their door steps and carry on business by extending credit and also through barter system. One disadvantage in the sale practices of the D.R. depots is that, they do not give credit facility to the tribals unlike the petty traders. It was also observed that the tribals derived some satisfaction by purchasing through bargaining and such provision was not there at the D.R. depots, where the prices were fixed. Moreover, some items like tobacco, bajra and jowar were not sold by the domestic requirement depots and for the purchase of these products the tribals had to rely upon the private merchants[36].

Another severe drawback that was observed in the functioning of the D.R. depots was lack of adequate number of salesmen in the Depot where the Shandy was being held. On the Shandy day, the sales at the D.R. depot would usually be high due to greater number of people coming from the surrounding villages. Therefore, the single salesman at the D.R. depot was unable to meet the requirements of the people. The tribals had to wait for a long time at the depot to fulfil their needs. Instead of waiting for a long time at the D.R. depots, it was observed that the tribals were making their purchases from the private merchants on the Shandy day.

The Corporation in order to promote industries in the tribal areas has established a few industrial units to process and grade selected items of minor forest and agricultural produce. Some of the industrial units established by the Corporation are honey and sheekakai processing units at Narsipatnam, soap making unit at Vizianagaram, gum processing plant at Nirmal and and niger seed oil unit at Paderu.

The Corporation has extended two benefits to the tribals in lieu of this activity. Firstly, it ensured a relative high price to the tribals for the supply of raw materials to these processing plants; and secondly to some extent, it provided employment to many tribals in the various operations involved in the processing of these raw materials.

The Girijan Corporation also started providing short-term agricultural credit to the tribals. The short-term loans were mainly intended to enable the tribals to purchase plough bullocks, high yielding varieties of seeds and fertilizers. The loans were provided to the tribals at subsidised rates of interest. This activity was, however, discontinued and it was revived since 1990-91.

During 1990-91, National Bank for Agricultural and Rural Development (NABARD) has recognised the GCC for advancing loans exclusively to the tribal farmer-members and avail re-financing benefit extended by the NABARD through APCOs. The GCC is the first institution in the country recognised by the NABARD for the financing of tribal farmers.

While coming to the microscopic view about GCC in the study area, the following dimensions have been observed which require an indepth analysis.

THE GIRIJAN CO-OPERATIVE CORPORATION LIMITED, UTNOOR DIVISION[37]

The GCC Limited, Utnoor Division is working in the District of Adilabad with its branches at Utnoor, Jainoor, Ichoda and Adilabad of the District. The GCC in Utnoor Division has been playing a major role in the interior areas of the district serving a majority of the population of tribals in particular on the following heads:

MINOR FOREST PRODUCE PROCUREMENT

The important MFP items procured by GCC in this Division are: Gum Karaya, Mohwa Flower, Mohwa Seed, Marking nuts, Wild brooms, Decamalli and Cleaning nuts, etc.

The progress in procurement of some of the major items during the year 1991-92, 1992-93 and 1993-94 upto June 1993 have been shown in Appendix-II.

PURCHASE OF AGRICULTURE PRODUCE FROM TRIBALS

The major items of Agriculture produce cultivated by the tribal farmers of this district are: Jowar, Pulses and Cotton. During 1990-91, the GCC had taken-up the purchase of agriculture produce on a large-scale. The quantities of agriculture produce purchased during 1991-92, 1992-93 and 1993-94 upto June, 1993 have been shown in Appendix-II.

COTTON PROCUREMENT

Cotton is a commercial crop, which has been growing extensively in Adilabad district. On an average, the cotton marketed in the district is roughly around 22 lakh quintals of which about three to four lakh quintals is from tribal cotton growers. Thus, cotton is the most important cash crop to the tribals of the district. Though there are regulated market-yards in the district, purchase of cotton is mostly done by private traders/commission agents and tribal farmers were forced to depend on these commission agents for the marketing of their produce. The C.C.I., which is a Government of India's organisation, purchases cotton in Adilabad district through Commission Agents. It was generally observed that the Commission Agents and private traders purchase cotton from tribals on credit basis and cheat them in weighment and in payment and inturn, they sell cotton to C.C.I. by charging huge margins[38].

In the light of this background, it was considered necessary to have institutional support to tribals in marketing their cotton. With a view to safe-guard the interests of tribals, G.C.C. for the first time entered the cotton market in Adilabad District in the year 1981-82. It continued its operations in a small way in 1982-83 and 1984-85. Later G.C.C. stopped it's cotton procurement operations for several reasons including financial constraints and also for the reason that it suffered heavy losses.

ROLE OF G.C.C. IN COTTON PROCUREMENT IN 1990-91[39]

Tribal farmers started demanding G.C.C. to enter cotton market advancing the major reason that they were at the mercy of private traders who were generally cheating them both in terms of weighment and abnormally delayed payments. After detailed examination of the issue and discussions held with District Administration, C.C.I., Marketing Department and I.T.D.A., Utnoor, GCC decided to purchase cotton from tribals during the season 1990-91 under the following categories.

(1) Direct purchase of cotton from loanees of GCC who were provided with short-term agricultural loans for cotton.

(2) Direct purchase of Cotton in head-loads from small tribal farmers and tribal wage earners who bring cotton in small quantities and who used to be mercilessly cheated by local petty merchants.

(3) Purchase of cotton to C.C.I. purchase centres - its sale to C.C.I. on the spot.

As in the case of 1990-91, even in 1991-92 season GCC purchased cotton is documented in Appendix-III[40].

PROCUREMENT PROGRAMME FOR 1992-93[41]

The GCC has decided to continue Cotton procurement operations in Adilabad district during 1992-93 season in a still bigger way particularly in the context of the fact that loaning operations have been intensified in all tribal areas. As against 7000 acres of cotton area covered under the loaning programme during 1991-92, in the year 1992-93 a total extent of about 25,000 acres was covered by cotton under loaning programme benefitting about 7500 tribal families. Cotton headloads from tribal labourers and small farmers will be purchased at all important D.R. Depots and Shandies. Branch-wise details and the list of Shandies have been presented in Appendix-IV.

DOMESTIC REQUIREMENT AND ESSENTIAL COMMODITIES

The GCC is catering to the needs of daily requirements of tribals through a wide network of 6 D.R. Depots and 13 Sub-depots scattered over the district in the interior and inaccessible scheduled and sub-plan areas. Through these D.R. depots the daily requirements viz. rice, oil, sugar, kerosene and wheat, and also such other items like salt, jaggery, dals, tea, tobacco, and cloth are sold.

The particulars furnished in Appendix-V reveal the steady increase in the turnover of the Utnoor division in the sales of Essential Commodities and D.R.s to the tribals from 1991-92 to June 1993.

The particulars of GCC in the distribution of essential commodities to strengthen the PDS is very much felt in the district. Accordingly 13 Sub-D.R. depots were opened in the interior areas of the district pursuant to the instructions of the District Administration and ITDA.

FORMATION OF V.D.S.S./V.T.D.A.S

A Novel scheme of *"Village Development Support System"* was proposed by the Corporation to involve the tribals in decision making process and the implementation of various schemes of the G.C.C. One such major area is loaning programme with the intensive involvement of the Tribal community at various stages viz., loanees identification, loan disbursement, and loan repayment. The V.D.S.S. Scheme's main focus is to facilitate community particulars in an organised manner in all the activities of G.C.C. and I.T.D.A. Based on the instructions of GCC and ITDA, the V.T.D.As formed in the loaning villages in Utnoor I.T.D.A. area i.e. Utnoor and Asifabad divisions are shown in Appendix-V.

In order to improve the economy of the tribal farmers and to inculcate modern methods of cultivation by taking advantage of the services of the ITDA and GCC working for the betterment and amelioration, the GCC has been implementing ST/SAO[42] loaning programme with the co-ordination of ITDA since 1990 in Adilabad District.

SAO LOANS IN 1990-91

During the year 1990-91 loaning programme was taken up on pilot basis in Branch Office, GCC Utnoor. Nine villages were identified and an amount of Rs.22.21 lakhs was disbursed to 561 members of tribal farmers and an amount of Rs.18.04 lakhs was recovered from them. The percentage of recovery was 81.2%. Thus during the year 1990-91 GCC made a break through in providing credit to tribal farmers by improving the recovery position to a large extent.

Encouraged by the tremendous response from the tribal farmers and also with the view to encourage them further, GCC has passed on the profits, it had earned in purchase of Cotton from tribal farmers by announcing a bonus of Rs.125/- per quintal to all tribal farmers who sold cotton to GCC during that year.

SAO LOANS DURING 1991-92

The new approach by GCC in providing credit to tribal farmers had a visible impact on all the tribals. There were representations from tribal leaders and farmers from all over the district to provide credit for SAO. Therefore GCC had further extended its operations to other branches of GCC in the District, viz. Asifabad and Ichoda in addition to the Utnoor branch. The particulars of number of villages identified, number of farmers, amount disbursed and amount recovered are mentioned in Appendix-VI. A majority of the tribals are accustomed to grow cotton crop. In order to provide proper marketing facility and save the tribals from local money-lenders, the GCC has purchased the cotton at the prevailing market rate and adjusted it to the loan account. In this process the GCC could recover the loans very effectively. The percentage of recovery has to be viewed against the adverse seasonal conditions that prevailed in that Khariff season.

SAO LOANING IN 1992-93

Action plan for issue of SAO loans during 1992-93 with a target of 6.00 crores covering 12,000 tribal families was prepared. As envisaged credit limit applications were prepared for SAO loaning programme for the year 1992-93 as per the guidelines issued from time to time amounting to Rs.4.28 crores.

LOANING PROGRAMME FOR THE YEAR 1993-94

In consultation with the VTDAs, Credit limit applications have been prepared for the eligible members for the Khariff 1993-94 as detailed in Appendix-VII.

After sanction of drawal applications so far an amount of Rs.69.67 lakhs has been disbursed as detailed in the statement which is shown in Appendix-VII.

THE GIRIJAN CO-OPERATIVE CORPORATION LIMITED: PALWANCHA DIVISION[43]

To keep close supervision over the Girijan Co-operative Corporation activities in Khammam District a Divisional Office was sanctioned and started functioning from 4-5-1972 with head-quarters at Kothagudem and subsequently it was shifted to its own building at Palwancha, on 1-11-1979. The Division consists of 5 branches namely, Bhadrachalam, Palwancha, Venkatapuram, Dammapeta and Yellandu with 151 D.R. depots and 2 Urban Depots, 88 Sub-Depots spread over in the entire remote corners of the forest area for the supply of daily requirements to the tribals including essential commodities such as rice, sugar, palmolene oil, kerosene, etc. The area of operations of this division is the entire district of Khammam with 24 forest ranges 5 Forest Divisions for the procurement of Minor Forest Produce and 31 Revenue Mandals.

During the year 1992 Palwancha Division is bifurcated into two divisions with head-quarters at Palwancha and Bhadrachalam. The Branch Offices at Palwancha, Dammapet and Yellandu come under the control of Palwancha division and the branch offices at Bhadrachalam, Venkatapuram and Chinthoor are under the control of Bhadrachalam Division. Subsequently the Branch Office, Palwancha is bifurcated into two Branches as Palwancha and Mangoor. The Mangoor branch is opened on 19-8-93 and is effectively functioning from 1-9-93. The branch office Dammapet is bifurcated into two branches as Dammapeta and Kukkunoor. The Kukkunoor branch is opened on 19-8-93 and is effectively functioning from 1-9-93.

More than 90% of the tribals are covered by the GCC services. To cater to the needs of the tribals, shandy points, D.R. depots and Sub-depots have been opened for the purchase of M.F.P. and to supply essential commodities and daily requirements. The branch-wise details are shown in Appendix-VIII.

PURCHASE OF M.F.P. AND A.P.

The first functional object of the GCC is to purchase outright MFP on monopoly basis from the tribals by paying fair price.

To fulfil this object the entire 24 forest ranges in Khammam district have been taken on monopoly basis from the forest department and kept open for the tribals for collection of minor forest produce. For easy identification of the tribal members and to protect the M.F.P. Pickers from the middlemen *"Giri Cards"* were distributed to all the tribals at free of cost. 98 Salesmen and 21 C.C.P.A.'s were designated as field staff have been authorised to purchase M.F.P. from the tribals at their door steps and also for distribution and collection of loans.

The M.F.P. & A.P. in terms of value collected from 1972-73 i.e., from the data of inception of the Division till to date and branch-wise particulars are shown in Appendix-IX.

SALE OF DAILY REQUIREMENTS

The second functional object is to supply Daily requirements such as rice, sugar, P.oil. kerosene and essential commodities such as dals, salt, tobacco, subsidised cloth, cigars, onions, edible oils, jowar, potato and chillies at a cheaper rates at the door steps of the tribals.

Accordingly 98 D.R. depots, 64 Sub-depots are functioning in nook and corners of the Scheduled Villages in the Sub-Plan area of Palwancha division. A Statement showing the unit-wise turnover of D.R.s for 1991-92 and 1992-93 and 1993-94 (upto 30-9-93) is enclosed in Appendix-X.

LOANING OPERATIONS OF G.C.C. OF THE DIVISION[44]

Crop Loans During 1990

From the year 1990, crop loans have been issued under (SAO) Seasonal Agricultural Operation Loans at tribal mandals of Dammapeta, Palwancha and Yellandu G.C.C. branch areas.

Consumption Loans

The G.C.C. has provided consumption loans to the tribals who had no land for cultivation and depended on collection of M.F.P. and also to Honey hunters.

NETWORK OF THE G.C.C. DURING FLOODS AND NATURAL CALAMITIES

During the floods and rainy season the G.C.C. has taken up active steps regarding the supply of daily requirements and essential commodities to the tribals.

As a part of this activity the G.C.C. is moving the D.R.s and stock of essential commodities to the remote and inaccessible corners well in advance for a period of 3 months to avoid complications in supply of D.R.s and essential commodities even in rainy season at the door steps of the tribals.

SUPPLY OF PROVISIONS TO HOSTELS

The GCC is supplying food provisions/essential commodities and other requirements to all S.T. hostels and Ashram Schools in Khammam district.

THE GIRIJAN CO-OPERATIVE CORPORATION LIMITED: ETURUNAGARAM DIVISION[45]

The jurisdiction of the branch offices in Eturnagaram division of GCC, extends to 13 mandals in Warangal and 4 mandals in Karimnagar districts.

The jurisdiction of Eturnagaram branch is found to be extensive rendering it difficult to supervise effectively, particularly interior and inaccessible areas. considering this fact and also considering the recent intensification of the activities of the GCC through loaning and other programmes, it was felt to bifurcate the Eturnagaram branch suitably into two branches. Presently one revenue mandal of Warangal district namely Bhupalpalli is in the jurisdiction of Mahadevpur branch in Karimnagar district. Thus the Manager, Mahadevpur has to correspond and cover two districts. Therefore, it was considered necessary to limit the jurisdiction of Mahadevpur branch to Karimnagar district only. In this background, from the areas of Eturnagaram branch and Mahadevpur branch a new branch with head-quarters at Mulug has been carved out and it had been functioning from 24-2-1991. After formation of Mulugu branch the mandals covered by each branch are as shown in Appendix-XI.

MINOR FOREST PRODUCE

Gum Karaya, Wild Brooms, Nuxvomica, Cleaning nuts, K.T. bundles, Mohwa seed and Mohwa flower are the main MFP items in Warangal division. Myrobalans, Marking nuts, Bee wax etc., are also available and to tap these new items, village-wise propaganda is taken-up to collect maximum minor forest produce. The branch-wise details of D.R. depots and the shandy particulars have shown in Appendix-XII.

In this division shandies are not the only places of purchase of MFP, D.R. depots also play an important role in purchase of MFP. The tribal can sell this MFP in D.R. depot and purchase his requirements there. Shandy Inspectors are also organising certain purchasing centres basing on the potentiality in the area of operation. The year-wise and branch-wise MFP procurement for the last 6 years in Eturnagaram division is shown in Appendix-XIII.

DOMESTIC REQUIREMENTS

By the end of 1988, there were only 65 D.R. depots in Eturnagaram division in the 3 branches for distribution of domestic requirements. In addition to essential commodities like rice, palmolene oil, sugar and kerosene oil, GCC is also supplying controlled cloth, dals, salt, matches, onions, garlic, turmeric, soaps, beedies etc., to the tribals through the D.R. depots. Branch-wise domestic requirement sales for the last 6 years in Eturnagaram division are shown in Appendix-XIII.

CREDIT SUPPLIED TO INSTITUTIONS

The GCC is supplying food provisions to Tribal Welfare Hostels and Ashram Schools in Warangal and Karimnagar districts from the Eturnagaram, Narsampet and Mahadevpur branches.

ORGANISATIONAL SETUP OF THE LOANING PROGRAMME

In order to streamline the loaning programme, issue of SAO loans under Khariff and Rabi to tribal farmers during the year 1992-93 and also in the ensuing years, decisions had been taken from time to time to strengthen the system by forming village elders committees now called as Village Tribal Development Associations, appointment of Village Liaison Workers, Agricultural Consultants, Agricultural officers, etc.

The branch-wise village tribal development associations formed and staff involved in loaning operations to achieve the task of providing credit to majority of tribals in this division has been presented in Appendix-XIV.

S.A.O. LOANS

During the year 1970-71 the Reserve Bank of India introduced a pilot scheme for channelising agricultural credit to tribal farmers and it was implemented in Warangal district. As the recovery of loans in the past was found to be not satisfactory and there was no definite source of funds to continue the loaning operations regularly the programme was discontinued and again it was revived.

For the first time, in the year 1990, the NABARD has recognised the GCC as a District Co-operative Central Bank for purposes of routing S.A.O., loans to tribals. The GCC has taken a decision to identify tribal villages where banking facilities are not available and where loaning programmes were not taken up extensively in previous years. In this background Kothaguda mandal in Narsampet branch was taken up for provision of S.A.O., loans during 1990 Khariff.

An amount of Rs.14.95 lakhs was issued as S.A.O., loans to tribals in Khariff 1990. Recovery operations were started immediately when crops were harvested. Recovery was made both in cash and kind. A new scheme was introduced through which the tribals are being paid the prevailing market rate on the date of purchase of agricultural produce. The GCC disposes off such produce when the market conditions are good. The margins earned by the GCC, in the disposal of such agriculture produce will be ploughed back to the tribals. Under this scheme a bonus rate of Rs.20/- per quintal for maize was already announced to the tribals in Kothaguda mandal who sold maize to GCC. It also purchased paddy towards repayment of loan from tribal loanees. Bonus to these loanees will also be declared at the end when the paddy is disposed off. This scheme is well received by tribals and from subsequent year onwards procurement of Agricultural Produce had gone up steeply.

Against Rs.14.95 lakhs disbursed as S.A.O., loans a sum of Rs.12.00 lakhs had since been collected as on 20-2-1991. Under the *"Incentives Scheme"*, villages which have repaid the loan with interest in full will be given a bonus of 40% of interest paid for first village, 30% of interest paid to second village and 20% for all other villages which repaid loan in full. Narsampet branch stood first in the state in the collection of loans. The details of loans disbursed and its recovery from 1990-91 to 1992-93 have been furnished in Appendix-XV. Besides, SAO loans amounting to Rs.150.97 lakhs during the year 1993-94 and an amount of Rs.26.39 lakhs during Rabi 1993-94 had been disbursed. The branch-wise details are furnished for both Khariff and Rabi in Appendix-XVI.

For the quantities of inputs that are distributed to tribal loanees under kind component during the 1993-94 Khariff season, the details are furnished in Appendix-XVII.

Thus, it can be surmised that, though the Corporation has been making all out efforts by implementing its marketing policies that relatively benefit the economic lot of the tribals, certain basic trends have also emerged out of its performance over the years[46]. They are:

(1) The expenditure pattern of the GCC on establishment and the maintenance cost had shown an upward trend and thereby developed a bureaucratic elite structure over the forest surplus and had its effect over the state revenue;

(2) Statutory monopoly rights over the collection of MFP has in a way led to the adoption of the suppressive price mechanism offered to the produce collected by the tribes. As a result, neither the State nor the community did benefit over the resource extraction, but only the intermediary functionaries of the structure were evolved and were benefited.

(3) The component of the 'co-operation' as a mode and principle did not make its presence in the marketing of the forest produce. An imposed official and a few staff of the Depot have again symbolised a centralised authority and there is no way by which tribal communities have a say in the fixation of the price to the produce collected;

(4) The efforts towards the periodical assessment of the purchase price to the produce collected by the tribals many a times is done arbitrarily. Genuine participation of the tribes in the whole process of fixation of the price was found to be totally absent although a few elite are incorporated in bodies at the apex level;

(5) Due to the absence of the village level tribal participation in the operations of GCC, the whole process of marketing by the state agency is a sort of unilateral dictation of the terms of trade and extractive network in the unequal exchange market circumstance;

(6) The differential surplus ratio of the revenue over the forest produce in the overall dealings of the sale-purchase policy and operations clearly indicate the substantial revenue to the GCC and on the other hand tribals get only a meagre share of their revenue as the returns are offered in the form of prices.

POSSIBLE POLICY INTERVENTIONS OVER THE MARKETING PATTERN OF G.C.C

A few steps may be taken in order to strengthen the tribal economy and these may be helpful to minimise the exploitative component that crept even into the marketing operations taken-up in tribal areas by the GCC[47]. They are:

(i) GCC should take necessary measures to ensure the remunerative procurement price to MFP items. It should also take necessary efforts to streamline the organisational aspects of it on a rational basis for providing the effective and useful services to the tribals;

(ii) The Government should take necessary steps to curb the wide variation between the purchase price and sale price and it should also offer higher prices for the produce of the tribals which benefit them.

(iii) Measures should be taken both by the forest department and GCC to assess the exact potential of MFP and notify the commercial items and provide adequate training methods and practices for the tribals to maximise the MFP collection in a more scientific and systematic way;

(iv) The price paid by the Corporation for the procurement of MFP was observed to be low compared to that of the private merchants. The Corporation may increase the price further by curtailing its overhead expenses which were exorbitant in nature;

(v) Mobile vigilance staff should be appointed to check the malpractices in the Shandy points and marketing centres;

(vi) New location of market centres and other Shandy points should be given preference where these centres do not exist. There is an imminent need to strengthen the Shandy culture at the Centre of the tribal villages;

(vii) GCC should take care as in relation to the curtailment of its overhead expenses and should also take necessary measures to prevent the fraudulent practices adopted by the field staff. Considerable measures should also be taken to curtail the expenditure on the establishment and pay-offs to the bureaucratic expansion at the intermediary levels;

(viii) GCC has to take care to provide better infra-structural facilities like construction of sheds, provision of drinking water and sanitation facilities in tribal villages as a policy matter;

(ix) Steps should be taken to establish the local market committees in each tribal village which is to be headed by the commonly accepted person among the tribal households. This will provide a greater check over the functioning of the local D.R. depots and ensure a sense of accountability. The Committee members should also have an access to the higher decision levels of the GCC to consult, complain about any event of malpractice that occurred at the village level; and

(x) Finally, valuable gem stones are collected illegally by the local traders and are smuggled out to the distant places like Bombay, Jaipur, where these are put to processing and sold to international markets. Systematically, this illicit gem trade is ignored by the state and the beneficiaries of the occasional pay-offs by these traders are known openly in the local areas. There should be a serious thinking over it by the state agencies operating in this region.

Finally, the researcher is of the opinion that the Government's policy is mainly oriented towards the development of tribal economy through institutional support which would not make much headway in its objective.

In sum, in the early traditional period of the State tribal economy, GCC has played the role of a progressive marketeer. But soon this has led to a kind of unquestionable operational freedom over the marketing process in the tribal areas in which local tribals have lesser opportunities to express their grievances against the exploitative price mechanism adopted even by the GCC. Thus, it led to a situation where as per the price mechanism-wise, it remained extractive oriented rather than being an emancipative agency. As per its growth, the GCC structure and establishment expenditure over the years grew over and above its normal size. This further gives scope for drawing a conclusion that in the elimination of the private oppressor through the state regulation in the marketing of the produce, necessary democratic control from the people should always be accorded a priority over other means. Otherwise it tends to pave the way for exclusive bureaucratic institutionalism that again kills the creativity of the state agencies dealing with the peoples' resources. The Girijan Co-operative Corporation's performance is a microscopic instance of this kind of overall attempts of the state trading in the tribal resources.

NOTES & REFERENCES

1. Saxena R.P. (1964), *Tribal Economy in Central India*, Firm K.L. Mukhopadhyay, Calcutta, p.207.
2. Tribal Economy is largely self-sufficient, unstructured and non-specialised.
3. Report of the *Committee of Special Multi-purpose Tribal Blocks*, Ministry of Home Affairs, New Delhi, 1960, p.131.
4. The All India Rural Credit Survey (1954) revealed that, out of the average borrowing of cultivating family during the year, which comes to Rs.210,3 per cent was borrowed from government, 3 per cent from co-operatives, 14 per cent from relatives, 2 per cent from landlords, 25 per cent from agricultural moneylenders, 45 per cent from professional moneylenders, 6 per cent from traders and slightly less than one per cent from

commercial banks and the remainder represents borrowings from other classes of traders.

5. For further details, see B. Janardhan Rao, (1987), *Land Alienation in Tribal Areas*, Kakatiya School of Public Administration, Warangal, pp.24-46.

6. Nair, V.M.(1968), 'Girijan Revolts, Marxists organise Armed Action by Andhra Tribes', *The Statesmen*, Calcutta, April 12.

7. Janardhan Rao, B.: *Land Alienation in Tribal Areas*, Op.cit., p.105 & 106.

8. Subba Rao, C. (1971), 'The Bullet Beat the Bow', *The Times Weekly Magazine*, Bombay, March, 21.

9. Mathus, B.S. (1971), *Co-operatives in India*, Sahitya Bhavan, Allahabad, p.357.

10. Government of India (1966), Report of the Committee on *Co-operative Marketing*, p.42.

11. Gopal Raja (1986), *Dynamics of Agricultural Marketing in Tribal India*, Rainbow Publications, Coimbatore, Tamil Nadu, p. 51.

12. Murali Krishna Rao, I. (1988), *Marketing in Tribal Economy*, Inter India Publications, New Delhi, p.42.

13. Tanniur, R. Rao (1976), 'Developing Countries : Role of Marketing', *Paper Presented at the 5th World Congress of Marketing*, held at New Delhi.

14. Syed Majdul Hasan (1983), 'Tribal Development in Andhra Pradesh - Focus on Awareness', *Business Standard*, Thursday, 23rd june.

15. All these had been observed by the researcher during his intensive field work in the three regions of Telangana, i.e., Adilabad, Khammam and Warangal.

16. The items include: beedi leaf, adda leaf, gums, tamarind, sopanuts, mohwa seed, nuxvomica, honey, etc. The collection and sale of these minor forest produce forms the major economic activity for vast majority of tribals and rural landless poor, providing subsistence income through trade and barter

17. Malayappan Committee Report, 1952, p.10

18. Murali Manohar, K., & Ramaiah, P. (1982), 'Marketing through Girijan Co-operative Corporation - A Study in Tribal Areas', *Indian Journal of Marketing*, Vol. XII, No.7, March, p.9.

19. This is a progressive measure while tackling the problem of marketing in scheduled areas. Hence, the GCC which was started with the sole aim of meeting the needs of the tribals in marketing and credit was not able to eliminate the exploitation of the private traders.
20. Raghava Rao, D.V. (1973), 'Marketing of Produce and Indebtedness among the Tribals', *A Report on a Study in Chinthalapally Block, Vishakapatnam District,* Andhra University, Waltair, p.70.
21. The GCC purchases as many as 22 items of minor forest produce. They are: 1. Gum Karaya, 2. Gum Thiruman, 3. Cleaning nuts, 4. K.T. bundles (in pairs), 5. Nuxvomica, 6. Mohwa seed, 7. Mohwa flower, 8. Wild brooms, 9. Tamarind seeded, 10. Taramind deseeded, 11. Tamarind seed, 12. Myrobalans, 13. Pungams seed, 14. R.S. roots, 15. Thatched grass, 16. Soapnuts, 17. Rock bee-honey, 18. Bee Wax, 19.Chiranji, 20. Amul Seed, 21. Bark, 22. Wet Karive Paku.
22. Presently he called as Credit-Cum-Procurement Assistant (CCPA).
23. Prior to the advent of the Corporation, the tribal used to sell MFP collected by him, to the plains-trader, in exchange for domestic requirements. It has resulted a heinous and the worst process of exploitation.
24. The tribals sell their produce to the Corporation at the Shandy and inturn they purchase the domestic requirements such as rice, kerosene, edible oils, cloth, etc., from the Depots of the Corporation. These Depots are called Domestic Requirement Depots or D.R. Depots.
25. For further details of fixation of the purchase price see *Girijan Co-operative Corporation Employee Union Dairy,* 1994, p.36.
26. This is through *G.O.Ms.No. 1477,* Revenue (T.W.-II) Department, dated 31-12-1970.
27. For further details of the fixation of the sale price see *Girijan Co-operative Corporation Employee Union Dairy,* 1994, p.37.
28. *Andhra Pradesh Forests,* Issued by A.P. Forest Department, Hyderabad, January, 1992, p.21.
29. Pratap D.R.: "A Study of the Andhra Pradesh Scheduled Tribes' Co-operative Finance and Development Corporation Limited", 1968, TCR & TI, Hyderabad, p.181.

30. For further details see Mohan Reddy, K., *Marketing of Minor Forest Produce - A Micro Level Study*, Unpublished M.Phil. Dissertation, submitted to Kakatiya University, Department of Economics, Warangal. 1989 pp.168-171.
31. Murali Krishna Rao, I.: *Marketing in a Tribal Economy*, Op.cit., p.275.
32. Janardhan Rao, B. (1989), 'Tribal Development in India', in *Rural Development*, (ed.), Murali Manohar, KASPA Publications, Warangal, pp.764-770.
33. Murali Krishna Rao, I.: *Marketing in a Tribal Economy*, Op.cit., pp.275-276.
34. The private merchants generally fix the price for the agricultural produce by coming to a common agreement among themselves. The Girijan Co-operative Corporation fixes the price for the agricultural produce by deducting nominal incidental charges from the nearest wholesale market price. The private merchants in order to attract the tribals to sell them the agricultural produce offer a slightly higher price than that offered by the Corporation.
35. Murali Krishan Rao, I.: *Marketing in a Tribal Economy*, Op.cit., p.281.
36. For further details see, Mohan Reddy, K., Op.cit., pp.152-157 & 168-173.
37. This information had been gathered from the following sources that had been collected by the Researcher from the GCC, Utnoor Divisional Office:

    (a) Note on Developmental Activities of GCC Ltd., Utnoor Division during the year 1993-94 (upto June 1994).

    (b) Note on S.A.O. Loaning Programme of Utnoor and Asifabad Divisions during the year 1993-94.

    (c) Procurement of Cotton by GCC from tribals in Adilabad District Action Plan for 1992-93.
38. This had also been observed by the researcher during his field work in the district.
39. During 1990-91, Government of India gave an export allotment of 5,000 bales of superior medium staple cotton to G.C.C. In association with Cotton Corporation of India, G.C.C. was able to successfully complete the export of Cotton. In this process, G.C.C. earned a clean profit of about Rs.54.00 lakhs. As G.C.C. is a

welfare institution and as the main idea of the export was to plough back profits to the tribal Cotton Growers, G.C.C. has paid a sum of Rs.126/- per quintal as bonus to tribals who sold cotton to GCC in 1990-91 season. This has created tremendous impact in the tribal areas as this is the first time any agency has ploughed back profits to tribal farmers in Andhra Pradesh.

40. During 1991-92 Cotton procurement operations were successfully completed. The tentative profit and loss account shows a net profit of Rs.11.32 lakhs. As per the policy of the GCC to plough back profits to the tribals, a bonus of Rs.40/- per quintal was declared benefitting 5194 loanee and non-loanee tribals who sold cotton to GCC in this year. It may be pertinent to mention here that GCC could disburse bonus inspite of un-favourable market trends that prevailed in Cotton trade during 1991-92 season.

41. Last year GCC purchased cotton as Agent to CCI. This year it is proposed to dispense with it and effect purchases directly in loaning villages to facilitate tribal farmers to have value addition to their produce.

42. In order to have peoples participation one educated tribal youth was selected as a liaison worker for every 100 farmers or a cluster of villages. For every 1000 farmer members one B.Sc., Agriculture Graduate has been appointed as Agricultural Consultant. The liaison worker will work as a link between the Agricultural Consultant and the tribal farmer by providing necessary assistance to the farmers for proper maintenance of crops. At the time of preparation of Credit limit applications also the indent for Seeds, Pesticides etc. are obtained as per the farmers' choice. The seeds, fertilizers and pesticides will be supplied as per the farmers' choice only. The Agricultural Consultants and agricultural department will provide necessary technical assistance to the tribal farmers from time to time for proper maintenance of crops. In order to impart proper knowledge to the liaison workers regarding the maintenance of books and Agricultural methods, a training has been given every year to refresh them with upto date knowledge in agricultural and other techniques. The liaison workers and agricultural Consultants have to work with close association with V.T.D.A. In order to have proper impact over the affairs the V.T.D.A. Presidents are authorised to disburse the remuneration to liaison workers and agricultural consultants. Thus the V.T.D.A.s are involved straight from identification of loannees, disbursement of loans and collection of loans.

43. (a) Brief notes on the Activities of Girijan Co-operative Cooperation Limited; Palwancha Division - Published by Palwancha Divisional Office, 1993-94.

    (b) Compiled from the various records of the Girijan Co-operative Corporation Limited; Palwancha Divisional Office, during the years 1993-94.

44. Loan recovery is accepted both in cash and kind for the advantage of the loanee. The kind component includes their surplus Agriculture Produce and also MFP.

45. Brief note on Activities of GCC, Eturnagaram Divisional Office, 1990-91 and 1993-94.

46. Janardhan Rao, B. & Mohan Reddy, K.: A Paper on 'Tribes, MFP and Role of GCC : A Note', presented at the National Seminar on *The share of Regulated Market Yards in the Marketed produce of various Agricultural commodities in Andhra Pradesh and Public Policy for increasing the share,* organised by Institute of Development and Planning Studies, Visakhapatnam, during 23rd - 25th August, 1993.

47. *Ibid;* A paper on Tribes FP and Role of GCC: A Note', *Op.cit.,* 1993.

5

SALIENT CHARACTERISTIC FEATURES OF THE STUDY AREA

The present chapter[1] throws light on some of the salient features of the study area and the socio-economic profile of the sample households so as to provide a backdrop for the analysis contained in other ensuing chapters in the thesis. Further, this chapter is divided into two sections. A brief profile of the entire study area had been discussed in Section-I and the Section-II had been devoted for an anlysis of the socio-economic profile of the sample households chosen for the present study.

The study area at a glance can be visualised in Table-1.

In view of the Table -1, the researcher had presented a brief profile of the study area hereunder. Prior to this, the researcher had also given a general explanation as in relation to the tribal population in the country as well as in the State and their growth rates in the State.

Different tribal groups are living in various degrees of economic backwardness in India and often they were referred as *Vanajati, Vanavasi, Adimjati, Adivasi* and *Aboriginals*, etc. Among all, *Adivasi or Scheduled Tribe*[2] is known most extensively. The largest concentration of tribal people in the entire world and outside Africa is in India[3]. The growth of the tribal population in the country and the concentration of Scheduled Tribes in various States during the post-independent era can be understood from Table -2. With the help of the Table, one can locate that the heavy concentration of them are in the States of Madhya Pradesh, Maharashtra, Orissa, Bihar, Gujarat, Rajasthan, Andhra Pradesh, and West Bengal with 22.72 per cent, 10.80 per cent, 10.38 per cent, 9.76 per cent, 9.10 per cent, 8.08 per cent, 6.20 per cent, and 5.62 per cent respectively. The total Scheduled Tribe population in the State of Andhra Pradesh as per 1991 Census is 41.99 lakhs. The comparative picture of Scheduled Tribe population in the State during 1961-1991 is presented in Table-3. The Table shows that there is a notable increase in the percentage of Scheduled Tribe population to the total population from 3.68 per cent in 1961 to 6.31 per cent in 1991. The maximum percentage increased had been observed in Warangal, i.e., from 2.13 per cent to 13.7 per cent, followed by Khammam, i.e., from 16.20 per cent to 25.20 per cent, Mahaboobnagar, i.e. from 0.30 per cent to 7.40 per cent and Nizamabad, i.e. from 0.10 per cent to 5.90 per cent. From the Table, one can also say that during 1961 Srikakulam stood at fourth place in the State and now it occupies 10th place with 5.80 per cent of tribal population.

Table 1
Study Area at A Glance

Name of the District	*Name of the Mandal*	*Name of the Village*
Khammam	Dammapet	Ankampalam
		Patwarigudem
Warangal	Tadvai	Narsapur
		Pambapur
		Katapur
Adilabad	Indravelli(B)	Anji
		Wadagon
		Indravelli(B)

Table 2
State-wise Percentage Distribution of Scheduled Tribe Population in India

Name of the State	*1951*	*1961*	*1971*	*1981*	*1991*
Madhya Pradesh	21.52	22.13	22.25	23.22	22.72
Orissa	13.37	14.00	13.45	11.45	10.38
Bihar	17.24	13.94	13.08	11.25	9.76
Gujarat	9.30	9.13	9.90	9.40	9.10

Contd.

Name of the State	*1951*	*1961*	*1971*	*1981*	*1991*
Rajasthan	7.88	7.79	8.28	8.10	8.08
Maharashtra	7.33	7.94	7.84	11.18	10.80
West Bengal	6.96	6.81	6.72	5.95	5.62
Andhra Pradesh	5.11	4.39	4.40	6.15	6.20
Assam*	6.90	6.84	4.26	–	4.24
Meghalaya	NA	NA	2.16	2.10	2.25
Nagaland	0.92	1.14	1.21	1.26	1.56
Tripura	0.85	1.19	1.20	1.13	1.25
Arunachal Pradesh**	NA	NA	0.98	1.75	0.81
Mizoram**	–	–	–	–	0.96
Manipur	0.86	0.83	0.89	0.75	0.93
Tamilnadu/Madras	0.61	0.84	0.38	1.00	0.85
Kerala	0.60	0.71	0.71	0.50	0.47
Karnataka/Mysore	0.36	0.64	0.61	3.53	2.82
Uttar Pradesh	–	–	0.53	0.45	0.43
Himachal Pradesh	0.12	0.34	0.38	0.38	0.32
Dadra & Nagar Haveli	NA	0.17	0.17	0.15	0.16
Lakshwadeep	0.06	0.08	0.08	0.08	0.07
Andaman & Nicobar Islands	NA	0.05	0.05	0.05	0.05
Goa, Daman & Diu	–	–	0.02	0.02	0.02
North East Frontier Agency	–	0.99	–	0.15	0.15
Punjab	0.01	0.05	–	–	–
Total	100.00	100.00	100.00	100.00	100.00

Note:

* Figures for India also exclude the population of Assam, where census could not be held in 1981.

** Arunachal Pradesh and Mizoram attained statehood on 20-02-1987 according to the notification issued on 11-02-1987.

Table 3
District-wise Scheduled Tribes Population in Andhra Pradesh as Per Census and Growth Rates from 1961-71, 1971-81, 1981-91

Name of the District	*S.T. Population (in lakhs)*				*Growth Rates*		
	1961	*1971*	*1981*	*1991*	*1961-71*	*1971-81*	*1981-91*
Srikakulam	1.92	2.12	1.05	1.34 (5.8)	10.40	(A)	27.6
Vizayanagaram	–	–	1.53	1.90 (9.0)	–	–	24.2
Vishakapatnam	2.14	3.00	3.54	4.69 (14.3)	40.2	18.0	32.5
East Godavari	1.00	1.19	1.43	1.76 (3.9)	19.0	20.2	23.1

Contd.

Name of the District	*S.T. Population (in lakhs)*				*Growth Rates*		
	1961	*1971*	*1981*	*1991*	*1961-71*	*1971-81*	*1981-91*
West Godavari	0.44	0.52	0.67	0.85 (2.4)	18.1	28.8	26.9
Krishna	0.37	0.51	0.67	0.92 (2.5)	37.8	31.3	37.3
Guntur	0.95	1.05	1.40	1.82 (4.4)	10.5	33.3	30.0
Prakasham	–	0.55	0.78	0.99 (3.6)	–	41.8	26.9
Kurnool	0.31	0.32	0.40	0.56 (1.9)	3.2	25.0	40.0
Nellore	1.32	1.30	1.77	2.14 (8.9)	(-) 1.5	36.1	20.0
Anantapur	0.49	0.65	0.82	1.11 (3.5)	32.6	26.1	35.3
Cuddapah	0.22	0.27	0.38	0.47 (2.1)	22.7	40.7	23.7
Chittor	0.51	0.67	0.79	1.05 (3.2)	31.4	17.9	32.9
Hyderabad	0.02	0.05	0.14	0.29 (0.9)	150.0(B)	180.0(B)	107.1
Ranga Reddy	–	–	0.73	1.09 (4.3)	–	–	49.3
Nizamabad	0.007	0.006	0.90	1.21 (5.9)	(-) 14.3	14000.0(B)	34.4
Medak	0.0008	0.001	0.68	0.95 (4.2)	25.0	67900.0(B)	39.7
Mahaboobnagar	0.05	0.06	1.55	2.27 (7.4)	20.0	2483.0(B)	46.4
Nalgonda	0.005	0.005	1.96	2.76 (9.7)	–	39100.0(B)	40.8
Warangal	0.33	0.43	2.93	3.85 (13.7)	30.3	581.4(B)	31.4
Khammam	1.71	2.02	4.30	5.59 (25.2)	18.1	112.9(B)	30.0
Karimnagar	0.13	0.16	0.61	0.83 (2.7)	23.1	281.2(B)	36.1
Adilabad	1.32	1.69	2.73	3.55 (17.0)	28.0	61.5	30.0
Total	13.2428	16.572	31.76	41.99 (6.31)	25.1	91.6	32.2

Note:
1. (A) Growth rate has not been calculated due to the bifurcation of the district.
2. (B) The large variation is due to the inclusion of different population groups Viz. Yerukalas, yanadies and sugalies in the Scheduled Tribes List.
3. Figures in parantheses indicate percentages of Scheduled Tribes population to total population of the concerned district.

Table 4
Decadal-wise Scheduled Tribe Population - Growth Rate

Year	*Scheduled Tribal Population*	*Variation*	*Percentage of Growth*
1951	7,66,679	–	–
1961	13,24,368	5,57,689	72.74
1971	16,57,657	3,33,289	25.16
1981	31,76,001	15,18,344	91.59
1991	41,99,481	10,23,480	32.22

The above Table -4 explains about the Scheduled Tribes population and their growth rates since 1951. While looking at the Table, one can say that from 1971 to 1981, there had been sudden spurt in the Scheduled Tribe population in the State, which is due to the inclusion of other groups - Lambadas, Yerukalas, Yanadies, etc., in the Scheduled Tribes list.

I

PROFILES OF THE DISTRICTS

Khammam District

Khammam district was formed on 1st October 1953 with five taluks, viz., Khammam, Yellandu, Bhoorgampadu, Palwancha (Kothagudem) and Madhira taluks, transferred from Warangal district. Khammam is one of the ten districts of Telangana region of Andhra Pradesh. It has an area of 15.8 lakh hectares and a total population of 22.15 lakhs. The district is flanked on the North by Madhya Pradesh and Orissa States; on the South by Krishna district; on the West by Warangal district and Nalgonda district and on the East by West Godavari district. The important rivers of Godavari, Shabari and Kinnerasani flow through the district.

The district is administered through four revenue divisions with the headquarters at Khammam, Kothagudem, Bhadrachalam and Palwancha. The district comprises of 46 revenue mandals and 46 mandal praja parishads. Khammam revenue division covers 17 mandals and the newly formed Palwancha revenue division covers the remaining ten mandals.

Warangal District

Warangal is an ancient town and the Warangal division in erstwhile Hyderabad State, formed the eastern portion of the Nizam's Dominions and extended from the river Penganga in the North to the Krishna in the South. It is bounded on the North by Karimnagar district; on the West by Medak district; on the South by Nalgonda district and by Khammam district on East and South-East. For the purpose of convenience, the administrative set-up of the district was divided into three revenue divisions and fifty revenue mandals.

Adilabad District

Adilabad district is situated in the Northern most part of Andhra Pradesh. The district, however, takes the fifth rank in area with an extent of 16,128 sq.kms. which accounts for 5.90 per cent of the total area of the State. It is the second largest district in the Telangana region of the State, next to Mahabubnagar.

The district is bounded on North by Yeotmal and Chanda districts of Maharashtra; on the East by Chanda district; on the South by Karimnagar and Nizamabad districts; and on the West by Nanded district of Maharashtra State.

The district is administered through the three revenue divisions, viz., Adilabad, Asifabad and Nirmal and it is an embodiment of 52 mandals and 11 panchayat samithies. Out of 11 panchayati samities, two panchayati samities, i.e., Utnoor and Wankidi are tribal blocks.

By and large, all the three districts have relatively higher percentage of tribals in the total population as per 1991 Census. The scheduled tribes form 25.22 per cent of the total population, their number is 5.58 lakhs in Khammam district. In Warangal district, their percentage is 13.7 per cent of the total population, their number is 3.8 lakhs. In Adilabad district, the tribals form 17.04 per cent of the total population, their number is 3.54 lakhs. In this respect, Khammam has a higher concentration of tribals in the district than the other two districts.

As tribals usually live in forests, the percentage of geographical area under forests has a crucial role for their well-being. Khammam district has the largest area under forests in the State. The percentage of forest area to geographical area is 52.60 and this is the highest proportion of forest area to total geographical area among all districts of the State, the total area being 8.08 lakh hectares.

In the district the total cropped area forms 24 per cent of the geographical area and of this cropped area, 35 per cent is irrigated. Since a greater portion of the cropped area is in plains area, the irrigation facilities are also provided in these areas. Hence, most of the forest area is unirrigated and cropped area is only a small per cent of the total area under forests in Warangal district as it is only 28.80, while it is 44.80 in Adilabad district. In Warangal district, the irrigated area is 31 per cent, whereas cropped area to total geographical area is 37 per cent. In Adilabad district, the percentage of irrigated area is nine per cent, while cropped area to geographical area is 40.80%.

Thus, among the three districts, the forest area as well as the tribal population is the highest in Khammam district. Besides these characteristics, this district has a higher proportion of agricultural labourers than the other two districts.

PROFILES OF THE MANDALS

Dammapet Mandal

The Dammapet mandal is in Palwancha division of Khammam district and it covers only 22 revenue villages having more number of hamlets under each village. The mandal is flanked on the North by Mulkalapalli; on the South by Kukkunoor; on the East by Aswaraopet and on the West by Sattupalli. The mandal has 21 inhabited and one uninhabited village with an area of 369 Sq. Kms. The mandal has one primary health centre, two doctors, three veterinary dispensaries, 11 rural veterinary dispensaries. All the villages are electrified. There is one sub-post office, 12 branch post offices and altogether 13 post offices, 2 RRBs, 2 branches of Andhra Bank, 23 fair price shops and one shandy point, one regulated market yard, 3 bus stops. It also has drinking water facility at the mandal headquarters.

Tadvai Mandal

It covers 73 villages. Forest area covers 67 percentage of the total land area and it is also covered under the sub-plan area and constitutes about 47 per cent of the tribal population to the total population of the mandal. In this mandal, only 15 villages are electrified. The boundaries of the mandal are as follows: Eturnagaram is on the North; Khammam district is on the South; in the East, Mangapet and in the West Govindaraopet. The mandal has 51 primary schools, three upper primary schools and two high schools, one allopathy and one unani dispensary are there. It has 11 post offices and only four villages in Mandal have been connected to pucca road. Four bus stops, eight fair price shops, two police stations, three primary agricultural co-operative societies, two commercial banks also provide facilities in this mandal.

Indravelli Mandal

The Indravelli mandal is in Utnoor revenue division and it covers 34 villages with an area of 306.5 Sq. Kms. The mandal is bounded on the North by Adilabad; on the South by Utnoor; on the East by Narnoor and on the West by Gudihatnoor. The mandal possesses one police station out-post; five RTC bus stops, 10 post offices, 18 primary schools, two upper primary schools, one high school, one private doctor, weekly market/ shandy on every Monday, one regulated market yard, two scheduled banks, two veterinary hospitals/dispensaries, 32 fair price shops, 30 electrified villages, six villages with pucca road, 20 villages covered under DRDA, 15 villages covered under S.C. Corporation, 29 villages covered under ITDA, 20 villages covered under B.C. Corporation and 16 villages covered under Women Welfare Corporation.

Thus, one mandal each had been selected from these three districts. The scheduled tribes population constitutes a percentage of 44.92 in Dammapet mandal of Khammam district, 46.80 in Tadvai mandal of Warangal district and 57.90 in Indravelli mandal of Adilabad district. Thus, all the mandals have about 45 per cent of their population as tribals. The forest area is 41.26 per cent, 86.40 per cent and 42.46 per cent of the total geographical area in Dammapet, Tadvai and Indravelli respectively. Thus, Tadvai mandal has a higher proportion of geographical area under forests than the other two mandals. Agricultural labourers as a percentage of the total population is 22.75 per cent, 20.90 per cent and 20.20 per cent in Dammapet, Tadvai and Indravelli mandals respectively signifying that in predominantly tribal populated areas also one-fifth of the population belongs to the category of agricultural labourers. This signifies the growth of agricultural production in the areas.

PROFILES OF SELECTED VILLAGES

Ankampalem Village

This village has six hamlets[4] with a total area of 3,885.38 hectares, having 1,909 population with 372 households, wherein male population is 964 and the female population is 945, forming 50.50 per cent and 49.50 per cent respectively. Of the total population, the scheduled castes population is too insignificant, i.e., only eight persons which accounts for just 0.42 per cent and the scheduled tribes population is 1,636 forming 85.70 per cent.

The literates in this village are 230 in number or 12 per cent of the total population, wherein male and female literates are 166 and 64, forming 8.70 per cent and 3.35 per cent to the total population respectively. The total main workers are 985, which accounts for 51.60 per cent of the total population; the cultivators are 334, agricultural labourers are 398, forming 17.50 per cent and 20.85 per cent respectively and together claim 38.35 per cent to the total population of the village; other workers are 62, accounts for 3.24 per cent, 187 are marginal workers, forming 9.80 per cent of the total population in the village. The non-workers in the village are 924 forming 48.40 per cent of the total population and they are engaged in the household industry, manufacturing, processing, servicing and repairs.

The total irrigated land is 51.61 hectares with a tank as a primary source. The unirrigated area in this village is 525.69 hectares, the culturable waste is 446.77 hectares and the area not available for cultivation is 40.06 hectares.

The village has facilities like a primary school, while a well is the prime source for drinking water. It has a post office and a community health worker. Though it is a road side village, it is 17 Kms. away from the shandy point, having bus facility and a pucca road. The nearest town is Kothagudam which is 24 Kms. away. The village was electrified for all practical purposes. The staple food in this village is rice and jowar.

Patwarigudem Village

This village consists of six hamlets[5] with a total area of 2,570.15 hectares, having 3,153 population with 622 households, wherein male population is 1,610 and the female population is 1,543, forming 51.06 per cent and 48.94 per cent respectively. Of the total population, the scheduled castes population is 386 and the scheduled tribes population is 1,520, forming 12.24 per cent and 48.20 per cent respectively. The literates in the village are 760, forming 24.10 per cent of the total population. Among the literates, the male and female literates are 498 and 262, forming 15.80 per cent and 8.30 per cent respectively. Of the total population, the total main workers are 1,595, which accounts for 50.58 per cent and the total non-workers are 1,558, which accounts for 49.42 per cent. Of the total population of the village, the cultivators are 692, agricultural labourers are 643, other workersare 245 and the marginal workers are 10, their percentage being 21.95 per cent, 20.40 per cent, 7.77 per cent and 0.32 per cent respectively, and another insignificant per cent, i.e., 0.15 is engaged in household industry, manufacturing, processing, servicing and repairs. Further, both cultivators and agricultural labourers together form major chunk of the total population, i.e., 42.35 per cent.

The total irrigated land is 101.17 hectares with a tank as a primary source. The unirrigated area in this village is 500.19 hectares, the culturable waste is 268.71 hectares, and the area not available for cultivation is 1,295.40 hectares. Out of the total geographical area, the forest area covers 404.68 hectares in the village.

The village is endowed with all the facilities like primary and middle schools, community health worker, post office, posts & telegraph office, bus stop, pucca road. The nearest town is Kothagudem which is 20 Kms. away. The village was electrified for all purposes. The prime source of drinking water in the village is a well. The staple food in this village is rice and jowar.

Narsapur Village

The total geographical area of the village is 31.97 hectares covering the total population of 549, wherein male and female population is 298 and 251, which accounts for 54.28 per cent and 45.72 per cent respectively. Of the total population, the scheduled castes population is 124, accounts for 22.58 per cent and the scheduled tribes population is 425, which accounts for 77.42 per cent of the total population in the village. Of the total population, the literates are only 58 which accounts for 10.56 per cent, whereas male literates are 47 and female literates are 11, forming 8.56 per cent and two per cent respectively. Of the total population, the total main workers are 342 and the non-workers are 207, which accounts for 62.30 per cent and 37.7 per cent respectively. Of the total population, 151 are cultivators, 178 are agricultural labourers, nine are other workers and four are engaged in household industry, manufacturing, processing, servicing and repairs, etc., which accounts for 27.50 per cent, 32.42 per cent, 1.64 per cent and 0.73 per cent respectively. Both cultivators and agricultural labourers in the village together form 59.92 per cent of the total population.

The total irrigated area in this village is 0.40 hectares with a tank as primary source. The unirrigated area is 31.16 hectares and the area not available for cultivation is 0.41 per cent.

The village is possessed with facilities like primary school, medical and posts & telegraphs facility each within a range of 5. Kms. The primary source of drinking water in the village is well and tank, it is having the bus facility within the radius of five Kms., having kaccha road. The nearest town is Warangal which is 95 Kms. away. The staple food in the village is rice and jowar.

Pambapur Village

The total geographical area of the village is 984.19 hectares with a population of 590 with 125 households. The male and female population constitute 278 and 312, forming 47.12 per cent and 52.88 per cent respectively. This village does not have any scheduled caste households and the scheduled tribes population is 433, which accounts for 73.40 per cent of the total population. Of the total population, the literates are 53 accounting for only about nine per cent of the total population in the village, wherein the male literates are 38, forming 6.44 per cent and the female literates are 15, forming 2.54 per cent of the total population of the village. Out of the total population of the village, the total main workers constitute 341 and the total non-workers constitute 249, forming 57.80 per cent and 42.40 per cent respectively. And further, of the total population, 130 are cultivators, 180 are agricultural labourers, two are engaged in household industry, manufacturing, etc.; 12 are other workers and the 17 are marginal workers forming 22.03 per cent, 30.51 per cent, 0.34 per cent, 2.03 per cent and 2.88 per cent respectively.

Out of the total geographical area, the village covers 766.87 hectares of forest area. Only 18.61 hectares of land is irrigated with a tank as primary source of irrigation. The unirrigated area in this village is 193.44 hectares and the area not available for cultivation is 4.85 hectares.

The village is endowed with the facilities like primary school, having medical facility within the radius of 5 Kms. The primary source of drinking water in the village is a well. It has a branch post office; having bus facility within the radius of 5 Kms., having a kaccha road, and the nearest town is Warangal which is 124 Kms., away from the village. The staple food in the village is rice and jowar.

Katapur Village

This village[6] has 509 households with 2,114 population. The total geographical area of the village is 239.98 hectares. Of the total population, the male and female population constitute 1,098 and 1,016, forming 51.94 per cent and 48.06 per cent respectively. Of the total population, the scheduled caste population and scheduled tribes population constitute 372 (17.60%) and 212 (10.03%) respectively. The total literates are 424 forming 20.05 per cent of the total population and among the literates male and female constitute 347 (16.41%) and 77 (3.64%) respectively. Of the total population, the total main workers are 810 (38.32%) and the total non-workers constitute 1,304 (61.68%). And, of the total population, the cultivators constitute 332, agricultural labourers are 198. Persons engaged in the household industry, manufacturing, etc., are 49; the other workers are 162 and the marginal workers are 69 which accounts for 15.70 per cent, 9.36 per cent, 2.34 per cent, 7.66 per cent and 3.26 per cent respectively.

Of the total geographical area, forest area is 15.78 hectares. The total irrigated area is 141.64 hectares with tank as a primary source of irrigation and the unirrigated area in this village is 55.84 hectares and the area not available for cultivation is 26.30 hectares of the total geographical area of the village.

The village has a primary school, middle and high school, having other medical facilities. The prime source of drinking water is a well. The village also has a branch post office, a shandy on every sunday, bus facility, and also a kaccha approach road. The nearest town is Warangal which is 118 Kms. away. The staple food in the village is rice and jowar.

Anji Village

This village has 100 households with 524 population with a total geographical area of 553.20 hectares. Of the total population, the male and female population constitute 258 and 266, forming 49.24 per cent and 50.76 per cent respectively. Of the total population, the scheduled castes population is 41 and the scheduled tribes population is 457, which accounts for 7.82 per cent and 87.22 per cent respectively. Of the total population, only 56 are literates forming 10.70 per cent, wherein male literates are 42 and the female literates are only 14, which constitutes only 8.03 per cent and 2.67 per cent of the total population respectively. Of the total population, 198 (37.78 per cent) are the total main workers and 326 (66.22%)

are the total non-workers in the village. Of the total population, cultivators are 67 (12.78%), agricultural labourers are 125 (23.85%), and other workers are only six forming 1.15 per cent.

It doesn't have any forest area and even doesn't have any irrigated area. The unirrigated area is 504.24 hectares; the culturable waste is 16.59 hectares and the area not available for cultivation is 31.97 hectares.

The village has a primary school, community health worker; having the posts & telegraphs facility within the radius of five Kms., having the shandy point on Monday and regulated market yard within the radius of five Kms., no bus facility; having kaccha approach road to village; well is the important source for drinking water in the village. The nearest town is Adilabad with 42 Kms. away from the village. The staple food is jowar.

Wadgaon Village

This village[7] has 319 households with 1,678 population, covering the total geographical area 1,327.37 hectares.

The total population of the village is 1,678, wherein the male and female population constitutes 838 and 840 forming 49.94 per cent and 50.06 per cent respectively. Of the total population, the scheduled caste population is 58 (3.45 per cent) and the scheduled tribe population is 1,430 (85.23 per cent). The literates are only 80 which accounts for 4.76 per cent of the total population in the village. Of the total population, the male literates are 68 with 4.05 per cent and the female literates constitute only 0.71. per cent. Of the total population, the main workers are 781 and the total non-workers are 897, forming 46.54 per cent and 53.46 per cent. And of the total population, 359 (21.4 per cent) are cultivators, 234 (13.95 per cent) are agricultural labourers, only two (0.12 per cent) are in household industry, manufacturing, processing, etc., 13 (0.77 per cent) are other workers and the remaining 173 (10.3 per cent) are marginal workers in the village.

The village has neither forest area nor the irrigated area. The unirrigated area in this village is 821.51 hectares; the culturable waste is 485.62 hectares and the area not available for cultivation is 20.24 hectares.

The village has a primary school and is having medical facility within a radius of above 10 Kms.; well is the primary source of drinking water in the village. It has a branch post office; having the Shandy point on Monday and the regulated market yard within a radius of above 10 Kms. from the village; having the facility within the radius of 5-10 Kms. away from the village; having the kaccha road. The nearest town is Adilabad which is 42 Kms. away; it was electrified for domestic purposes. The main staple food in the village is jowar as in the case of Anji village.

Indravelli Village (Buzurg)

This village is the mandal headquarter with a total geographical area of 1,696.03 hectares.

The total population of the village is 6,108 with 1,090 households. Of the total population, the male and female population constitute 3,814 and 2,924 which accounts for 52.13 per cent and 47.87 per cent respectively. Of the total population, the scheduled castes population is 999 constituting 16.35 per cent and the scheduled tribes population is 1,191 accounting for 19.50 per cent. The literates are 1,781 forming 29.16 per cent of the total population; and among the literates, the male and female literates are 1,370 (22.43 per cent) and 411 (6.73 per cent) of the total population in the village. Of the total population, the total main workers are 1,993 and the total non-workers are 4,115 which accounts for 32.63 per cent and 67.37 per cent respectively. And, of the total population, the cultivators are 423 forming 6.93 per cent; the agricultural labourers are 653 constituting 10.68 per cent; the persons engaged in the household industry, manufacturing, processing, etc., are 31 forming 0.50 per cent; the other workers are 881 with 14.42 per cent and the marginal workers are constituting only 0.08 per cent. Inspite of being a mandal headquarter, both the cultivators and agricultural labourers together constitute a major chunk of the total main workers in the village accounting for 17.61 per cent of the total population.

This village has 147.71 hectares of forest area and it is not having any irrigated area. The unirrigated area in the village

Table 5

Land and Irrigation Intensities in the Sample Villages

Particulars (Area in Hectares)	*V1*	*V2*	*V3*	*V4*	*V5*	*V6*	*V7*	*V8*
Total Geographical Area	3885.38	2570.15	31.97	984.19	239.98	553.20	1327.37	1696.30
Cultivated Area	578.30	601.36	31.56	212.05	197.48	504.24	821.51	1278.80
Percentage of Cultivated Area to Total Geographical Area	14.88	23.40	98.72	21.55	82.30	91.15	61.90	75.40
Total Cropped Area	1025.05	870.07	31.56	212.05	197.48	520.83	1307.03	1390.09
% of 4 to 1	26.38	33.85	98.72	21.55	82.30	94.15	98.46	81.96
Area Irrigated	52.61	101.17	0.40	18.61	141.64	–	–	–
Percentage of Area Irrigated to Total Cultivated Area (% of 6 to 2)	9.10	16.82	1.26	8.77	71.72	–	–	–
Cropping Intensity (4/2*100)	177.25	144.68	100.00	100.00	100.00	103.30	159.10	108.70

Note: V_1 = Ankampalem; V_2 = Patwarigudem; V_3 = Narsapur;
V_4 = Pambapu V_5 = Katapur; V_6 = Anji;
V_7 = Wadagon; V_8 = Indravelli(B)

And hereafter refers to the same for all the tables in this chapter is 1,278.80 hectares; the culturable waste is 111.29 hectares and the area not available for cultivation is 158.23 hectares.

This village has a primary school, middle school, high school and also adult literacy centre. It has community health worker and registered private medical practitioner. Well is the primary source for drinking water in the village. It has the posts & telegraphs facility. The village has both Shandy point on Monday and the Regulated Market Yard and also has bus facility with pucca approach road to the village. The nearest town is Adilabad which is 46 Kms. away and got electrification for all purposes. The prime staple food is jowar and rice.

While having an idea over the entire study area, it is essential to peep into the prominent salient features of the eight villages that had been taken-up for the present study. All the important salient features of the study villages have been mentioned hereunder in the form of comparative statistics.

Table-5 shows the land and irrigation intensities in the study villages. While looking at the Table, in the case of the percentage of cultivated area to total geographical area, V_3 stood first with 98.72 per cent followed by V_6, V_5, V_8, V_7, V_2, V_4 and V_1 with 91.15 per cent; 82.30 per cent, 75.40 per cent, 61.90 per cent, 23.40 per cent, 21.55 per cent and 14.88 per cent respectively. As per the percentage of cropped area to the total geographical area, V_6, V_7 and V_8 stood first on an average followed by V_3, V_5, V_4, V_2, and V_1. Despite the cropped and cultivated areas, V_6, V_7 and V_8 do not have any percentage of irrigated area and whereas V_5 ranked first with 71.72 per cent of irrigated areas followed by V_2, V_1, V_4 and V_3. Though V_6, V_7 and V_8 lack percentage of area irrigated, these villages have slightly higher cropping intensities when compared with the villages-V_3, V_4 and V_5 and with regard to the cropping intensities, V_1 and V_2 occupied highest ranks among the sample villages. Therefore, one can deduce from the table taking into account the percentage of area irrigated as it is one of the indicators to assess the development of the region in the sample villages-V_6, V_7 and V_8 in Adilabad district are the backward villages relative to that of V_3, V_4 and V_5 in Warangal district and at the same time V_2, V_1 in Khammam district.

Table-6 and 7 are corollaries to the above table (5.5) and depict district-wise, mandal-wiseand village-wise percentages of different aspects of the geographical and demographical setting of the study area.

While looking at the Table-6 it can be said that Khammam district has a preponderant position over the other two study areas, in the case of percentage of forest area to total geographical area, percentage of irrigated area and percentage of scheduled tribes population in the district. The Warangal district in the study area dominates over the other two study areas with regard to aspects like percentage of workers, percentage of cultivators and cropping intensity. The Adilabad district has an edge over other study areas in the case of percentage of non-workers, percentage of cultivated area to total geographical area, percentage of cropped area to geographical area, and percentage of scheduled castes population. Moreover, Adilabad district has a marginal (9%) per cent of irrigated area to the total cropped area and further the cropping intensity is also less; percentage of literacy is also very marginal however, the percentage of non-workers is the highest. Further, while looking at the same Table and the Table-7, a similar tendency can be observed even in the case of respective sample mandals and in the case of sample villages. Therefore, from the above analysis, one will be able to deduce the fact that among the districts of the study area, the Adilabad district is to be considered as the most backward district where *'the speed and the level of development'* especially in the case of agriculture has not been commensurate with the other two sample districts in the study area. The sole reason for such backwardness is very low per cent of irrigated area to the total cropped area. And further, even though the district has cultivated area more or less on par with the two other sample districts, as it lacks irrigation facilities the yields of crops grown in the dry cultivated area have not increased substantially.

Apart from the above information, the availability of general infrastructural facilities will also have an important bearing on the path of the development of any region. Therefore, the infrastructural facilities and amenities available in the sample villages had also been presented in Table-8.

Table 6

District-Wise and Mandal-Wise Percentages of Different Aspects in the Study Area

Particulars (in %)	*State (A.P.)*	*Khammam District*	*Dammapeta Mandal*	*Warangal District*	*Tadvai Mandal*	*Adilabad District*	*Indravelli Mandal*
Literacy	36.82	33.47	31.66	32.60	26.20	26.78	14.77
Workers	45.06	43.30	49.40	45.30	49.70	41.73	44.25
Non-workers	54.94	56.70	50.60	54.70	50.30	58.27	55.75
Cultivators	11.86	11.78	16.03	14.70	21.55	14.14	19.32
Agricultural Labourers	17.50	20.94	22.75	19.06	20.90	14.60	20.20
Forest Area to Total Geographical Area	23.20	52.60	41.26	28.80	86.40	44.80	42.46
Irrigated Area	39.90	38.40	34.80	31.30	68.85	9.00	N.A
Cultivated Area to total geographical area	38.05	28.92	44.57	30.50	3.10	45.14	43.03
Cropped Area to Geographical area	46.36	30.27	45.08	37.00	3.50	40.80	43.03
Cropping intensity	121.86	104.65	101.15	142.80	125.30	102.64	100.00
S.C. Population	15.92	16.25	11.68	17.20	9.90	18.53	9.40
S.T. Population	6.32	25.23	44.92	13.70	46.80	17.04	57.90

Table 7
Percentage Particulars of Different Strata in the Regions Village-Wise

Particulars (in %)	V_1	V_2	V_3	V_4	V_5	V_6	V_7	V_8
Literacy	12.00	24.10	10.56	9.00	20.05	10.70	4.76	29.16
Main workers	51.60	50.58	62.30	57.80	38.32	37.78	46.54	32.63
Non-workers	48.40	49.42	37.70	42.20	61.68	62.22	53.46	67.37
Cultivators	17.50	21.95	27.50	22.03	15.70	12.78	21.40	6.93
Agricultural Labourers	20.85	20.40	32.42	30.51	9.36	23.85	13.95	10.68
Forest Area to Total Geographical Area	72.58	15.75	Nil	77.92	6.57	Nil	Nil	8.71
Irrigated Area	9.10	16.82	1.26	8.77	71.72	–	–	–
Cultivated Area to total geographical area	14.88	23.40	98.72	21.55	82.30	91.15	61.90	75.40
Cropped Area to Geographical area	26.38	33.85	98.72	21.55	82.30	94.15	98.46	81.96
Cropping Intensity	177.25	144.68	100.00	100.00	100.00	103.30	159.10	108.70
S.C. Population	0.42	12.42	22.58	Nil	17.60	7.82	3.45	16.35
S.T. Population	85.70	48.20	77.42	73.40	10.03	87.22	85.23	19.50

Table 8
Infrastructural Facilities in the Sample Villages

Particulars	*V1*	*V2*	*V3*	*V4*	*V5*	*V6*	*V7*	*V8*
Major Crops	Paddy Cashew Nuts Jowar	Paddy Cashew Nuts Jowar	Paddy Ground Nuts Micrhi Jowar	Paddy Ground Nuts Micrhi Jowar	Paddy Cashew Nuts Micrhi Jowar	Paddy Jowar Micrhi Cotton	Jowar Paddy Cotton Mirchi	Paddy Cotton Jowar Mirchi Tobacco
Staple Foods	Rice Jowar	Rice Jowar	Rice Jowar	Rice Jowar	Rice Jowar	Jowar	Jowar	Jowar Rice
Education % of Literacy	12.00 Primary	24.10 primary middle and High School	10.56 primary	9.00 primary	20.05 High School	1.07 primary	4.76 primary	29.16 primary middle High School
Power	Yes	Yes	Yes	Yes	Yes	Yes	Yes	Yes
Approach Road	Pucca	Pucca	Kaccha	Kaccha	Kaccha	Kaccha	Kaccha	Pucca
Distance in Km.s								
Surface Road	1	1	18	16	14	4	8	NA
Mandal	17	14	18	16	14	4	8	NA
Major Town	24 Kothagudem	20 Kothagudem	95 Warangal	124 Warangal	118 Warangal	42 Adilabad	42 Adilabad	46 Adilabad
Medical	LA, RMP	LA, RMP	5	5	LA, RMP	CHW	10	CHW, RP & Others
Banks	4	1	3	2	LA	4	8	LA

Contd.

Particulars	V1	V2	V3	V4	V5	V6	V7	V8
P & T	BPO	BPO & PT	3	BPO	BPO	4	BPO	BPO
PHC	4	LA	18	16	14	4	8	LA
Shandy	17	14	3	2	LA	4	8	LA
Nearest Regulated Market Yard	17	14	51	50	48	4	8	LA
Bus Stand	LA	LA	3	2	LA	4	8	LA
Fair Price Shop	YES	YES	NO	NO	YES	NO	NO	YES

Note:
B.P.O.= Branch Post Office; LA = Locally Available; P&T = Post & Telegraphs
PHC = Primary Health Centre; CHW = Community Health Worker;
RP = Registered Private Practitioner; RMP = Registered Medical Practitioner;
NA = Not Applicable

Out of the eight sample villages, only three villages have pucca approach road and most of the villages have schooling facility and were electrified. It is evident that the attention of most of the households in the villages have been turning towards the commercial crops like cashewnuts, groundnut, cotton, mirchi and tobacoo. Most of the villages are far away from the major town in the district and some of the villages are far away even from the Mandal headquarters. By and large, the sample villages didn't have satisfactory infrastructural facilities and this limits physical access to formal markets for both the tribal and non-tribal farmers in the sample villages; which phenomenon is seen more in the case of tribal and other small farmers when compared to the non-tribals. Even if such physical access existed in some of the sample villages, it did not safeguard and guarantee actual or economic access, especially in the case of tribal and other non-tribal marginal and small farmers too. Some times this is not an exception even to large farmers - both in the tribals and non-tribal communities as well. Therefore, it is to be concluded that, the physical access to economic benefits or returns to the tribal farmers in particular and even non-tribal farmers in general is a necessary though not a sufficient condition for the growth of markets in the tribal areas.

II

The socio-economic background of the tribal and non-tribal households in general and the sample respondents in particular had been ascertained through the collection of primary data during the field investigation by the researcher in the eight villages in three mandals of the three districts, viz., Khammam, Warangal and Adilabad.

The age-wise distribution of the sample respondents had been depicted in Table - 9.

While looking at the Table, it can be said that most of the sample respondents in the study area were in the age group of 25-40 years, accounting for 45.3 per cent followed by the age group of 40-55 years with 32 per cent. Among the three districts, Warangal had the highest per cent in the age group of 25-40 (51.0 per cent) followed by Khammam and Adilabad with 43 per cent and 42 per cent respectively. Therefore, from the table it can be inferred that the age group upto 40 years constitute the *"effective working group"* which confirms the active involvement in the collection of minor forest produce and also pursuing the agricultural activities effectively.

Table 9
Age-Wise Distribution of the Sample Respondents Region-Wise

		Region		
Age in Years	*Khammam*	*Warangal*	*Adilabad*	*Row Total*
< 25	8 (24.2)	17 (51.5)	8 (24.2)	33
–	(8.0)	(17.0)	(8.0)	(11.0)
25-40	43(31.6)	51(37.5)	42(30.9)	136
	(43.0)	(51.0)	(42.0)	(45.3)
40-55	37(38.5)	22(22.9)	37(38.5)	96
	(37.0)	(22.0)	(37.0)	(32.0)
55+	12(34.3)	10(28.6)	13(37.1)	35
	(12.0)	(10.0)	(13.0)	(11.7)
Column Total	100 (33.3)	100 (33.3)	100 (33.3)	300 (100.0)
Chi-square	Value	DF		Significance
Pearson	11.0701	6		0.0862
Likelihood Ratio	11.0714	6		0.0861
Mantel-Haenszel Test for Linear Association	0.0284 r = 0.009	1		0.8660
Statistic		Value		Approximate Significance
Phi		0.1920		0.0862 *1
Cramer's V		0.1920		0.0862 *1

* 1 Pearson Chi-square probability

Source: Field Study and hereafter refers to the same.
Note: Figures in parentheses indicate row-wise and column-wise percentages and hereafter refers to the same.

Further, from the table it can also be said that the chi-square and the other chi-square based measures have been found to be statistically significant at 10 per cent level, but the M-H test for linear association has not been found significant. Further, the correlation co-efficient is also weak as it represents the weak association between the age groups and the region.

The primary occupation of the respondents had been presented in Table -10. This clearly shows that most of the tribal and non-tribal sample households' primary occupation is agriculture in the former case 90 per cent and the latter 93.3 per cent followed by the occupation of the collection of Minor Forest Produce constituting 3.8 per cent among the sample tribal households. Among the non-tribal households, no household reported the occupation of the collection of minor forest produce. Therefore, the data presented in the Table confirms that the primary occupation of agriculture has a preponderant position over the other occupations as it lends support to the hypothesis that most of the village economies are embedded with agricultural activities rather than the other occupations. A similar trend had also been observed even in the case of region-wise configuration in the study area and this had been depicted in Table -10 (A).

Chi-square tests and other measures based on chi-square had also been estimated and have not been found statistically significant and the correlation co-efficient is also weak though it is positive. Thus, it reveals that the two variables used in the Table are independent of each other and no variable would influence the other. But, while looking at the region-wise analysis, these tests and measures have been found to be statistically significant at 10 per cent level whereas the likelihood ratio was found to be statistically significant at 5 per cent level. But the M-H test for linear association has been found to be non-significant and further the correlation co-efficient is also very weak and it does not form any association between the variables considered in the Table.

As Table -10(B) is a corollary to the above tables, it reveals about the particulars of region-wise subsidiary occupations of the sample tribal and non-tribal households.

Subsidiary occupations contribute substantially to the earnings of the tribals. The Table shows the region-wise distribution of subsidiary occupation for tribal and non-tribal

Table 10
Primary Occupation Particulars of the Sample Respondents Group-wise

Group-wise Category	*Occupation Particulars*								
	No Occu-pation	*Agri-culture*	*MFP*	*Agri-culture & Wage Labour*	*Employee*	*Agri-culture + MFP*	*Agri+ Culture & Wage Labour+ MFP*	*Others**	*Row Total*
Tribals	1 (0.4) (100.0)	216 (90.0) (79.4)	9 (3.8) (90.0)	8 (3.3) (88.0)	4 (1.7) (100.0)	1 (0.4) (100.0)	1 (0.4) (100.0)	–	240 (80.0)
Non-Tribals	–	56 (93.3) (20.0)	–	2 (3.4) (20.0)	–	–	–	2 (3.3) (100.0)	60 (20.0)
Column Total	1 (0.3)	272 (90.7)	9 (3.0)	10 (3.3)	4 (1.3)	1 (0.3)	1 (0.3)	2 (0.7)	300 (100.0)

Chi-square	*Value*	*DF*	*Significance*
Pearson	10.8782	7	0.1440
Likelihood Ratio	10.8641	7	0.1446
Mantel-Haenszel Test for Linear Association	0.8138 r = 0.052	1	0.3669

Statistic	*Value*	*Approximate Significance*
Phi	0.1904	0.1440 *1
Cramer's V	0.1904	0.1440 *1

* 1 Pearson Chi-square probability

*Others include the occupations like carpentry, tailoring and other caste occupations respondents. Less than five per cent of the total tribal population has no subsidiary occupation in all the districts except for a maximum of five per cent being found in Adilabad district. In contrast, non-tribals have a higher percentage of those who have no subsidiary occupation in Khammam followed by Adilabad and Warangal, the percentages being 70.0, 40.0 and 15.0 respectively. A finding of significance is that in all the districts between 40 to 50 per cent of tribal population is engaged in the collection of MFP. But in the case of agricultural/wage labour, a relatively more irrigated district like Khammam has a lesser percentage, i.e., 22.5, while both Warangal and Adilabad have relatively higher percentages, they being 45, 42.5 respectively. Hence, here a surmise can be either tribal areas in Khammam district did not receive irrigation facilities or even if irrigation facilities are there, the tribals have not been absorbed as agricultural labourers. Among those who are engaged in other occupations, the percentage is higher for Khammam than the other two districts. This may indicate a diversification of the activities that the tribals are undertaking in Khammam district.

Table 10(A)

Occupational (Primary) Distribution of the Sample Respondents Region - Wise

	Region			
Occupation Details	*Khammam*	*Warangal*	*Adilabad*	*Row Total*
No Occupation	1(100.0) (1.0)	–	–	1 (0.3)
Agriculture	85(31.3) (85.0)	97(35.7) (97.0)	90(33.1) (90.0)	272 (90.7)
MFP	8(88.9) (8.0)	–	1(11.1) (1.0)	9 (3.0)
Agricultural/ Wage Labour	4(40.0) (4.0)	1(10.0) (1.0)	5(50.0) (5.0)	10 (3.3)
Employee	1(25.0) (1.0)	1(25.0) (1.0)	2(50.0) (2.0)	4 (1.3)
Agriculture plus MFP	–	–	1(100.0) (1.0)	1 (0.3)

Contd.

	Region			
Occupation Details	*Khammam*	*Warangal*	*Adilabad*	*Row Total*
Agricultural/ Wage Labour plus MFP	–	–	1(100.0) (1.0)	1 (0.3)
Others	1(50.0) (1.0)	1(50.0) (1.0)	–	2 (0.7)
Column Total	100 (33.3)	100 (33.3)	100 (33.3)	300 (100.0)

Chi-square	Value	DF	Significance
Pearson	22.7681	14	0.0641
Likelihood Ratio	26.0851	14	0.0252
Mantel-Haenszel Test for Linear Association	0.0232	1	0.8788
		r = 0.008	

Statistic	Value	Approximate Significance	
Phi	0.2754	0.0641	*1
Cramer's V	0.2754	0.0641	*1

* 1 Pearson Chi-square probability

Chi-square test, Phi and Cramer's V had been estimated and except for M-H test for linear association, all other tests show that the null hypothesis that the variables are independent is rejected by all tests in the case of Khammam and Warangal. In the case of Adilabad, the M-H test for linear association is found to be non-significant. But the other tests were proved to be significant.

Further, from the Tables -10, 10(A) and 10(B), it can be inferred that forestry is one of the main contributors to the tribal economy, and it has been contributing either as a main occupation or as a subsidiary occupation. Therefore, it can be said that those who are having agriculture as main occupation in the case of tribals, collection of minor forest produce is only as a subsidiary occupation during the off season and thus lends support to the generally held hypothesis that the tribal economy is dichotomised both with agriculture and forestry.

Table 10(B)

Subsidiary Occupational Distribution of Respondents Group-Wise and Region-Wise

	Region								
	Khammam			*Warangal*			*Adilabad*		
Details of Subsidiary Occupation	*Tribal*	*Non-Tribal*	*Row Total*	*Tribal*	*Non-tribal*	*Row Total*	*Tribal*	*Non-Tribal*	*Row Total*
No Subsidiary Occupation	2 (12.5) (2.5)	14 (87.5) (70.0)	16 (16.0)	3 (50.0) (3.8)	3 (50.0) (15.0)	6 (6.0)	4 (3.3) (5.0)	8 (66.7) (40.0)	12 (12.0)
MFP	37 (100.0) (46.3)	–	37 (37.0)	38 (100.0) (47.5)	–	38 (38.0)	34 (100.0) (42.5)	–	34 (34.0)
Agri./ Wager Labour+ MFP	18 (100.0) (22.5)	–	18 (18.0)	36 (100.0) (45.0)	–	36 (36.0)	34 (100.0) (42.5)	–	34 (34.0)
Others*	23 (79.3) (28.8)	6 (20.7) (30.0)	29 (29.0)	3 (15.0) (3.8)	17 (85.0) (85.0)	20 (20.0)	8 (40.0) (10.0)	12 (60.0) (60.0)	20 (20.0)
Column Total	80 (80.0)	20 (20.0)	100 (100.0)	80 (80.0)	20 (20.0)	100 (100.0)	80 (80.0)	20 (20.0)	100 (100.0)

Chi-Square	Value	DF	Significance
Pearson	59.3211	3	0.0000
Likelihood Ratio	58.4545	3	0.0000
M-H Test for Linear Association	10.6381	1	0.0011

r = 0.327

Chi-Square	Value	DF	Significance
Pearson	74.6875	3	0.0000
Likelihood Ratio	74.8543	3	0.0000
M-H Test for Linear Association	24.4957	1	0.0000

r = 0.497

Chi-Square	Value	DF	Significance
Pearson	53.3333	3	0.0000
Likelihood Ratio	57.8836	3	0.0000
M-H Test for Linear Association	0.9158	1	0.3385

r = 0.096

Statistic	Value	Approximate significance	
Phi	0.7702	0.0000	*1
Cramer's V	0.7702	0.0000	*1

*1 Pearson Chi-Square Probability

Statistic	Value	Approximate significance	
Phi	0.8642	0.0000	*1
Cramer's V	0.8642	0.0000	*1

*1 Pearson Chi-Square Probability

Statistic	Value	Approximate significance	
Phi	0.7303	0.0000	*1
Cramer's V	0.7303	0.0000	*1

*1 Pearson Chi-Square Probability

* Others include the occuaptions like agriculture, agricultural/wage labour, employee, agriculture plus MFP, agriculture plus agricultural/wage labour, forest labour, tailoring, taddy tapping, and rearing of cows/goats.

From the above analysis, one will be able to surmise that the occupational pattern of the sample households in the study area had shown the uneven distribution. Therefore, occupations other than cultivation are more or less supplementary and subsidiary to agriculture.

The high rate of illiteracy among the sample tribal and non-tribal households in the study area underscores the absence of adequate schooling facilities in the tribal areas which *ipso facto* means the lack of communication facilities. The literacy standards of the sample households had been depicted in Table-11. The Table clearly shows that among the three districts, the Khammam district had the higher per cent of sample illiterates followed by Warangal and Adilabad, the percentages being 79, 74 and 54 respectively. This finding is contrary to the generally held notion that as Adilabad district is a backward district, it should have high rate of illiteracy. While looking at the differences among the sample tribal and non-tribal households, the rate of illiteracy is a glaring phenomenon as it had been more pronounced on the part of the sample tribal households than the non-tribal households in the study area. This finding lends supports to the generally held hypothesis that the rate of illiteracy among the tribals is higher when compared with the non-tribal households as it is due to the socio-economic status of the respective groups and moreover the non-tribals have an edge over the tribals in receiving the education due to the more accessibility of the schooling facilities.

Further, the table reveals that most of the sample non-tribal households have received the higher education of 45 per cent in Adilabad and in the case of Warangal and Khammam 20 per cent and 10 per cent respectively. But in the case of sample tribal households, a deplorably low figure of around five per cent in Adilabad and 3.8 per cent each in Khammam and Warangal claimed to have had education other than primary level By and large, one will be able to surmise that the problem of illiteracy is more wide-spread, in the tribal areas which has far reaching implications for the tribals.

Table 11
Group-Wise and Region-Wise Literacy Status of the Respondents

Literacy Particulars	Region: Khammam Tribal	Khammam Non-Tribal	Khammam Row Total	Warangal Tribal	Warangal Non-tribal	Warangal Row Total	Adilabad Tribal	Adilabad Non-Tribal	Adilabad Row Total
Illiterate	70 (88.6)	9 (11.4)	79	63 (85.1)	11 (14.9)	74	51 (94.4)	3 (5.6)	54
	(87.5)	(45.0)	(79.0)	(78.8)	(55.0)	(74.0)	(63.8)	(15.0)	(54.0)
Primary	7 (43.8)	9 (56.3)	16	14 (73.7)	5 (26.3)	19	25 (75.8)	8 (24.2)	33
	(8.8)	(45.0)	(16.0)	(17.5)	(25.0)	(19.0)	(31.3)	(40.0)	(33.0)
Others	3 (60.0)	2 (40.0)	5	3 (42.9)	4 (57.1)	7	4 (30.8)	9 (69.2)	13
	(3.8))	(10.0)	(5.0)	(3.8)	(20.0)	(7.0)	(5.0)	(45.0)	(13.0)
Column Total	80	20	100	80	20	100	80	20	100
	(80.0)	(20.0)	(100.0)	(80.0)	(20.0)	(100.0)	(80.0)	(20.0)	(100.0)

Chi-Square	Value	DF	Significance	Chi-Square	Value	DF	Significance	Chi-Square	Value	DF	Significance
Pearson	18.0488	2	0.0001	Pearson	7.7289	2	0.0209	Pearson	27.1051	2	0.0000
Likelihood Ratio	15.3869	2	0.0004	Likelihood Ratio	6.4061	2	0.0406	Likelihood Ratio	24.3051	2	0.0000
M-H Test for Linear Association	12.8744	1	0.0003	M-H Test for Linear Association	7.0185	1	0.0080	M-H Test for Linear Association	24.8584	1	0.0000
	r = 0.360				r = 0.266				r = 0.501		

Statistic	Value	Approximate significance		Statistic	Value	Approximate significance		Statistic	Value	Approximate significance	
Phi	0.4248	0.0001	*1	Phi	0.2780	0.0209	*1	Phi	0.5206	0.0000	*1
Cramer's V	0.4248	0.0001	*1	Cramer's V	0.2780	0.0209	*1	Cramer's V	0.5206	0.0000	*1

*1 Pearson Chi-Square Probability   *1 Pearson Chi-Square Probability   *1 Pearson Chi-Square Probability

The Chi-square tests and other chi-square based measures had been estimated for the data reported in the Table and they had also been found to be very much significant, indicating the inter-dependability of the variables used in the Table. And further, the correlation co-efficients calculated for the three districts also confirm the similar finding and it had the highest in Adilabad followed by Khammam, and Warangal, the correlation co-efficients being 0.501, 0.360 and 0.266 respectively.

The pattern of size of operational land holdings have been shown in Tables-12 and 12(A) with which one will be able to deduce the economic viability of the sample households. The former depicts the differences among the sample tribal and non-tribal households in the study area and the latter reports the regional configuration of the land possession of the sample households in the study areas.

Table 12
Group-Wise Distribution of Sample Households as Per Size of Operational Land Holding

	Size of Operational Land Holding (in Acres)					
Group-wise Category	*Not Applicable*	*≤2.50*	*2.50 - 5.00*	*5.00 - 10.00*	*10.00 +*	*Row Total*
Tribals	11(4.6)	37(15.4)	87(36.3)	81(33.8)	24(10.0)	240
	(84.6)	(84.1)	(87.0)	(84.4)	(51.1)	(80.0)
Non-Tribals	2(3.3)	7(11.7)	13(21.7)	15(25.0)	23(38.3)	60
	(15.4)	(15.9)	(13.0)	(15.6)	(48.9)	(20.0)
Column Total	13	44	100	96	47	300
	(4.3)	(14.7)	(33.3)	(32.0)	(15.7)	(100.0)

Chi-Square	Value	DF	Significance
Pearson	29.4399	4	0.0000
Likelihood Ratio	24.8965	4	0.0000
Mantel-Haenszel Test for Linear Association	12.6834	1	0.0003

r = 0.205

Statistic	Value	Approximate Significance
Phi	0.3132	0.0000 *1
Cramer's V	0.3132	0.0000 *1

* 1 Pearson Chi-square probability

The small and marginal farmers among the tribal households account for 51.7 per cent, whereas among the non-tribals, they account for only 33.4 per cent. Thus, it can be said that the small and marginal tribal farmers both in terms of absolute and relative sense outweigh the same category in non-tribals. But in the case of medium and big farmers, the sample non-tribals had a higher percentage than the tribal farmers in the study area as their percentages are 64.5 and 43.8 respectively. In absolute figures, the landless households among the sample tribal households are relatively more than the sample non-tribal households; but in terms of percentage, the difference is not much between the sample tribal and non-tribals, though tribals have the higher percentage.

Chi-square measures and other related statistics were found to be significant statistically and it connotes the inter-dependability of the variables. A similar conclusion can also been drawn with the help of the correlation co-efficient (r = 0.205).

The region-wise data in the Table -12(A) confirms that the small and marginal farmers are more in Warangal followed by Khammam and Adilabad with 55 per cent, 53 per cent and the 36 per cent respectively. But in the case of medium and big farmers, Adilabad had a preponderant position over the other two districts-Khammam and Warangal and the percentages being 57 and 43 in each of the two districts respectively.

The estimated chi-square measures and other related statistics were found to be statistically significant. Pearson, Phi and Cramer's V were found to be significant at 8 per cent level and the likelihood ratio at 5 per cent level. But the M-H test for linear association has not been found to be significant and similarly the strength of association between the variables in the Table had also been proved to be weak with the help of correlation co-efficient (r = 0.069).

Table -13 deals with the region-wise distribution of sample households as per the type of irrigation system.

At this juncture, it is very essential to distinguish between the public and private irrigation systems. The public irrigation systems includes the tanks, canals, kuntas, streams and lift irrigation, etc., whereas the private irrigation system includes the wells and the tube-wells possessed by the households in their own lands.

Table 12(A)
Land size Distribution of the Sample Respondents Region-wise

	Region			
Land Size in Acres	*Khammam*	*Warangal*	*Adilabad*	*Row Total*
Not Applicable	4(30.8) (4.0)	2(15.4) (2.0)	7(53.8) (7.0)	13 (4.3)
≤2.50	20(45.5) (20.0)	14(31.8) (14.0)	10(22.7) (10.0)	44 (14.7)
2.50 – 5.00	33(33.0) (33.0)	41(41.0) (41.0)	26(26.0) (26.0)	100 (33.3)
5.00 – 10.00	23(24.0) (23.0)	36(37.5) (36.0)	37(38.5) (37.0)	96 (32.0)
10.00+	20(42.6) (20.0)	7(14.9) (7.0)	20(42.6) (20.0)	47 (15.7)
Column Total	100 (33.3)	100 (33.3)	100 (33.3)	300 (100.0)

Chi-square	Value	DF	Significance
Pearson	20.7616	8	0.0078
Likelihood Ratio	22.1063	8	0.0047
Mantel-Haenszel Test for Linear Association	1.4589 r = 0.069	1	0.2270

Statistic	Value	Approximate Significance
Phi	0.2630	0.0781 *1
Cramer's V	0.2630	0.0781 *1

* 1 Pearson Chi-square probability

The Table reveals that Adilabad did not account much for the public irrigation system. Though it had some mixed category, on the whole most of the households (74 per cent) in the district depend on rain-water, whereas this accounts for 45 per cent and 2 per cent in Khammam and Warangal districts respectively. Further, the Table reveals that relatively

Warangal is in an advantageous position with regard to the types of irrigation systems when compared to the Khammam district. This finding may not tally with the finding for the overall district figures for the two districts. However, in light of all these aspects, one can conclude that Adilabad is the least developed than the other two districts in the study area and moreover it had also been observed that the district demonstrated and exhibited the practice of dry land agriculture.

Table 13
Region-wise Distribution of Sample Households As Per Type of Irrigation System

	Region			
Type of Irrigation System	*Khammam*	*Warangal*	*Adilabad*	*Row Total*
Not Applicable	3(33.3)	1(11.1)	5(55.6)	9
	(3.0)	(1.0)	(5.0)	(3.0)
Public	6(18.8)	26(81.3)	–	32
	(6.0)	(26.0)		(10.7)
Private	1(50.0)	–	1(50.0)	9
	(1.0)		(1.0)	(0.7)
Both	10(71.4)	3(21.4)	1(7.1)	14
	(10.0)	(3.0)	(1.0)	(4.7)
Rainfed	45(37.2)	2(1.7)	74(61.2)	121
	(45.0)	(2.0)	(74.0)	(40.3)
Both + Rainfed	6(60.0)	4(40.0)	–	10
	(6.0)	(4.0)		(3.3)
Public + Rainfed	23(24.2)	64(67.4)	8(8.4)	95
	(23.0)	(64.0)	(8.0)	(31.7)
Private + Rainfed	6(35.3)	–	11(64.7)	17
	(6.0)		(11.0)	(5.7)
Column Total	100	100	100	300
	(33.3)	(33.3)	(33.3)	(100.0)

Chi-square	Value	DF	Significance
Pearson	182.4420	14	0.0000
Likelihood Ratio	218.2576	14	0.0000
Mantel-Haenszel Test for Linear Association	0.0062	1	0.9371
	r = 0.004		

Statistic	Value	Approximate Significance
Phi	0.7798	0.0000 *1
Cramer's V	0.7798	0.0000 *1

* 1 Pearson Chi-square probability

Further, the regional variations, and the dependability between the type of irrigation system and the region is well evidenced by the pearson chi-square, chi-square likelihood ratio and phi and Cramer's V statistic. But the linear association between the variables has been refuted by the M-H test and it had also been proved by the weak positive correlation co-efficient (r = 0.004).

Tribal and non-tribal group-wise and region-wise agricultural incomes of the sample households have been shown in Table -14. Of the three districts, Khammam district has greater than one-half of the households (65 per cent) possessing agricultural incomes Rs.10,000, but in the case of Adilabad less than one-half of the sample households that is 38 per cent, and in the case of Warangal less than one-fourth that is 19 per cent of the households were in earning incomes less than or equal to Rs.10,000/-. Further, it also reveals that a smaller percentage of the sample households earn incomes Rs.35,000 or more and even among the three districts, Khammam had relatively higher percentage followed by Warangal and Adilabad with 11 per cent, 8 per cent and 7 per cent respectively.

Further, the Table also reveals the inequalities between the sample tribal and non-tribal households as in relation to the agricultural incomes within the districts. These inequalities are more prominent in Khammam followed by Adilabad and Warangal. For instance, while taking the income level of Rs.35,000 +, in the Khammam district, 50 per cent of the non-tribals have this level and whereas tribals figured very low with 1.3 per cent and a similar tendency had also been observed in the case of sample tribal and non-tribal households in Adilabad district with 1.3 per cent and 30.0 per cent respectively. But in the case of Warangal, a minute difference has been observed among the sample tribal and non-tribal households for the aforesaid income level. Therefore, from the above analysis, it can be inferred that the income inequalities are more stark even if one takes group-wise, and the region-wise configurations of tribals and non-tribals in the study area in general and in particular the income inequalities are more

Table 14

Group-Wise and Region-Wise Agricultural Incomes of the Sample Households

	Region								
	Khammam			Warangal			Adilabad		
Size of Agricultural Incomes	*Tribal*	*Non-Tribal*	*Row Total*	*Tribal*	*Non-tribal*	*Row Total*	*Tribal*	*Non-Tribal*	*Row Total*
Not Applicable	4 (100.0)	–	4	2 (100.0)	–	2	4 (80.0)	1 (20.0)	5
	(5.0)		(4.0)	(2.5)		(2.0)	(5.0)	(5.0)	(5.0)
≤ 10,000	59 (90.8)	6 (9.2)	65	17 (18.5)	2 (10.5)	19	34 (89.5)	4 (10.5)	38
	(73.8)	(30.0)	(65.0)	(21.3)	(10.0)	(19.0)	(42.5)	(20.0)	(38.0)
10,000 – 20,000	13 (92.9)	1 (7.1)	14	34(81.0)	8 (19.0)	42	32 (86.5)	5 (13.5)	37
	(16.3)	(5.0)	(14.0)	(42.5)	(40.0)	(42.0)	(40.0)	(25.0)	(37.0)
20,000 – 35,000	3 (50.0)	3 (5.0)	6	20 (69.0)	9 (31.0)	29	9 (69.2)	4 (30.8)	13
	(3.8)	(15.0)	(6.0)	(25.0)	(45.0)	(29.0)	(11.3)	(20.0)	(13.0)
35,000 +	1 (9.1)(1.3)	10 (90.9)	11	7 (87.5)	1 (12.5)	8	1 (14.3)	6 (85.7)	7
		(50.0)	(11.0)	(8.8)	(5.0)	(8.0)	(1.3)	(30.0)	(7.0)
Column Total	80	20	100	80	20	100	80	20	100
	(80.0)	(20.0)	(100.0)	(80.0)	(20.0)	(100.0)	(80.0)	(20.0)	(100.0)

Chi-Square	Value	DF	Significance	Chi-Square	Value	DF	Significance	Chi-Square	Value	DF	Significance
Pearson	45.1011	4	0.0000	Pearson	4.0777	4	0.3955	Pearson	22.9397	4	0.0001
Likelihood Ratio	37.8359	4	0.0000	Likelihood Ratio	4.4408	4	0.3496	Likelihood Ratio	18.4064	4	0.0010
M-H Test for Linear Association	37.7674	1	0.0000	M-H Test for Linear Association	1.5744	1	0.2095	M-H Test for Linear Association	13.1900	1	0.0002
	r = 0.617				r = 0.126				r = 0.365		

Statistic	Value	Approximate significance		Statistic	Value	Approximate significance		Statistic	Value	Approximate significance	
Phi	0.6715	0.0000	*1	Phi	0.2019	0.3955	*1	Phi	0.4789	0.0001	*1
Cramer's V	0.6715	0.0000	*1	Cramer's V	0.2019	0.3955	*1	Cramer's V	0.4789	0.0001	*1

*1 Pearson Chi-Square Probability   *1 Pearson Chi-Square Probability   *1 Pearson Chi-Square Probability

stark in Khammam and Adilabad than in Warangal. The researcher had also observed and enquired the reasons for such inequalities from the sample respondents and it was informed to that it could be due to the enormous influx of non-tribals along with the merchant capital, which has been thriving in these areas. If one takes Adilabad district, most of the well endowed non-tribals migrated to this district from the neighbouring state of Maharashtra and in Khammam, most of the advanced sections of non-tribals of Andhra region with technical expertise migrated to the tribal areas in the district. But in the case of Warangal one can also see the influx of non-tribals in the tribal areas but most of them belonged to the peasant category and here one should note that there had been a difference among the non-tribals who migrated into the tribal belts of Warangal, Khammam and Adilabad. In contrast to the peasant non-tribal infiltration in Warangal district, in Khammam and Adilabad, the non-tribal infiltraters were either merchants utilising their capital for usury or advanced sections of peasantry with technical expertise with which they opened up a new vista in the realm of tribals' exploitation.

The estimated chi-square tests and other measures based on chi-square were found to be significant both in Khammam and Adilabad, which exhibits the inter-dependability and the similar trend had also been observed in respect of correlation co-efficients (r=0.617 and r=0.365 for Khammam and Adilabad). But they were not found to be significant in the Warangal district and thereby reject the inter-dependability and the same finding had also been confirmed by its correlation co-efficient (r = 0.126).

Table-15 shows the MFP incomes of the sample households. This Table reveals that among the three districts, Warangal had a preponderant position over the other two districts by having the 57 per cent of the sample households with regard to the income level of Rs.4,000+. Khammam and Warangal have 42 per cent of the households in each district obtaining the income level of less than or equal to Rs.4,000/-. The data within the districts also corroborates the finding. Thus, it can be inferred from the above analysis that the

Table 15
Group-wise and Region-wise MFP Incomes of the Sample Households

	Region								
	Khammam			*Warangal*			*Adilabad*		
Size of MFP Incomes	*Tribal*	*Non-tribal*	*Row Total*	*Tribal*	*Non-tribal*	*Row Total*	*Tribal*	*Non-tribal*	*Row Total*
Not Applicable	14 (4102) (17.5)	20 (58.8) (100.0)	34 (34.0)	3 (13.0) (3.8)	20 (87.0) (100.0)	23 (23.0)	10 (33.3) (12.5)	20 (66.7) (100.0)	30 (30.0)
≤ 4,000	42 (100.0) (52.5)	–	42 (42.0)	20 (100.0) (25.0)	–	20 (20.0)	42 (100.0) (52.5)	–	42 (42.0)
4,000 +	24 (100.0) (30.0)	–	24 (24.0)	57 (100.0) (71.3)	–	57 (57.0)	28 (100.0) (35.0)	–	28 (28.0)
Column Total	80 (80.0)	20 (20.0)	100 (100.0)	80 (80.0)	20 (20.0)	100 (100.0)	80 (80.0)	20 (20.0)	100 (100.0)

dependence on the collection of minor forest produce in the sample villages is still more in the Warangal district than in the other two districts, though it is relatively developed in agriculture when compared to the Adilabad district.

The region-wise and tribal and non-tribal group-wise incomes obtained by way of agricultural/wage labour of the sample households have been shown in Table-16.

The Table reveals that, out of the total sample, 157 (52.33 per cent) households obtained their incomes by way of agricultural labour. Out of 240 tribal households, 129 tribal households have this income, accounting for 53.75 per cent, whereas in the case of non-tribals, only 28 households have the income from this source, forming 46.66 per cent. It clearly shows that the proportion of tribal households having income from agricultural labour outweigh the proportion of non-tribal households. Region-wise configuration shows that Khammam district has a slightly higher percentage with 55 per cent of the households' income from the above mentioned source followed by Adilabad and Warangal with 54 per cent and 48 per cent respectively. Further, while taking into account the distinction of tribal and non-tribal, relatively higher number of tribal households (both in absolute terms and relative percentages) depend on the wage labour incomes when compared to the non-tribal households in both Khammam and Warangal districts. The converse is true in the case of Adilabad district. By and large, one will be able to say that these incomes also contribute to their total earnings, though not to a substantial extent.

All the estimated chi-square measures and other related statistics in all the three districts were found to be statistically non-significant leading to conclude that the variables are independent of each other and did not have any association and the weak correlation co-efficients in the districts shown in the Table also corroborate the above finding.

Non-casual labour incomes (depicted in Table-17) are hypothesised to be dependent on the level of development of the area in non-agricultural sectors. In this respect Khammam district is able to absorb more labour than the other two

Table 16
Agricultural/wage Labour Incomes of the Sample Households Group-wise and Region-wise

	Region								
	Khammam			*Warangal*			*Adilabad*		
Size of Agricultural/ Wage Labour Incomes	*Tribal*	*Non-Tribal*	*Row Total*	*Tribal*	*Non-tribal*	*Row Total*	*Tribal*	*Non-Tribal*	*Row Total*
Not Applicable	32 (71.1)	13 (28.9)	45	43 (82.7)	9 (17.3)	52	36 (78.3)	10 (21.7)	46
	(40.0)	(65.0)	(45.0)	(53.0)	(45.0)	(55.0)	(45.0)	(50.0)	(46.0)
≤ 3,000	22 (91.7)	2 (8.3)	24	27 (81.8)	6 (18.2)	33	24 (85.7)	4 (14.3)	28
	(27.5)	(10.0)	(24.0)	(33.8)	(30.0)	(33.0)	(30.0)	(20.0)	(28.0)
3,000 +	26 (83.9)	5 (16.1)	31	10 (66.7)	5 (33.3)	15	20 (76.9)	6 (23.1)	26
	(32.5)	(25.0)	(31.0)	(12.5)	(25.0)	(15.0)	(25.0)	(30.0)	(26.0)
Column Total	80	20	100	80	20	100	80	20	100
	(80.0)	(20.0)	(100.0)	(80.0)	(20.0)	(100.0)	(80.0)	(20.0)	(100.0)

Chi-Square	Value	DF	Significance	Chi-Square	Value	DF	Significance	Chi-Square	Value	DF	Significance
Pearson	4.5542	2	0.1025	Pearson	1.9704	2	0.3733	Pearson	0.8122	2	0.6662
Likelihood Ratio	4.8167	2	0.0899	Likelihood Ratio	1.7757	2	0.4115	Likelihood Ratio	0.8534	2	0.6526
M-H Test for Linear Association	2.2597	1	0.1327	M-H Test for Linear Association	1.3417	1	0.2467	M-H Test for Linear Association	0.0000	1	1.0000
	r = 0.151				r = 0.116				r = 0.000		

Statistic	Value	Approximate significance		Statistic	Value	Approximate significance		Statistic	Value	Approximate significance	
Phi	0.2134	0.1025	*1	Phi	0.1403	0.3733	*1	Phi	0.0901	0.6662	*1
Cramer's V	0.2134	0.1025	*1	Cramer's V	0.1403	0.3733	*1	Cramer's V	0.0901	0.6662	*1

*1 Pearson Chi-Square Probability   *1 Pearson Chi-Square Probability   *1 Pearson Chi-Square Probability

Table 17
Group-wise and Region-wise Non-casual Labour Incomes of the Sample Households

	Region								
	Khammam			*Warangal*			*Adilabad*		
Size of Non-Casual Labour Incomes	*Tribal*	*Non-Tribal*	*Row Total*	*Tribal*	*Non-tribal*	*Row Total*	*Tribal*	*Non-Tribal*	*Row Total*
Not Applicable	53 (82.8)	11 (17.2)	64	71 (86.6)	11 (13.4)	82	66 (82.5)	14 (17.5)	80
	(66.3)	(55.0)	(64.0)	(88.8)	(55.0)	(82.0)	(82.5)	(70.0)	(80.0)
≤ 5,000	23 (92.0)	2 (8.0)	25	5 (41.7)	7 (58.3)	12	3 (50.0)	3 (50.0)	6
	(28.8)	(10.0)	(25.0)	(6.3)	(35.0)	(12.0)	(3.8)	(15.0)	(6.0)
5,000 +	4 (36.4)	7 (63.6)	11	4 (66.7)	2 (33.3)	6	11 (78.6)	3 (21.4)	14
	(5.0)	(35.0)	(11.0)	(5.0)	(10.0)	(6.0)	(13.8)	(15.0)	(14.0)
Column Total	80	20	100	80	20	100	80	20	100
	(80.0)	(20.0)	(100.0)	(80.0)	(20.0)	(100.0)	(80.0)	(20.0)	(100.0)

Chi-Square	Value	DF	Significance	Chi-Square	Value	DF	Significance	Chi-Square	Value	DF	Significance
Pearson	15.6573	2	0.0004	Pearson	13.9100	2	0.0009	Pearson	3.7053	2	0.1568
Likelihood Ratio	12.9890	2	0.0015	Likelihood Ratio	11.4939	2	0.0031	Likelihood Ratio	3.0182	2	0.2211
M-H Test for Linear Association	5.7456	1	0.0165	M-H Test for Linear Association	7.8653	1	0.0050	M-H Test for Linear Association	0.5937	1	0.4409
	r = 0.241				r = 0.282				r = 0.077		

Statistic	Value	Approximate significance		Statistic	Value	Approximate significance		Statistic	Value	Approximate significance	
Phi	0.3956	0.0004	*1	Phi	0.3729	0.0009	*1	Phi	0.1924	0.1568	*1
Cramer's V	0.3956	0.0004	*1	Cramer's V	0.3729	0.0009	*1	Cramer's V	0.1924	0.1568	*1

*1 Pearson Chi-Square Probability   *1 Pearson Chi-Square Probability   *1 Pearson Chi-Square Probability

districts as 36 per cent of the sub-sample of the Khammam district have non-casual labour income in contrast with Warangal and Adilabad, whose percentages are 18 and 20 respectively. Among those who earn less than Rs.5,000/- per annum, tribals constitute a higher relative percentage than non-tribals in Khammam district, but in the case of those who earn more than Rs.5,000/- the relative percentages are uniformly higher for non-tribals than tribals in all the districts. A comparison of tribals alone shows that this percentage is higher for Adilabad than the other two districts. Various chi-square tests, phi and Cramer's V statistic are statistically significant in Khammam and Warangal which is also reflected in the correlation co-efficient which is 0.241 for Khammam and 0.282 for Warangal. This signifies that there is a linear association among variables in a way attesting the hypothesis that geographical location matters in the generation of non-casual labour incomes for tribals.

A district-wise comparison of the total incomes of the sample households (Table-18) will reveal the well-being of tribals in different districts. Among those whose annual income is less than Rs.15,000/- among tribals, the percentage is relatively higher in Khammam district which is 70 per cent followed by 15 per cent in Warangal and 32.5 per cent in Adilabad. In the income range of Rs.15,000-25,000, the percentage is higher for Adilabad than the other two districts. In the income range of Rs.25,000 - 35,000, Warangal has a higher percentage than the other two districts and even for more than Rs.35,000 income group, the percentage is higher in Warangal than the other two districts. A significant finding is that for non-tribals, the percentage values are higher for Rs.35,000/- income group in Khammam followed by Adilabad and Warangal. The correlation co-efficient has relatively higher values of 0.677 and 0.337 in Khammam and Adilabad respectively and in these two districts, all the chi-square values, phi and Cramer's V are found to be statistically significant.

Total expenditure depends not only on total incomes but also on the geographical areas in which they live. Table -19 reveals that, wherever the incomes generated are relatively

Table 18
Total Incomes of the Sample Households Group-Wise and Region-Wise

	Region								
	Khammam			*Warangal*			*Adilabad*		
Size of Total Incomes	*Tribal*	*Non-Tribal*	*Row Total*	*Tribal*	*Non-tribal*	*Row Total*	*Tribal*	*Non-Tribal*	*Row Total*
≤ 15,000	56 (94.9)	3 (5.1)	59	12 (75.0)	4 (25.0)	16	26 (86.7)	4 (13.3)	30
	(70.0)	(15.0)	(59.0)	(15.0)	(20.0)	(16.0)	(32.5)	(20.0)	(30.0)
15,000 – 25,000	19 (86.4)	3 (13.6)	22	37 (82.2)	8 (17.8)	45	40 (87.0)	6 (13.0)	46
	(23.8)	(15.0)	(22.0)	(46.3)	(40.0)	(45.0)	(50.0)	(30.0)	(46.0)
25,000 – 35,000	4 (66.7)	2 (33.3)	6	14 (70.0)	6 (30.0)	20	10 (83.3)	2 (16.7)	12
	(5.0)	(10.0)	(6.0)	(17.5)	(30.0)	(20.0)	(12.5)	(10.0)	(12.0)
35,000 +	1 (7.7)	12 (92.3)	13	17 (89.5)	2 (10.5)	19	4 (33.3)	8 (66.7)	12
	(1.3)	(60.0)	(13.0)	(21.3)	(10.0)	(19.0)	(5.0)	(40.0)	(12.0)
Column Total	80	20	100	80	20	100	80	20	100
	(80.0)	(20.0)	(100.0)	(80.0)	(20.0)	(100.0)	(80.0)	(20.0)	(100.0)

Chi-Square	Value	DF	Significance	Chi-Square	Value	DF	Significance	Chi-Square	Value	DF	Significance
Pearson	51.9076	3	0.0000	Pearson	2.7046	3	0.4394	Pearson	18.6413	3	0.0003
Likelihood Ratio	44.1475	3	0.0000	Likelihood Ratio	2.7437	3	0.4328	Likelihood Ratio	14.8066	3	0.0019
M-H Test for Linear Association	45.4889	1	0.0000	M-H Test for Linear Association	0.3777	1	0.5388	M-H Test for Linear Association	11.3092	1	0.0007
	r = 0.677				r = 0.061				r = 0.337		

Statistic	Value	Approximate significance		Statistic	Value	Approximate significance		Statistic	Value	Approximate significance	
Phi	0.7204	0.0000	*1	Phi	0.1644	0.4394	*1	Phi	0.4317	0.0003	*1
Cramer's V	0.7204	0.0000	*1	Cramer's V	0.1644	0.4394	*1	Cramer's V	0.4317	0.0003	*1

*1 Pearson Chi-Square Probability   *1 Pearson Chi-Square Probability   *1 Pearson Chi-Square Probability

Table 19
Total Expenditures of the Sample Households Group-Wise and Region-Wise

	Region								
	Khammam			*Warangal*			*Adilabad*		
Size of Total Expenditures	*Tribal*	*Non-Tribal*	*Row Total*	*Tribal*	*Non-tribal*	*Row Total*	*Tribal*	*Non-Tribal*	*Row Total*
≤ 10,000	27 (96.4)	1 (3.6)	28	1 (100.0)	–	1	6 (85.7)	1 (14.3)	7
	(33.8)	(5.0)	(28.0)	(1.3)		(1.0)	(7.5)	(5.0)	(7.0)
10,000 – 15,000	38 (95.0)	2 (5.0)	40	26 (81.3)	6 (18.8)	32	38 (92.7)	3 (7.3)	41
	(47.5)	(10.0)	(40.0)	(32.5)	(30.0)	(32.0)	(47.5)	(15.0)	(41.0)
15,000 – 25,000	13 (76.5)	4 (23.5)	17	34 (77.3)	10 (22.7)	44	29 (78.4)	8 (21.6)	37
	(16.3)	(20.0)	(17.0)	(42.5)	(50.0)	(44.0)	(36.3)	(40.0)	(37.0)
25,000 +	2 (13.3)	13 (86.7)	15	19 (82.6)	4 (17.4)	23	7 (46.7)	8 (53.3)	15
	(2.5)	(65.0)	(15.0)	(23.3)	(20.0)	(23.0)	(8.8)	(40.0)	(15.0)
Column Total	80	20	100	80	20	100	80	20	100
	(80.0)	(20.0)	(100.0)	(80.0)	(20.0)	(100.0)	(80.0)	(20.0)	(100.0)

Chi-Square	Value	DF	Significance	Chi-Square	Value	DF	Significance	Chi-Square	Value	DF	Significance
Pearson	52.1472	3	0.0000	Pearson	0.5836	3	0.9001	Pearson	14.7422	3	0.0020
Likelihood Ratio	45.2405	3	0.0000	Likelihood Ratio	0.7773	3	0.8548	Likelihood Ratio	13.5127	3	0.0036
M-H Test for Linear Association	38.7544	1	0.0000	M-H Test for Linear Association	0.0042	1	0.9478	M-H Test for Linear Association	11.0101	1	0.0009
r = 0.625				r = 0.006				r = 0.333			

Statistic	Value	Approximate significance		Statistic	Value	Approximate significance		Statistic	Value	Approximate significance	
Phi	0.7221	0.0000	*1	Phi	0.7640	0.9001	*1	Phi	0.3839	0.0020	*1
Cramer's V	0.7221	0.0000	*1	Cramer's V	0.7640	0.9001	*1	Cramer's V	0.3839	0.0020	*1

*1 Pearson Chi-Square Probability *1 Pearson Chi-Square Probability *1 Pearson Chi-Square Probability

high, the expenditures are relatively high. As a greater proportion among tribals have annual incomes of less than Rs.15,000/- in Khammam, the percentage of those whose expenditure is less than Rs.10,000 is also relatively high. In the next expenditure group of Rs.10,000 - 15,000/-, the percentage is the same for Khammam and Adilabad, but it is lesser in Warangal. But it is relatively high for non-tribals in this district than the other two districts. In the next expenditure group of Rs.15,000 - 25,000, the percentages are relatively higher for Warangal and Adilabad at 42.5 and 36.3 respectively for tribals and they are also relatively high for non-tribals at 50.0 and 40.0 in the above two districts than Khammam, whose percentage is only 20.0. In the expenditure group of more than Rs.25,000/- among tribals, the percentage is the highest in Warangal, while the percentages are relatively high for non-tribals at 65 per cent and 40 per cent in Khammam, and Adilabad respectively. The chi-square values, phi and Cramer's V ratios are statistically significant at Khammam and Adilabad where the correlation co-efficients are 0.625 and 0.333 respectively.

SUMMING UP

Khammam district has a preponderant position over the other two study areas. In the case of percentage of forest area to total geographical area, percentage of irrigated area and in the case of the scheduled tribes population in the district. Warangal district in the study area dominates over the other two study areas with regard to the aspects like percentage of workers, percentage of cultivators with slightly higher percentages and cropping intensity. Adilabad district has an edge over in the case of percentage of non-workers, percentage of cultivated area to total geographical area, percentage of cropped area to geographical area, and percentage of scheduled castes population. Moreover, Adilabad district has only a marginal i.e., nine per cent of irrigated area to the total cropped area in the district and further the cropping intensity is also less; percentage of literacy is also very marginal and moreover, the percentage of non-workers is the highest. A similar tendency had also been observed even in the case of respective sample mandals and in the case of sample villages. Therefore, from the above analysis, one will be able to deduce the fact that among the districts of the study area, the Adilabad district is to be considered as the least developed district.

The availability of general infrastructural facilities will also have an important bearing on the path of the development of any region. By and large, the villages didn't have satisfactory infrastructural facilities and this limits physical access to formal markets for both the tribal and non-tribal farmers in the sample villages. Even if such physical access existed in some of the sample villages, it did not safeguard and guarantee actual or economic access, especially in the case of tribal and other non-tribal marginal and small farmers too. Some times this is not an exception even to large farmers - both in the tribals and non-tribals as well. Thus, the physical access to economic benefits or returns to the tribal farmers in particular and even non-tribal farmers in general is a necessary though not a sufficient condition for the growth of markets in the tribal areas.

The socio-economic analysis of the sample tribal and non-tribal households reveal that most of the sample households in the study area were aged less than 40 years, which can be considered as the *'effective working group'*, whose involvement in the collection of MFP and pursuit of the agricultural activities is active and effective. The region-wise and tribal and non-tribal group-wise configuration with regard to the primary occupation lends support to generally held hypothesis that most of the village economies in tribal areas had undergone a transition from forest-based economies to agriculturally oriented economies. The subsidiary occupations in the sample villages contribute substantially to the earnings of the tribals. Thus, both the primary and subsidiary occupation-wise details of the sample households confirms that those who are having agriculture as main occupation in the case of tribals will tend to depend on the collection of MFP only as a subsidiary occupation during the off-season.

As per the educational status, the high rate of illiteracy among the sample tribal and non-tribal households in the study area, which under-scores the lack of adequate schooling facilities in the tribal areas and particularly the rate of illiteracy is more rampant on the part of the sample tribal households than the non-tribal sample households and in turn reflects their socio-economic status.

The region-wise, and tribal and non-tribal group-wise configuration of the size of operational holdings reveals that the sample tribal households preponderate over the sample non-tribal households in the case of the small and marginal farmers and the reverse is held true in the case of the medium and big farmers. Thus, it confirms the uneven distribution in possessing the size of operational holdings in the study area.

The region-wise, the tribal and non-tribal group-wise agricultural incomes of the sample households reveals the uneven distribution of agricultural incomes and exhibit greater inequalities among the sample tribal and non-tribal households as well as among the sample households in different regions. But even these inequalities are more stark among the tribals than among non-tribals. Further, if one looks at the entire study area, these inequalities are more in Khammam and Adilabad than in Warangal.

The MFP incomes of the sample households reveal that among the three districts, Warangal had a dominant position over the other two districts in the study area. Hence, it can be surmised that the dependence on the collection of MFP in the sample villages is prevalent to a certain extent though the households had bestowed much attention towards agriculture. But incomes from MFP are also substantial additions to the agricultural incomes of the tribal households in the study area. The agricultural wage labour incomes also contribute to the total earnings and incomes of the sample tribal and non-tribal households, though they do not add substantially to the total earnings of the tribal households.

The non-casual labour incomes in the study area reveal that Khammam district is able to absorb more labour than the rest of the districts in the study area as 36 per cent of the Khammam district have non-casual labour incomes contrast to Warangal and Adilabad with 18 per cent and 20 per cent respectively. A comparison of tribals shows the percentage is higher at Adilabad than in the other two districts.

Thus, the total incomes and expenditures of the sample households also demonstrate the uneven distribution of incomes and expenditures among the sample tribal and non-tribal households in all the districts. Albeit, total incomes and expenditures of sample non-tribal households were on the higher side than the incomes and expenditures of the sample tribal households. This pattern reveals that wherever the incomes generated are relatively high, the expenditures are also relatively high.

Finally, one will be able to surmise that the socio-economic characteristics like pattern and size of operational holding of tribal and non-tribal households, their education, occupations, incomes from agriculture and other than agriculture, debt, and expenditures vividly reflect the weaker economic status of the tribals and as well as the small and marginal farmers in the case of non-tribals. Thus, the poor economic conditions, the lack of free availability of institutional credit and the lack of adequate institutional marketing facilities heighten the prospects for the pauperisation of the households and inturn contributes for the linked transactions of the households. Further they will lead to a further deterioration of the economic status of the poor, small and marginal farmers and inturn make them to depend more on the non-institutional credit as well as non-institutional marketing that had been in vogue in the sample villages.

NOTES & REFERENCES

1. This chapter had been written based on the information provided by the village elders, concerned Mandal revenue Officers and the Statistical Assistants of the study area and this had been collected by the researcher with the help of village schedule, apart from the other main schedules administered to the households in the sample villages. Besides the above information, the other relevant statistics presented in this chapter had been compiled from the latest Districts Census Hand Books, Mandal Gananka Dharishinies, based on 1991 Census data published by the concerned Chief Planning Officers and other Census Abstracts

and Reports of 1951, 1961, 1971, 1981 and 1991 for having the tribal population in the country and the state as well. Hence, the researcher had not mentioned source for each table separately and, therefore, hereafter in this chapter for all the tables references are the same. The analysis made in Section-II is primarily based on the field survey.

2. The term *'Tribe'* is derived from a Latin root, the Middle English term *'Tribuz'*, meaning the three divisions into which the early Romans were grouped, came to evolve into the modern English 'Tribe'. The word *'Tribe'* as generally understood in the literture on Anthropology *is a social group speaking a distinctive language and possessing a distinctive culture that makes it off from other tribes.*

3. Report of *Scheduled Areas and Scheduled Tribes Commission*, Government of India, New Delhi, 1961, p.4.

4. They are: Erragumpa, Lankalapalli, Arepenta, Kodisagattu, Bolligattu, Kodisalagudem.

5. They are: Malapalli, Chillagumpu, Parklagandi, Pakalagudem, Kothur, Sudhapalli.

6. It has only one hamlet, i.e., Jaggaram.

7. This village has eight Hamlets. They are: Naikpodugu, Todsmaguda, Pathaguda, Kolamguda, Mamiguda, Palaguda, Lingapur and Jaithaguda.

6

LINKAGES OF CREDIT WITH PRODUCT MARKETS–AN EMPIRICAL EVIDENCE

On the supply side, there are formal[1] and informal[2] financial institutions to provide the credit to the farmers, wherein the former is associated with complex procedures and cumbersome formalities and the latter with simple, easy and flexible procedures marked by the personal relations and timely supply of the required credit to the farmers by linking the credit to the input and output markets and also by charging higher interest rates. Further, on the demand side, one will be able to identify the small and poor farmers on the one side associated with a low literacy level, lower caste status, lower incomes, small size of operated land holding, higher family size, and higher worker dependent ratio and on the other side larger farmers endowed with high human and physical resources. Despite having the institutional infrastructure and formal credit available in the rural and tribal areas, leaving the interior belts of the tribal areas, small, poor and tribal farmers repeatedly will tend to depend on the *'modus operandi'* of the non-institutional lenders that are available in the area, with evidence of linkages with other factor and product markets and also due to the backwardness of the region and also due to the institutional bottlenecks[3] of the formal credit market.

The imperfections beset with the capital market in the rural areas of the developing countries has engaged the attention of a number of economists and social scientists[4] as access to credit is far more easier for some groups than the others. A well established fact attested by a number of studies[5] is in respect of supplying of credit by the formal agencies, according to which poor farmers have seldom benefitted and consequently the primary advantage has accrued to the large farmers. It has also been observed by the researcher during his field visits. Therefore, it can be said that the market for loans in the case of certain groups of borrowers may be severely restricted and limited to the extent possible.

In the light of the above background,this chapter had been devoted for an examination of the nature of the credit market with specific purpose to analyse the interlinking[6] of the various agrarian markets in the tribal areas with special reference to the interlinkages of credit with input and product markets. The analysis presented here is primarily based on the field work. The extent of the interlinked credit transactions across the households had also been undertaken in this chapter. Further, the regional, tribal and non-tribal diversity in the extent of these transactions and the household characteristic features contributing to this sort of credit transactions had also been examined. The access to the formal and informal agencies that existed in the study area had also been undertaken in this chapter.

Assessment on extension of institutional credit facilities in tribal areas is based on comparison between the number of borrowers drawn into the institutional net-work to that of borrowers who still remain in the clutches of non-institutional agencies (Table -1). It is also presumed that borrowers from non-institutional sources also have linked transactions. The percentage of borrowers out of total respondents is relatively higher for Khammam sub-sample than the other two sub-samples. Between tribals and non-tribals, it is relatively high for tribals, which indicates that tribals have been drawn into the vortex of credit markets. Here, this finding is contrary to the existing hypothesis that credit tends to gravitate towards

Table 1
Extent of Credit Transactions in Study Area

Particulars	*Study Area/Size of the Sample*					
	Total Sample Size	*Khammam Sub-Sample*	*Warangal Sub-Sample*	*Adilabad Sub-Sample*	*Sub-Sample of Tribals*	*Sub-Sample of Non-Tribals*
Total No. of Households Surveyed	300 (100.00)	100 (100.00)	100 (100.00)	100 (100.00)	240 (100.00)	60 (100.00)
Total No. of Borrowers	234 (78.00)	84 (84.00)	81 (81.00)	69 (69.00)	191 (79.60)	43 (71.67)
Total No. of Non-Borrowers	66 (22.00)	16 (16.00)	19 (19.00)	31 (31.00)	49 (20.40)	17 (28.33)
No. of Borrowers from Institutional Sources	138 (15.00)	48 (57.15)	40 (49.38)	50 (72.46)	116 (60.73)	22 (51.16)
No. of Borrowers from Non-Institutional Sources	54 (23.10)	23 (27.38)	21 (25.92)	10 (14.50)	47 (24.60)	7 (16.28)
No. of Borrowers from Institutional and Non-Institutional Sources	42 (17.90)	13 (15.47)	20 (24.70)	9 (13.04)	28 (14.67)	14 (32.56)
No. of Linked Borrowers	80 (34.20)	28 (33.33)	36 (44.44)	16 (23.18)	61 (31.94)	19 (44.18)
No. of Non-Linked Borrowers	74 (31.60)	49 (58.33)	15 (18.52)	10 (14.50)	50 (26.18)	24 (55.82)
No. of Borrowers who did not respond	80 (34.20)	7 (8.34)	30 (37.04)	43 (62.32)	80 (41.88)	-

Source: Field Study

Note:

1. Figures in parantheses indicate percentages.
2. The percentage of borrowers and non-borrowers to the total number of house-holds survyed andwhereas the other percentages in the table referred to the total number of borrowers in the sample.

the better off farmers as it was held by Ghatak[7] and Sarap[8]. Among borrowers, the percentage of those who borrowed from institutional sources is relatively high in Adilabad than in the other two districts, though the percentage for borrowers in this district is the lowest among the three districts. As a corollary to this is that the percentage of those who borrowed from non-institutional sources is the lowest here, but it is relatively high for Khammam among the three districts. In the case of tribals Vs non-tribals, the percentage for tribals is relatively higher for both borrowers from purely institutional sources and purely non-institutional sources than non-tribals, but for borrowers from both the sources, it is higher for non-tribals than tribals. Among the districts, such a category has a relatively higher percentage in Warangal district than the other two districts. Of the total borrowers those who revealed that they have linked transactions had a higher percentage in Warangal, while in Adilabad it is relatively lower in percentage. The variations in this percentage have an association with the category of borrowers from both institutional and non-institutional sources. Among the non-tribals percentage is relatively high for those with non-linked transactions than with linked transactions, but in the case of linked transactions the percentage is higher for non-tribals than the percentage for tribals. All those who did not respond to the question on linked transactions, were tribals and among these the percentage is higher for Adilabad than the other two districts. While the data attests to the fact of growing institutionalisation of credit in tribal areas, it also reveals the prevalence of linked transactions among borrowers signifying the nexus among credit, labour and commodity markets. Thus, the growing institutionalisation of credit in tribal areas refutes the usually held hypothesis that the formal financial institutions in the tribal areas are not accessible.

The details of the loan-wise distribution of the sample households had been shown in Table -2. Among the three districts, 16 per cent, 19 per cent and 31 per cent of the households in the sub-samples of Khammam, Warangal and Adilabad respectively did not have any loan. This had been

Table 2
Loan-Wise Distribution of Sample Households Group-Wise and Region-Wise

No. of Loans	Region: Khammam Tribal	Khammam Non-tribal	Khammam Row Total	Warangal Tribal	Warangal Non-tribal	Warangal Row Total	Adilabad Tribal	Adilabad Non-tribal	Adilabad Row Total
No Loan	13 (81.2)	3 (18.8)	16	14 (73.7)	5 (26.3)	19	22 (71.0)	9 (29.0)	31
	(16.2)	(15.0)	(16.0)	(17.5)	(25.0)	(19.0)	(27.5)	(45.0)	(31.0)
One Loan	59 (87.4)	7 (10.6)	66	49 (83.1)	10 (16.9)	59	51 (87.9)	7 (12.1)	58
	(73.8)	(35.0)	(66.0)	(61.3)	(50.0)	(59.0)	(63.8)	(35.0)	(58.0)
More than	8 (44.4)	10 (55.6)	18	17 (77.3)	5 (22.7)	22	7 (63.6)	4 (36.4)	11
One Loan	(10.0)	(50.0)	(18.0)	(21.3)	(25.0)	(22.0)	(8.8)	(20.0)	(11.0)
Column Total	80	20	100	80	20	100	80	20	100
	(80.0)	(20.0)	(100.0)	(80.0)	(20.0)	(100.0)	(80.0)	(20.0)	(100.0)

Chi-Square	Value	DF	Significance	Chi-Square	Value	DF	Significance	Chi-Square	Value	DF	Significance
Pearson	17.3453	2	0.0001	Pearson	0.9191	2	0.6315	Pearson	5.7017	2	0.0577
Likelihood Ratio	14.5412	2	0.0007	Likelihood Ratio	0.8982	2	0.6382	Likelihood Ratio	5.5861	2	0.0612
M-H Test for Linear Association	10.5238	1	0.0011	M-H Test for Linear Association	0.0544	1	0.8155	M-H Test for Linear Association	0.1628	1	0.6865
	r = 0.326				r = 0.023				r = 0.040		

Statistic	Value	Approximate significance		Statistic	Value	Approximate significance		Statistic	Value	Approximate significance	
Phi	0.4164	0.0001	*1	Phi	0.0958	0.6315	*1	Phi	0.2387	0.0577	*1
Cramer's V	0.4164	0.0001	*1	Cramer's V	0.0958	0.6315	*1	Cramer's V	0.2387	0.0577	*1
*1 Pearson Chi-Square Probability				*1 Pearson Chi-Square Probability				*1 Pearson Chi-Square Probability			

Source: Field Study and hereafter refers to the same.

Note: Figures in parentheses indicate row-wise and column-wise percentages and hereafter refers to the same.

ascribed to their economic status, that is, either some of them are landless labourers or some of them are self-sufficient, who are capable of self-financing their agriculture and other needs. This category of non-borrowers is more prominent among tribals and their percentage is relatively higher at Adilabad district. Of those who borrowed one loan the relative percentage is higher for tribals in Khammam district constituting 73.8 per cent followed by Adilabad forming 63.8 per cent and Warangal with 61.3 per cent. In the case of non-tribals, this percentage is relatively higher in Warangal district account for 50 per cent, which is lesser than the percentage for the tribals of any one of the three districts. In the case of those who borrowed more than one loan, the data confirms the hypothesis that the non-tribals are in an advantageous position than the tribals. This may be due to the more accessibility of the institutional and non-institutional credit agencies for non-tribals in the study areas. In all the districts, their relative percentages are higher than the tribals. Here also, among the tribals the absolute number as well as relative percentage is higher in Warangal than in the other two districts.

Further, the inter-dependence among the variables considered here is found to be statistically significant at 5 per cent level only in Khammam district by whatever measure it had been tested-whether it is Pearson, likelihood ratio, M-H test for linear association in the case of Chi-square and Phi and Cramer's V and at 10 per cent significant level for Pearson, likelihood ratio in the case of Chi-square and Phi and Cramer's V in Adilabad district.

The particulars of the distribution of sample households as per sources of loan had been presented in Table -3. In the study area, the households who borrowed from the institutional sources is relatively higher in Adilabad with 50 per cent followed by Khammam and Warangal with 48 per cent and 40 per cent respectively. Even in the case of tribal borrowers, it is higher in Adilabad with 53.8 per cent followed by Khammam with 47.5 per cent and Warangal with 43.8 per cent. But in the case of non-tribal borrowers from the institutional sources, Khammam stood first with 50 per cent

Table 3
Distribution of Sample Households As Per Sources of Loan Group-Wise and Region-Wise

	Region								
Sources of Loans	*Khammam*			*Warangal*			*Adilabad*		
	Tribal	*Non-tribal*	*Row Total*	*Tribal*	*Non-tribal*	*Row Total*	*Tribal*	*Non-tribal*	*Row Total*
Not Applicable	13 (81.3) (16.3)	3 (18.8) (15.0)	16 (16.0)	14 (73.7) (17.5)	5 (26.3) (25.0)	19 (19.0)	22 (71.0) (27.5)	9 (29.0) (45.0)	31 (31.0)
Institutional	38 (79.2) (47.5)	10 (20.8) (50.0)	48 (48.0)	35 (87.5) (43.8)	5 (12.5) (25.0)	40 (40.0)	43 (86.5) (53.8)	7 (14.0) (35.0)	50 (50.0)
Non-Institutional	22 (95.7) (27.5)	1 (4.3) (5.0)	23 (23.0)	16 (76.2) (20.0)	5 (23.8) (25.0)	21 (21.0)	9 (90.0) (11.3)	1 (10.0) (5.0)	10 (10.0)
Institutional + Non-Institutional	7 (53.8) (8.8)	6 (46.2) (30.0)	13 (13.0)	15 (75.0) (18.8)	5 (25.0) (25.0)	20 (20.0)	6 (66.7) (7.5)	3 (33.3) (15.0)	9 (9.0)
Column Total	80 (80.0)	20 (20.0)	100 (100.0)	80 (80.0)	20 (20.0)	100 (100.0)	80 (80.0)	20 (20.0)	100 (100.0)

Chi-Square	Value	DF	Significance	Chi-Square	Value	DF	Signifi-cance	Chi-Square	Value	DF	Signifi-cance
Pearson	9.1158	3	0.0277	Pearson	2.3829	3	0.4968	Pearson	4.3306	3	0.2279
Likelihood Ratio	9.3392	3	0.0251	Likelihood Ratio	2.4920	3	0.4767	Likelihood Ratio	4.2739	3	0.2333
M-H Test for Linear Association	0.8928	1	0.3447	M-H Test for Linear Association	0.1547	1	0.6940	M-H Test for Linear Association	0.1576	1	0.6913
	r = 0.094				r = 0.039				r = 0.039		

Statistic	Value	Approximate significance		Statistic	Value	Approximate significance		Statistic	Value	Approximate significance	
Phi	0.3019	0.0277	*1	Phi	0.1543	0.6315	*1	Phi	0.2081	0.2279	*1
Cramer's V	0.3019	0.0277	*1	Cramer's V	0.1543	0.6315	*1	Cramer's V	0.2081	0.2279	*1
*1 Pearson Chi-Square Probability				*1 Pearson Chi-Square Probability				*1 Pearson Chi-Square Probability			

followed by Adilabad with 35 per cent and Warangal with 25 per cent. Further, it also reveals that the households who borrowed from the non-institutional sources, Khammam stood first with 23 per cent followed by Warangal and Adilabad forming 21 per cent and 10 per cent respectively. Thus, in Adilabad this is nearly less than the one-half of the percentage observed in the other two districts. A similar tendency had also been observed even for the sample tribal borrowers accounting for 27.5 per cent, 20 per cent and 11.3 per cent respectively. But in the case of non-tribal borrowers Warangal had a dominant position in the entire study area with 25 per cent followed by Khammam and Adilabad with 5 per cent each. Therefore, this data also confirms the generally held hypothesis that the tribal borrowers depend more on non-institutional sources than the non-tribal households. It is reported that the tribals are at the vicinity of the money-lenders or merchants who give them loan whenever a household is in need of it to meet the immediate needs. Further, this Table also reveals that the percentage for sample tribal borrowers who obtained the loans from the institutional sources is relatively higher than the sample non-tribal borrowers in the entire study area. This observation is in contrast to the findings of Sarap[9]. This had been attributed to the fact that in the recent past the institutions created for the upliftment of the tribals - ITDA and GCC - have been rendering services to them while offering the loans both in kind and cash and further it is due to the revival of the discontinued SAO loaning operations by the GCC. This had been the highest in Adilabad district owing to the yeoman services of ITDA and GCC in the researcher's study villages. Further, the researcher had also observed that this does not mean that the tribal households are economically worthy enough and more accessible to the formal lending agencies in the area.

Chi-square tests and other related statistics had also been estimated for all the districts and were found to be non-significant statistically for Warangal and Adilabad, whereas in Khammam they were found to be significant at 5 per cent level, but the M-H test for linear association is not statistically significant.

Table -4 shows the distribution of the sample borrowers according to the purpose of the loan by region-wise. The Table vividly brings out that most of the borrowers obtained the loans for agricultural inputs and related to land development activities. This had been the highest in Warangal followed by Adilabad and Khammam with 68 per cent, 63 per cent and 38 per cent respectively. The purpose like marriages and social ceremonies has a very low percentage signifying the growing peasant culture of tribals. The purpose like domestic needs figured significantly in Khammam with 31 per cent. For this, during the field trip the researcher had observed that most of the tribal borrowers in the district obtained the consumption loan to the tune of Rs.500/- from the GCC on behalf of the assistance scheme for gum pickers. Further, it is to be noted that the Chi-square tests estimated have been found to be very much significant, indicating the inter-dependency and strong association between the variables under consideration.

Table 4
Region-Wise Distribution of Sample Households As Per Purpose of Borrowing

	Region			
Purposes of Borrowing	*Khammam*	*Warangal*	*Adilabad*	*Row Total*
Not Applicable	16(24.3) (16.0)	19(28.8) (19.0)	31(46.9) (31.0)	66 (22.0)
Agricultural inputs and related land development activities(1)	38(22.5) (38.0)	68(40.2) (68.0)	63(37.3) (63.0)	169 (56.3)
Marriages and social ceremonies (2)	2(66.7) (2.0)	1(33.3) (1.0)	–	3 (1.0)
Domestic needs (3)	31(88.6) (31.0)	1(2.9) (1.0)	3(8.6) (3.0)	35 (11.7)
Others(4)	2(28.6) (2.0)	4(57.1) (4.0)	1(14.3) (1.0)	7 (2.3)
One Plus Two	3(60.0) (3.0)	1(20.0) (1.0)	1(20.0) (1.0)	5 (1.7)
One Plus Three	5(50.0) (5.0)	4(40.0) (4.0)	1(10.0) (1.0)	10 (3.3)
One Plus Four	–	1(100.0) (1.0)	–	1 (0.3)

Contd.

	Region			
Purposes of Borrowing	*Khammam*	*Warangal*	*Adilabad*	*Row Total*
Two Plus Three	3(100.0) (3.0)	–	–	3 (1.0)
Three Plus Four	–	1(100.0) (1.0)	–	1 (0.3)
Column Total	100 (33.3)	100 (33.3)	100 (33.3)	300 (100.0)

Chi-square	Value	DF	Significance
Pearson	81.7344	18	0.0000
Likelihood Ratio	83.3275	18	0.0000
Mantel-Haenszel Test for Linear Association	27.8643 r = 0.305	1	0.0000

Statistic	Value	Approximate Significance
Phi	0.5219	0.0000 *1
Cramer's V	0.5219	0.0000 *1

* 1 Pearson Chi-square probability

As Table -4 (A) is a corollary to the above table, it explains about the purpose for which the sample borrowers had spent the borrowed amount. While looking at the Table, it had been observed that a considerable percentage of the borrowers diverted the loan amount for other purposes. This had been the highest in Adilabad followed by Warangal and Khammam with 50.70 per cent, 49.40 per cent, and 40.50 per cent respectively and the remaining sample borrowers reported that the amount had been spent for the borrowed purpose only. During the field study, it had also been observed that most of the borrowers diverted the productive loan amount[10] to the unproductive purposes like ordinary and conspicuous consumption and other social functions and ceremonies.

The Pearson and likelihood ratio Chi-square tests as well as Phi and Cramer's V had also been estimated and were found to be significant statistically at 10 per cent level indicating the inter-dependability between the variables.

Table 4 (A)
Region-Wise Distribution of Sample Households As Per Loan Amount Spent

Purposes of which Loan is Spent	Region			
	Khammam	*Warangal*	*Adilabad*	*Row Total*
Not Applicable	16(24.3) (16.0)	19(28.8) (19.0)	31(46.9) (31.0)	66 (22.0)
Spent on borrowed purpose	50(40.0) (50.0)	41(32.8) (41.0)	34(27.2) (34.0)	125 (41.7)
Diversified	34(31.2) (34.0)	40(36.7) (40.0)	35(32.1) (35.0)	109 (36.3)
Column Total	100 (33.3)	100 (33.3)	100 (33.3)	300 (100.0)

Chi-square	Value	DF	Significance
Pearson	8.9445	4	0.0625
Likelihood Ratio	8.7068	4	0.0688
Mantel-Haenszel Test for Linear Association	1.2708	1	0.2596
	r = 0.065		

Statistic	Value	Approximate Significance
Phi	0.1726	0.0625 *1
Cramer's V	0.1726	0.0625 *1

* 1 Pearson Chi-square probability

The source of formal loan exclusively borrowed by the sample households had been explained by using the logit analysis. Here the specification of the variables included in the model are: dummy dependent variable: 1 if the household has borrowed from formal sources, O, other-wise. The explanatory variables included in the model are number of loans (V_{27}), amount taken (V_{31}), amount outstanding (V_{33}), agricultural incomes (V_{138}), MFP incomes (V_{139}) and the total expenditures of the households (V_{143}). This had been carried out for all the sub-samples. Table -5 shows the final results of logistic regression model for the sub-sample of borrowers from formal agencies of total sample households surveyed.

For the logistic regression model with V_{28} as dependent variable, the -2LL value that contains only the constant is

316.8134. The Chi-square value for -2LL with 227 degrees of freedom is 256.558 leading us to reject the null hypothesis revealing that this model differs significantly from the perfect model. Since the model chi-square and improvement chi-square has the same value of 60.256 with 6 degrees of freedom, it leads us to reject the null hypothesis. But the goodness of fit statistic leads us to a different conclusion as in the case of -2LL Chi-square indicating that this does not differ significantly from the perfect model with the large observed significance level.

Table 5
Maximum Likelihood Estimation (Dummy Dependent Variable: 1 if the Household has Borrowed from Formal Sources, 0 - Otherwise): Total Sub-Sample (N = 234)

-2 Log Likelihood 316.8134

	Chi-Square	df	Significance
-2 Log Likelihood	256.558	227	0.0866
Model Chi-Square	60.256	7	0.0000
Improvement	60.256	6	0.0000
Goodness of Fit	254.332	227	0.1028

Classification Table

Predicted

Observed	Other than formal sources	Formal sources	Per cent correct
Other than formal sources	42	54	43.75
formal sources	7	131	94.93
			Overall 73.93%

Variables in the Equation

Variable	B	S.E.	Wald	DF	Sig.	R	Exp(B)
V_{27}	-3.0805	0.5461	31.8172	1	0.0000	-0.3068	0.0459
V_{31}	0.3890	0.2454	2.5128	1	0.1129	0.0402	1.4754
V_{33}	0.0911	0.1945	0.2193	1	0.6396	0.0000	1.0953
V_{138}	-0.2113	0.1323	2.5503	1	0.1103	-0.0417	0.8096
V_{139}	-0.0421	0.0955	0.1943	1	0.6594	0.0000	0.9588
V_{143}	0.1699	0.1556	1.1924	1	0.2748	0.0000	1.1852
Constant	3.4882	0.6008	33.7078	1	0.0000		

V_{27} = Number of Loans; V_{31} = Amount taken
V_{33} = Amount Outstanding; V_{138} = Agricultural Incomes
V_{139} = M.F.P. Incomes; V_{143} = Total Expenditures

And hereafter refers to the same

The classification table presented in Table - 5 shows that out of a total of 234, a total of 61 cases were misclassified. Of those who had borrowed loans from other than institutional sources, 43.75 per cent were correctly classified. Among those who borrowed from institutional sources 94.93 per cent were correctly classified. Overall 73.93 per cent of the 234 borrowers were correctly classified. Here, we would like to see small estimated probability for borrowers from non-institutional sources and large estimated probabilities for borrowers from institutional sources. Here, the estimated probability for the borrowers who have borrowed from the institutional sources is relatively high.

These co-efficients can be interpreted as the change in the log odds associated with a one unit change in the regressors. Therefore, when V_{27} changes from 0 to 1, the odds are decreased by a factor of 0.0459. When V_{31} changes from 0 to 1, the odds are increased by factor of 1.47. But in the case of V_{138}, the odds are decreased by a factor of 0.80. Thus, by increasing the value of V_{27} and V_{138} by one unit, it decreased the log odds by -3.0805 and -0.2113 respectively. But by increasing the value of V_{31} by one unit, it increased the log odds by about 0.3890.

The final results of the maximum likelihood estimates of the binary logit for the sub-sample of Khammam had been shown in Table - 6.

The value -2LL for the logistic model that contains only the constant is 114.7285. The Chi-square value of -2LL is 98.389 with 77 degrees of freedom has been found to be statistically significant leading us to reject the null hypothesis. Since the model Chi-square and improvement have the same value of 16.340 with 6 degrees of freedom they have been found to be statistically significant leading us to reject the null hypothesis for both the model Chi-square and improvement. But the goodness of fit statistic produces a different conclusion when compared with -2LL Chi-square, revealing that this model does not differ significantly from the perfect model as it is due to the large observed significance level.

From the classification table, it can be noted that of the borrowers with other than institutional sources 41.67 per cent were correctly classified and of the borrowers who had borrowed from the institutional sources 89.58 per cent were correctly predicted. In the overall borrowers of 84, 69.05 per cent were correctly classified. Further, the off-diagonal entries of the classification table shows that 15 and 5 borrowers who had borrowed from other than institutional sources and from the institutional sources of a total of 20 respectively were not correctly predicted with their respective associations. The estimated probability in the former case is greater than one-half and in the case of latter, the estimated probability is lesser than one-half. Further, it is to be noted that the estimated probability from the institutional sources is higher than the borrowers from the non-institutional sources.

Table 6
Maximum Likelihood Estimation of Dichotomous Logit Relationship (Dummy Dependent Variable: 1 if the Household has Borrowed from Formal Sources, 0 - Otherwise): Khammam Sub-Sample (N = 84)

-2 Log Likelihood 114.7285

	Chi-Square	df	Significance
-2 Log Likelihood	98.389	77	0.0507
Model Chi-Square	16.340	6	0.0120
Improvement	16.340	6	0.0120
Goodness of Fit	84.387	77	0.2642

Classification Table

Predicted

Observed	Other than formal sources	Formal sources	Per cent correct
Other than formal sources	15	21	41.67
formal sources	5	43	89.58
			Overall 69.05%

Variables in the Equation

Variable	B	S.E.	Wald	DF	Sig.R	Exp(B)	
V_{27}	-2.0755	0.7867	6.9596	1	0.0083	-0.2079	0.1255
V_{31}	-0.5543	0.4037	1.8847	1	0.1698	0.0000	0.5745
V_{33}	0.7636	0.4513	2.8628	1	0.0906	0.0867	2.1459
V_{138}	-0.3334	0.2409	1.9150	1	0.1664	0.0000	0.7165
V_{139}	0.0544	0.1779	0.0935	1	0.7598	0.0000	1.0559
V_{143}	0.5606	0.2848	3.8756	1	0.0490	0.0000	1.7518
Constant	2.0829	0.9265	5.0543	1	0.0246		

As the change in the log odds are associated with a one unit change in the regressors, when V_{33} and V_{143} change from 0 to 1, the odds are increased by a factor of 2.14 and 1.05 respectively. But in the case of V_{27}, as it has a negative Co-efficient, the odds are decreased by a factor of 0.12. Thus, by increasing the value of V_{33} and V_{143} by one unit, it increased the log odds by about 0.76 and 0.56 respectively. But by increasing the value of V_{27} by one unit, it decreased the log odds by -2.07.

Table 7
Maximum Likelihood Estimation of Dichotomous Logit Relationship (Dummy Dependent Variable: 1 if the Household has Borrowed from formal Sources, 0 - Otherwise): Warangal Sub-Sample (N = 81)

-2 Log Likelihood 112.2775

	Chi-Square	df	Significance
-2 Log Likelihood	88.780	74	0.1158
Model Chi-Square	23.498	6	0.0006
Improvement	23.498	6	0.0006
Goodness of Fit	77.916	74	0.3553

Classification Table

Observed	Predicted: Other than formal sources	Predicted: Formal sources	Per cent correct
Other than formal sources	20	21	48.78
Formal sources	2	38	95.00
			Overall 71.60%

Variables in the Equation

Variable	B	S.E.	Wald	DF	Sig.	R	Exp(B)
V_{27}	-2.9672	0.8330	12.6896	1	0.0004	-0.3086	0.0514
V_{31}	0.2921	0.3916	0.5562	1	0.4558	0.0000	1.3392
V_{33}	-0.0587	0.3489	0.0283	1	0.8665	0.0000	0.9430
V_{138}	-0.0532	0.2176	0.0597	1	0.8070	0.0000	0.9482
V_{139}	0.0420	0.1490	0.0793	1	0.7782	0.0000	1.0429
V_{143}	-0.0641	0.2704	0.0562	1	0.8126	0.0000	0.9379
Constant	3.3783	1.1718	8.3117	1	0.0039		

The results of the maximum likelihood estimates of the binary logit for the sub-sample of Warangal district are shown in Table -7.

The value of -2LL for the logistic model that contains only the constant is 112.2775. The Chi-square value of -2LL is 88.780 with 74 degrees freedom and it has not been found to be statistically significant. The goodness of fit also confirms the similar finding with large observed significance level. The model Chi-square and Improvement have the same value of 23.498 with 6 degrees of freedom and have been found to be statistically significant.

From the classification table it can be visualised that of the total sample borrowers in the district, 48.78 per cent of borrowers who had other than the institutional sources were correctly classified and in the case of the institutional sources 95 per cent of borrowers were correctly predicted. Of the total borrowers, 71.60 per cent were correctly assigned their respective associations and remaining per cent were misclassified. The off-diagonal entries show the misclassified borrowers in the sample. Of the total, 2 and 21 were misclassified from the institutional sources and from non-institutional sources respectively. Here, the estimated probability for misclassification in the former is too less and in the case of latter, it is greater than one-half. Further, it is to be noted that the estimated prediction for correctly classified cases in the case of institutional sources outweigh than those in the case of non-institutional sources.

When V_{27} changes from 0 to 1, as it has a negative Co-efficient, the odds are decreased by a factor of 0.05. Thus, by increasing the value of V27 by one unit, it decreased the log odds by about -3.0.

Table-8 depicts the final out come of the maximum likelihood estimates of the binary logit model for the sub-sample of Adilabad.

The value of -2LL for the logistic model that contains only the constant is 81.2157. The Chi-square value of -2LL is 38.319 with 62 degrees of freedom and has not been found to be statistically significant leading us to accept the null hypothesis and the goodness of fit also confirms the similar finding with large observed significance. The model Chi-square and improvement have the same value of 42.897 with 6 degrees of freedom and have been found to be statistically significant.

Table 8
Maximum Likelihood Estimation of Dichotomous Logit Relationship (Dummy Dependent Variable: 1 if the Household has Borrowed from formal Sources, 0 - Otherwise): Adilabad Sub-Sample (N = 69)

-2 Log Likelihood 81.2157

Chi-Square	df		Significance
-2 Log Likelihood	38.319	62	0.9922
Model Chi-Square	42.897	6	0.0000
Improvement	42.897	6	0.0000
Goodness of Fit	46.533	62	0.9284

Classification Table

Observed	Predicted: Other than formal sources	Predicted: Formal sources	Per cent correct
Other than formal sources	14	5	73.68
Formal sources	3	47	94.00
			Overall 88.41%

Variables in the Equation

Variable	B	S.E.	Wald	DF	Sig.	R	Exp(B)
V_{27}	-10.6880	3.2994	10.4938	1	0.0012	-0.3234	0.0000
V_{31}	1.7445	0.7772	5.0386	1	0.0248	0.1934	5.7229
V_{33}	1.6097	0.8180	3.8728	1	0.0491	0.1519	5.0013
V_{138}	0.3202	0.4634	0.4775	1	0.4895	0.0000	1.3774
V_{139}	0.2613	0.4178	0.3912	1	0.5317	0.0000	1.2986
V_{143}	-0.1881	0.4691	0.1608	1	0.6884	0.0000	0.8285
Constant	7.5239	3.1385	5.7469	1	0.0165		

From the classification table, it can be seen that 5 sample borrowers who had other than non-institutional sources were not predicted correctly and similarly in the case of borrowers who had institutional sources 3 of them were mis-classified. Therefore, the entire misclassification in the table accounts only for 11.59 per cent. The misclassification rate in both the cases are far lesser than the one-half of the estimated probabilities. Further, it can also be visualised from the table that of the borrowers who had other than institutional sources 73.68 per cent were correctly classified and of the borrowers who had institutional sources 94 per cent were correctly predicted. Of all 69 borrowers, 88.41 per cent were classified under their respective associations correctly. In the case of borrowers who had institutional sources the estimated probability for correctly predicted cases is higher than the borrowers who had other than institutional sources for the loaning operations.

Further, when V_{31} and V_{33} change from 0 to 1, the odds are increased by a factor of 5.72 and 5.00 respectively. But in the case of V_{27} as it has a negative Co-efficient, the odds are decreased by a factor of 0.00. Thus, by increasing the value of V_{31} and V_{33} by one unit, it increased the log odds by about 1.74 and 1.61 respectively. But by increasing the value of V_{27} by one unit, it decreased the log odds by about -10.68.

Table -9 shows the final results of the logit model for the sub-sample of tribal households.

The value of -2LL for the logistic model that only contains the constant is 255.9123. The Chi-square value of -2LL is 212.949, with 184 degrees of freedom and has been found to be statistically significant and the goodness of fit also confirms the similar finding at the 10 per cent significance level. Since the model Chi-square and improvement have the same value of 42.963 with 6 degrees of freedom they were found to be statistically significant.

From the classification table, it can be seen that the borrowers who had borrowed from non-institutional sources is 38.67 per cent and were correctly classified, whereas 95.69 per cent were correctly assigned their association in the case of the borrowers who have the institutional sources for obtaining the loan of the 191 borrowers, 73.30 per cent were classified correctly. Further, of the total of 51 misclassified borrowers, 46 cases and 5 cases, accounted for 61.33 per cent and 4.31 per cent from the former and latter respectively. Here, it is to be noted that the estimated probability in the case of former is higher than the one-half and conversely it was true in the case of latter. The estimated probability for the borrowers who had the institutional sources outweigh the estimated probability of the other party in the classification table.

In terms of odds, when V_{91} changes from 0 to 1, the odds are increased by a factor of 2.07. But in the case of V_{27}, as it has a negative co-efficient the odds are decreased by a factor of 0.04. Likewise, by increasing the value of V_{91} by one unit, it increased the log odds by about 0.73. But by increasing the value of V_{27} by one unit, it decreased the log odds by about -3.11.

Table-10 depicts the solution of the logit model for the sub-sample of non-tribal households.

The value of -2LL for the logistic model that only contains the constant is 59.5874. The Chi-square value of -2LL is 29.805 with 37 degrees of freedom and has been found to be non-significant and the goodness of fit also confirms the similar finding with the large observed significance level. The model Chi-square and improvement have the same value of 29.783 with 5 degrees of freedom but were found to be significant statistically.

Table 9
Maximum Likelihood Estimation of Dichotomous Logit Relationship (Dummy Dependent Variable: 1 if the Household has Borrowed from Formal Sources, 0 - Otherwise): Sub-Sample of Tribals (N = 191)

-2 Log Likelihood 255.9123

	Chi-Square	df	Significance
-2 LogLikelihood	212.949	184	0.0707
Model Chi-Square	42.963	6	0.0000
Improvement	42.963	6	0.0000
Goodness of Fit	209.037	184	0.0995

Classification Table

Predicted

Observed	Other than formal sources	Formal sources	Per cent correct
Other than formal sources	29	46	38.67
Formal sources	5	111	95.69
			Overall 73.30%

Variables in the Equation

Variable	B	S.E.	Wald	DF	Sig.	R	Exp(B)
V_{27}	-3.1120	0.6253	24.7689	1	0.0000	0-0.2983	0.0445
V_{31}	0.7309	0.3145	5.4019	1	0.0201	0.1153	2.0770
V_{33}	0.0699	0.2563	0.0744	1	0.7851	0.0000	1.0724
V_{138}	-0.0601	0.1576	0.1455	1	0.7029	0.0000	0.9417
V_{139}	-0.0106	0.1122	0.0090	1	0.9244	0.0000	0.9894
V_{143}	-0.1313	0.2042	0.4131	1	0.5204	0.0000	0.8770
Constant	3.2942	0.6875	22.9597	1	0.0000		

In terms of odds, when V_{31} changes from 0 to 1, the odds are increased by a factor of 2.07. But in the case of V_{27}, as it has a negative co-efficient the odds are decreased by a factor of 0.04. Likewise, by increasing the value of V_{31} by one unit, it increased the log odds by about 0.73. But by increasing the value of V_{27} by one unit, it decreased the log odds by about -3.11.

Table 10

Maximum Likelihood Estimation of Dichotomous Logit Relationship (Dummy Dependent Variable: 1 if the Household has Borrowed from Formal Sources, 0 - Otherwise): Sub-Sample of Non-Tribals (N=43)

-2 Log Likelihood 59.5874

	Chi-Square	df	Significance
-2 LogLikelihood	29.805	37	0.7936
Model Chi-Square	29.783	5	0.0000
Improvement	29.783	5	0.0000
Goodness of Fit	28.230	37	0.8495

Classification Table

	Predicted		
Observed	Other than formal sources	Formal sources	Per cent correct
Other than formal sources	16	5	76.19
Formal sources	3	19	86.36
			Overall 81.40%

Variables in the Equation

Variable	B	S.E.	Wald	DF	Sig.	R	Exp(B)
V_{27}	-5.2977	1.7654	9.0048	1	0.0027	-0.3429	0.0050
V_{31}	-0.2431	0.5254	0.2140	1	0.6436	0.0000	0.7842
V_{33}	0.7065	0.4996	2.0001	1	0.1573	0.0016	2.0269
V_{138}	-0.8000	0.3541	5.1036	1	0.0239	-0.2282	0.4493
V_{143}	1.1555	0.4251	7.3871	1	0.0066	0.3007	3.1756
Constant	5.6418	1.9666	8.2305	1	0.0041		

The classification table documented at the bottom of the Table - 10 denotes the predictions to the observed outcomes. Of the borrowers 76.19 per cent who had loans from non-institutional sources were correctly classified, whereas 86.36 per cent of the sample borrowers who obtained the loans from the institutional sources were correctly predicted. Of 43 sample borrowers among the total sample non-tribal households 81.40 per cent were able to predict their respective association and the remaining 18.60 per cent of the total sample non-tribal borrowers were unable to assign their respective associations. Of the total of 8 misclassified borrowers 5 cases, and 3 cases accounted for 23.81 per cent and 13.64 per cent respectively. Here, it is to be noted that the estimated probabilities for both the misclassified borrowers were greater than the one-half. Further, it is also to be noted that the correctly classified estimated probability of the latter outweigh the former correctly classified estimated probability.

As V_{143} changes from 0 to 1, the odds are increased by a factor of 3.17. But in the case of V_{27} and V_{138}, as they have negative co-efficients, the odds are decreased by the factors of 0.005 and 0.44. Thus, by increasing the value of V_{143} by one unit, it increased the log odds by about 1.15. But by increasing the values of V_{27} and V_{138} by one unit, it decreased the log odds by about -5.29 and 0.80 respectively.

The position one enjoys in the ritual hierarchy entails one to borrow higher amounts and hence non-tribals often borrow amounts, which are normally higher than the amounts borrowed by tribals as shown in Table-11. In a relative sense, the percentage of those who borrowed in the Rs.5,000+ amount is higher for the non-tribals than tribals in Khammam and Adilabad. In Khammam this dependence among variables is conclusively supported by all the tests, as they reject the null hypothesis. In Adilabad, only likelihood ratio test is found to be statistically significant at 10 per cent level.

A perusal of the amount outstanding of the sample households as shown in Table -12 confirms the hypothesis that non-tribals have often amounts outstanding in higher quantum than tribals[11]. It is more evident in the case of Khammam district, where 50 per cent among non-tribals have amounts outstanding more than Rs.5000/-. Like-wise tribals in Warangal district have relatively a higher percentage in the Rs.2000 - Rs.5000 amount outstanding. All the tests indicate that they are statistically significant in Khammam district. In Adilabad, except M-H test for linear association, other

Table 11
Distribution of Sample Households As Per Amount taken Group-Wise and Region-Wise

Particulars of Amount Taken	Region								
	Khammam			Warangal			Adilabad		
	Tribal	Non-tribal	Row Total	Tribal	Non-tribal	Row Total	Tribal	Non-tribal	Row Total
Not Applicable	13 (81.3) (16.3)	3 (18.8)(15.0)	16 (16.0)	14 (73.7) (17.5)	5 (26.3) (25.0)	19 (19.0)	22 (71.0) (27.5)	9 (29.0) (45.0)	31 (31.0)
≤ 5,000	65 (92.9) (81.3)	5 (7.1) (25.0)	70 (70.0)	46 (82.1) (57.5)	10 (17.9) (50.0)	56 (56.0)	41 (89.1) (51.3)	5 (10.9) (25.0)	46 (46.0)
5,000 +	2 (14.3) (2.5)	12 (85.7) (60.0)	14 (14.0)	20 (80.0) (25.0)	5 (20.0) (25.0)	25 (25.0)	17 (73.9) (21.3)	6 (26.1) (30.0)	23 (23.0)
Column Total	80 (80.0)	20 (20.0)	100 (100.0)	80 (80.0)	20 (20.0)	100 (100.0)	80 (80.0)	20 (20.0)	100 (100.0)

Chi-Square	Value	DF	Significance	Chi-Square	Value	DF	Signifi-cance	Chi-Square	Value	DF	Signifi-cance
Pearson	49.7717	2	0.0000	Pearson	0.6344	2	0.7281	Pearson	4.5099	2	0.1048
Likelihood Ratio	41.1609	2	0.0000	Likelihood Ratio	0.6069	2	0.7382	Likelihood Ratio	4.6991	2	0.0954
M-H Test for Linear Association	19.9144	1	0.0000	M-H Test for Linear Association	0.2041	1	0.6513	M-H Test for Linear Association	0.2272	1	0.6335
	r = 0.448				r = 0.045				r = 0.047		

Statistic	Value	Approximate significance		Statistic	Value	Approximate significance		Statistic	Value	Approximate significance	
Phi	0.7054	0.0000	*1	Phi	0.0796	0.7281	*1	Phi	0.2123	0.1048	*1
Cramer's V	0.7054	0.0000	*1	Cramer's V	0.0796	0.7281	*1	Cramer's V	0.2123	0.1048	*1

*1 Pearson Chi-Square Probability   *1 Pearson Chi-Square Probability   *1 Pearson Chi-Square Probability

Table 12
Amount Outstanding of the Sample Households Group-Wise and Region-Wise

Particulars of Amount Outstanding	Khammam Tribal	Khammam Non-tribal	Khammam Row Total	Warangal Tribal	Warangal Non-tribal	Warangal Row Total	Adilabad Tribal	Adilabad Non-tribal	Adilabad Row Total
Not Applicable	23 (85.2) (28.8)	4 (14.8) (20.0)	27 (27.0)	29 (76.3) (36.3)	9 (23.7) (45.0)	38 (38.0)	44 (72.1) (55.0)	17 (27.9) (85.0)	61 (61.0)
£ 2,000	53 (94.6) (66.3)	3 (5.4) (15.0)	56 (56.0)	25 (86.2) (31.3)	4 (13.8) (20.0)	29 (29.0)	28 (100.0) (35.0)	–	28 (28.0)
2,000 -5,000	4 (57.1) (5.0)	3 (42.9) (15.0)	7 (7.0)	19 (76.0) (23.8)	6 (24.0) (30.0)	25 (25.0)	6 (75.0) (7.5)	2 (25.0) (10.0)	8 (8.0)
5,000 +	–	10 (100.0) (50.0)	10 (10.0)	7 (87.5) (8.0)	1 (12.5) (5.0)	8 (8.0)	2 (66.7) (2.5)	1 (33.3) (5.0)	3 (3.0)
Column Total	80 (80.0)	20 (20.0)	100 (100.0)	80 (80.0)	20 (20.0)	100 (100.0)	80 (80.0)	20 (20.0)	100 (100.0)

Chi-Square	Value	DF	Significance	Chi-Square	Value	DF	Significance	Chi-Square	Value	DF	Significance
Pearson	50.2438	3	0.0000	Pearson	1.5518	3	0.6703	Pearson	9.8189	3	0.0201
Likelihood Ratio	44.4709	3	0.0000	Likelihood Ratio	1.6258	3	0.6535	Likelihood Ratio	15.0753	3	0.0017
M-H Test for Linear Association	30.1849	1	0.0000	M-H Test for Linear Association	0.1668	1	0.6828	M-H Test for Linear Association	1.3612	1	0.4233
r = 0.552				r = 0.041				r = 0.117			

Statistic	Value	Approximate significance		Statistic	Value	Approximate significance		Statistic	Value	Approximate significance	
Phi	0.7088	0.0000	*1	Phi	0.1245	0.6703	*1	Phi	0.3133	0.0201	*1
Cramer's V	0.7088	0.0000	*1	Cramer's V	0.1245	0.6703	*1	Cramer's V	0.3133	0.0201	*1

*1 Pearson Chi-Square Probability   *1 Pearson Chi-Square Probability   *1 Pearson Chi-Square Probability

measures based on Chi-square were found to be statistically significant. In both these districts there is dependence among the variables.

Table -13 depicts the usurious interest rates that are often charged for the loans borrowed from non-institutional sources and even in charging these interest rates there is a distinction between tribals and non-tribals. The often held hypothesis is that tribals are charged higher rates of interest than non-tribals. Of the 240 tribals, 20 per cent did not borrow, whereas this percentage is 28 among 60 sample non-tribals. Interest free loans[12], are a rare category and its percentage is infinitesimal. A majority among the tribals as well as non-tribals were paying less than and equal to 18 per cent. The above hypothesis finds validity if interest rates as high as 120 per cent are observed: the percentage for tribals here is 6.3 per cent, while it is 3.3 per cent for non-tribals. In general in the case of all loans bearing more than 36 per cent, the relative percentages are higher for tribals than non-tribals. Even among composite category cases, that is part of the loan bearing 18 per cent and the other part bearing a higher percentage, the relative percentages are higher for tribals. Here, except for M-H test for linear association, which is not statistically significant even at 10 per cent level, all other tests are found to be statistically significant.

Table 13
Group-Wise Distribution of Sample Households As Per Percentage Rate of Interest

	Group-Wise Distribution		
Percentage Rate of Interest	*Tribals*	*Non- Tribals*	*Row Total*
Not Applicable	49(74.2) (20.4)	17(25.8) (28.3)	66 (22.0)
Interest Free	2(66.7) (0.8)	1(33.3) (1.7)	3 (1.0)
≤18	116(85.9) (48.3)	19(14.1) (31.7)	135 (45.0)
18 - 24	1(100.0) (0.4)	-	1 (0.3)

Contd.

Percentage Rate of Interest	Group-Wise Distribution Tribals	Non- Tribals	Row Total
24 - 36	4(57.1) (1.7)	3(42.9) (5.0)	7 (2.3)
36 - 48	10(83.3) (4.2)	2(16.7) (3.3)	12 (4.0)
48 - 60	16(100.0) (6.7)	-	16 (5.3)
60 - 100	7(100.0) (2.9)	-	7 (2.3)
120 +	15(88.2) (6.3)	2(11.8) (3.3)	17 (5.7)
Interest Free+ ≤18	-	7(100.0) (11.7)	7 (2.3)
≤18 + 24 - 36	8(57.1) (3.3)	6(42.9) (10.0)	14 (4.7)
≤18 + 36 - 48	3(50.0) (1.3)	3(50.0) (5.0)	6 (2.0)
≤ 18 + 48 - 60	9(100.0) (3.8)	-	9 (3.0)
Column Total	240 (80.0)	60 (20.0)	300 (100.0)

Chi-square	Value	DF	Significance
Pearson	52.5829	12	0.0000
Likelihood Ratio	51.7404	12	0.0000
M-H Test for Linear Association	1.6862	1	0.1940

r = 0.075

Statistic	Value	Approximate Significance
Phi	0.4186	0.0000 *1
Cramer's V	0.4186	0.0000 *1

* 1 Pearson Chi-square probability

Table -14 depicts whether the sample borrowers have the linked or the non-linked transactions. Among the three districts, Warangal has the highest linked borrowers with 36 per cent, followed by Khammam with 28 per cent and Adilabad with 16 per cent. A similar trend had also been observed even among the borrowers of sub-samples of tribal and non-tribal

Table 14
Type of Sample Borrowers Group-Wise and Region-Wise

Type of Borrowers	*Region*								
	Khammam			*Warangal*			*Adilabad*		
	Tribal	*Non-tribal*	*Row Total*	*Tribal*	*Non-tribal*	*Row Total*	*Tribal*	*Non-tribal*	*Row Total*
Not Applicable	20 (87.0) (25.0)	3 (13.0) (15.0)	23 (23.0)	44 (89.8) (55.5)	5 (10.2) (25.0)	49 (49.0)	65 (87.8) (81.3)	9 (12.2) (45.0)	74 (74.0)
Linked	21 (75.0) (26.3)	7 (25.0) (35.0)	28 (28.0)	26 (72.2) (32.5)	10 (27.8) (50.0)	36 (36.0)	14 (87.5) (17.5)	2 (12.5) (10.0)	16 (16.0)
Non-Linked	39 (79.6) (48.8)	10 (20.4) (50.0)	49 (49.0)	10 (66.7) (12.5)	5 (33.3) (15.0)	15 (15.0)	1 (10.0) (1.3)	9 (90.0) (45.0)	10 (10.0)
Column Total	80 (80.0)	20 (20.0)	100 (100.0)	80 (80.0)	20 (20.0)	100 (100.0)	80 (80.0)	20 (20.0)	100 (100.0)

Khammam

Chi-Square	Value	DF	Significance
Pearson	1.1382	2	0.5660
Likelihood Ratio	1.1890	2	0.5518
M-H Test for Linear Association	0.3072	1	0.5793

r = 0.055

Statistic	Value	Approximate significance	
Phi	0.1066	0.5660	*1
Cramer's V	0.1066	0.5660	*1

*1 Pearson Chi-Square Probability

Warangal

Chi-Square	Value	DF	Significance
Pearson	5.9665	2	0.0506
Likelihood Ratio	6.1490	2	0.0462
M-H Test for Linear Association	5.4559	1	0.0195

r = 0.234

Statistic	Value	Approximate significance	
Phi	0.2442	0.0506	*1
Cramer's V	0.2442	0.0506	*1

*1 Pearson Chi-Square Probability

Adilabad

Chi-Square	Value	DF	Significance
Pearson	34.0287	2	0.0000
Likelihood Ratio	26.7409	2	0.0000
M-H Test for Linear Association	23.5539	1	0.0000

r = 0.487

Statistic	Value	Approximate significance	
Phi	0.5833	0.0000	*1
Cramer's V	0.5833	0.0000	*1

*1 Pearson Chi-Square Probability

households as well with 32.5 per cent, and 50 per cent; 26.3 per cent, and 35 per cent; and 17.5 per cent and 10 per cent for Warangal, Khammam and Adilabad respectively. Further, the Table also reveals that both in Warangal and Khammam the sub-sample of non-tribal household borrowers are relatively higher than the tribal borrowers and the reverse is true in the case of Adilabad district. Thus, the data confirm that the developed villages and the economically well-off people have more linkages of credit with product markets as it is evident in Warangal and Khammam and further this finding is contrary to Adilabad district as it had exhibited that the poor and the tribal borrowers have more linkages and this might be due to most of the non-tribal borrowers in the district obtaining their loans from the formal credit agencies, indicating that they have more access to the formal lending agencies in the area than others.

Further, the non-parametric tests had also been estimated for the data presented in the table and they have been found to be very much significant in Adilabad district and also found to be significant at 5 per cent level in Warangal district. But they were found to be non-significant statistically with large observed significance level in Khammam district.

Table - 15 presents the extent of commitment against the loan of the sub-sample borrowers of tribal and non-tribal households. The table reveals that most of the households (72.7 per cent) were not under the purview of the commitment against the loan and among those households even some of them did not have any loan and some of them did not respond to the question. While looking at the column-wise percentages, among the tribals the linked borrowers have a relatively higher percentage (12.9%) and they have the commitment to sell their crop to the lender at whatever price that is offered to them in lieu of the loan. In the case of a small percentage of borrowers crop will be sold at Rs.150/- per bag, and in some other cases it will be sold at Rs.200/- per bag. But in the case of linked borrowers among non-tribals most of them i.e., 26.7 per cent have the commitment only to sell their crop to the lender, whereas in other cases the crop will be sold at Rs.150/- per bag. Therefore, it reveals that relatively more number of tribals have the commitment to sell their crop at the pre-determined rates at the time of taking the loan from the lender and this sort of practice is not found to be very much significant in the case of linked borrowers among non-tribals though they have commitment. While looking at the row-wise percentages, the table further reveals that among the sub-sample of linked borrowers most of them i.e., 88.2 per cent linked borrowers among tribals have the commitment to sell their crop at the rate of Rs.150/- per bag and in the case of non-linked borrowers among non-tribals this percentage is only 11.8 followed by Rs.235/- per bag and the crop will be sold. Therefore, the row-wise percentages also confirm the similar finding as in the case of column-wise percentages. Thus, one will be able to say that this sort of practice[13] is more prominent among the tribals than the non-tribals leading to the exploitative relations among the two parties - lender and lessee[14].

Table 15
Group-wise Distribution of Sample Households As Per Nature of Commitment Against Loan

	Group-Wise Distribution		
Type of Commitment Against loan	*Tribals*	*Non- Tribals*	*Row Total*
Not Applicable	179(82.1) (74.6)	39(17.9) (65.0)	218 (72.7)
By Doing Labour Work	1(33.3) (0.4)	2(66.7) (3.3)	3 (1.0)
Crop will be Sold	31(66.0) (12.9)	16(34.0) (26.7)	47 (15.7)
Crop will be sold at Rs. 150 per bag	15(88.2) (6.3)	2(11.8) (3.3)	17 (5.7)
Crop will be sold at Rs. 200 per bag	8(100.0) (3.3)	-	8 (2.7)
Crop will be sold at Rs. 215 per bag	2(100.0) (0.8)	-	2 (0.7)
Crop will be sold at Rs. 225 per bag	1(100.0) (0.4)	-	1 (0.3)
Crop will be sold at Rs. 235 per bag	3(75.0) (1.3)	1(25.0) (1.7)	4 (1.3)

Contd.

Column Total	240 (80.0		60 (20.0)	300 (100.0)
Chi-square	**Value**	**DF**	**Significance**	
Pearson	14.0156	7	0.0509	
Likelihood Ratio	14.5267	7	0.0425	
M-H Test for Linear Association	0.6429 r = 0.014	1	0.7998	

Statistic	Value	Approximate Significance	
Phi	0.2161	0.0509	*1
Cramer's V	0.2161	0.0509	*1

* 1 Pearson Chi-square probability

The Chi-square tests and other related statistics had also been estimated and were found to be statistically significant at 5 per cent level. But, the Mantel-Haenszel Test for linear association has not been found significant statistically.

As Table -15(A) is a corollary to the above, it depicts the region-wise distribution of sample households as per the extent of commitment against the loan. In Khammam 19 per cent of the borrowers made an agreement with the lenders that the crop will be sold to the concerned lender, while in other cases, the condition that crop will be sold at the rate of Rs.200/- per bag and it accounts for 5 per cent. In Warangal district 17 per cent of the linked borrowers made an agreement that the crop will be sold at the rate of Rs.150/- per bag followed by the condition that the crop will be sold to the lender with 16 per cent. Finally in Adilabad district, 12 per cent of the linked borrowers have the condition that they would sell their crop to the concerned lender. Barring those conditions mentioned above, the remaining conditions depicted in the table may not be high indeed. A similar tendency had also been observed even in the total sample size also. The condition that the crop will be sold at the rate of Rs.150/- per bag had been prevailing only in Warangal district and the rest of the linked borrowers in the two districts did not have that agreement with the lenders, which is a highly exploitative one than all other conditions presented in the Table. Therefore, the table reveals

Table 15(A)
Region-Wise Distribution of Sample Households As Per Nature of Commitment Against Loan

	Region			
Nature of Commitment Against Loan	*Khammam*	*Warangal*	*Adilabad*	*Row Total*
Not Applicable	72(33.0) (72.0)	63(28.9) (63.0)	83(38.1) (83.0)	218 (72.7)
By Doing Labour Work	2(66.7) (2.0)	-	1(33.3) (1.0)	3 (1.0)
Crop will be sold	19(40.4) (19.0)	16(34.0) (16.0)	12(25.5) (12.0)	47 (15.7)
Crop will be sold at Rs.150 per bag	--	17(100.0) (17.0)	--	17 (5.7)
Crop will be sold at Rs.200 per bag	5(62.5) (5.0)	3(37.5) (3.0)	--	8 (2.7)
Crop will be sold at Rs.215 per bag	1(50.0) (1.0)	--	1(50.0) (1.0)	2 (0.7)
Crop will be sold at Rs.225 per bag	--	--	1(100.0) (1.0)	1 (0.3)
Crop will be sold at Rs.235 per bag	1(25.0) (1.0)	1(25.0) (1.0)	2(50.0) (2.0)	4 (1.3)
Column Total	100 (33.3)	100 (33.3)	100 (33.3)	300 (100.0)

Chi-square	Value	DF	Significance
Pearson	48.5859	14	0.0000
Likelihood Ratio	55.7709	14	0.0000
Mantel-Haenszel Test for Linear Association	1.1813	1	0.2770
	r = 0.062		

Statistic	Value	Approximate Significance
Phi	0.4024	0.0000 *1
Cramer's V	0.4024	0.0000 *1

* 1 Pearson Chi-square probability

that the sub-sample of linked borrowers in the Warangal district relatively are more prone to the subtle type of exploitation when compared with the borrowers in two other districts in the study area, though Warangal is a relatively developed district when compared with the Adilabad district and at the same time it is also relatively less developed when compared with the Khammam district.

Further, non-parametric tests had also been estimated and they were found to be very much significant, but the M-H test for linear association was not found to be statistically significant.

Table 16
Region-Wise Distribution of Sample Households As Per Mode of Repayment of Loan

	Region			
Mode of Repayment Particulars	*Khammam*	*Warangal*	*Adilabad*	*Row Total*
Not Applicable	17(25.0) (17.0)	20(29.4) (20.0)	31(45.6) (31.0)	60 (22.7)
Cash to Cash	55(40.1) (55.0)	45(32.8) (45.0)	37(27.0) (37.0)	137 (45.7)
Cash to Labour	3(75.0) (3.0)	-	1(25.0) (1.0)	4 (1.3)
Cash to Kind	6(13.6) (6.0)	18(40.90) (18.0)	20(45.5) (20.0)	44 (14.7)
Cash to Labour and Cash	-	2(100.0) (2.0)	-	2 (0.7)
Input to Output	1(100.0) (1.0)	-	-	1 (0.3)
Cash to Cash and Output	18(40.9) (18.0)	15(34.1) (15.0)	11(25.0) (11.0)	44 (14.7)
Column Total	100 (33.3)	100 (33.3)	100 (33.3)	300 (100.0)

Chi-square	Value	DF	Significance
Pearson	27.3561	12	0.0068
Likelihood Ratio	29.8358	12	0.0029
Mantel-Haenszel Test for Linear Association	1.1613	1	0.2811

r = 0.062

Statistic	Value	Approximate Significance
Phi	0.3019	0.0068 *1
Cramer's V	0.3019	0.0068 *1

* 1 Pearson Chi-square probability

Table 17
Literacy-Wise Distribution of Sample Respondents As Per Type of Borrowers

	Type of Borrowers			
Literacy Level	*Not Applicable*	*Linked*	*Not-Linked*	*Row Total*
Illiterate	100(48.3) (68.5)	56(27.1) (70.0)	51(24.6) (68.9)	207 (69.0)
Primary	35(51.5) (24.0)	18(26.5) (22.5)	15(22.1) (20.3)	68 (22.7)
Others	11(44.0) (7.5)	6(24.0) (7.5)	8(32.0) (10.8)	25 (8.3)
Column Total	146 (48.7)	80 (26.7)	74 (24.7)	300 (100.0)

Chi-square	Value	DF	Significance
Pearson	1.0390	4	0.9038
Likelihood Ratio	1.0028	4	0.9093
Mantel-Haenszel Test for Linear Association	0.0652	1	0.7983
	r = 0.014		

Statistic	Value	Approximate Significance
Phi	0.0588	0.9038 *1
Cramer's V	0.4161	0.9038 *1

* 1 Pearson Chi-square probability

In tribal areas, all the relations are not monetised as it is evident from Table -16. Once a loan is taken, it may be repaid in cash form, or labour form or output form. Or the loan itself may be in the form of inputs to be repaid finally in the form of output. These relations signify the relative significance of non-monetised transactions in tribal areas. In all the districts, it is cash to cash form which is more predominant, though the relative importance of it is more in Khammam than in the other two districts. Among other forms, cash to labour is not found to be prevalent, while cash to kind is relatively more important in Warangal and Adilabad. The other form which is of relevance is cash to cash and output in all the districts. The Pearson and likelihood ratio and Chi-square tests were found to be statistically significant confirming the hypothesis that there is a regional configuration to the form of repayment. A finding of significance from the Table is that in all the districts there is a greater degree of monetisation of transactions, though Khammam ranks first followed by Warangal and Adilabad.

Table 18
Type of Sample Borrowers As Per the Size of Agricultural Incomes

		Type of Borrowers		
Size of Agricultural Incomes	*Not Applicable*	*Linked*	*Not-Linked*	*Row Total*
Not Applicable	8(72.7) (5.5)	1(9.1) (1.3)	2(18.2) (2.7)	11 (3.7)
≤10,000	58(47.5) (39.7)	24(19.7) (30.0)	40(32.8) (54.1)	122 (40.7)
10,000 - 20,000	53(57.0) (36.3)	23(24.7) (28.8)	17(18.3) (23.0)	93 (31.0)
20,000 - 35,000	20(41.7) (13.7)	21(43.8) (26.3)	7(14.6) (9.5)	48 (16.0)
35,000 +	7(26.9) (4.8)	11(42.3) (13.8)	8(30.8) (10.8)	26 (8.7)
Column Total	146 (48.7)	80 (26.7)	74 (24.7)	300 (100.0)

Chi-square	Value	DF	Significance
Pearson	24.3124	8	0.0020
Likelihood Ratio	24.2101	8	0.0021
Mantel-Haenszel Test for Linear Association	0.3372 r = 0.033	1	0.5614

Statistic	Value	Approximate Significance
Phi	0.2846	0.0020 *1
Cramer's V	0.2013	0.0020 *1

* 1 Pearson Chi-square probability

It is often hypothesised that literacy brings a change in the outlook of an individual and the borrower would desist linked transactions. The relationship between literacy and linked transactions had been presented in Table -17.

Of the 300 respondents, 26.7 per cent have linked transactions, while 24.7 per cent have no linked transactions. Under each category as per the level of literacy of the borrowers, there is not much difference in the percentages implying that literacy may not be a causative factor for the distinction between linked and non-linked transactions. The same hypothesis is found to be valid in the case of all the tests indicating that both these variables are independent.

Table 19

Distribution of Type of Borrowers As Per MFP Incomes

		Type of Borrowers		
Size of MFP Incomes	*Not Applicable*	*Linked*	*Not-Linked*	*Row Total*
Not Applicable	35(40.2)	26(29.9)	26(29.9)	87
	(24.0)	(32.5)	(35.1)	(29.0)
≤4,000	59(56.7)	23(22.1)	22(21.2)	104
	(40.4)	(28.8)	(29.7)	(34.7)
4,000 +	52(47.7)	31(28.4)	26(23.9)	109
	(35.6)	(38.8)	(35.10)	(36.3)
Column Total	146	80	74	300
	(48.7)	(26.7)	(24.7)	(100.0)

Chi-square	Value	DF	Significance
Pearson	5.4671	4	0.2426
Likelihood Ratio	5.4772	4	0.2417
Mantel-Haenszel Test for Linear Association	0.4231	1	0.5153
	r = 0.037		

Statistic	Value	Approximate Significance
Phi	0.1350	0.2426 *1
Cramer's V	0.0954	0.2426 *1

* 1 Pearson Chi-square probability

One hypothesis that had been examined here is whether the increase in the amount borrowed has any association with the increase in the number of those who have linkages. This had been examined in Table -18. Though the percentages do not increase, with an increase in the amount borrowed, they are relatively higher than the percentage for non-linked transactions, under each borrowed amount category, except for less than Rs.10,000/-. Thus, there is an association between the variables and this is confirmed by the Pearson, likelihood ratio tests as well as Phi and Cramer's V statistics.

The distribution of type of borrowers by their MFP incomes is shown in Table -19. Here it is important to note that even the sub-sample of non-tribal linked and non-linked borrowers would also come under the category of 'not applicable' due to the fact that no non-tribal household had the MFP income. The table clearly shows that borrowers with higher MFP incomes have more linked transactions as compared with the borrowers of non-linked transactions and conversely borrowers with lesser MFP incomes have non-linked transactions as compared with the borrowers of linked transactions. Therefore, the data confirms the hypothesis that higher the MFP incomes, higher the linked transactions and lesser the MFP incomes lesser the non-linked transactions and it suggests a positive relationship between the MFP incomes of the borrowers and the transactions they have. Further, Chi-square tests and the other related statistics had also been estimated and were found to be non-significant statistically.

Table-20 portrays the distribution of type of sample borrowers with respect to the agriculture/wage labour incomes. Those who did not have the agricultural/wage incomes have linked transactions with 52.5 per cent followed by the sub-sample borrowers who have rupees 3000/- and the remaining per cent of them have above Rs.3000/-. More or less, a similar tendency can also be observed even in the sub-sample of non-linked borrowers. Here data reveal that the sub-sample borrowers who did not have neither agricultural incomes nor wage incomes figure in the linked as well as non-linked transactions. Therefore, it is to be inferred from the above analysis that with no wage incomes, both the transactions were prominent and further as these incomes move upward, both of these transactions move downwards. Thus, the data confirms the inverse relationship for both the transactions observed in the study area. Further, it is to be noted that a similar trend and finding had also been observed in the case of the incomes obtained by way of non-casual labour and this had been presented in Table-21.

Chi-square tests and other related statistics have not been found statistically significant, which signifies that the variables in the Table -20 are independent. But the same had been found to be statistically significant in the case of the data reported in the Table -21.

Table 20
Distribution of Type of Borrowers As Per Agricultural/Wage Labour Incomes

	Type of Borrowers			
Size of Agricultural/ Wage Labour Incomes	*Not Applicable*	*Linked*	*Not-Linked*	*Row Total*
Not Applicable	63(44.1) (43.2)	42(29.4) (52.5)	38(26.6) (51.4)	143 (47.7)
≤ 3,000	43(50.6) (29.5)	26(30.6) (32.5)	16(18.8) (21.6)	185 (28.3)
3,000 +	40(55.6) (27.4)	12(16.7) (15.0)	20(27.8) (27.0)	72 (24.0)
Column Total	146 (48.7)	80 (26.7)	74 (24.7)	300 (100.0)

Chi-square	Value	DF	Significance
Pearson	6.6433	4	0.1559
Likelihood Ratio	7.1066	4	0.1303
Mantel-Haenszel Test for Linear Association	1.1787 r = 0.060	1	0.2989

Statistic	Value	Approximate Significance
Phi	0.1488	0.1559 *1
Cramer's V	0.1052	0.1559 *1

* 1 Pearson Chi-square probability

Table-22 delineates the distribution of sample households by the type of borrowers. Among those who have linked transactions most of the borrowers, 36.3 per cent, were in the income range of Rs.15,000/- to 25,000/-. In the range of Rs. less than or equal to 15,000, 26.3 per cent were observed and in the range of Rs. 25,000 - Rs. 35,000 the percentage was 15.0, while in the case of above Rs. 30,000/- class it was 22.5 per cent. Thus, this confirms a hypothesis that as size of the income increases, linked transactions will also increase and after attaining a level of income, say Rs. 25,000 in this sample, it had a downward trend, indicating the *'positive relationship'* works upto a certain point only. Further, the table reveals the

Table 21
Distribution of Type of Borrowers As Per Incomes of Non-Casual Labour

Size of Non Casual Labour Incomes	*Type of Borrowers* *Not Applicable*	*Linked*	*Not-Linked*	*Row Total*
Not Applicable	123(54.4) (84.2)	61(27.0) (76.3)	42(18.6) (56.8)	226 (75.3)
≤ 5,000	8(18.6) (5.5)	12(27.9) (15.0)	23(53.5) (31.1)	43 (14.3)
5,000 +	15(48.4) (10.3)	7(22.6) (8.8)	9(29.0) (12.2)	31 (10.3)
Column Total	146 (48.7)	80 (26.7)	74 (24.7)	300 (100.0)

Chi-square	Value	DF	Significance
Pearson	27.8632	4	0.0000
Likelihood Ratio	26.9422	4	0.0000
Mantel-Haenszel Test for Linear Association	9.0052 r = 0.173	1	0.0026

Statistic	Value	Approximate Significance
Phi	0.3047	0.0000 *1
Cramer's V	0.2155	0.0000 *1

* 1 Pearson Chi-square probability

reverse trend in the case of the borrowers who did not have the linked transactions and here data confirms the inverse and negative relationship as it denotes that as size of total incomes increases, the non-linked transactions will decrease and vice-versa. A similar tenency had also been observed even in the case of the total expenditure of the sample households and the data had been presented in Table -23.

Further, for both the total incomes and expenditures the Chi-square tests and other related statistics have been found to be statistically significant at 5 per cent level. But the M-H test for linear association has not been found to be statistically significant.

Table 22
Distribution Of Type Of Borrowers As Per Total Incomes

	Type of Borrowers			
Size of Total Incomes	*Not Applicable*	*Linked*	*Not-Linked*	*Row Total*
≤15,000	51(48.6) (34.9)	21(20.0) (26.3)	33(31.4) (44.6)	105 (35.0)
15,000 - 25,000	63(55.8) (43.2)	29(25.7) (36.3)	21(18.6) (28.4)	113 (37.3)
25,000 - 35,000	18(47.4) (12.3)	12(31.6) (15.0)	8(21.1) (10.8)	38 (12.7)
35,000 +	14(31.8) (9.6)	18(40.9) (22.5)	12(27.3) (16.2)	44 (14.7)
Column Total	146 (48.7)	80 (26.7)	74 (24.7)	300 (100.0)

Chi-square	Value	DF	Significance
Pearson	13.1926	6	0.0400
Likelihood Ratio	13.1845	6	0.0400
Mantel-Haenszel Test for Linear Association	0.3796	1	0.5378

r = 0.035

Statistic	Value	Approximate Significance
Phi	0.2097	0.0400 *1
Cramer's V	0.1482	0.0400 *1

* 1 Pearson Chi-square probability

Among the mean values for different variables as depicted in Table -24, for borrowers with linked and non-linked transactions, the literacy status cannot explain the difference as the differences have a variegated nature. If the hypothesis is that borrowers with non-linked transactions are presumed to have a higher literacy status than borrowers with linked transactions, such a phenomenon can be observed for the total sub-sample of borrowers, for the sub-sample of borrowers in Warangal and for the non-tribals sub-sample in Adilabad. But in the case of tribals sub-sample and sub-sample of Khammam, the reverse tendency can be observed. In the case of family size, borrowers with linked transactions have a higher family size than borrowers with non-linked transactions for all sub-samples. As regards agricultural incomes, except for Adilabad sub-sample, in all other sub-samples the borrowers with linked transactions have a higher mean agricultural income than borrowers with non-linked transactions. The reverse phenomenon is observed for MFP incomes, again the stray case being Adilabad sub-sample, where those with linked transactions have higher mean MFP income than those with non-linked transactions. Incomes from agricultural/wage labour do not show any pattern though in Adilabad sub-sample there is a wide gulf in the mean values of the borrowers with linked transactions and borrowers with non-linked transactions, where the linked group is having a higher mean value than the non-linked group. For tribals sub-group this tendency is reversed, though the difference is not much. In the case of overall sub-sample also the difference is much, but here the linked group has a lower mean value when compared to non-linked group. Incomes from non-casual labour also do not represent any pattern, though the divergence between mean incomes of the linked group and non-linked group is very wide for the Khammam sub-sample, where the non-linked group has a higher mean income than the linked group. Except for Adilabad sub-sample and non-tribals, the mean total expenditures are generally higher for linked group than the non-linked group. Another variable examined for analysis is the proportion of male workers to total workers, which is relatively high for linked group than non-linked group, once again the exception being Adilabad, where a reversal of this tendency is observed. Contrary to the above observation, the mean worker dependent ratio is uniformly higher for non-linked group in all the sub-samples. On the basis of this analysis, a generalisation could be that the group of borrowers with linked transactions when compared with the group of borrowers with non-linked transactions have a lower mean literacy status, higher mean family size, higher mean agricultural income, lower mean MFP income, lower mean income from agricultural/wage labour, lower level of income with respect to incomes from non-agricultural labour, a relatively higher mean total expenditures, a higher proportion of mean male workers to total workers and a lesser worker-dependent ratio.

Table 23
Distribution of Type of Borrowers As Per Total Expenditures

		Type of Borrowers		
Size of Total Expenditure	*Not Applicable*	*Linked*	*Not-Linked*	*Row Total*
≤10,000	12(33.3)	7(19.4)	17(47.2)	36
	(8.2)	(8.8)	(23.0)	(12.0)
10,000 - 15,000	63(55.8)	27(23.9)	23(20.4)	113
	(43.2)	(33.8)	(31.1)	(37.7)
15,000 - 25,000	51(52.0)	27(27.6)	20(20.4)	98
	(34.9)	(33.8)	(27.0)	(32.7)
25,000 +	20(37.7)	19(35.8)	14(26.4)	53
	(13.7)	(23.8)	(18.9)	(17.7)
Column Total	146	80	74	300
	(48.7)	(26.7)	(24.7)	(100.0)

Chi-square	Value	DF	Significance
Pearson	16.2331	6	0.0125
Likelihood Ratio	14.9378	6	0.0207
Mantel-Haenszel Test for Linear Association	0.3453	1	0.5567
	r = 0.033		

Statistic	Value	Approximate Significance
Phi	0.2326	0.0125 *1
Cramer's V	0.1644	0.0125 *1

* 1 Pearson Chi-square probability

Table 24
Mean Rates Of The Variables With Linked and Non-Linked Borrowers

Variable	Total Sub-Sample (N=154)		Khammam Sub-Sample (N=77)		Warangal Sub-Sample (N=51)		Adilabad Sub-Sample (N=26)		Tribals' Sub-Sample (N=111)		Non-Tribals' Sub-Sample (N=43)	
	Linked (N=80)	Non-linked (N=74)	Linked (N=28)	Non-Linked (N=49)	Linked (N=36)	Non-linked (N=15)	Linked (N=16)	Non-Linked (N=10)	Linked (N=61)	Non-linked (N=50)	Linked (N=19)	Non-Linked (N=24)
V8	1.40	1.47	1.42	1.22	1.33	1.73	1.50	2.30	1.26	1.18	1.84	2.08
V15	5.46	5.02	5.18	4.96	5.49	5.09	5.88	5.44	5.68	5.29	6.28	5.98
V138	20,750	15,450	18,750	11,500	23,300	18,300	18,400	30,500	17,850	9,800	30,000	27,250
V139	4,020	4,180	2,700	4,320	5,100	6,400	3,860	200	5,280	6,200	–	–
V140	985	2,280	2,070	2,700	930	730	2,060	750	2,010	2,260	920	2,330
V141	1,340	2,020	1,440	3,660	1,220	1,060	1,500	1,400	1,000	1,640	3,630	4,230
V143	17,150	15,600	16,250	12,850	18,300	16,000	16,250	28,500	15,050	10,700	24,000	25,800
V150	48.10	47.92	53.30	48.60	48.30	44.72	38.54	49.33	46.77	45.92	52.36	52.08
V153	11.30	13.42	9.06	9.90	11.57	18.13	14.62	23.80	10.73	12.42	13.14	15.50

V_8 = Literacy Status
V_{15} = Family Size
V_{138} = Agricultural incomes
V_{139} = MFP incomes
V_{140} = Incomes from agricultural/wage labour
V_{141} = Incomes from non-casual labour
V_{143} = Total expenditures
V_{150} = Proportion of male workers to total workers
V_{153} = Worker-dependent ratio

In view of the specifities that are beset with the formal and other than formal sources of loans for the borrowers, here an attempt had been made by the researcher to identify the specific characteristic features of the different sub-sample households to analyse why the households opt for either linked or non-linked transactions. This had been undertaken with the help of the logit analysis. Here the specification of the variables included in the model are: dependent variable: dummy dependent variable 1 if the household has linked transactions, O-otherwise. The explanatory variables included in the model are: agricultural incomes (V_{138}), M.F.P. incomes (V_{139}) and the total expenditures of the households (V_{143}).

Table 25
Maximum Likelihood Estimation of Dichotomous Logit Relationship (Dummy Dependent Variable: 1 if the Household is Linked Borrower, 0 - Otherwise): Total Sub-Sample (N = 154)

-2 Log Likelihood 213.2555

	Chi-Square	df	Significance
-2 Log Likelihood	198.818	150	0.0047
Model Chi-Square	14.437	3	0.0024
Improvement	14.437	3	0.0024
Goodness of Fit	153.260	150	0.4109

Classification Table

Predicted

Observed	Non-linked	Linked	Per cent correct
Non-linked	41	33	55.41
Linked	31	49	61.25
			Overall 58.44%

Variables in the Equation

Variable	B	S.E.	Wald	DF	Sig.	R	Exp(B)
V_{138}	0.5193	0.1545	11.2924	1	0.0008	0.2087	1.6809
V_{143}	-0.4321	0.1652	6.8396	1	0.0089	-0.1506	0.6491
V_{139}	0.1162	0.0970	1.4364	1	0.2307	0.0000	1.1233
Constant	-0.6169	0.4019	2.3565	1	0.1248		

V_{138} = Agricultural Incomes
V_{143} = Total Expenditures of the Households
V_{139} = M.F.P. Incomes
And hereafter refers to the same

The results of the maximum likelihood estimates of the binary logit model are given in Table-25. The value of -2LL for the logistic model that contains only the constant is 213.2555. The Chi-square value for -2LL is 198.818, since the observed significance level is small, we reject the null hypothesis that the model fits. The Goodness of fit statistic in the last row of the table leads us to a different conclusion which indicates that this model does not differ significantly from the perfect model.

Table 26

Maximum Likelihood Estimation of Dichotomous Logit Relationship (Dummy Dependent Variable: 1 if the Household is Linked Borrower, 0 - Otherwise): Khammam Sub-Sample (N = 77)

-2 Log Likelihood 100.9441

	Chi-Square	df	Significance
-2 Log Likelihood	92.557	73	0.0609
Model Chi-Square	8.387	3	0.0387
Improvement	8.387	3	0.0387
Goodness of Fit	76.034	73	0.3810

Classification Table

Predicted

Observed	Non-linked	Linked	Per cent correct
Non-linked	43	6	87.76
Linked	20	8	28.57
			Overall 66.23%

Variables in the Equation

Variable	B	S.E.	Wald	DF	Sig.	R	Exp(B)
V138	0.4106	0.2221	3.4189	1	0.0645	0.1186	.5078
V143	-0.3254	0.2349	1.9189	1	0.1660	0.0000	0.7223
V139	-0.1600	0.1893	0.7140	1	0.3981	0.0000	0.8522
Constant	-0.5684	0.5992	0.9001	1	0.3428		

Since the model Chi-square and improvement have the same value of 14.437 with 3 degrees of freedom and were found to be statistically significant leading us to reject the null hypotheses for both the model Chi-square and the improvement. From the classification table, it can be seen that 41 cases with non-linked transactions were correctly predicted and like-wise 49 cases with the linked transactions were also correctly predicted. A total of 64 were misclassified, of which 33 cases were with non-linked and 31 cases were with linked transactions. The overall percentage is 58.44, which has been correctly classified. Here, we naturally expect the small estimated probabilities for linked transactions and large estimated probabilities for non-linked cases. Hence, this table can be interpreted as whether for each predicted groups, the estimated probability is greater or less than one-half. In this case the estimated probabilities for the predicted group cannot be correctly assessed though each predicted correctly classified cell has greater than 50 per cent.

Table 27
Maximum Likelihood Estimation of Dichotomous Logit Relationship (Dummy Dependent Variable: 1 if the Household is Linked Borrower, 0 - Otherwise): Warangal Sub-Sample (N = 51)

-2 LogLikelihood 61.7913

	Chi-Square	df	Significance
-2 Log Likelihood	58.578	47	0.1199
Model Chi-Square	3.214	3	0.3599
Improvement	3.214	3	0.3599
Goodness of Fit	49.748	47	0.3644

Classification Table

	Predicted		
Observed	Non-linked	Linked	Per cent correct
Non-linked	1	14	6.67
Linked	0	36	100.00
			Overall 72.55%

Variables in the Equation

Variable	B	S.E.	Wald	DF	Sig.	R	Exp(B)
V_{138}	0.2742	0.2910	0.8880	1	0.3460	0.0000	1.3155
V_{143}	-0.0146	0.3530	0.0017	1	0.9669	0.0000	0.9855
V_{139}	-0.0855	0.1675	0.2603	1	0.6099	0.0000	0.9181
Constant	0.0390	0.9418	0.0017	1	0.9670		

As V_{138} changes from 0 to 1 the odds are increased by a factor of 1.68 as shown in the column Exp (B) in Table-25. Likewise as V_{143} changes the odds are decreased only by a factor of 0.65. By increasing the value of V_{138} by one unit, log odds are increased by about 0.51 i.e., the value of the Co-efficient for V_{138} and similarly by increasing the value of V_{143} by one unit log odds are decreased by about -0.43 as it has a negative Co-efficient.

The final results of the maximum likelihood estimates of the binary logit model for the sub-sample of Khammam are shown in Table-26.

Table 28
Maximum Likelihood Estimation Of Dichotomous Logit Relationship (Dummy Dependent Variable: 1 If The Household Is Linked Borrower, 0 - Otherwise): Adilabad Sub-Sample (N = 26)

-2 Log Likelihood 34.6464

	Chi-Square	df	Significance
-2 Log Likelihood	14.757	22	0.8725
Model Chi-Square	19.890	3	0.0002
Improvement	19.890	3	0.0002
Goodness of Fit	15.490	22	0.8404

Classification Table

	Predicted		
Observed	Non-linked	Linked	Per cent correct
Non-linked	9	1	90.00
Linked	2	14	87.50
			Overall 88.46%

Variables in the Equation

Variable	B	S.E.	Wald	DF	Sig.	R	Exp(B)
V138	0.3834	0.6409	0.3577	1	0.5498	0.0000	1.4672
V143	-0.3470	0.6099	0.3236	1	0.5694	0.0000	0.7068
V139	2.9404	1.4423	4.1560	1	0.0415	0.2495	18.9231
Constant	-2.0316	2.2870	0.7891	1	0.3744		

The value of -2LL for the logistic model that contains only the constant is 100.9441. The Chi-square value of -2LL is 92.557 but it has been found to be statistically significant at 10 per cent level. The Goodness of fit statistic was not found to be significant leading to a different conclusion to that of -2LL in the model. Since the model Chi-square and improvement with 3 degrees of freedom were found to be statistically significant and they have the same value of 8.387.

The classification table shows that 51 cases had been correctly classified. The overall percentage of correctly classified cases is 66.23, which is greater than 50 per cent.

The logistic regression Co-efficients in the model shows that only V_{138} was found to be statistically significant at 10 per cent level. The 'R' value is 0.1186 and positive in the case of V_{138} reveals that by increasing the value of V_{138}, the odds increased by a factor of 1.5 and thereby increasing the value of V_{138} by one unit, increased the log odds by about 0.4106.

The final solution of the model for the sub-sample of Warangal district has been depicted in Table - 27.

The value of -2LL for the logistic model that contains only the constant is 61.7913. The Chi-square value for -2LL is 58.578 with 47 degrees of freedom. Since the observed significance level is large and has not been found to be statistically significant, we do not reject the null hypothesis that the model fits. Hence,this model does not differ significantly from the perfect model.

Model Chi-square and Improvement have the same value of 3.214 and have not been found to be statistically significant leading to acceptance of null hypothesis for both the model Chi-square and the Improvement.

The Goodness of fit statistic in the last row of the table leads us to a similar conclusion which indicates that this model does not differ significantly from the perfect model.

The classification table compares our predictions to observed outcomes. From the Table it can be seen that only 1 sample household without linked transactions was correctly predicted by the model not to have the linked transactions. Similarly, 36 were with linked transactions were correctly predicted to have the linked transactions. The off-diagonal entries of the classification table shows that a total of 14 households were mis-classified and the entire misclassification is associated only with the non-linked transactions. Of the households with non-linked transactions only 6.67 per cent were correctly classified, whereas of the house-holds with linked transactions cent per cent were correctly classified. Overall, 72.55 per cent of the 51 households were correctly classified. Here the estimated probabilities for the predicted group of borrowers with non-linked transactions cannot be correctly assessed.

The lower part of the Table-27 shows the logistic regression Co-efficients and its other related statistics. The value of B only in the case of V_{138} is positive, that is by increasing the value of V_{138}, the odds increased by a factor 1.3 and thereby increasing the value of V_{138} by one unit, increased the log odds by about 0.2742. By and large, this regression model also does not yield any satisfactory result as in the case of Khammam sub-sample excepting for the positive association of V_{35} with respect to V_{138}.

The final solution of the maximum likelihood estimates of the binary logit model for the sub-sample of Adilabad had been presented in Table -28.

The value of -2LL for the logistic model that contains only the constant is 34.6464. The Chi-square value for -2LL is 14.757 with 47 degrees of freedom and is very large and has not been found to be statistically significant. But the goodness of fit statistic leads us to a similar conclusion with large observed significance level indicating that this model does not differ significantly from the perfect model as in the case of -2LL Chi-square. Since the model Chi-square and Improvement have the same value of 19.890 with 3 degrees of freedom they have been found to be statistically significant for both the model Chi-square and Improvement.

From the classification table, it can be seen that 9 households without linked transactions were correctly predicted by the model not to have the linked transactions. Similarly, 14 borrowers with linked transactions were correctly classified to have the linked transactions. The off-diagonal entries show that a total of 3 households were misclassified, wherein 1 borrower and 2 borrowers were associated with non-linked and respectively. Of the borrowers with non-linked transactions, 90 per cent were correctly classified, whereas of the borrowers with linked transactions 87.50 per cent were correctly predicted. Hence out of 26 borrowers 86.46 per cent were correctly classified. In this case, by and large, the estimated probabilities for the predicted group of borrowers of both the non-linked and linked transactions were correctly assessed as it has been evident from the classification table.

Table 29
Maximum Likelihood Estimation Of Dichotomous Logit Relationship (Dummy Dependent Variable: 1 If The Household Is Linked Borrower, 0 - Otherwise): Sub-Sample Of Tribals (N = 111)

-2 LogLikelihood 152.7867

	Chi-Square	df	Significance
-2 Log Likelihood	128.088	107	0.0806
Model Chi-Square	24.699	3	0.0000
Improvement	24.699	3	0.0000
Goodness of Fit	112.876	107	0.3300

Classification Table

	Predicted		
Observed	Non-linked	Linked	Per cent correct
Non-linked	32	18	64.00
Linked	14	47	77.05
			Overall 71.17%

Variables in the Equation

Variable	B	S.E.	Wald	DF	Sig.	R	Exp(B)
V138	0.5256	0.2173	5.8495	1	0.0156	0.1587	1.6915
V143	0.1273	0.2913	0.1910	1	0.6621	0.0000	1.1358
V139	-0.2558	0.1535	2.7771	1	0.0956	-0.0713	0.7743
Constant	-0.7628	0.5327	2.0501	1	0.1522		

As V_{138} is changing from 0 to 1, and the values of the other independent variables remain the same, the log odds for linked transactions, increased by 0.38 or in odds, they are increased by a factor of 1.46 as shown in the Exp (B) column in the Table-28. But in the case of V_{143}, as it has a negative Co-efficient, the odds decrease by a factor of 0.70. As V_{139} changes from 0 to 1, the odds are increased by a factor of 18.92. By and large, by increasing the value of V_{138} by one unit, it increased the log odds by about 0.38. By increasing the value of V_{143} by one unit, it decreased the log odds by about -0.34. Finally, in the case of increasing the value of V_{139} by one unit, it increased the log odds by about 2.94.

The results of the maximum likelihood estimates of the binary logit model for the sub-sample of tribal households have been shown in Table-29.

The value of -2LL for the logistic model that contains only the constant is 152.7867. The Chi-square value of -2LL is 120.088 with 107 degrees of freedom and has been found statistically significant at 10 per cent level. Since the model chi-square and Improvement have the same value of 24.699 with 3 degrees of freedom they had been found to be statistically significant. But the goodness of fit statistic yields a different conclusion to that of -2LL Chi-square indicating that this model does not differ significantly from the perfect model with the large observed significant level.

From classification table in the estimated model, it can be visualized that, of the borrowers with non-linked transactions 64 per cent were correctly classified and of the borrowers with linked transactions 77.05 per cent were correctly predicted. Therefore, of 111 borrowers 77.17 per cent were correctly predicted. Further, the off-diagonal entries of the classification table shows that 18 borrowers and 14 borrowers of a total of 32 with non-linked and linked transactions were not correctly predicted with their respective associations and in both the cases the estimated probability is lesser than the one-half.

When V_{138} changes from 0 to 1, the odds are increased by a factor of 1.70 and similarly when V_{143} changes from 0 to 1, the odds are increased by a factor of 1.13. But in the case of V_{139} as it has a negative Co-efficient, the odds decrease by factor of 0.77. Thus, by increasing the value of V_{138} by one unit, it increased the log odds by about 0.52 and the increased log odds by about 0.12 can be found in the case of V_{143}. But by increasing the value of V_{139} by one unit, it decreased the log odds by about -0.25.

The final results of the maximum likelihood estimates of the binary logit model for the sub-sample of non-tribal households have been shown in Table -30.

The value of -2LL for the logistic model that contains only the constant is 59.0279. The Chi-square value of -2LL is 55.236 with 40 degrees of freedom and has been found to be statistically significant. Since the model chi-square and Improvement have the same value of 3.792 with 2 degrees of freedom have been found to be statistically significant. But the goodness of fit statistic leads us to a different conclusion as compared with -2LL Chi-square, indicating that this model does not differ significantly from the perfect model with a large observed significance level.

Table 30
Maximum Likelihood Estimation of Dichotomous Logit Relationship (Dummy Dependent Variable: 1 if the Household is Linked Borrower, 0 - Otherwise): Sub-Sample of Non Tribals (N = 43)

-2 Log Likelihood 59.0279

	Chi-Square	df	Significance
-2 Log Likelihood	55.236	40	0.0550
Model Chi-Square	3.792	2	0.1502
Improvement	3.792	2	0.1502
Goodness of Fit	42.524	40	0.3629

Classification Table

	Predicted		
Observed	Non-linked	Linked	Per cent correct
Non-linked	19	5	79.17
Linked	11	8	42.11
			Overall 62.79%

Variables in the Equation

Variable	B	S.E.	Wald	DF	Sig	R	Exp(B)
V_{138}	0.4091	0.2326	3.0937	1	0.0786	0.1361	1.5054
V_{143}	-0.4121	0.2368	3.0284	1	0.0818	-0.1320	0.6622
Constant	-0.5233	0.7380	0.5028	1	0.4783		

From the classification table, it can be said that of the borrowers with non-linked transactions 79.17 per cent were correctly predicted and of the borrowers with linked transactions 42.11 per cent were correctly classified. Combining all the cases, 62.79 per cent of 43 borrowers were correctly assigned with their respective predicted groups. Further, the off-diagonal entries of the classification table shows that 5 borrowers and 11 borrowers of the total of 17 with non-linked and linked transactions were not correctly predicted with their respective associations and further the estimated probability for wrongly assigned cases are lesser than the one-half in the case of those who had non-linked transactions and the estimated probability for the same is greater than one-half in the case of the borrowers who had linked transactions. Therefore, the estimated probabilities for the predicted group cannot be correctly assessed in the case of linked transactions group.

As V_{138} changes from 0 to 1 the odds are increased by a factor of 1.50. But in the case of V_{139}, as it has a negative Co-efficient, the odds are decreased by a factor of 0.66. Thus, by increasing the value of V_{138} by one unit, it increased the log odds by about 0.40. But by increasing the value of V_{143} by one unit, it decreased the log odds by about -0.41.

Table 31
Influence of Explanatory Variables on Linkage

	Influnece On Linkage In The Case Of					
Explanatory Variables*	*Total sub-sample*	*Khammam sub-sample*	*Warangal sub-sample*	*Adilabad sub-sample*	*Tribals' sub-sample*	*Non-Tribals' sub-sample*
V_8	-	+	-	X	+	-
V_{138}	+	+	+	+	+	+
V_{139}	+	-	-	+	-	X
V_{140}	+	+	+	X	+	+
V_{141}	+	-	+	X	-	+
V_{143}	-	-	-	-	+	-
V_{150}	-	+	+	X	+	-
V_{153}	-	+	-	X	-	-

* These relationships are based on ceterisparibus condition.

Note: + (Plus) sign means the variable is positively correlated and - (minus) sign means that the variable is negatively correlated with linkage which is the dependent variable. X signifies that the influence of a particular factor has not been investigated.

For the notation of Variables See Table -24

Prior to the taking up of the discriminant analysis, the researcher intends to summarise the direction of variables based on the logistic regression Co-efficients of the explanatory variables initially[15] included in the logit model for identifying the positive and negative influences of the explanatory variables on linkages.

Among the various causative factors influencing linkages, some are exhibiting positive impact while others are exerting a negative impact as shown in Table -31. An improvement in literacy status of the respondents has an overall negative influence on linkages in the overall sample, but it has positive influence in Khammam sub-sample and tribals sub-sample. Agricultural incomes and incomes from agricultural wage labour have a positive influence on linkages. In the case of MFP incomes, tribals have a negative impact, signifying that an increase in MFP income would weaken the linkage effect. The same finding had been observed in the case of incomes from non-casual labour. The total expenditure has a negative influence on the linkage variable, but for tribals it has a positive influence. Further, the influence is positive for the proportion of male workers to total workers. The worker-dependent ratio has a negative impact on linkage variable in the case of tribals sub-sample. Hence in the case of tribals, an improvement in certain variables like literacy status of the borrowers, agricultural incomes, incomes from agricultural labour, total expenditures and proportion of male workers to total workers, contrary to certain earlier hypotheses, leads to an increase in linkages rather than diminishing it. On the other hand, a rise in MFP incomes, incomes from non-casual labour and worker-dependent ratio reduce these linkages and lends support to the observation of earlier studies.

At this juncture, it is pertinent to cull out the relative magnitude of the explanatory variables which demonstrate the basic household characteristic features that may influence the sample borrowers' decisions going for linked transactions. Here this had been done with the help of the discriminant function analysis which is often used to identify the variables that are important for distinguishing between the groups for different sub-sample strata. Here in the present study based on a collection of variables such as proportion of female workers to total workers (V_{150}), worker-dependent ratio (V_{153})

literacy particulars of the sample respondents (V_8), agricultural incomes (V_{138}), total expenditures of the households (V_{143}), MFP incomes (V_{139}), incomes from agricultural/wage labour (V_{140}), and incomes from non-casual labour (V_{141}), two mutually exclusive groups such as borrowers who have linked transactions and those who have non-linked transactions had been distinguished.

Table-32 shows the univariate F-values for the different sample strata used in the analysis. This indicates that significant differences exist among group means for the variables like V_{138}, V_{143}, V_8 and V_{153} in the case of total sub-sample; V_{138}, V_{141} and V_{139} in the case of sub-sample of Khammam; V_{153}, V_{138}, V_{140} and V_8 in the case of Warangal; V_{139}, and V_{150} in the case of Adilabad; and finally V_{138}, V_{140}, V_{139}, and V_{150} in the case of sub-sample of tribal households in the study area of the eight variables hypothesised to affect borrowers opting for linked transactions. The observed significance of F-values had also been shown in the table,with which one will be able to reject the hypothesis that all group means are equal. The univariate F-values indicate the potential power of each individual in discriminating between linked transactions and others.

A number of discriminant functions were computed to develop the best over all model. The first model incorporated all the eight variables mentioned above. The result of the first computation showed that some of the variables like V_{150}, V_{139}, V_{140} and V_{141} did not contribute significantly to the overall model. Only V_{138}, V_{143}, V_8 and V_{153} contributed significantly to the overall explanatory power of the discriminant function. The elimination of insignificant variables has been done by examining the size of calculated F-ratios of the variables. The same procedure has been adopted for all sub-sample discriminant functions with eight variables. But variables like V_{138}, V_{141} and V_{139} in the case of Khammam; V_{153}, V_{138}, V_{140} and V_8 in the case of Warangal; V_{139} and V_{150} in the case of Adilabad; and finally V_{138}, V_{139}, V_{140} and V_{150} in the case of sub-sample of tribal households contributed to the overall explanatory power of the discriminant function. Therefore, it shows that significant

Table 32

Linked Borrowers and Others: Relative Importance of Variables of Different Sample Strata

Total Sub-Sample		*Sub-Sample of Khammam*		*Sub-Sample of Warangal*		*Sub-Sample of Adilabad*		*Sub-Sample of Tribals*	
Sl.No. of Variables	*F-Ratios*	*Sl.No. of Variables*	*F-Ratios*	*Sl.No. of Variables*	*F-Ratios*	*Sl.No.of Variables*	*F-Ratios*	*Sl.No. of Variables*	*F-Ratios*
V138	657071 (0.0211)	V138	5.55364 (0.0850)	V183	3.09128 (0.0000)	V139	27.9562 21.3790	V138	(0.0113) (0.0000)
V143	6.52091 (0.0019)	V141	4.00566 (0.02233)	V138	2.71305 (0.7065)	V150	19.9976 (0.0000)	V140	12.5412 (0.0000)
V8	4.90884 (0.0028)	V139	3.07408 (0.0329)	V140	2.62589 (0.0613)	–	–	V139	9.23279 (0.0000)
V153	4.02810) (0.0113)	–	–	V8	2.35460 (0.0677)	–	–	V150	7.22139 (0.0000)

Note:

i. Figures in Parantheses indicate the significance level

ii. For the notation of Variables See Table -24

differences exist among group means for three, four, two, and four of the eight variables included in the model for the districts of Khammam, Warangal, Adilabad and for sample tribal households respectively.

Thus, the discriminant function was estimated and the calculated F-values for the above mentioned variables have been found to be statistically significant at 1 per cent level, revealing that the function is also highly significant with respect to the above mentioned variables for the total sub-sample strata presented in the analysis.

The relative importance of each of these variables individually in their power to discriminate between the two groups in the total distance measured were also calculated with the help of all the co-efficients and the mean differences. The final results for the sample strata have been depicted in Table-33.

The results show that the variables which contributed to the classification of the overall sample households into linked borrowers and othersin the order of importance were: agricultural incomes (V_{138}), total expenditures of the households (V_{143}), education (V_8), and worker-dependent ratio (V_{153}) of the households. The weights calculated for these variables to the total distance measured were 49.40, 32.50, 9.60 and 8.50 respectively.

The discriminant function was also estimated for the sub-sample of Khammam district and the calculated F-ratios for the above mentioned variables have been found to be statistically significant at 5 per cent level, indicating that the discriminant function is also highly significant with respect to the variables– V_{138}, V_{142} and V_{139}. The relative importance of each of these variables separately in their power to discriminate between the two groups in the total distance measured were also calculated and the final results show that the variables which contributed to the classification of the households into linked borrowers and others in the order of importance were agricultural incomes, incomes from non-casual labour, and MFP incomes of the households. The weights calculated for these variables to the total distance measured were 39.70, 34.00 and 26.00 respectively.

Table 33

Linked Borrowers and Others: Percentage Contribution of Individual Variables (Only Significant Variables) to the Total Distance Measured of Different Sample Strata

Total Sub-Sample		*Sub-Sample of Khammam*		*Sub-Sample of Warangal*		*Sub-Sample of Adilabad*		*Sub-Sample of Tribals*	
Sl.No. of Variables	*Percentage Contribution*	*Sl.No. of Variables*	*Percentage Contribution*	*Sl.No. of Variables*	*Percentage Contribution*	*Sl.No.of Variables*	*Percentage Contribution*	*Sl.No. of Variables*	*Percentage Contribution*
V138	49.40	V138	39.70	V183	33.80	V139	62.35	V138	52.30
V143	32.58	V141	34.00	V138	24.40	V150	37.65	V140	21.25
V8	9.60	V139	26.00	V140	23.40	–	–	V139	15.70
V153	8.50	–	–	V8	18.40	–	–	V150	18.75

Note: For the notation of variables See Table-24.

The discriminant function was also estimated separately for the sub-sample of Warangal district and the calculated F-ratios for the above mentioned variables have been found to be statistically significant at 10 per cent level, revealing that the function is significant with respect to the variables like V_{153}, V_{138}, V_{140} and V_8. The variables which contributed to the classification of the households into the linked borrowers and others in the order of importance were agricultural incomes, worker-dependent ratio, incomes for agricultural/wage labour, and education of the households. The weights calculated for these variables to the total distance measured were 33.80, 24.40, 23.40 and 18.40 respectively.

Similarly, the analysis was also carried out separately for the sub-sample of Adilabad district and also for the sub-sample of tribal households. The calculated F-values for both the discriminant functions have been found to be very much significant statistically with the observed significance level of 0.00 with respect to the variables like V_{139} and V_{150}; and V_{138}, V_{140}, V_{139} and V_{150} for the sub-sample of tribals. The relative importance of each of these characteristics in their power to discriminate between the two groups in the total distance measured were calculated and the final results show that the variables which contributed to the classification of the farmers into linked borrowers and others in the order of importance were MFP incomes and proportion of male workers to the total workers of the households in the case of Adilabad district; and agricultural incomes, incomes from agricultural/wage labour, MFP incomes and proportion of male workers to total workers of the households in the case of the sub-sample of tribal households in the entire study area. In the case of Adilabad the weights calculated for these variables to the total distance measured were 62.35 and 37.65 per cent each and in the case of sub-sample of tribal households were 52.30, 21.25, 15.70, 10.75 respectively.

Table -34 shows the summary of the classification results of different sub-sample strata in the study area. The diagonal elements are the number of cases classified correctly into the groups. From the aforesaid variables the discriminant function

Table 34
Classification Results Of Different Sample Strata

CLASSIFICATION RESULTS			PREDICTED GROUP MEMBERSHIP	
Sample Strata	*ACTUAL GROUP*	*NO. OF CASES*	*NON-LINKED (0)*	*LINKED (1)*
For Total Sub-Sample (N=154)	GROUP (0) NON-LINKED	74	51 (68.9)	23 (31.1)
	GROUP LINKED (1)	80	31 (38.8)	49 (61.3)
PER CENT OF GROUPED CASES CORRECTLY CLASSIFIED: 64.94%				
For Sub-Sample of Khammam (N=77)	GROUP (0) NON-LINKED	49	32 (65.3)	17 (34.7)
	GROUP LINKED (1)	28	7 (25.0)	21 (75.0)
PER CENT OF GROUPED CASES CORRECTLY CLASSIFIED: 68.83%				
For Sub-Sample of Warangal (N=51)	GROUP (0) NON-LINKED	15	9 (60.0)	6 (40.0)
	GROUP LINKED (1)	36	10 (27.8)	26 (72.2)

Contd.

CLASSIFICATION RESULTS			*PREDICTED GROUP MEMBERSHIP*	
Sample Strata	*ACTUAL GROUP*	*NO. OF CASES*	*NON-LINKED (0)*	*LINKED (1)*
	PER CENT OF GROUPED CASES CORRECTLY CLASSIFIED: 68.63%			
For Sub-Sample of Adilabad (N=26)	GROUP (0) NON-LINKED	10	10 (100.0)	0 (0.0)
	GROUP LINKED (1)	16	2 (12.5)	14 (87.5)
	PER CENT OF GROUPED CASES CORRECTLY CLASSIFIED: 92.31%			
For Sub-Sample of Tribals (N=111)	GROUP (0) NON-LINKED	50	40 (80.0)	10 (20.0)
	GROUP LINKED (1)	61	23 (37.7)	38 (62.3)
	PER CENT OF GROUPED CASES CORRECTLY CLASSIFIED: 70.27%			

Note: *Figures in Parentheses indicate percentages.*

was fitted in order to predict whether a household is likely to be a linked borrower or another. To predict the group membership, a critical Z-score has to be calculated. Below this score, households are placed in one group. There are various criteria upon which the establishment of critical Z-score can be based. But here the researcher derived the group membership on the basis of prior probability for the group to which a particular household belongs to. The prior probability can be estimated in several ways. If the sample is considered representative of the population, the observed proportions of cases in each group can serve as estimates of the prior probabilities. In this case, we have a different classification results for different sub-sample strata presented in the Table -34.

Out of 154 cases for whom all information is available 74 cases or 48 per cent belong to the group of non-linked, and 80 cases which account for 52 per cent belong to the group of linked borrowers. The prior probability example, of 74 cases in the group of non-linked borrowers, 51 were predicted correctly to be members of group 0 (non-linked borrowers) accounting for 68.9 per cent, while 23 (31.1 per cent) were assigned incorrectly to group 1 (linked borrowers). Similarly, 49 out of 80 (61.3 per cent) of the Group 1 (linked borrowers) cases were identified correctly, and 31 (38.8 per cent) were misclassified to Group 0 (non-linked borrowers). Thus, the predicted group membership correctly classified shows the non-linked transactions group has a higher percentage than the linked transactions group. Therefore, the overall percentages of cases classified correctly is 64.94 per cent i.e., 100 out of 154. By and large, the percentage of misclassification is not very much high and therefore one will be able to say that the function is a significant one.

For the sub-sample of Khammam, out of 77 cases,49 or 63.64 per cent belonged to linked transactions group, while 28 or 36.36 per cent belong to non-linked transactions group. Of the 49 cases, 32 cases and 17 cases were correctly and incorrectly assigned in the case of non-linked borrowers and the respective percentages are 65.3 and 34.7, whereas in the case of linked borrowers 21 out of 28 cases were classified correctly and only 7 out of 28 cases were misclassified to the group of non-linked borrowers and they account for 75 per cent and 25 per cent respectively. Therefore, it is to be said that the percentage of predicted group membership correctly classified for the linked borrowers group outweigh the percentage of correctly classified for the non-linked borrowers group. Thus, the overall percentage of 'Grouped' cases correctly classified is 68.83. Thus, here also the percentage of misclassification is not much and it is also to be noted that the function is a significant one.

For the sub-sample of Warangal, 15 and 36 cases out of 51 cases for whom all information is available belong to non-linked and linked groups which account for 29.40 per cent and 70.60 per cent respectively. It reveals that the linked borrowers outweigh the non-linked borrowers in the district. Of the 15 cases, 9 cases were correctly classified, forming 60 per cent of the total non-linked borrowers and the remaining 40 per cent were misclassified to linked borrowers group. Whereas, of the 36 cases, 26 cases or 72.2 per cent of the total linked borrowers were correctly predicted and the remaining 10 cases (27.8 per cent) were mis-classified to the non-linked borrowers. Therefore, the percentage of correctly predicted cases in the linked borrowers group is much higher than the percentage of correctly predicted cases in the non-linked borrowers group. Further, the overall per cent of 'Grouped' cases correctly classified is 68.63 and misclassifi-cation rate is not high. Therefore, the fitted discriminant function to the sub-sample of Warangal district with respect to the aforesaid variables is also considered to be a significant one.

For the sub-sample of Adilabad, 10 and 16 out of 26 cases belong to non-linked and linked groups and the respective percentages 38.46 and 61.54. Here also the linked borrowers are more than the non-linked borrowers in the sample. Cent per cent cases were correctly predicted in the case of non-linked group of borrowers, whereas among the linked group borrowers, 14 out of 16 cases, implying 87.5 per cent were correctly predicted for their group membership and the remaining two cases (12.5 per cent) were incorrectly assigned to the non-linked group of borrowers. Here the percentage of correctly predicted cases among the non-linked group borrowers is higher than the percentage of correctly classified among the linked group borrowers. Thus, the overall per cent of 'Grouped' cases correctly classified and predicted is 92.31 and with which one will be able to say that the per cent and the rate of misclassification is non-significant. Therefore, one has to surmise that the fitted discriminant function of V_{35} with respect to the variables– V_{139} and V_{150} was to be more significant though the number of cases are less when compared with all other sub-samples presented in the Table. Thus, it is revealing that these variables have the potential power individually in discriminating between the linked borrowers and others in this area. Perhaps, this might be due to small sample size with only two discriminating variables. This is highly powerful and significant function when compared to all other discriminant functions that have been fitted in the analysis, though they too are significant functions.

Finally, for sub-sample of tribal households in the study area, 50 and 61 cases out of 111 for whom all the information is available belong to linked and non-linked groups and the respective percentages are 45.05 and 54.95. Here also the percentage of linked borrowers group is higher than the percentage of non-linked borrowers group.

Among the non-linked group borrowers 40 cases or 80 per cent were correctly predicted and the remaining 10 cases or 20 per cent were incorrectly assigned to the linked borrowers group, whereas among the linked group borrowers 38 cases or 62.3 per cent were correctly classified into the linked group and the remaining 23 cases or 37.7 per cent were misclassified into the non-linked group. Here on should also note that the per cent of correctly predicted among the non-linked group borrowers is higher than the per cent of correctly classified or predicted among the linked borrowers group as in the case of the sub-sample of Adilabad district. Thus, the overall per cent of 'Grouped' cases correctly classified is 70.27 and therefore, the rate of misclassified is not much high. And hence, one

Table 35

Pooled-Within-Groups Correlations

Strictire Matrices									
Pooled-within-groups correlations between discriminating variables and canonical discriminant functions (Variables ordered by size of correlation within function)									
Total Sub-Sample (N=154)		*Sub-Sample of Khammam (N=77)*		*Sub-Sample of Warangal (N=51)*		*Sub-Sample of Adilabad (N=26)*		*Sub-Sample of Tribals (N=111)*	
Variables	*Function 1*	*Variables*	*Function 1*	*Variables*	*Function 1*	*Variables*	*Function 1*	*Variables*	*Function 1*
V138	-0.63226	V138	-0.76560	V153	-0.55509	V139	0.81845	V138	0.84838
V140	0.40506	V139	0.65273	V138	0.51192	V138	-0.36907	V143	0.58049
V153	0.28258	V143	-0.48242	V143	0.41704	V143	-0.33308	V139	-0.26248
V139	0.24513	V141	0.41591	V8	-0.41305	V150	-0.30701	V140	-0.09517
V143	-0.21724	V8	-0.30146	V140	0.19572	V140	0.27354	V141	-0.06059
V141	0.21339	V140	0.18869	V141	-0.11156	V8	-0.23728	V150	0.05610
V8	0.13647	V150	-0.15962	V139	0.02963	V153	-0.15735	V153	0.04040
V150	-0.07295	V153	0.14731	V150	0.01685	V141	-0.13881	V8	-0.0.01229

Note: For the notation of Variables See Table -24

will be able to conclude that the fitted discriminant function with respect to the above mentioned variables was found to be more significant, indicating the power of individual variables in discriminating between the linked and the non-linked borrowers' group.

To summarise all the above discriminant functions by taking into account the F-ratios, relative percentage contribution and the per cent of correctly predicted group membership, it is to be surmised that all the discriminant functions fitted with respect to the aforesaid explanatory variables have been found to be significant as they have lesser percentage of misclassification rate when compared with the per cent of 'Grouped' cases correctly classified in the analysis.

Therefore, linked borrowers compared to others demonstrate household characteristics that clearly exhibit why a household may opt for linked credit borrowings. Out of the eight variables included in the model, the aforesaid variables in each of the sub-sample were found to be very useful in classifying the households into linked borrowers and others. In a theoretical and empirical sense these variables are realistic and have the potential power while discriminating the linked borrowers and others in the researcher's study area.

A pooled with in groups correlation have been presented in Table -35. Another way to assess the contribution of a variable to the discriminant function is to examine the correlations between the values of the function and the values of the variables. For each case the value of the discriminant function is computed and the pearson correlation co-efficients between it and the original variables are obtained. These, however, are simple bivariate correlations, so they are not affected by relationships with the other variables. Hence the table shows the pooled within groups correlations of the different sub-sample strata that had been considered for the analysis.

The Table indicates that V_{138} has the largest correlation in absolute value with the discriminant function. The correlation Co-efficient is -0.6322. The negative sign indicates that small function values are associated with the large agricultural

Table 36
Unstandardized and Standardized Canonical Discriminant Function Coefficients

Total Sub-Sample (N=154)			*Sub Sample of Khammam (N=77)*			*Sub Sample of Warangal (N=51)*			*Sub Sample of Adilabad (N=26)*			*Sub Sample of Tribals (N=111)*		
Variables	*A*	*B*	*Variables*	*A*	*B*	*Variables*	*A*	*B*	*Variables*	*A*	*B*	*Variables*	*A*	*B*
V153	0.2677	0.3064	V138	-0.2486	-0.6431	V153	-0.4690	-0.5691	V150	-4.4558	-0.6014	V150	1.5568	0.2287
V8	0.4204	0.3438	V139	0.2516	0.4261	V8	-0.4210	-0.4293	V139	1.1555	0.9962	V138	0.6073	1.1111
V138	-0.6935	-1.7705	V141	0.3279	0.5516	V138	0.3931	0.7889	–	–	–	V139	-0.1973	-0.3331
V143	0.5237	1.1645	–	–	–	V140	0.2644	0.5475	–	–	–	V140	0.1834	0.4517
Constant	-0.1275	–	Constant	-0.1071	–	Constant	-0.9360	–	Constant	0.4800	–	Constant	-2.2795	–

A = Unstandardized Func. 1

B = Standardized Func. 1

Note: For the notation of Variables see Table -24

incomes and the larger values are associated with lesser agricultural incomes. This confirms the inverse relationship with V_{138} and V_{35}. The second variable i.e., V_{140} has the highest positive correlation with the discriminant function followed by V_{153}, V_{139}, V_{141} and V_8. The V_{143} has the negative correlation with the discriminant function, indicating that the small function value when compared with V_{138}, indicating the highest contribution to the discriminant function next to V_{138} and it also confirms the inverse relationship with V_{143} and V_{35}.

Pooled with in groups correlations for the sub-sample of Khammam indicates that V_{138} has the largest correlation in absolute value with the discriminant function, the value being -0.7656 and it indicates that small function values are associated with larger agricultural incomes and vice-versa. Besides V_{138}, negative associations with the function for V_{153},V_{143} and V_8 can also be observed from the Table. V_{140} has the highest positive correlation with the function. Such positive associations are also observed for V_{139}, V_{141} and V_{150}. A similar trend had also been observed in the case of V_{138} and V_{139} for the sub-sample of Warangal in that order. While V_{140} has the highest positive correlation with the function followed by V_{153}, V_{143}, V_8 and V_{150}. the sub-sample of Adilabad presented in the table indicates that V_{139} has the highest positive correlation with the discriminant function. V_{138} relatively has the second largest negative correlation with the function value followed by V_{143} and V_{150}. In the case of sub-sample of tribal households V_{138} has the highest positive correlation with the discriminant function, indicating the linear relationship with the function followed by V_{143}. V_{139} relatively has the third highest negative correlation with function value, which indicates that the small function values are associated with the presence of V_{139}, V_{140} and V_{141} in that order.

By and large, Table-35 gives the within structure Co-efficients for all the sub-samples of different strata. Further, it should be noted that these Co-efficients are smaller than the total structure Co-efficients shown in Table-36, but the rankings from the largest absolute magnitude to the smallest are similar although not identical. Some of the Co-efficients could be larger or much smaller or even have the opposite sign from their total counterparts in Table -36.

By looking at the groups of the variables, with co-efficients of different signs, we can determine which variable values result in large and small functional values. For instance, the total sub-sample presented in the table clearly reveals that V_{138} has a larger value and hence it leads to a small value for the function. But larger values for V_{143} will increase the value of the function. Large function values are associated with large linked transactions, while small function values are associated with non-linked transactions.

As Table -36 is a corollary to the Table -35, it depicts the total structure co-efficients of both the unstandardized and standardized canonical discriminant function co-efficients. Since the variables are correlated, it is not possible to assess the importance of an individual variable. The value of the co-efficient for a particular variable also depends on the other variables included in the function. Here, variables with large co-efficients are thought to contribute more to the overall discriminant function. This can be done by examining the magnitude of the standardised co-efficients (ignoring the signs); the larger the magnitude, the greater is that variable's contribution to the discriminant function and conversely which is also true to the function. Keeping this in view, the researcher made an attempt to analyse the standardised discriminant function co-efficients as shown in Table-36 for the different sub-sample strata.

Considering total sub-sample, V_{138} makes the greatest contribution followed by V_{143}, V_8 and V_{153}. V_8 has the 3rd rank and the difference in the values between V_{143} and V_8 is quite large. But in the case of unstandardized Co-efficients though V_{138} has the first rank and V_{143} has second rank and V_8 has the third rank, the difference between V_{143} and V_8 is not much.

For the sub-sample of Khammam, the table shows that V_{138} makes the highest contribution for the linked borrowers followed by V_{141} and V_{139} for the function and the reverse is true in the case of unstandardised co-efficients for the function.

In the case of sub-sample of Warangal, V_{138} has the major contribution for the linked transactions by having the highest co-efficient followed by V_{153}, V_{140} and V_8 for their contribution to the linked transactions of the sample borrowers in the area. But in the case of Adilabad only two variables are found to be relevant for making the borrowers to have the linked transactions and between them V_{139} makes a greater contribution to have the linkages followed by V_{150}.

Finally, while taking into account the sub-sample of tribal households, V_{138} makes the highest and the significant contribution for the borrowers to have the linked transactions followed by V_{140}, V139 and V_{150} as the causative factors for the discriminant function to make it more effective, which implies that they have a decisive role for the sample tribal households to have the linked transactions instead of non-linked transactions in the study area.

Table 37
Eigen Values and Measures of Importance

Canonical Discriminant Function For	*Eigen Value*	*Relative Percentage*	*Canonical Correlation*
Sub-Sample of Adilabad(N=26)	1.7389	70.96	0.7968
Sub-Sample of Tribals(N=111)	0.2725	11.12	0.4628
Sub-Sample of Warangal(N=51)	0.2047	8.35	0.4123
Sub-Sample of Khammam(N=77)	0.1263	5.15	0.3349
Total Sub-Sample (N=154)	0.1081	4.42	0.3124

Table -37 gives the results of the comparison of the five non-zero eigen values, and they have been presented in the order of descending magnitude. Therefore, taken together, all the functions do not necessarily provide perfect discrimination, but atleast one will be able to identify the order of their importance. They cannot be interpreted directly as they are from different functions. Therefore, one has to compare the relative magnitudes to see how much of the total discriminating power each has. To make such comparisons, the eigen values had been converted into relative percentages. Thus, the first function that is for the sub-sample of Adilabad, contains 70.96 per cent of the total discriminating power followed by other functions and perhaps this might be due to the small number of cases having the discriminating power only with the two variables out of the eight variables incorporated in the function. Therefore, the relative percentages tells whether the function is weak relative to the other and further it tells about the differences between the groups that they are not equal.

Another way to judge the substantive utility of a discriminant function is by examining the canonical correlation Co-efficient, which as a measure of association demonstrates the degree of relatedness between the groups and the discriminant function. A high Co-efficient, such as found for the first function in the Table-37 indicates that a strong relationship exists between the groups and the first discriminant function. The other functions, however have a rather low value, which indicates a weak association as surmised from the relative percentage[16].

Table 38
Residual Discrimination and Tests of Significance

Functions Derived Lambda	*Wilk's*	*Chi-Square*	*Degrees of Freedom*	*Significance Level*
For Total Sub-Sample (N=154)	0.9024	15.402	4	0.0039**
Sub-Sample of Khammam (N=77)	0.8878	8.744	3	0.0329**
Sub-Sample of Warangal (N=51)	0.8300	8.755	4	0.0675***
Sub-Sample of Adilabad (N=26)	0.3651	23.174	2	0.0000*
For Sub-Sample Tribals (N=111)	0.7859	25.786	4	0.0000*

* Statistically significant at 1% level
** Statistically significant at 5% level
*** Statistically significant at 10% level

Therefore, from the above table one will be able to conclude that even though the first function is always the 'most' powerful in a relative sense as measured by the relative percentage, it may only be weakly related to the groups as measured by the canonical correlation. To supplement for the above, the residual discrimination and tests of significance had also been presented in Table -38 to have an idea over the test for the statistical significance of the discriminant functions proceeds indirectly. To have an idea over the real discrimination Wilk's Lambda also called U-statistic is taken into account in the analysis.

While looking at the table for total sub-sample, the Chi-square test for Lambda is found to be statistically significant. $A\lambda = 0.9024$ is transformed to $\chi 2 = 15.402$ with four degrees of freedom. The observed significance level is 0.0039. The table shows for all the sub-samples presented, Chi-square test for Lambda is found to be significant. Thus, one will be able to surmise that the estimated discriminant function for all the sub-samples of different strata with the aforesaid explanatory variables had the potential power with respect to their power to discriminate between the two mutually exclusive groups of linked borrowers and non-linked borrowers in the study area.

SUMMING UP

The broad conclusions that emerged from the above analysis are as given hereunder:

The credit facilities in the tribal areas attest the fact that the percentage for tribals is relatively higher for both borrowers from exclusively institutional sources and exclusively from non-institutional sources than non-tribals, but for borrowers from both the sources, it is higher for non-tribals than tribals. This clearly shows the growing institutionalisation of credit in tribal areas. The existence of linked transactions among the sub-sample borrowers demonstrates the nexus between the credit and product markets. Among the borrower households the data confirms the hypothesis that the non-tribals are in an advantageous position than the tribals. This indicates the accessibility of the institutional and non-institutional credit agencies for them in the study area. The data further reveals that the sample tribal borrowers who obtained the loans from the institutional sources are relatively higher in number than the sample non-tribal borrowers due to the operations of the institutions like ITDA and GCC created for the upliftment of the tribals. Further, it had been observed that most of the borrowers obtained the loans for agricultural inputs, and land development activities. Other purposes like marriages, ceremonies and the domestic needs did not figure as the needs for borrowing significantly among the sample borrowers. It had also been observed that a majority of the borrowers had diverted their loan amount for the other purposes in the sense that from productive purpose to the unproductive purposes like ordinary and conspicuous consumption.

The sources of formal loan exclusively borrowed by the different sub-sample borrowers had been analysed by using the logit model by making use of the dummy dependent variable : 1 if the household has borrowed from formal sources and O - other wise with some of the specific household characteristics as explanatory variables. The entire analysis supports the argument that mere having the formal lending agencies in the tribal areas does not guarantee and safeguard the interests of the tribal households and as well the small and marginal non-tribal peasants in the tribal areas as it is due to the potential power of the larger farmers over the formal credit agencies that had been there in the study area and moreover also due to the asset based lending policies adopted and practiced by the formal lending agencies. Low literacy level, lower caste status, lower incomes, small size of operated land holding, higher family size, and higher worker-dependent ratio badly affect the small, marginal, poor and tribal farmers of the sample households while getting the loans from the formal lending agencies. Thus, the lending policies of the formal credit agencies deter the small, poor and tribal farmers to obtain the loans from them and also even deter them for approaching them to obtain the loans in the study area. Therefore, it can be inferred from the above analysis that merely establishing the formal lending agencies[17] in the tribal areas do not ensure effective and efficient access of the formal credit to the needy tribal farmers and other needy small and marginal farmers among the non-tribal households and thus establishing them reveals only the physical accessibility of the institutions to the area for the big and large farmers who are endowed with high physical and human resources.

In tribal areas, a variety of credit relations and transactions had been found to be prevalent in the study area as a whole. These relations signify the relative significance of non-monetised transactions in tribal areas. In all the districts under consideration for the study, the prevalent mode is cash to cash form which is more prominent, despite the relative importance of it being more in Khammam than in the other two districts. Among other forms, cash to labour is not found to be prevalent, while cash to kind is relatively more important in Warangal and Adilabad. The other form which is of relevance is cash to cash and output in all the districts. Therefore, it can be said that in all the districts there is a greater degree of monetisation of transactions, though Khammam ranks first followed by Warangal and Adilabad.

On the basis of the analysis of linked and non-linked transactions in the study area, it can be said that the group of borrowers with linked transactions when compared with the group of borrowers with non-linked transactions have a lower mean literacy status, higher mean family size, higher mean agricultural income, lower MFP income, lower mean income from agricultural wage labour, lower level of income with respect to incomes from non-agricultural labour, a relatively higher mean total expenditures, a higher proportion of mean male workers to total workers and a lesser worker-dependent ratio.

The logistic regression analysis and the discriminant function analysis had also been taken up to identify the specific household characteristics of those who opt for either the linked or non-linked transactions with respect to the different sub-sample strata.

Among various causative factors influencing linkages, some are exhibiting positive impact while others are exerting a negative impact. An improvement in literacy status of the respondents has an overall negative influence on linkages in the overall sample, but it has a positive influence in Khammam sub-sample and tribals' sub-sample. Agricultural incomes and incomes from agricultural/wage labour have a positive influence on linkages. In the case of MFP incomes, it has a negative impact in the case of tribals, signifying that an increase in MFP income would weaken the linkage effect. The same finding had also been observed in the case of incomes from non-casual labour. The total expenditure has a negative influence on the linkage variable, but for tribals it has a positive influence. Further, the influence is positive for proportion of male workers to total workers. The worker-dependent ratio has a negative impact on linkage variable in the case of tribals sub-sample. Hence, in the case of tribals, an improvement in certain variables like literacy status of the borrowers, agricultural incomes, incomes from agricultural labour, total expenditures and proportion of male workers to total workers, contrary to certain earlier hypotheses, leads to an increase in linkages, rather than diminishing it. On the other hand, a rise in MFP incomes, incomes from non-casual labour and worker-dependent ratio reduce these linkages and this observation lends support to the observation of earlier studies.

From the discriminant function analysis, one will be able to draw the conclusion that the linked borrowers compared to others demonstrate the specific household characteristics that may clearly exhibit why the household may be going for the linked credit borrowings. Out of the eight explanatory variables fitted in the discriminant function, the relative magnitude of each variable contributed to the function to the total distance measured for the different sub-sample strata.

While taking the total sub-sample discriminant function, agricultural incomes, total expenditures, literacy status and worker-dependent ratio contributed to the same hierarchical order to the function and explain the households' decision for opting for the linked transactions in the study area. In the case of Khammam sub-sample, the hierarchical order of the relative contribution to the function are agricultural incomes, incomes from non-casual labour, and M.F.P. incomes and these variables played a vital role in regard to the households decisions to have the linked borrowings. In the case of Warangal sub-sample, the relative magnitude of the variables for the discriminant function are agricultural incomes, worker-dependent ratio, incomes from agricultural/wage labour and finally the literacy status that have had the potential power to discriminate between the linked and non-linked borrowings of the sample households in the district. But in the case of Adilabad, only two variables - MFP incomes, proportion of male workers to total workers - significantly contributed to the discriminant function and thus these two variables signify the households' decision-making process whether to go for the linked borrowings or not. Finally, in the case of sub-sample of tribals in the study area, the relative magnitude of the variables by the total distance measured to the discriminant function are agricultural incomes, incomes from agricultural/ wage labour, MFP incomes and proportion of male workers to total workers that have a significant bearing in regard to the households decisions going for the linked transactions in the area.

From the above analysis, it can also be said that the relative contribution of agricultural incomes to the function can be found in the total sub-sample, sub-sample of Khammam, sub-sample of Warangal and the sub-sample of tribals in the study area. Its relative contribution to the function is relatively higher in the case of sub-sample of tribals followed by total sub-sample, Khammam sub-sample and the Warangal sub-sample with the percentage contribution of 52.30, 40.40, 39.70 and 33.80 respectively. The percentage contribution (32.50) of the total expenditures to the function can only be seen in the case of total sub-sample of the study area. The relative percentage contribution of the literacy status to the function was only associated with the sub-sample of Warangal and the total sub-sample with 18.40 and 9.60 respectively. A similar finding had also been observed even in the case of worker-dependent ratio. Its relative percentage contribution is relatively higher in Warangal with 24.40 followed by the total sub-sample with 8.50. The relative percentage contribution (34.00) of the incomes from non-casual labour to the discriminant function can only be visualised in the sub-sample of Khammam. The relative contribution of MFP incomes to the function can be seen in the case of sub-sample of Khammam, sub-sample of Adilabad and the sub-sample of tribals in the study area. Its percentage contribution was the highest in Adilabad followed by Khammam and the sub-sample of tribals with 62.35, 26.00 and 15.70 respectively. The relative percentage contribution of agricultural/wage labour incomes to the function is apparent in the sub-sample of Warangal followed by the sub-sample of tribals with 23.40 and 21.25 respectively. Finally, the relative percentage contribution of proportion of male workers to total workers to the discriminant function can only be seen in the case of sub-sample of Adilabad followed by the sub-sample of tribals with 37.65 and 10.75. By and large, though these variables attest the regional diversification to the function, one will be able to say that in a theoretical and empirical sense these variables are realistic and have the potential power while discriminating the linked borrowers and others in the researchers' study area with different sub-sample strata that had been analysed here.

NOTES & REFERENCES

1. The formal agencies include GCC, Govt., ITDA, Co-operatives, Commercial Banks and Regional Rural Banks, that are expected to provide cheaper credit in the form of subsidised interest rates to the households.

2. The informal agencies include landlords, money-lenders, traders and merchants, indigenous bankers, friends and relatives which are expected to provide credit with relatively higher rates of interest than in the formal credit market.

3. Narayana Reddy, M.V., *Access and Cost of Borrowing of Formal and Informal Credit in Two Villages of Guntur District,* An M.Phil. dissertation submitted to the Centre for Economic and Social Studies, Begumpet, Hyderabad, 1991, p.3.

4. (a) Griffin, K. *The Political Economy of Agrarian Change,* London, Macmillan, 1979

   (b) Ladman, J.R. & Adams, D.W., "The Rural Poor and Recent Performance of Formal Rural Financial Markets in the Dominican Republic", *Canadian Journal of Agricultural Economics,* Vol.26, No.1, 1978, pp.43-50.

(c) Lipton, M., Agricultural Finance and Rural Credit in Poor Countires' *World Development,* Vol.4, No.7, 1976,pp.543-553.

(d) Ruttan,V.W, "Assistance to Expand Agricultural Production" *World Development,* Vol.14, No.1,1986, pp.39-63.

(e) Braverman, A. & Guasih, J.L., "Rural Credit Markets and Institutions in Developing Countries: Lessons for policy analysis from practice and modern theory", *World Development,* Vol.14, No.10, 1986, pp.1253-1267.

5. In addition to the earlier mentioned studies (in reference-4) the following studies provided enough empirical evidence for the above finding. They are:

(a) Lele, U, 'Co-operatives and the Poor: A Comparative Perspective", *World Development,* Vol.9, No.1, 1981, pp. 55-72.

(b) Rao, C.H.H. 'Farm Size and Credit Policy', *Economic and Political Weekly,* Vol.5, No.52, 1970, pp.157-162.

(c) ————: *'Technological Change and Distribution of Gains in Indian Agriculture,* Macmillan, New Delhi - 1975.

(d) Egger, P., 'Banking for the Rural Poor : Lessons from some Innovative Savings and Credit Schemes', *International Labour Review,* Vol.125, 1996, pp. 447-462.

(e) Sarap, Kailas : *Interlinked Agrarian Markets in Rural India,* Sage Publications, New Delhi, 1991.

6. An interlinked transaction is one where two or more interdependent exchanges are simultaneously agreed upon. *Braverman and Srinivasan* defined these contracts as 'transactions in more than one commodity or service made between the same pair of individuals and linked in an essential way so that declining contracts would be infeasible or costly for atleast one part'. For details also see infra *Chapter-II.*

7. Ghatak, S. 'Rural Credit and the Cost of Borrowing : Inter State variations in India", *Journal of Developing Areas,* Vol.18, No.1, 1977, pp.21-34.

8. Sarap, K., "Transactions in Rural Credit Markets in Western Orissa, India", *The Journal of Peasant Studies,* Vol.15, No.1, 1987, pp.83-107.

9. His data clearly attested the fact that small and marginal farmers have less access to formal credit institutions in the survey area because of the asset-based and caste-biased lending policies of

the formal agencies. For a detailed discussion see Sarap, K., *Interlinked Agrarian Markets in Rural India,* Sage Publications, New Delhi, 1991, pp.53-75.

10. Here it is to be stated that the amount of working capital that can be mobilised depends on the amount of land he owns, which is often a good proxy for the total wealth of the households.

11. This finding supports the observation made by James that almost 62.39 per cent of the total overdues of the sample farm households is accounted for by the large farmers. For a detailed discussion see James V.E., "Credit Rationing, Rural Savings and Financial Policy in Developing Countries", Asian Development Bank, *Staff Working paper,* No.13, Sept. 1982, Manila.

12. It had been discussed elaborately in chapters - V & IX.

13. In this case the simple interest formula was used to calculate the explicit interest rate : $R = I X 100/p.nX12$, where '*R*' is the explicit interest rate per annum; *I* is the actual interest payments; '*P*' is the principal loan amount and '*n*' is the duration of loan in months which is estimated by using the 'monthly products method'. Therefore, by doing so if the crop is be sold at the rate of Rs.150/ - per bag, the claculated explicit interest rate is 133.44 per cent per annum, if it is Rs.200/- per bag, then the explicit interest is 50.04 per cent, if it is Rs.215/- per bag, then it would be 31.68 per cent, if it is Rs.225/- per bag, then it would be 22.80 per cent and if it is Rs.235/- per bag, then it would be 12.80 per cent. Besides, in this condition the lenders used to charge usual rate of interest ranging from 10 per cent to 50 per cent. Therefore, if one includes these rates of interest, with the calculated explicit interest rates then the actual rate of interest charged by the money lenders would become very high, which is an intolerable one and they were shown in the rate of interest table presented in this chapter. Therefore, this type of linkages of credit with product market will lead to the exploitative relations as mentioned earlier.

14. As per J.M. Rao, the dominant party-dictates the terms of exchange, while the weaker is obliged to accept it. The poorer the households in general, the more acute the need for consumption and other loans, the easier for the lender to extract a higher proportion of their income by more exploitative terms and conditions of lending through interlinked transactions. It also makes it possible to extract a surplus even out of a low output of the peasant households by depressing their consumption level to the extent possible. According to Desai, however, the nature

of interlokcing of transactions differs according to the relative power of the contracting parties and the strategies adopted by different parties involved in the exchange process. For a detailed discussion see Rao, J.M. 'Interest Rates in Backward Agriculture', *Cambridge Journal of Economics,* Vol.4, No.2, 1980, pp.159-167. Also See Desai, M. et. al. *Agrarian Power and Agricultural Productivity in South Asia,* Oxford University Press, Delhi, 1984 and also see Sarap, K., *Interlinked Agrarian Markets in Rural India,* Op.cit., 1991.

15. Initially the researcher included in the logit model the explanatory variables V_8, V_{138}, V_{139}, V_{140}, V_{141}, V_{143}, V_{150} and V_{153} and latter with the help of *'trial and error'* method only the variables mentioned in the analysis had been included in the model for predicting the direction of the variables with linked credit decisions.

16. Here, one should note that the canonical correlation in Table - 37 is influenced by small number of cases (N = 26). Larger samples have greater difficulty yielding high correlations, because they are typically more heterogenous in nature.

17. Iqbal considered that the growth of the formal lending agencies will be able to create the competition among the formal and informal lenders and this competition reduces the monopoly power of the latter. For further details see Iqbal, F. 'The Determinants of Money-lender Interest Rates : Evidence from Rural India', *The Journal of Development Studies,* Vol.24, No.3, 1988, pp.364-378.

7

DETERMINANTS OF MARKETABLE SURPLUS AND MARKETED SURPLUS IN THE TRIBAL AREAS-A STATISTICAL ANALYSIS

The present chapter throws light on the marketable surplus and marketed surplus of various products of the tribal and non-tribal sample house-holds that had been randomly chosen for the study. This chapter intends to analyse the influence of various other factors' over the marketable and marketed surplus. The factors that contribute to the variation in the marketable and marketed surplus have been examined by the application of multiple regression analysis to understand the causal relationships, and the analysis of variance had also been taken-up to have an idea over the significance levels of various other influencing factors on them.

Besides their significance as highlighted above, one hypothesis regarding indigenous markets is that these markets may not be conducive for a greater portion of final product being marketed as they are still undeveloped. Hence the percentage of marketed surplus in the total product or the percentage of marketable surplus out of total product can be indicators of the marketing consciousness developed among tribals as juxtaposed to self consumption. The concepts of marketable and marketed surplus are being considered as crucial variables in the process of economic development. An increase in the marketable and marketed surplus either from qualitative angle or quantitative point of view or both is one of the most desired means for the rapid economic development of an agrarian economy[1]. Several connotations[2] have been used by various authors in their studies to define the concept of marketable surplus. Inspite of many terms in vogue, 'marketable and marketed surpluses' are being widely used. 'Marketable surplus represents the theoretical surplus available for disposal with the producer left after his genuine requirements of the family consumption, payment of wages in kind, feed and seed have been met'[3]. Therefore, it is the proportion of the total output that should normally be brought for sales. To put it in another way, excess of output over sectoral retentions refer to what is termed as the marketable surplus. Sectoral retentions of farm output may be partly for consumption purposes (domestic consumption) or for further use in farming operations such as for seed, animal feed, wage payments to agricultural labourers in kind, etc.[4]. While marketed surplus refers to that portion of the marketable surplus which is being actually disposed off in the market a distinction is important here between the terms marketable surplus which is an *'exante'* concept referring to the surplus planned to be marketed and the term marketed surplus, which is an *'expost'* concept referring to the actual amount marketed during a period (usually in an agricultural year).

Most of the empirical studies on marketable and marketed surplus of agricultural commodities particularly done in India by and large analyse the relations of marketable and marketed surplus with respect to the size group of farms, their income levels, prices, productivity and other related variables.

Hence, multivariate regression analysis had been carried out for both marketable surplus and marketed surplus as regressand and other indepen-dent variables, leaving out price variable. As a corollary to the analysis, the mean values and standard deviations have also been analysed.

Table-1 shows the mean values and the standard deviations of the listed variables used in the multiple regression analysis.

Table 1
Means and Standard Deviations of the Listed Variables used in Multiple Regression Analysis

	Mean Values						Standard Deviations					
Variables	*Total N=300*	*Khammam N=100*	*Warangal N=100*	*Adilabad N=100*	*Tribals N=240*	*Non-Tribals N=60*	*Total N=300*	*Khammam N=100*	*Warangal N=100*	*Adilabad N=100*	*Tribals N=240*	*Non-Tribals N=60*
V15	5.88	5.76	5.70	6.20	5.758	6.40	2.392	2.226	2.612	2.318	2.39	2.352
V22	0.423	0.18	0.38	0.710	0.313	0.867	1.161	0.914	0.838	1.546	0.918	1.780
V25	31.575	5.25	38.75	50.75	32.075	29.575	29.85	18.90	26.45	22.60	29.775	30.35
V31	4,890	4,590	5,400	4,680	4,224	12,858	4,602	5,550	4,221	3,870	3,201	12,570
V35	0.760	1.260	0.660	0.360	0.671	1.117	0.823	0.812	0.728	0.659	0.800	0.825
V50	678.60	498	802	736	650	793.40	376.40	300.20	392.40	364	337.20	491.20
V61	55.925	59.25	58.50	50.0	50.0	59.575	29.925	39.675	22.825	23.575	29.40	31.925
V62	52.825	56.0	54.75	47.75	52.50	54.175	27.75	37.8	20.625	20.75	27.80	27.675
V63	60.425	53.75	62.75	64.75	60.825	58.75	27.25	32.825	21.175	25.40	26.825	29.05
V64	5.185	2.4	3.50	9.65	6.395	0.067	6.835	4.845	4.295	8.265	7.03	—
V142	18,950	15,400	22,850	18,600	17,105	26,335	11,535	12,075	10,735	10,615	10,230	13,465

Source: Field Study and hereafter refers to the same.

v_{15} = size of the family
v_{25} = percentage of area under commercial crops
v_{35} = commitment against loan
v_{61} = marketable surplus as percentage of total agricultural produce
v_{63} = percentage of produce consumed
v_{142} = total incomes
v_{22} = no. of acres under double crop
v_{31} = amount taken
v_{50} = total amount spent on shandy/marketing
v_{62} = marketed surplus as percentage of total agricultural produce
v_{64} = percentage of MFP consumed

The mean value for V_{15} shows that the family size is around six and the district-wise comparison shows that Adilabad has a relatively higher value than Khammam and Warangal. Contrary to the hypothesis that tribals have large sized families, in the sample the size of the family for nontribals is relatively higher than the tribals. The standard deviations do not show much variation, though it is slightly higher for Warangal district than the other two districts. V_{22} has the overall average of 0.423 acres and this value is the least for Khammam. Adilabad has the higher value of 0.710 acres. If tribal and non-tribal distinction is taken into account, the mean value for tribals is 0.313 acres, while it is 0.867 acres for non-tribals, reflecting the differences between them in land possession even in tribal areas. The standard deviations show that Adilabad has a relatively higher value and even non-tribals also have relatively higher values for standard deviations.

The mean value for V_{25} shows that 31.575 per cent of the total area is under commercial crops, but there are wide variations among the districts. Khammam district has a very low value of 5.25 per cent, while Adilabad has a very high value of 50.75 per cent and Warangal has the value of 38.75 per cent. But their standard deviations do not reflect these differences as they are 18.90, 22.60 and 26.45 respectively. A phenomenon here is that tribals have a relatively higher per cent of area under commercial crops than non-tribals in the study area as their mean values are 32.075 and 29.575 respectively. Even the standard deviations show that the tribals have a lesser value than non-tribals, the difference being marginal. V_{31} shows that the mean value for the total sample is Rs.4,890/-. Only Warangal district has a higher mean value which is above average for the whole sample. The tribal and non-tribal difference also shows that the amount taken by the non-tribals is three times more than the amount taken by the tribals. The comparison of standard deviations show that among the districts, it is relatively high for Khammam, and in the case of non-tribals, it is about four times to that of tribals, indicating a wider variation than in the case of tribals around their mean values. V_{35} shows the inter-linkages between the two parties, where one party is the lender of the loan and the other party is lessee. The mean value for the sample shows that the commitment is on the relatively high side and this phenomena is more evident in the case of Khammam district, which is considered as more developed than Adilabad. Likewise the non-tribals in the sample have a greater commitment against loan than the sample tribal households in the study area. Except for Adilabad and Warangal all other standard deviation values are nearer to each other.

The marketing charges and the amount spent on the shandy day is shown here as V_{50}. The mean value for the sample Rs.678.60. In the case of Warangal and Adilabad the mean values are relatively higher than Khammam. The value for non-tribals is also relatively higher than the value for tribals and the standard deviations for non-tribals is also higher than the standard deviations for the tribals indicating that more charges are being paid by non-tribals. A comparison of V_{61} and V_{62} shows that the percentage of produce as marketable surplus is relatively higher than the percentage of produce as marketed surplus for all the three districts uniformly. Both these values are relatively higher in Khammam than in Adilabad and differences also persist in the case of tribals and non-tribals. One observation is that the percentage of marketed surplus is higher than the percentage of marketable surplus in the case of tribals, indicating around 2.5 per cent of the produce as *'forced sales'* and the differences are not much in the case of Standard deviations. V_{63} has a mean value of 60.425 per cent and the district-wise comparison shows that Khammam has a relatively lower value of 53.75 per cent when compared to the value of 64.75 per cent for Adilabad. This finding confirms the generally held hypothesis that the tribals retain a greater percentage of output than non-tribals for self-consumption, and these values are 60.825 per cent and 58.75 per cent respectively. Among the standard deviations, Khammam has relatively higher values than the other two districts.

The mean value for V_{64} is 5.185 per cent indicating that the self-consumption of MFP is on the lower side when compared to V_{63}. The district-wise comparison of the percentages show wide variations as they are 2.4, 3.5 and 9.65 for Khammam, Warangal and Adilabad respectively. For Adilabad, the value of standard deviation is also relatively high as it is 8.265, while the other two values are 4.845 and 4.295 for Khammam and Warangal respectively. Thus, Adilabad has relatively higher self consumption of MFP as the items collected like Mohwa Flower, Mohwa Seed, Hill Brooms are more used for self-consumption than in the other districts.

Finally, the mean value for V_{142} is Rs.18,950/- and Adilabad is nearer to this value, whereas the value for Warangal is relatively on the high side with Rs.22,850/-, while it is relatively lower for Khammam with Rs.15,400/-. But Khammam has relatively higher value for Standard deviation than others.

The difference between tribals and non-tribals is considerable as non-tribals earn one and half times more to the incomes of the tribals. Standard deviations also show a difference as the standard deviations for non-tribals are relatively higher than the standard deviations for tribals.

By and large, in the literature on agricultural economics, marketable surplus is presumed to depend on the price of the product,but marketable surplus for all products as a percentage of total agricultural production depends on various other factors. In tribal areas, besides marketing the crops raised on their lands, they also market their minor forest produce. Therefore, as in the case of cross-sectional sample study, many variables related to households such as size of the family, total incomes of the households, amount taken as a loan, commitment against loan, total amount spent on marketing aspect will also be reckoned as important variables having either association with or influencing marketable surplus.

Among the other variables, percentage of area under commercial crops, number of acres under double crop, percentage of produce consumed and percentage of MFP consumed were also considered as relevant variables in respect of marketable surplus. The analysis is carried out through a correlation table, depicting bi-variate correlation co-efficients for all the variables and also through multiple regression analysis, where marketable surplus as percentage of total agricultural produce is considered as a dependent variable.

Table 2
Inter-correlations Between the Variables
(Total Sample Size: N = 300)

Variables	*Co-relation Co-efficients*									
	V_{15}	V_{22}	V_{25}	V_{31}	V_{35}	V_{50}	V_{61}	V_{62}	V_{63}	V_{64}
V_{15}	1.000	-0.036	0.076	0.105	-0.010	0.206	0.021	-0.008	0.082	-0.040
V_{22}	-0.036	1.000	0.180	0.077	-0.047	0.361	0.156	0.126	-0.095	-0.037
V_{25}	0.076	0.180	1.000	0.181	-0.279	0.356	0.087	0.088	0.129	0.267
V_{31}	0.105	0.077	0.181	1.000	0.213	0.350	0.337	0.284	-0.190	-0.145
V_{35}	-0.010	-0.047	-0.279	0.213	1.000	-0.032	0.102	0.066	-0.089	-0.176
V_{50}	0.206	0.361	0.356	0.350	-0.032	1.000	0.270	0.201	-0.101	0.009
V_{61}	0.021	0.156	0.087	0.337	0.102	0.270	1.000	–	-0.625	-0.200
V_{62}	-0.008	-0.126	0.088	0.284	0.066	0.201	–	1.000	0.584	-0.164
V_{63}	0.082	-0.095	0.129	-0.190	-0.089	-0.101	-0.625	0.584	1.000	0.172
V_{64}	-0.040	-0.037	0.267	-0.145	-0.176	0.009	-0.200	-0.164	0.172	1.000
V_{142}	0.461	0.249	0.280	0.514	0.042	0.644	0.367	-0.282	-0.195	-0.153

In the inter-correlation table (Table-2), it is evident that either in the case of negative correlation or positive correlation, the value is not higher than 0.70. While the table seeks to examine primarily correlation of various other variables with respect to marketable surplus and marketed surplus, other inter correlations among variables had also been considered. Marketable surplus as percentage of agricultural produce, V61 has a negative association with self-consumption and the value of correlation coefficient is 0.625. This confirms the inverse relationship between these two variables, which had also been attested by other studies. Likewise marketed surplus has also an inverse relationship, but its coefficient is -0.584. Among other variables it has a positive association with total incomes of the household, but the coefficient has a value of 0.367. The value is 0.282 for marketed surplus signifying that their association has not yet become strong. The amount taken as a loan has a positive association with the marketable as well as marketed surplus and its value is 0.337. Here also loan is not strongly associated with either marketable surplus or marketed surplus. All other variables have weak correlation coefficients with respect to marketable or marketed surplus. Among other inter-correlations, the correlation of total income of the household with other variables seems to be stronger than other intercorrelations.

Table 3
Inter-correlations Between the Variables
(Khammam Sub Sample: N = 100)

Variables	Co-rrelation Co-efficients									
	V_{15}	V_{22}	V_{25}	V_{31}	V_{35}	V_{50}	V_{61}	V_{62}	V_{63}	V_{64}
V_{15}	1.000	-0.068	-0.078	0.198	-0.032	0.150	0.037	0.053	0.006	-0.049
V_{22}	-0.068	1.000	0.442	-0.123	-0.213	0.016	0.058	0.078	0.003	-0.099
V_{25}	-0.078	0.442	1.000	0.245	-0.139	0.443	-0.006	0.008	0.090	-0.084
V_{31}	0.198	-0.123	0.245	1.000	0.129	0.622	0.297	0.257	-0.233	-0.149
V_{35}	-0.032	-0.213	-0.139	0.129	1.000	0.226	-0.021	-0.027	-0.037	0.276
V_{50}	0.150	0.016	0.443	0.622	0.226	1.000	0.084	0.081	-0.022	-0.094
V_{61}	0.037	0.058	-0.006	0.297	-0.021	0.084	1.000	–	0.759	-0.143
V_{62}	0.053	0.078	0.008	0.257	-0.027	0.081	–	1.000	-0.746	-0.121
V_{63}	0.006	0.003	0.090	-0.233	-0.037	-0.022	-0.759	-0.746	1.000	0.094
V_{64}	-0.049	-0.099	-0.084	-0.149	0.276	-0.094	-0.143	-0.121	0.094	1.000
V_{142}	0.451	0.025	0.278	0.705	0.020	0.560	0.332	0.282	-0.243	-0.133

Table - 3 shows the inter-correlations in Khammam region between the variables chosen for analysis. In this region marketable surplus (V_{61})and marketed surplus (V_{62}) display a similar tendency in their relationship with other variables except that marketable surplus and per cent of area under commercial crops, V_{25} are negatively associated but their relationship is weak, whereas it is positive and weak for marketed surplus. Among other variables both are highly negatively correlated with per cent of produce consumed (V_{63}) and these values are higher than the values for total sample size. Another variable which is positively associated with these variables, but has a lesser value in the vicinity of 0.3 for the correlation coefficient is the total incomes of the households, V_{142}. Like-wise both are positively correlated with amount taken, V_{31} but are negatively associated with almost zero value with respect to the variable V_{35}, commitment against the loan. Among other intercorrelations, V_{142} displays better correlation with other variables. Its correlation with V_{31} is the highest among positive values. Like-wise total amount spent on shandy, V_{50}, is highly correlated with amount taken, V_{31}, its value being 0.622. V_{50} is also correlated in a better manner with per cent of area under commercial crops. Thus marketing at shandy depends to a certain extent on the extent of irrigation facilities.

Table 4
Inter-correlations Between the Variables
(Warangal Sub Sample: N = 100)

Variables	*Co-rrelation Co-efficients*									
	V_{15}	V_{22}	V_{25}	V_{31}	V_{35}	V_{50}	V_{61}	V_{62}	V_{63}	V_{64}
V_{15}	1.000	0.090	0.097	0.027	0.041	0.292	0.009	-0.095	0.125	0.068
V_{22}	0.090	1.000	-0.022	0.168	-0.051	0.458	0.292	0.230	-0.304	-0.135
V_{25}	0.097	-0.022	1.000	0.129	0.114	0.075	0.150	0.122	0.011	0.239
V_{31}	0.027	0.168	0.129	1.000	0.318	0.143	0.274	0.190	-0.244	-0.100
V_{35}	0.041	-0.051	0.114	0.318	1.000	-0.274	0.009	-0.026	0.071	0.175
V_{50}	0.292	0.458	0.075	0.143	-0.274	1.000	0.574	0.454	-0.514	-0.076
V_{61}	0.009	0.292	0.150	0.274	0.009	0.574	1.000	–	-0.658	-0.036
V_{62}	-0.095	0.230	0.122	0.190	-0.026	0.454	–	1.000	-0.559	-0.004
V_{63}	0.125	-0.304	0.011	-0.244	0.071	-0.514	-0.658	-0.559	1.000	0.046
V_{64}	0.068	-0.135	0.239	-0.100	0.175	-0.076	-0.036	-0.004	0.046	1.000
V_{142}	0.553	0.412	0.132	0.319	0.015	0.764	0.405	0.263	-0.323	-0.065

Table-4 depicts the inter-correlations between the variables that had been used in the multiple regression analysis in Warangal district. The marketable surplus variable and marketed surplus variable in the case of Warangal sub-sample are negatively correlated with per cent of produce consumed, but the values are on the low side when compared with either total sample size or Khammam sub-sample. Here V_{142} has a positive association with V_{62} and V_{61} but the value for V_{61} is better associated with V_{142} than V_{62}, the inferene being that marketable surplus varies with total incomes of the households. Though many variables have positive associations, total amount spent on shandy has a better association with respect to marketable as well as marketed surplus than in the case of Khammam sub-sample. Here number of acres under double crop is better associated with V_{61} and V_{62} than per cent of area under commercial crops showing a contrasting result than that had been observed in Khammam. This could be due to growing of paddy as a double crop in Warangal instead of opting for commercial crops as in the case of Khammam, where irrigation facilities are available. Here also V_{35} has almost no correlation with either of the variable and V_{31} has a positive but weak association with the two variables. Among other variables,here also, V_{142} has a better association with all other variables, than any other variable. The expenses on shandy is negatively correlated having a value - 0.51 with the per cent of produce consumed (V_{63}). Thus, Warangal sub-sample displays a different kind of interrelationships in contrast to Khammam sub-sample.

Table 5
Inter-correlations Between the Variables
(Adilabad Sub Sample: N = 100)

Variables	*Co-rrelation Co-efficients*									
	V_{15}	V_{22}	V_{25}	V_{31}	V_{35}	V_{50}	V_{61}	V_{62}	V_{63}	V_{64}
V_{15}	1.000	-0.136	0.094	0.097	0.058	0.169	0.065	0.030	0.121	-0.223
V_{22}	-0.136	1.000	-0.001	0.214	0.282	0.473	0.312	0.247	-0.167	-0.158
V_{25}	0.094	-0.001	1.000	0.315	0.066	0.239	0.628	0.677	-0.041	-0.019
V_{31}	0.097	0.214	0.315	1.000	0.390	0.323	0.515	0.472	-0.101	-0.218
V_{35}	0.058	0.282	0.066	0.390	1.000	0.501	0.276	0.171	-0.049	-0.292
V_{50}	0.169	0.473	0.239	0.323	0.501	1.000	0.430	0.315	-0.044	-0.075
V_{61}	0.065	0.312	0.628	0.515	0.276	0.430	1.000	–	-0.316	-0.266
V_{62}	0.030	0.247	0.677	0.472	0.171	0.315	–	1.000	-0.236	-0.211
V_{63}	0.121	-0.167	-0.041	-0.101	-0.049	-0.044	-0.316	-0.236	1.000	0.205
V_{64}	-0.223	-0.158	-0.019	-0.218	-0.292	-0.075	-0.266	-0.211	0.205	1.000
V_{142}	0.455	0.335	0.310	0.427	0.419	0.541	0.495	0.398	-0.176	-0.314

Inter-correlations between the variables for Adilabad district are shown in Table-5. Adilabad sub-sample shows a another pattern of inter-correlations among variables. Here among all the variables intercorrelated with V_{61} and V_{62}, V_{25} that is per cent of area under commercial crops has the highest positive value for correlation coefficient for V_{61} as well as V_{62}. This finding is due to raising of cotton crop by many tribals in the study area. Here V_{31} has also a better relationship and V_{35} has a positive relationship instead of negative relationship as in the case of other sub-samples with respect to V_{61} and V_{62}. Even V_{50} has a positive and better relationship than observed in the case of other samples. But V_{63} has a weaker relationship though the value is negative as inthe case of other sub-samples.Thus,marketing consciousness seems to be high in this region than in the other two regions. Among other variables, V_{142} has a better association with all other variables including V_{61} and V_{62}, though the values are relatively low, when compared with values for V_{25}. Here V_{35}, commitment against loan has a positive relationship with amount spent on shandy and the value of correlation coefficient is 0.501. Like-wise family size and amount taken show a better positive relationships here. Here number of acres under double crop is better associated with total amount spent on shandy than in other sub-samples. Thus Adilabad sub-sample shows better inter-correlations among variables that influence marketing of products.

Table 6
Inter-correlations Between the Variables
(Tribals' Sub Sample: N = 240)

Variables	*Co-rrelation Co-efficients*									
	V_{15}	V_{22}	V_{25}	V_{31}	V_{35}	V_{50}	V_{61}	V_{62}	V_{63}	V_{64}
V_{15}	1.000	-0.061	0.112	0.114	-0.042	0.241	-0.001	-0.019	0.132	0.000
V_{22}	-0.061	1.000	0.110	0.130	-0.144	0.309	0.120	0.117	-0.062	0.059
V_{25}	0.112	0.110	1.000	0.304	-0.337	0.361	0.049	0.067	0.218	0.293
V_{31}	0.114	0.130	0.304	1.000	-0.009	0.320	0.282	0.230	-0.108	-0.046
V_{35}	-0.042	-0.144	-0.337	-0.009	1.000	-0.202	0.066	0.047	-0.096	-0.108
V_{50}	0.241	0.309	0.361	0.320	-0.202	1.000	0.215	0.154	-0.051	0.099
V_{61}	-0.001	0.120	0.049	0.282	0.066	0.215	1.000	-	0.577	-0.206
V_{62}	-0.019	0.117	0.067	0.230	0.047	0.154	-	1.000	-0.545	-0.176
V_{63}	0.132	-0.062	0.218	-0.108	-0.096	-0.051	-0.577	-0.545	1.000	0.214
V_{64}	0.000	0.059	0.293	-0.046	-0.108	0.099	-0.206	-0.176	0.214	1.000
V_{142}	0.478	0.170	0.344	0.462	-0.120	0.616	0.302	0.222	-0.123	-0.047

Inter-correlations between the variables for tribals are shown in Table-6. The intercorrelations among variables for the tribal sub-sample shows that V_{142} has a positive but weaker association with V_{61} and V_{62}. As in the case of other sub-samples they are associated in a better manner with V_{63} and the correlation coefficients are negative as in the case of other sub-samples signifying that per cent of produce consumed will have an inverse relationship with either marketed surplus or marketable surplus. In this sub-sample, number of acres under double crop has a better relationship than per cent of area under commercial crops, though both the correlation coefficients are very weak. Likewise V_{35}, that is commitment against loan, is almost uncorrelated with either V_{61} or V_{62}, while V_{31}, that is amount taken, has a better relationship with either of the two variables. Similarly amount spent on shandy, V_{50} has also a lesser value, when compared with some other sample values. Among other intercorrelations V_{142}, has a better association with other variables. Here family size and total income have a better value for correlation coefficient, while number of acres under double crop and amount spent on shandy also signify a better association than many other associations. In the case of this sub-sample the per cent of area under crop is positively related to amount taken, but negatively related to commitment against loan, though both the values cannot be considered to be on the high side.

Table 7
Inter-correlations Between the Variables
(Non-tribals' Sub Sample: N = 60)

Variables	*Co-rrelation Co-efficients*									
	V_{15}	V_{22}	V_{25}	V_{31}	V_{35}	V_{50}	V_{61}	V_{62}	V_{63}	V_{64}
V_{15}	1.000	-0.060	-0.050	0.033	-0.007	0.067	0.072	0.026	-0.089	-0.022
V_{22}	-0.060	1.000	0.380	-0.071	-0.001	0.398	0.217	0.158	-0.157	-0.064
V_{25}	-0.050	0.380	1.000	0.068	-0.056	0.394	0.238	0.179	-0.202	0.196
V_{31}	0.033	-0.071	0.068	1.000	0.477	0.349	0.481	0.462	-0.353	-0.131
V_{35}	-0.007	-0.001	-0.056	0.477	1.000	0.295	0.182	0.127	-0.043	-0.178
V_{50}	0.067	0.398	0.394	0.349	0.295	1.000	0.399	0.339	-0.222	-0.105
V_{61}	0.072	0.217	0.238	0.481	0.182	0.399	1.000	–	-0.789	-0.142
V_{62}	0.026	0.158	0.179	0.462	0.127	0.399	–	1.000	-0.731	-0.138
V_{63}	-0.089	-0.157	-0.202	-0.353	-0.043	-0.222	-0.789	0.731	1.000	-0.153
V_{64}	-0.022	-0.064	0.196	-0.131	-0.178	-0.105	-0.142	0.138	-0.153	1.000
V_{142}	0.390	0.262	0.203	0.513	0.237	0.681	0.556	0.508	-0.404	-0.062

Table-7 presents the correlation matrix for non-tribal sample households which gives the product moment correlation coefficient for each pair of variables. The nontribal sub-sample as a contrast to tribal sub-sample displays better relationships in the case of certain variables. For instance both V_{61} and V_{62} have better values for correlation coefficients with respect to V_{63}, than in the case of tribal sub-sample. Like-wise they have a better positive association with respect to V_{142} than what we observe in the case of tribal sub-sample. Both V_{61} and

V_{62} are also associated in a better manner in respect of V_{31} and V_{50}. The marketed surplus and marketable surplus are positively correlated to commitment against loan. Among other variables V_{142} as in the case of tribal sub-sample, displays association in respect of other variables, where these values are observed to be on the higher side than the values observed in the case of tribal sub-sample. Number of acres under double crop is associated with per cent of area under commercial crops, while per cent of area under commercial crops has a relatively high value for its correlation coefficient, 0.394 with respect to V_{50}, that is expenses on marketing. Here V_{31} has a better association with V_{35}, that is amount taken against a commitment and total amount spent on marketing has a higher value for its correlation coefficient with respect to V_{142}, that is total incomes of the households. Hence this sub-sample displays different characteristics when contrasted with tribal sub-sample.

Table-8 presents the results of multiple regression analysis for different sub-sample strata for marketable surplus (V_{61}) as regressand. For the total sample households the regressors like V_{63}, V_{142}, V_{31}, V_{25}, V_{64} have been found to be statistically significant and they do account for 48.1 per cent of variation in the dependent variable, V_{61}. For Khamm sub-sample, only two regressors – V_{69} and V_{142} have been found to be statistically significant and account for 60 percent of total variation in the regressand, V_{61}. For Warangal sub sample, V_{63} and V_{50} have been found to be statistically significant and they do account for 51 per cent of total variation in the endogenous variable, i.e., V_{61}. For Adilabad sub sample the explanatory variables like V_{25}, V_{31}, V_{63} and V_{22} have been found to be statistically significant and 62 per cent of total variation in the predictand is due to the above variables. For the sub-sample of tribals, explanatory variables like V_{63}, V_{142} and V_{31} have been found to be statistically significant and they do account for 40.4 per cent of total variation in the predictand. For the sub sample of non-tribals, the controlled variables like V_{63}, V_{64} and V_{142} have been found to be statistically significant and they do account for 74.4 percent of total variation in the response variable, i.e., V_{61}.

Table 8
Multiple Regression Analysis for Marketable Surplus (V_{61}) as Regressand

Explanatory Variables	*Total Sample*	*Khammam Sub-Sample*	*Warangal Sub-Sample*	*Adilabad Sub-Sample*	*Sub-Sample of Tribals*	*Sub-Sample of Non-Tribals*
Constant	3.2540	3.9235	3.0782	1.0192	3.0838	3.6715
	(0.1679)	(0.2629)	(0.3380)	(0.2257)	(0.1924)	(0.3346)
	[0.0000]	[0.0000]	[0.0000]	[0.0000]	[0.0000]	[0.0000]
V_{15}	NFSS	NFSS	NFSS	NFSS	NFSS	NFSS
V_{22}	NFSS	NFSS	NFSS	0.1306	NFSS	NFSS
				(0.0402)		
				[0.0016]		
V_{25}	0.1249	NFSS	NFSS	0.5537	NFSS	NFSS
	(0.0471)			(0.0699)		
	[0.0085]			[0.0000]		
V_{31}	0.0919	NFSS	NFSS	0.2309	0.1605	NFSS
	(0.0386)			(0.0502)	(0.0625)	
	[0.0179]			[0.0001]	[0.0010]	
V_{35}	NFSS	NFSS	NFSS	NFSS	NFSS	NFSS
V_{50}	NFSS	NFSS	0.1488	NFSS	NFSS	NFSS
			(0.0386)			
			[0.0002]			
V_{63}	-0.6304	-0.8706	-0.5319	-0.2140	-0.5921	-0.7961
	(0.0484)	(0.0800)	(0.0894)	(0.0599)	(0.0556)	(0.8283)
	[0.0000]	[0.0000]	[0.0000]	[0.0006]	[0.0000]	[0.0000]
V_{64}	-0.0831	NFSS	NFSS	NFSS	NFSS	-0.5869
	(0.0396)					(0.1708)
	[0.0370)					[0.0011]
V_{142}	0.0751	0.1033	NFSS	NFSS	0.0967	0.1180
	(0.0267)	(0.0435)			(0.0326)	(0.0353)
	[0.0053]	[0.0196]			[0.0034]	[0.0015)
R	0.6938	0.7739	0.7129	0.7854	0.6351	0.8624
R^2	0.4813	0.5990	0.5083	0.6169	0.4033	0.7438
$\bar{R}^2$	0.4725	0.5907	0.4982	0.6008	0.3958	0.7301
F-Value	54.5799	72.4504	50.1473	38.2557	53.1895	54.2078
	[0.0000]	[0.0000]	[0.0000]	[0.0000]	[0.0000]	[0.0000]

Note:
( ) First bracket indicates standard errors
[ ] Second bracket indicates the significance level and in the case of F-value figures in these brackets refer to the significance level
NFSS = Not Found Statistically Significant

All the F-values computed through ANOVA, are statistically significant. While the overall sample size has a value of 54.5799, the Khammam sub sample has the highest value among all the sub-samples indicating that the fitted regression line is a better fit for this sub-sample. The F-value is the lowest for the Adilabad sub-sample though it is a good fit. There is not much difference between tribal sub-sample and nontribal sub-sample as far as their F-values are concerned.

One finding, therefore, is that regional, tribal and non-tribal differences are more persistent in the study area. Percentage of produce consumed, V_{63} is a common variable for all the regression equations and it has been found to be statistically significant. V_{142} has been found to be statistically significant only for the total sample size, for Khammam sub-sample, for tribal and non-tribal sub-sample regression equations. V_{31} has been found to be statistically significant for the fitted regression equations of the total sample, for Adilabad district and for sub-sample equation of tribal households. V_{25} has been found to be statistically significant for the fitted regression equations of total sample and for Adilabad district. V_{64} has been found to be statistically significant only for the total sample and for the sub-sample of non-tribal households. V_{50} explanatory variable has been found to be statistically significant only for the sub-sample of Warangal district's fitted regression equation. And finally, V_{22} regressor has been found to be statistically significant only for the sub-sample of Adilabad district's fitted regression equation. Therefore, from the above analysis it is to be inferred that the marketable surplus depends on various factors and different regressors have been exerting influence on regressand in a variegated manner and it might be due to wide differences in the regions and also due to the stark differences among the tribal and non-tribal sample households in different regions of the study area.

The marketed surplus is also known as the households realised or actual produce that has been marketed or sold by the households. As it is less than theoretical surplus, it also depends on various factors in addition to the price of a product. It is generally held that the realised surplus depends on several other factors like the type of crops that have been grown by the households, size of the family, number of acres under double crop, percentage of area under commercial crops, amount taken, commitment against loan, total amount spent on shandy/marketing under different charges, percentage of produce consumed and percentage of minor forest produce consumed and also the total incomes of the households. Altogether six regression models have been estimated to the fitted data with explanatory variables such as V_{15}, V_{22}, V_{25}, V_{31}, V_{35}, V_{50}, V_{63}, V_{64} and V_{142} with respect to percentage of marketed surplus as total agricultural produce (V_{62}) as dependent variable. The final results were shown in Table -9.

For the total sample households, the regressors - V_{63}, V_{31} and V_{25} have been found to be statistically significant and do account for 39 per cent of variation in the dependent variable. For Khammam sub-sample, only one regressor, i.e., V_{63} has been found to be statistically significant and about 56 per cent of variation in the regressand is due to this variable. For Warangal sub-sample, the regressors V_{63} and V_{50} are statistically significant and they account for 35.1 per cent of variation in the predictand. For Adilabad sub-sample, the explanatory variables V_{25}, V_{31}, V_{22} and V_{63} have been found to be statistically significant and they account for 59.4 per cent of the total variation in the dependent variable. For the sub-sample of tribals, V_{63}, V_{25} and V_{31} have been found to be statistically significant and they do account for 35 per cent of the total variation in the endogenous variable. For the sub sample of non-tribals V_{63}, V_{64} and V_{142} have been found to be statistically significant and they account for 64 per cent of the total variation in the predictand.

The F-values are found to be statistically significant. The first three F-values for marketed surplus as regressand are higher than the F-values computed for marketable surplus as regressand. Thus for total sample size, Khammam sub-sample and Warangal sub-sample, these values are higher than the values for marketable surplus implying that these regressions are not only better fits than earlier fits but marketing of products can be explained through the variables included as explanatory variables. In the case of other three sub-samples the regression fits for marketable surplus as regressand have slightly higher values. In the case of marketed surplus as regressand, the tribal sub-sample has a higher F-value than non-tribal sub-sample, as the explanatory variables can explain in a better manner the marketing behaviour of tribals than non-tribals.

Table 9
Multiple Regression Analysis for Marketed Surplus (V_{62}) as Regressand

Explanatory Variables	*Total Sample*	*Khammam Sub-Sample*	*Warangal Sub-Sample*	*Adilabad Sub-Sample*	*Sub-Sample of Tribals*	*Sub-Sample of Non-Tribals*
Constant	3.1871 (0.1462) [0.0000]	4.0859 (0.1948) [0.0000]	2.8902 (0.3511) [0.0000]	0.8356 (0.2046) [0.0000]	3.1628 (0.1718) [0.0000]	3.2384 (0.3447) [0.0000]
V_{15}	NFSS	NFSS	NFSS	NFSS	NFSS	NFSS
V_{22}	NFSS	NFSS	NFSS	0.0921 (0.0364) [0.0131]	NFSS	NFSS
V_{25}	0.1253 (0.0435) [0.0043]	NFSS	NFSS	0.5485 (0.0634) [0.0000]	0.1429 (0.0535) [0.0081]	NFSS
V_{31}	0.1091 (0.0342) [0.0016]	NFSS	NFSS	0.1489 (0.0455) [0.0015]	0.1277 (0.0586) [0.0303]	NFSS
V_{35}	NFSS	NFSS	NFSS	NFSS	NFSS	NFSS
V_{50}	NFSS	NFSS	0.0954 (0.0401) [0.0193]	NFSS	NFSS	NFSS
V_{63}	-0.5835 (0.0477) [0.0000]	-0.8585 (0.0774) [0.0000]	-0.4314 (0.0929) [0.0000]	-0.1300 (0.0543) [0.0186]	-0.5861 (0.0569) [0.0000]	-0.6451 (0.0853) [0.0000]
V_{64}	NFSS	NFSS	NFSS	NFSS	NFSS	-0.4888 (0.1759) [0.0074]
V_{142}	NFSS	NFSS	NFSS	NFSS	NFSS	0.0905 (0.0364) [0.0161]
R	0.6241	0.7458	0.5922	0.7705	0.5886	0.7989
R^2	0.3895	0.5563	0.3507	0.5936	0.3465	0.6383
$\bar{R}^2$	0.3833	0.5518	0.3373	0.5765	0.3382	0.6189
F-Value	62.9538 [0.0000]	122.8883 [0.0000]	26.2043 [0.0000]	34.7013 [0.0000]	41.7217 [0.0000]	32.9511 [0.0000]

Note:
( ) First bracket indicates standard errors
[ ] Second bracket indicates the significance level and in the case of F-value figures in these brackets refer to the significance level
NFSS = Not found statistically significant

By examining the above points, one will be able to say that there had been lot of differences between the regions and between the tribal and non-tribal households. Only V_{63} regressor is common for all the regression equations. V_{31} regressor is found to be statistically significant only in the first, fourth and fifth regression equations, which refers to the total sample, for Adilabad and for tribal households respectively. V_{25} regressor is found to be statistically significant in the first, fourth and fifth regression equations, which refers to the total sample, Adilabad and tribal households respectively. V_{50} is statistically significant only in Warangal district. V_{22} is statistically significant only in Adilabad district. V_{64} and V_{142} are found to be statistically significant only in the case of non-tribal households. It is also to be noted that only V_{63}, V_{31} and V_{25} have been found to be statistically significant both in total sample and sub-sample of tribals' regression equations. Therefore, with respect to the marketed surplus, different regressors have been influencing dependent variable in a variegated manner and further there had been regional, and tribal and non-tribal differences as it is evident by the percentage contribution of total variation in the regressand. Therefore, it is to be stated that the marketed surplus depends on various factors. The regional differences might be due to the geo-climatic and economic conditions and the tribal and non-tribal differences may be due to their socio-economic conditions of the households.

SUMMING UP

The inferences drawn from the above analysis can be summarised as hereunder:

The average family size is about six and Adilabad has a relatively higher value than Khammam and Warangal. The family size among the non-tribal households is relatively higher than the tribal households in the study area and this is in contrast to the usually held hypothesis that the tribals have large sized families than the non-tribal households. The relatively high family size among the non-tribal households is due to the existence of the joint family system in the study area. If tribal and non-tribal distinction in the case of land possession is taken into account, the mean value for tribals is 0.313 acres, while it is 0.867 acres for non-tribals.

The tribal and non-tribal differences also show that the amount taken by the non-tribals is three times more than the amount taken by the tribals. The mean value for the inter-linkages between the two parties, where one party is the lender of the loan and the other party is lessee shows that the commitment is on the relatively high side and this phenomenon is more evident in the case of Khammam, which is considered as relatively developed than Adilabad. Like-wise, the sub-sample of non-tribals have a greater commitment against loan than the sub-sample of tribal households in the study area.

The study also points out that the percentage of produce as marketable surplus is relatively higher than the percentage of produce as marketed surplus for all the three districts uniformly. Both these values are relatively higher in Khammam than in Adilabad and the differences also persist in the case of tribals and non-tribals. One observation is that the percentage of marketed surplus is higher than the percentage of marketable surplus in the case of tribals, indicating around 2.5 per cent of the produce as *'forced sales'*. Regarding the total incomes of the sample households, the difference between tribals and non-tribals is considerable as non-tribals earn one and half times more to the incomes of the tribals.

In Khammam district V_{31} has a strong positive association (r=0.705) with V_{142} indicating a positive relationship between the total incomes of the sample households and the commitment against the loan. V_{62} has a strong negative association (r=0.746) with V_{63} revealing the inverse relationship between percentage of produce marketed and the percentage of produce consumed. A similar relationship had also been observed even in the case of percentage of marketable surplus and the percentage of produce consumed (r=-0.759). In Warangal district, V_{50} is positively associated with V_{142} (r=0.764) revealing a better linear relationship between the total incomes of the sample households and the amount spent on shandy/marketing.

Though some of the positive and negative associations have been observed in Adilabad district as in the case of Khammam and Warangal, the very high product moment correlation co-efficients in the range of 0.702 to 0.99 were not observed in this district. A similar tendency had also been observed in the case of total sample size even in the case of sub-sample of tribal households.

In the case of non-tribal sample households, V_{61} has a strong negative association with V_{63} (r=-0.789) revealing a perfect inverse relationship between the percentage of marketable surplus and the percentage of produce consumed. A similar relationship had also been observed even in the case of percentage of produce marketed and the percentage of produce consumed (r=-0.731).

As far as the marketable surplus is concerned one will be able to surmise that regional, tribal and non-tribal differences are more persistent in the study area. V_{63} regressor is common in all the regression equations that has been found to be statistically significant. V_{142} has been found to be statistically significant in the total sample size, in Khammam sub-sample, in tribal and non-tribal sub-sample regression equations. V_{31} regressor has been found to be statistically significant for the fitted regression equations of the total sample, for Adilabad district and for sub-sample equation of tribal households. V_{25} has been found to be statistically significant for the fitted regression equations of total sample and for Adilabad district. V_{64} stimulus had been found to be statistically significant only for the total sample and for the sub-sample of non-tribal households. V_{50} explanatory variable has been found to be statistically significant only for the sub-sample of Warangal district's fitted regression equation. And finally, V_{22} regressor has been found to be statistically significant only for the sub-sample of Adilabad district's fitted regression equation. Therefore, from the above analysis it is to be inferred that the marketable surplus depends on various factors and different regressors have been exerting their influence on regressand in a dissimilar manner and it might be due to the non-uniformities in the regions and also due to the stark differences among the tribal and non-tribal sample households in different regions of the study area.

By examining the inferences pertaining to the marketed surplus, one will be able to say that there had been a lot of difference between the regions and between the tribal and non-tribal households. Only 63 regressor is common for all the regression equations. V_{31} regressor is found to be statistically significant only in the first, fourth and fifth regression equations, that refer to the total sample, Adilabad and tribal sample households respectively. V_{25} regressor is statistically significant in the first, fourth and fifth regression equations, which refer to the total sample, Adilabad and tribal sample households respectively. V_{50} variable is statistically significant only in Warangal district. V_{22} is statistically significant in Adilabad district. V_{64} and V_{142} regressors are statistically significant only in the case of non-tribal households' regression equation. Further, it is also to be noted that only the regressors like V_{63}, V_{31} and V_{25} are statistically significant both in total sample and sub-sample of tribals' regression equations.

Therefore, with respect to the marketed surplus different regressors have been influencing in a variegated manner and further are regional, tribal and non-tribal differences as it is evidenced by their proportionate contribution to total variation of the regressand. Thus, it can be stated that marketed surplus depends on various factors in a cross-section sample. The regional differences might be due to the geo-climatic and economic conditions and the tribal and non-tribal differences may be due to the socio-economic conditions of the tribal households.

NOTES & REFERENCES

1. Natarajan, B., (1961), 'Problems of Marketable Suprlus in Indian Agriculture', *Indian Journal of Agricultural Economics,* Vol.XVI, No.1, January-March, p.55.
2. To mention a few it is referred to as an agricultural surplus, producers' surplus, market arrivals, market supply, economic

supply, marketable surplus, marketed supply and surplus for disposals, etc.

3. Bansil, P.C., (1961), 'Problems of Marketable Surplus', *Indian Journal of Agricultural Economics,* Vol.XVI, No.1, January-March, p.26.
4. Panchamukhi, P.R., (1975), "Rapporteur's Report on Mobilisation of Rural Surpluses for Development", *Indian Journal of Agricultural Economics,* Vol. XXX, No.3, p.68.

8

MARKETING PATTERN IN TRIBAL AREAS–MICRO LEVEL FINDINGS

In economics the concept of market is used in two senses: One, a comprehensive *'allocative'* sense, and the other in a narrow *'exchange'* sense. While the former includes the exchange aspect as well, the latter does not contain allocative function of market. The present study uses market in the narrow sense, as an exchange mechanism. Therefore, exchange as a specific institution, penetrates through social fabric of the society. But quite often the market is said to be *'perfect'* when each buyer has full knowledge, and the ability to use it, of what every seller is demanding, and each seller has full knowledge, and the ability to use it as he is aware of what buyer is offering. But in practice, this is a rare phenomenon to have perfect knowledge of the conditions of the market, as all the sellers and buyers involved in the act of marketing do not fit into the realistic and empirical situations. This is simply due to imperfections saddled with the practical situations, since the marketing principle emerged from the socio-economic device to facilitate the needs of people. Therefore, in a hierarchical system of marketing, people do not know each other personally, and when more and more kinds of goods appear, the market may be more fully a matter of an effort to sell at the highest price and buy at the lower; then buyer and seller alike *'shop around'*, and who the man is, who buys or sells does not matter as compared with the opportunity to get the best price[1]. Therefore the marketing of a product in the tribal areas requires an intimate knowledge of the habits, culture and the financial status of the people living in the area. Hence it had been observed that the functions of modern marketing have limited applicability in the tribal shandies[2].

Ever since the money economy has entered the tribal areas, marketing for the products grown in tribal areas had become a permanent problem for the tribals in the country. As it is a basic problem, there are no proper marketing facilities in scheduled areas to dispose-off their produce and no pucca roads to carry their produce into the adjoining markets situated in plain areas. In this nexus, tribals mostly depend on petty traders and businessmen to obtain their domestic requirements. Due to the absence of transport facilities, ignorance and innocence of tribals, the traders and business-cum-money-lenders exploit the tribal community. Thus, the ignorance of the tribal community on the prevailing market rates of domestic goods and their products also is one of the major causes of exploitation. In view of this, one of the basic tenets of the tribal economy is the existence of periodical markets and these markets reflect the marketing pattern in the tribal areas. In view of their periodicity, these markets are often known as weekly, fortnightly or bi-weekly markets.

Further in view of the severe exploitation that had been perpetrated by the petty traders and private merchants, the Government had taken up many remedial measures to extricate tribals from the clutches of moneylenders and petty traders; various State Governments had taken-up several protective measures among which the Girijan Co-operative Corporation[3] was one that had been established to eliminate the petty and private traders and merchants from tribals areas and also to render its services for the betterment of tribal households. Thus, the introduction of the Corporation served as a first step to introduce the tribal seller as well as buyer to a well knitted organised marketing institution that is supposed to dispense a fair deal both to the sellers and buyers. Despite, the presence of GCC tribals face many odds both from physical and social environment[4]. Thus, by looking at the overall marketing system in the tribal areas, one will be able to classify the tribal markets into the two broad categories: institutional and non-institutional marketing agencies[5].

In the the light of the above discussion, this Chapter had been devoted for examining the various facets involved in the indigenous marketing pattern in tribal areas based on the field findings and it also throws light on the *'modus operandi'* of the GCC. It also incorporates the sample tribal households' suggestions and views in regard to the strengthe-ning of the Corporation and to make it function effectively and efficiently.

A majority of households, 85 per cent, in the study area visited the shandies and a few of them (2 per cent) exclusively visited the regulated market and 11 per cent of them had visited both the shandy and the regulated market simultaneously. Those who had attended the shandy points had a specific purpose usually to purchase the goods offered for sale either by the traders in the shandy or by GCC's D.R. depots at the vicinity of shandy points and further the same buyers in the shandy sometimes also act as sellers to both the people as well as the GCC D.R. depots and the details had been depicted in Table - 1. Among the sample tribal households, 73.8 per cent had visited the shandy for both the activities of buying and selling and only 6.7 per cent of them visited the shandy exclusively for the sake of buying domestic requirements. But 9.6 per cent of the sample tribal households visit the shandy for buying the domestic requirements and for meeting the relations. It was not uncommon in the study area to find people visiting the shandy on social matters like settling the matrimonial alliances and their disputes as well. Among the non-tribal households, 95 per cent of them do not visit the shandy. The Table clearly shows the distinction between the sample tribal and non-tribal households. The distinction observed reflects the hiatus between tribal households and non-tribal households.

The number of visits in a month made by the sample tribal households to the shandy point had been shown in Table -2. Among those who visited shandy, 37.5 per cent of the sample

Table 1
Group-Wise Distribution of Sample Households As Per Purpose of Visiting the Shandy

	Purpose of the Visiting the Shandy										
Group Wise Category	*Not Applicable*	*1*	*2*	*3*	*4*	*5*	*6*	*7*	*8*	*9*	*Row Total*
Tribals	1 (0.4) (1.7)	16 (6.7) (88.9)	177 (73.8) (100.0)	2 (0.8) (66.7)	6 (2.5) (100.0)	1 (0.4) (100.0)	2 (0.8) (100.0)	23 (9.6) (100.0)	7 (2.9) (100.0)	5 (2.1) (100.0)	240 (80.0)
Non-tribals	57 (95.0) (98.3)	2 (3.3) (11.1)	–	1 (1.7) (33.3)	–	–	–	–	–	–	60 (20.0)
Column Total	58 (19.3)	18 (6.0)	177 (59.0)	3 (1.0)	6 (2.0)	1 (0.3)	2 (0.7)	23 (7.7)	7 (2.3)	5 (1.7)	300 (100.0)

Source: Field Study and hereafter refers to the same

Note: Figures in parentheses indicate row-wise and column-wise percentages and hereafter refers to the same.

1 = To buy domestic requirements and others,
2 = To sell produce and to buy domestic requirements and others
3 = To buy domestic requirements and others plus social matters,
4 = To buy domestic requirements and others plus meeting relations,
5 = To buy domestic requirements and others plus matrimonial alliances
6 = Two Plus social matters
7 = Two Plus meeting relations,
8 = Two plus matrimonial alliances,
9 = Two plus settlings disputes

tribal households were attending the shandy point once in a month, 26.3 per cent visited twice in a month and 17.9 per cent each in thrice and four times in a month visited to the shandy point. Thus, the frequency of visits in a month reflects one's own simultaneous dual role as a seller and as a buyer.

Table 2
Group-Wise Distribution of Sample Households As Per Frequency in a Month

	Frequency in a Month					
Group-wise Category	*Not Applicable*	*Once*	*Twice*	*Thrice*	*Four Times*	*Row Total*
Tribals	1(0.4) (1.6)	90(37.5) (100.0)	63(26.3) (100.0)	43(17.9) (100.0)	43(17.9) (100.0)	240 (80.0)
Non-Tribals	60(100.0) (98.4)	–	–	–	–	60 (20.00)
Column Total	61 (20.3)	90 (30.0)	63 (21.0)	43 (14.3)	43 (14.3)	300 (100.0)

Table-3 shows the distribution of sample households according to the products sold by them in the shandy points. It had been observed that a majority of the sample tribal households (79.2 per cent) visited the shandy points for selling the minor forest produce and others for selling agricultural produce, selling of cattle did not figure much and the mixed category accounts only for 7.9 per cent.

Table 3
Group-Wise Distribution of Sample Households As Per Produce Sold in the Shandy

	Produce Sold in the Shandy					
Group-wise Category	*Not Applicable*	*MFP*	*AP*	*Cattle*	*MFP & AP*	*Row Total*
Tribals	23(9.6) (27.7)	190(79.2) (100.0)	7(2.9) (100.0)	1(0.4) (100.0)	19(7.9) (100.0)	240 (80.0)
Non-Tribals	60(100.0) (72.3)	–	–	–	–	60 (20.00)
Column Total	83 (27.7)	190 (63.3)	7 (2.3)	1 (0.3)	19 (6.3)	300 (100.0)

MFP = Minor Forest Produce
AP = Agricultural Produce

Table 4

Group-Wise Distribution of Sample Households As Per Nature of Weights and Measures

	Nature of Weights & Measures used in Sale							
Group-Wise Category	*No Response*	*Standard Weights & Measures (1)*	*Country Measures (2)*	*Both (3)*	*Approxi-mation (4)*	*1 + 4*	*2 + 4*	*Row Total*
Tribals	2 (0.8) (3.5)	176 (73.3) (100.0)	2 (0.8) (66.7)	30 (12.5) (96.8)	26 (10.8) (92.9)	4 (1.7) (100.0)	–	240 (80.0)
Non-Tribals	55 (91.7) (96.5)	–	1 (1.7) (33.3)	1 (1.7) (3.2)	2 (3.3) (7.1)	–	1 (1.7) (100.0)	60 (20.0)
Column Total	57 (19.0)	176 (58.7)	3 (1.0)	31 (10.3)	28 (9.3)	4 (1.3)	1 (0.3)	300 (100.0)

Table-4 shows whether malpractices are there in the use of weights and measures. A variety of weights and measures were observed to be in use in the shandy points, besides from selling and buying through the approximation. Of the total tribal sample, a majority of them (73.3 per cent) reported that the standard weights and measures are being used and only 10.8 per cent reported the approximation[6].

Table 5
Region-Wise Distribution of Sample Households As Per Reasons for the Need of the Shandy Inspector

	Region			
Reasons for having the Shandy Inspector	*Khammam*	*Warangal*	*Adilabad*	*Row Total*
Not Applicable	44(40.4) (44.0)	29(26.6) (29.0)	36(33.0) (36.0)	109 (36.3)
Informs MFP Prices	10(66.7) (10.0)	3(20.0) (3.0)	2(13.3) (2.0)	15 (5.0)
Marketing of MFP	31(27.4) (31.0)	43(38.1) (43.0)	39(34.5) (39.0)	113 (37.7)
Both	15(23.8) (15.0)	25(39.7) (25.0)	23(36.5) (23.0)	63 (21.0)
Column Total	100 (33.3)	100 (33.3)	100 (33.3)	300 (100.0)

Chi-square	Value	DF	Significance
Pearson	15.3498	6	0.0177
Likelihood Ratio	15.0748	6	0.0196
Mantel-Haenszel Test for Linear Association	3.6653 r = 0.110	1	0.0555

Statistic	Value	Approximate Significance	
Phi	0.2261	0.0177	*1
Cramer's V	0.2261	0.0177	*1

* 1 Pearson Chi-square probability

The Shandy Inspectors, now called *Credit-Cum-Procurement Assistants* (CCPAs) are normally appointed by the GCC in the tribal areas to purchase the MFP from the tribal households at the shandy points and they are empowered to confiscate the MFP purchased by the private merchants at the shandy points. Questions regarding the role of Shandy Inspector to the sample tribal households had been posed. Out of 240, 93.75 per cent said that the Shandy Inspector is known to them. Of the total sample, 75 per cent, of the sample households reported that the Shandy Inspectors are needed. The remaining sample households were included in the 'Not Applicable' category, that had been presented in Table -5. The Table reveals that 37.7 per cent of them stated that the Shandy Inspector is needed for marketing of MFP alone, whereas 21 per cent said that he is needed for both in the case of marketing of MFP as well as in the case of information of MFP prices. The regional diversity is clearly visible from the Table. The chi-square and the other measures based on chi-square were found to be statistically significant.

Region-wise distribution of the sample households whether they received the help or not by the Shandy Inspector is shown in Table -6. Here 'Not Applicable' refers to non-tribal households. Among the sample tribal households, a majority of them reported that they did not receive any sort of help from the Shandy Inspector and this is relatively high in Khammam forming 41 per cent followed by Adilabad and Warangal accounting for 26 per cent and 22 per cent respectively.

Among the sample tribal households those who had received help from the Shandy Inspector fall under different heads like marketing of MFP, in the weighment of their product, securing reasonable prices, removing exploitation of non-tribals and other mixed categories. A relatively high per cent of the sample tribal households received the help in both the cases that is in the sale of MFP and securing reasonable prices. This percentage is relatively high in Adilabad followed by warangal and Khammam with 31, 29 and 17 respectively. Only 13.7 per cent of them received help from the Shandy Inspector in the case of marketing of MFP and it is relatively high in Adilabad followed by Warangal and Khammam. The other categories of help received by them do not have a significant proportion, while 30 per cent did not receive any help. Further, the Chi-square and other measures based on chi-square were found to be statistically significant at 10 per cent level.

Table 6
Region-wise Distribution of Sample Households As Per the Help of Shandy Inspector

	Region			
Particulars of the Help Received	*Khammam*	*Warangal*	*Adilabad*	*Row Total*
Not Applicable	20(33.3) (20.0)	20(33.3) (20.0)	20(33.3) (20.0)	60 (20.0)
Not helping(1)	41(46.1) (41.0)	22(24.7) (22.0)	26(29.2) (26.0)	89 (29.7)
Marketing of MFP (2)	12(29.3) (12.0)	14(34.1) (14.0)	15(36.6) (15.0)	41 (13.7)
Weighing(3)	–	1(33.3) (1.0)	2(66.7) (2.0)	3 (1.0)
Securing Reasonable Prices (4)	3(60.0) (3.0)	1(20.0) (1.0)	1(20.0) (1.0)	5 (1.7)
Two Plus Three	4(23.5) (4.0)	10(58.8) (10.0)	3(17.6) (3.0)	17 (5.7)
Two Plus Four	17(22.1) (17.0)	29(37.7) (29.0)	31(40.3) (31.0)	77 (25.7)
Four Plus Removing Exploitation of Nontribals	–	1(100.0) (1.0)	–	1 (0.3)
Two Plus Removing Exploitation of Non-tribals	2(100.0) (2.0) (0.7)	–	–	2
Three Plus four	1(20.0) (1.0)	2(40.0) (2.0)	2(40.0) (2.0)	5 (1.7)
Column Total	100 (33.3)	100 (33.3)	100 (33.3)	300 (100.0)

Chi-square	Value	DF	Significance
Pearson	26.6318	18	0.0861
Likelihood Ratio	27.6834	18	0.0670
Mantel-Haenszel Test for Linear Association	2.8899	1	0.0891
	r = 0.098		

Table 7
Region-Wise Distribution of Sample Households As Per Problems with the Shandy Inspector

	Region			
Problems	*Khammam*	*Warangal*	*Adilabad*	*Row Total*
Not Applicable/	87(35.4)	86(35.0)	73(29.7)	246
No Problems	(87.0)	(86.0)	(73.0)	(82.0)
Underweighment (1)	–	1(8.3)	11(91.7)	12
		(1.0)	(11.0)	(4.0)
Excessive	3(20.0)	3(20.0)	9(60.0)	15
Driages (2)	(3.0)	(3.0)	(9.0)	(5.0)
One Plus Two	5(31.3)	4(25.0)	7(43.8)	16
	(5.0)	(4.0)	(7.0)	(5.3)
One Plus Three	--	4(100.0)	--	4
		(4.0)		(1.3)
One Plus Under	1(100.0)	–	–	1
rate the quality	(1.0)			(0.3)
Two Plus Under	–	1(100.0)	–	1
rate the quality		(1.0)		(0.3)
One Plus Two Plus	4(80.0)	1(20.0)	–	5
Under rate the quality	(4.0)	(1.0)		(1.7)
Column	100	100	100	300
Total	(33.3)	(33.3)	(33.3)	(100.0)

Chi-square	Value	DF	Significance
Pearson	42.8628	14	0.0000
Likelihood Ratio	45.4755	14	0.0000
Mantel-Haenszel Test for Linear Association	0.2246	1	0.6355
	r = 0.027		

Statistic	Value	Approximate Significance
Phi	0.3779	0.0000 *1
Cramer's V	0.3779	0.0000 *1

* 1 Pearson Chi-square probability

In Table-7 the problems encountered by the sample households with the Shandy Inspector while marketing the MFP are presented. The Table reveals that only 18 per cent of the sample households are having problems such as underweighment, excess driages, underrating the quality while selling their produce to the Shandy Inspectors at the shandy

Table 8
Marketing Pattern of MFP of Sample Households Group-Wise and Region-Wise

Details of Marketing Pattern	*Region*								
	Khammam			*Warangal*			*Adilabad*		
	Tribal	*Non-tribal*	*Row Total*	*Tribal*	*Non-tribal*	*Row Total*	*Tribal*	*Non-tribal*	*Row Total*
Not Applicable	14 (41.2) (17.5)	20 (58.8) (100.0)	34 (34.0)	3 (13.0) (3.8)	20 (87.0) (100.0)	23 (23.0)	10 (33.3) (12.5)	20 (66.7) (100.0)	30 (30.0)
Only Institutional	41 (100.0) (51.3)	–	41 (41.0)	5 (100.0) (6.3)	–	5 (5.0)	3 (100.0) (3.8)	–	3 (3.0)
Institutional + Non Institutional	25 (100.0) (31.3)	–	25 (25.0)	72 (100.0) (90.0)	–	72 (72.0)	67 (100.0) (83.8)	–	67 (67.0)
Column Total	80 (80.0)	20 (20.0)	100 (100.0)	80 (80.0)	20 (20.0)	100 (100.0)	80 (80.0)	20 (20.0)	100 (100.0)

points. Among the three study areas, relatively a high percentage of such cases is apparent in Adilabad followed by Warangal and Khammam[7].

Further except the Mantel-Haenszel test for linear association, all the estimated tests and measures were found to be statistically significant.

Among the total sample households, only 213 households 71.0 per cent are engaged in the collection of MFP. The marketing pattern of MFP is shown in Table -8. It depicts both the channels of marketing simultaneously that are preferred mostly by tribals in Warangal and Adilabad districts, the percentages being 90.0 and 83.8 respectively. Exclusively institutional channel had been preferred by 51.3 per cent in Khammam.

Table 9
Region-Wise Distribution of Sample Households As Per Percentage of MFP Marketed

	Region			
Percentage of MFP Marketed	*Khammam*	*Warangal*	*Adilabad*	*Row Total*
Not Applicable	34(39.1) (34.0)	23(26.4) (23.0)	30(34.5) (30.0)	87 (29.0)
≤ 50	--	--	1(100.0) (1.0)	1 (0.3)
50 - 75	--	2(28.6) (2.0)	5(71.4) (5.0)	7 (2.3)
75 +	66(32.2) (66.0)	75(36.6) (75.0)	64(31.2) (64.0)	205 (68.4)
Column Total	100 (33.3)	100 (33.3)	100 (33.3)	300 (100.0)

Table -9 shows that most of the households had marketed more than 75 per cent of MFP collected. As the households consume Mohwa-flower, Mohwa-seed and wild-brooms as all other MFP items are marketed. This had been ascribed to the reason that they are unable to fetch high returns even if they are marketed due to the low procurement prices for these items. The tribal MFP collectors had obtained incomes, though not substantial, from the collection of MFP during the off-season and thus, it provides an off-farm employment to them[8].

Table -10 deals with MFP sold to the Corporation. In all the districts, among those tribals who sell less than 75 per cent of their MFP, the percentage is relatively high in Warangal district followed by Adilabad and Khammam. But among those who sell more than 75 per cent of their MFP to the Corporation, Warangal district has a higher percentage than Khammam which comes next and Adilabad has still lesser percentage.

It had been observed that almost all the sample tribal households are selling items like wild-brooms, honey and K.T. bundles in open market to get higher prices than the prices offered by the Corporation. So, there is a need to enhance the prices of these MFP items by the Corporation to induce the tribals to sell their produce to GCC only and the same opinion was also expressed by the sample tribal households.

Besides selling MFP to the Corporation, tribals also purchase some items for consumption purpose from the Corporation, though the expenditure on GCC items is not very high as depicted in Table -11. The expenditure is less than 10 per cent for 52.5 per cent of tribals in Warangal, while it is 23.5 per cent and 17.5 per cent in Khammam and Adilabad respectively. But the percentage of expenditure is more than 10 per cent for 82.5 per cent of the tribals in Adilabad followed by 76.3 per cent in Khammam. In Warangal this percentage is 47.5.

Table - 12 depicts the region-wise distribution of the sample households in the study area according to the percentage of agricultural produce sold to GCC and sold to other than GCC. It reveals that 9.7 per cent of the sample households sold their agricultural produce to the Corporation. Among the three districts in the study area, only 29 per cent of the sample tribal households of Adilabad district had sold their agricultural produce to the Corporation. Further, the chi-square and other measures based on the chi-square were found to be statistically significant.

Table 10

Distribution of Sample Households As Per Percentage MFP Sold to GCC Group-Wise and Region-Wise

Percentage of MFP sold to GCC	Region								
	Khammam			*Warangal*			*Adilabad*		
	Tribal	*Non-tribal*	*Row Total*	*Tribal*	*Non-tribal*	*Row Total*	*Tribal*	*Non-tribal*	*Row Total*
Not Applicable	15 (42.9) (18.8)	20 (57.1) (100.0)	35 (35.0)	4 (16.7) (5.0)	20 (83.3) (100.0)	24 (24.0)	17 (45.9) (21.3)	20 (54.1) (100.0)	37 (37.0)
≤ 75	27 (100.0) (33.8)	–	27 (27.0)	35 (100.0) (43.8)	–	35 (35.0)	32 (100.0) (40.0)	–	32 (32.0)
75 +	38 (100.0) (47.5)	–	38 (38.0)	41 (100.0) (51.2)	–	41 (41.0)	31 (100.0) (38.8)	–	31 (31.0)
Column Total	80 (80.0)	20 (20.0)	100 (100.0)	80 (80.0)	20 (20.0)	100 (100.0)	80 (80.0)	20 (20.0)	100 (100.0)

Table 11
Distribution of Sample Households As Per Percentage of Amount goes to GCC in Consumption Expenditure Group-Wise and Region-Wise

	Region								
Percentage of Amount goes to GCC	*Khammam*			*Warangal*			*Adilabad*		
	Tribal	*Non-tribal*	*Row Total*	*Tribal*	*Non-tribal*	*Row Total*	*Tribal*	*Non-tribal*	*Row Total*
Not Applicable	–	20 (100.0) (100.0)	20 (20.0)	–	20 (100.0) (100.0)	20 (20.0)	–	20 (100.0) (100.0)	20 (20.0)
≤ 10	19 (100.0) (23.8)	–	19 (19.0)	42 (100.0) (52.5)	–	42 (42.0)	14 (100.0) (17.5)	–	14 (14.0)
10 +	61 (100.0) (76.3)	–	61 (61.0)	38(100.0) (47.5)	–	38 (38.0)	66(100.0) (82.5)	–	66 (66.0)
Column Total	80 (80.0)	20 (20.0)	100 (100.0)	80 (80.0)	20 (20.0)	100 (100.0)	80 (80.0)	20 (20.0)	100 (100.0)

Table 12

Distribution of Sample Households As Per Percentage of Produce Sold to GCC and Other than GCC

	Percentage of agricultural produce sold to GCC				*Percentage of agricultural produce sold to other than GCC*			
	Region				*Region*			
	Khammam	*Warangal*	*Adilabad*	*Row total*	*Khammam*	*Warangal*	*Adilabad*	*Row total*
Not Applicable	100 (36.9) (100.0)	100 (36.9) (100.0)	71 (26.2) (71.0)	271 (90.3)	25 (52.1) (25.0)	5 (10.4) (5.0)	18 (37.5) (18.0)	48 (16.0)
≤ 25	–	–	3 (100.0) (3.0)	3 (1.0)	–	–	4 (100.0) (4.0)	4 (1.3)
25 - 50	–	–	9 (100.0) (9.0)	9 (3.0)	–	–	5 (100.0) (5.0)	5 (1.7)
50 – 75	–	–	5 (100.0) (5.0)	5 (1.7)	–	–	9 (100.0) (9.0)	9 (3.0)
75 +	–	–	12 (100.0) (12.0)	12 (4.0)	75 (32.21) (75.0)	95 (40.6) (95.0)	64 (27.4) (64.0)	234 (78.0)
Column Total	100 (33.3)	100 (33.3)	100 (33.3)	300 (100.0)	100 (33.3)	100 (33.3)	100 (33.3)	300 (100.0)

Chi-Square	Value	DF	Significance	Chi-Square	Value	DF	Significance
Pearson	64.2066	8	0.0000	Pearson	55.2083	8	0.0000
Likelihood Radio	70.1875	8	0.0000	Likelihood Radio	60.7302	8	0.0000
Mantel –Haenszel	41.7804	1	0.0000	Mantel –Haenszel	0.0201	1	0.8870
Test for Linear Association	r=0.373			Test for Linear Association	r=0.008		

Static	Value	Approximate Significance	Static	Value	Approximate Significance
phi	0.4626	0.0000 *1	phi	0.4289	0.0000 *1
Cramer's V	0.4626	0.0000 *1	Cramer's V	0.4289	0.0000 *1

* 1 Pearson Chi-Square Probability   * 1 Pearson Chi-Square Probability

As in regards the percentage of agricultural produce sold to other than the Corporation[9], 78 per cent of the total sample households had sold more than 75 per cent of their produce to others. Among the three districts, the entire category of households who marketed their produce both in Warangal and Khammam had sold more than 75 per cent of the produce to other than the Corporation, whereas in the case of Adilabad, 64 per cent had sold more than 75 per cent of their agricultural produce to others. This percentage in Khammam and Warangal are 95 and 75 respectively. Thus, among the districts, Warangal leads the entire study area followed by Khammam and Adilabad. Due to a variety of reasons like lower agricultural prices offered by the institution, intimacy with the private traders and village merchants and also due to the produce which is also not bought by GCC a majority of the sample households did not prefer to sell it to GCC.

Only 14 per cent of the sample households in Adilabad district had sold their produce to both the Corporation as well as to the private merchants and this is in the case of cotton in particular. Thus, it had been observed that the Corporation in Adilabad district entered into the domain of cotton procurement.

Except the Mantel-Haenszel test for linear association, the chi-square and other chi-square based measures were found to be statistically significant. But the weak correlation co-efficient (r=0.008) confirms the non-significance of linear association.

The reasons for selling the produce to the private merchants are shown in Table-13. The 'Not Applicable' category includes the sample households of both those who had not marketed their produce and those who had marketed their produce exclusively to the institutions - GCC and CCI. From the Table, it had been observed that among the 55 sample households who had sold their produce to the private merchants, 18.3 per cent of them reported that the produce had not been bought by the Corporation. This response had been the highest in Khammam constituting 36 per cent followed by Warangal and Adilabad forming 18 per cent and one per cent respectively. From the table, it had also been observed that 16.3 per cent of the sample households claimed that the price offered by the private merchants is higher than the price offered by the Corporation and it had been more prominent in Adilabad followed by Warangal and Khammam with 39 per cent, eight per cent and two per cent respectively.

Table 13
Reasons for Selling the Produce to Private Merchants Region-Wise

	Region			
Reasons	*Khammam*	*Warangal*	*Adilabad*	*Row Total*
Not Applicable	20(50.0) (20.0)	4(10.0) (4.0)	16(40.0) (16.0)	40 (13.3)
A	2(4.1) (2.0)	8(16.3) (8.0)	13(79.6) (39.0)	49 (16.3)
B	15(45.5) (15.0)	9(27.3) (9.0)	9(27.3) (9.0)	33 (11.0)
C	10(30.3) (10.0)	15(45.5) (15.0)	8(24.2) (8.0)	33 (11.0)
D	36(65.5) (36.0)	18(32.7) (18.0)	1(1.8) (1.0)	55 (18.3)
A + B	–	4(100.0) (4.0)	–	4 (1.3)
A + C	--	7(36.8) (7.0)	12(63.2) (12.0)	19 (6.3)
A + D	2(5.3) (2.0)	27(71.1) (27.0)	9(23.7) (9.0)	38 (12.7)
B + C	3(27.3) (3.0)	2(18.2) (2.0)	6(54.5) (6.0)	11 (3.7)
B + D	1(50.0) (1.0)	1(50.0) (1.0)	–	2 (0.7)
C + D	9(75.0) (9.0)	3(25.0) (3.0)	–	12 (4.0)
A + B + D	–	1(100.0) (1.0)	–	1 (0.3)
A + C + D	–	1(100.0) (1.0)	–	1 (0.3)
B + C + D	2(100.0) (2.0)	–	–	2 (0.7)
Column Total	100 (33.3)	100 (33.3)	100 (33.3)	300 (100.0)

Contd.

Chi-square	Value	DF	Significance
Pearson	164.2498	26	0.0000
Likelihood Ratio	185.4056	26	0.0000
Mantel-Haenszel Test for Linear Association	5.9262	1	0.0149
	r = 0.140		

A = Price is higher than GCC
B = Intimacy with private merchant
C = Gives loan and to pay off the loan
D = Produce not bought by GCC

Further, the Table reveals that 11 per cent said that either intimacy with private merchants or their offering of loans are the reasons to sell their produce to the private merchants. Besides, some other mixed reasons were also added factors for selling their produce to the private merchants instead to the Corporation. Therefore, from the above analysis, it can be said that the private traders and merchants played a predominent role in the domain of purchasing the agricultural produce from the sample households.

It had been observed that almost all the sample households had preferred to sell their produce soon after the harvesting and a similar tendency had also been observed in all the districts in the study area due to their eagerness to clear-off their loans and to meet their immediate consumption requirements. Further, all the estimated measures were found to be statistically significant.

The tribals sell their produce to the Corporation and inturn purchase their domestic requirements like rice, kerosene, matches, oils, controlled cloth, pulses, etc., from the D.R. depots of the GCC. Region-wise respondents' satisfaction rate over the quality of commodities supplied by the Corporation through its D.R. depots is shown in Table -14.

Here, the category of 'Not Applicable' includes the sample of non-tribal households as they were not concerned with the matter. Only 33.3 per cent of the sample households expressed their satisfaction over the quality of commodities supplied by the domestic requirement depots and this had been the highest in Warangal accounting for 43 per cent followed by Khammam and Adilabad with 33 per cent and 20 per cent. Of the sample households 27.3 per cent expressed their dissatisfaction over the quality of commodities that had been supplied by the Corporation through its depots and this had been relatively higher in Khammam followed by Adilabad and Warangal with 33 per cent, 32 per cent and 17 per cent respectively. Hence a certain section of the sample tribal households are sceptical about the quality of the commodities supplied by the Corporation. All the estimated tests were also found to be statistically significant except for the Mantel-Haenszel test for linear association.

Table 14
Respondents' Satisfaction Rate Over the Quality of Commodities Supplied by the Corporation (DR Depots)

Satisfaction Rate	*Region*			*Row Total*
	Khammam	*Warangal*	*Adilabad*	
Not Applicable	20(33.3) (20.0)	20(33.3) (20.0)	20(33.3) (20.0)	60 (20.0)
Highly Satisfied	4(100.0) (4.0)	--	--	4 (1.3)
Satisfied	33(34.4) (33.0)	43(44.8) (43.0)	20(20.8) (20.0)	96 (32.0)
Dissatisfied	25(39.1) (25.0)	12(18.8) (12.0)	27(42.2) (27.0)	64 (21.3)
Indifferent	10(17.2) (10.0)	20(34.5) (20.0)	28(48.3) (28.0)	58 (19.3)
Highly Dissatisfied	8(44.4) (8.0)	5(27.8) (5.0)	5(27.8) (5.0)	18 (6.0)
Column Total	100 (33.3)	100 (33.3)	100 (33.3)	300 (100.0)

Chi-square	Value	DF	Significance
Pearson	29.9778	10	0.0008
Likelihood Ratio	31.9756	10	0.0004
Mantel-Haenszel Test for Linear Association	2.5972 r = 0.093	1	0.1070

Contd.

Statistic	Value	Approximate Significance
Phi	0.3161	0.0008 *1
Cramer's V	0.3161	0.0008 *1

* 1 Pearson Chi-square probability

Table -15 shows their reasons for dissatisfaction, of all the reasons, low quality, higher prices, closure of store very often, heavy loss of time at the depots during the busy agricultural season and supplying the insufficient quantity are claimed to be the prime reasons[10]. By and large, despite its weakness in some of the areas, on the whole one can also draw the conclusion that here the line of activity of the Corporation is considered to be successful itself to cater to the needs of the tribals on behalf of the channel of civil supplies through its D.R. depots to some extent. Therefore, in light of this background, almost all the consumable articles are being supplied at the subsidised rates.

Table 15
Grievances of Sample Households with regard to the D.R. Depots Region-Wise

	Region			
Grievances	*Khammam*	*Warangal*	*Adilabad*	*Row Total*
Not Applicable	67(30.7) (67.0)	83(38.1) (83.0)	68(31.2) (68.0)	218 (72.7)
Low Quality(1)	2(66.7 (2.0)	–	1(33.3) (1.0)	3 (1.0)
Higher Prices(2)	1(33.3) (1.0)	–	2(66.7) (2.0)	3 (1.0)
Closure of Store(3)	2(25.0) (2.0)	–	6(75.0) (6.0)	8 (2.7)
Time loss is high (4)	1(50.0) (1.0)	–	1(50.0) (1.0)	2 (0.7)
Insufficient Quantity(5)	3(100.0) (3.0)	–	–	3 (1.0)
One Plus Two	2(100.0) (2.0)	–	–	2 (0.7)
One Plus Three	4(36.4) (4.0)	1(9.1) (1.0)	6((54.5) (6.0)	11 (3.7)

Contd.

	Region			
Grievances	*Khammam*	*Warangal*	*Adilabad*	*Row Total*
One Plus Four	2(40.0) (2.0)	1(20.0) (1.0)	2(40.0) (2.0)	5 (1.7)
Two Plus Three	1(16.7) (1.0)	3(50.0) (3.0)	2(33.3) (2.0)	6 (2.0)
Two Plus Four	1(50.0) (1.0)	–	1(50.0) (1.0)	2 (0.7)
Three Plus Four	8(34.8) (8.0)	8(34.8) (8.0)	7(30.4) (7.0)	23 (7.8)
Three Plus Five	1(100.0) (1.0)	–	–	1 (0.3)
One Plus Two Plus Three	3(37.5) (3.0)	2(25.0) (2.0)	3(37.5) (3.0)	8 (2.7)
One Plus Two Plus Five	1(100.0) (1.0)	–	–	1 (0.3)
One Plus Three Plus Four	1(33.3) (1.0)	1(33.3) (1.0)	1(33.3) (1.0)	3 (1.0)
Column Total	100 (33.3)	100 (33.3)	100 (33.3)	300 (100.0)

The sample tribal households who had visited the shandies had three primary sources from whom they would make their purchases. The sources are: Village Showkaries, Local Shandy points, and the D.R. depots of the GCC. Table - 8.16 explains about the region-wise sample tribal households' preference to buy their day-to-day purchases. The Table reveals that 20 per cent of the sample non-tribals were included in the 'Not Applicable' category as they were not concerned with this question. Among the sample households, 38.3 per cent of the tribals expressed their preference to make their purchases both from the domestic requirement depots of the Corporation plus the village showkaries and this had been the highest in Adilabad with 46 per cent followed by Khammam and Warangal with 42 per cent and 27 per cent respectively. But 30.7 per cent of the sample tribal households had preferred to make their purchases from the three main sources simultaneously. Warangal has relatively higher percentage followed by Adilabad and Khammam accounting for 39 per cent, 34 per cent and 19 per cent respectively. Only a six per cent of them preferred to make their purchases exclusively from the village showkaries. Thus, it had been observed that no household preferred to make their purchases exclusively from a single source and their purchases depend on the availability of the items from the said sources and inturn reflecting their needs from time to time. Further, all the estimated tests had also been found to be statistically significant.

Table 16
Region-Wise Sample Households' Preference to Buy Commodities

	Region			
Preferential Particulars	*Khammam*	*Warangal*	*Adilabad*	*Row Total*
Not Applicable	20(33.3) (20.0)	20(33.3) (20.0)	20(33.3) (20.0)	60 (20.0)
Village Showkari	15(83.3) (15.0)	3(16.7) (3.0)	–	18 (6.0)
GCC + Village Showkari	42(36.5) (42.0)	27(23.5) (27.0)	46(40.0) (46.0)	115 (38.3)
GCC + Local Shandy	2(28.6) (2.0)	5(71.4) (5.0)	–	7 (2.3)
Village Show-kari+ Local Shandy	2(25.0) (2.0)	6(75.0) (6.0)	–	8 (2.7)
GCC + Village Showkari + Local Shandy	19(20.7) (19.0)	39(42.4) (39.0)	34(37.0) (34.0)	92 (30.7)
Column Total	100 (33.3)	100 (33.3)	100 (33.3)	300 (100.0)

Chi-square	Value	DF	Significance
Pearson	45.7285	10	0.0000
Likelihood Ratio	52.0105	10	0.0000
Mantel-Haenszel Test for Linear Association	3.7516 r = 0.112	1	0.0527

Statistic	Value	Approximate Significance
Phi	0.3904	0.0000 *1
Cramer's V	0.3904	0.0000 *1

* 1 Pearson Chi-square probability

A variety of reasons are responsible for the sample tribal households to make their purchases from D.R. depots of the Corporation for meeting their requirements as shown in Table–17. Among all the reasons expressed by the households, 23.3 per cent of them had preferred to make their purchases from the D.R. depots owing to the better and graded price in the depots and this reason had attracted the highest response in Adilabad followed by Warangal with 39 per cent and 28 per cent, respectively. The other reasons among all the districts are variegated in nature.

Table-18 clearly reveals that of the total sample, 18 per cent of them had claimed both the availability of multiple variety of items and non-availability of item with GCC plus availability of credit as the reasons for purchasing the essential commodities from the village showkaries and the private merchants and this percentage had been the highest in Adilabad followed by Warangal and Khammam with 25 per cent, 18 per cent and 11 per cent respectively.

As a corollary to the above Tables -17 and 18, Table -19 portrays about the region-wise sample households' opinion about the rating of quality of commodities. The Table clearly shows that 33.3 per cent of the sample households opined that the commodities bought from the village showkari had a better quality when compared to the items bought from the D.R. Depots of the Corporation. Among the three districts, in Warangal a relatively higher per cent (32) of the households reported that the commodities bought from the D.R. Depots of the Corporation had the better quality rather than the commodities bought from the showkaries. A 25 per cent of sample households said that the commodities obtained from both the sources had the better quality and it had been the highest in Adilabad followed by Khammam and Warangal constituting 29 per cent, 28 per cent and 18 per cent respectively. Further, except the M-H test for linear association, chi-square, likelihood ratio chi-square, phi and Cramer's V were found to be statistically significant at 10 per cent level.

Table 17
Reasons for Buying from Corporation (D.R. Depots) Region-Wise

	Region			
Reasons	*Khammam*	*Warangal*	*Adilabad*	*Row Total*
Not Applicable	37(43.0) (37.0)	29(33.7) (29.0)	20(23.3) (20.0)	86 (28.7)
Assured Marketing(1)	4(28.6) (4.0)	3(21.4) (3.0)	7(50.0) (7.0)	14 (4.7)
Better/Graded Price(2)	3(4.3) (3.0)	28(40.0) (28.0)	39(55.7) (39.0)	70 (23.3)
Perfect weighing & Measurement(3)	7(63.6) (7.0)	1(9.1) (1.0)	3(27.3) (3.0)	11 (3.7)
Free from malpractices(4)	10(27.0) (10.0)	10(27.0) (10.0)	17(45.9) (17.0)	37 (12.3)
Better Quality(5)	1(100.0) (1.0)	–	–	1 (0.3)
One Plus Two	2(100,0) (2.0)	--	--	2 (0.7)
One Plus Three	–	1(100.0) (1.0)	–	1 (0.3)
One Plus Four	–	2(100.0) (2.0)	–	2 (0.7)
One Plus Five	–	1(100.0) (1.0)	–	1 (0.3)
Two Plus Three	3(30.0) (3.0)	5(50.0) (5.0)	2(20.0) (2.0)	10 (3.3)
Two Plus Four	5(22.7) (5.0)	10(45.5) (10.0)	7(31.8) (7.0)	22 (7.3)
Two Plus Five	1(10.0) (1.0)	5(50.0) (5.0)	4(40.0) (4.0)	10 (3.3)
Three Plus Four	14(82.4) (14.0)	2(11.8) (2.0)	1(5.9) (1.0)	17 (5.7)
Three Plus Five	2(50.0) (2.0)	2(50.0) (2.0)	–	4 (1.3)
Four Plus Five	6(100.0) (6.0)	–	–	6 (2.0)
Two Plus Three Plus Four	3(100.0) (3.0)	–	–	3 (1.0)
One Plus Two Plus Three+Four	2(66.7) (2.0)	1(33.3) (1.0)	–	3 (1.0)
Column Total	100 (33.3)	100 (33.3)	100 (33.3)	300 (100.0)

Table 18
Reasons for Buying from Village Showkari Region-Wise

	Region			
Reasons	*Khammam*	*Warangal*	*Adilabad*	*Row Total*
Not Applicable	22(32.8) (22.0)	25(37.3) (25.0)	20(29.9) (20.0)	67 (22.3)
Better Quality(1)	–	–	1(100.0) (1.0)	1 (0.3)
Two*(2)	7(46.7) (7.0)	5(33.3) (5.0)	3(20.0) (3.0)	15 (5.0)
Credit(3)	–	10(43.5) (10.0)	13(56.5) (13.0)	23 (7.7)
Long Acquaintance (4)	1(100.0) (1.0)	–	–	1 (0.3)
Time loss is high(5)	–	2(100.0) (2.0)	–	2 (0.7)
One Plus Two	7(70.0) (7.0)	3(30.0) (3.0)	--	10 (3.3)
One Plus Three	6(21.4) (6.0)	8(28.6) (8.0)	14(50.0) (14.0)	28 (9.3)
One Plus Four	4(100.0) (4.0)	--	--	4 (1.3)
Two Plus Three	11(20.4) (11.0)	18(33.3) (18.0)	25(46.3) (25.0)	54 (18.0)
Two Plus Five	1(4.3) (1.0)	10(43.5) (10.0)	12(52.2) (12.0)	23 (7.7)
Three Plus Four	6(30.0) (6.0)	7(35.0) (7.0)	7(35.0) (7.0)	20 (6.7)
Three Plus five	1(25.0) (1.0)	1(25.0) (1.0)	2(50.0) (2.0)	4 (1.3)
One Plus Two Plus three	13(61.9) (13.0)	7(33.3) (7.0)	1(4.8) (1.0)	21 (7.0)
One Plus Two Plus Four	3(100.0) (3.0)	–	–	3 (1.0)
One Plus Three Plus Four	8(88.9) (8.0)	–	1(11.1) (1.0)	9 (3.0)
One Plus Three Plus Five	2(66.7) (2.0)	–	1(33.3) (1.0)	3 (1.0)
Two Plus Three Plus Four	4(100.0) (4.0)	–	–	4 (1.3)
Two Plus Three Plus Five	–	2(100.0) (2.0)	–	2 (0.7)
One Plus Two Plus Three+Four	4(66.7) (4.0)	2(33.3) (2.0)	--	6 (2.0)
Column Total	100 (33.3)	100 (33.3)	100 (33.3)	300 (100.0)

* Availability of Multiple variety and the item is not available with GCC

Table 19
Region-Wise Sample Households' Opinion about the Rating of Better Quality of Commodities

	Region			
Satisfied about the Quality of the Product	*Khammam*	*Warangal*	*Adilabad*	*Row Total*
Not Applicable	20(33.3) (20.0)	20(33.3) (20.0)	20(33.3) (20.0)	60 (20.0)
GCC	17(26.2) (17.0)	32(49.2) (32.0)	16(24.6)) (16.0)	65 (21.7)
Village Showkari	35(35.0) (35.0)	30(30.0) (30.0)	35(35.0) (35.0)	100 (33.3)
Both	28(37.3) (28.0)	18(24.0) (18.0)	29(38.7) (29.0)	75 (25.0)
Column Total	100 (33.3)	100 (33.3)	100 (33.3)	300 (100.0)

Chi-square	Value	DF	Significance
Pearson	10.8753	6	0.0923
Likelihood Ratio	10.6460	6	0.0999
Mantel-Haenszel Test for Linear Association	0.0176 r = 0.007	1	0.8944

Statistic	Value	Approximate Significance
Phi	0.1903	0.0923 *1
Cramer's V	0.1903	0.0923 *1

* 1 Pearson Chi-square probability

Table-20 elicits the sample households' opinion as in regard to the getting of remunerative price when produce is (includes both MFP and agricultural produce) sold to formal and informal marketing agencies existing in the study area. It shows that 39 per cent expressed that they are not getting the remunerative price irrespective of the marketing agency to whom the produce was sold. Here Adilabad had the highest per cent of sample households followed by Khammam and Warangal with 46 per cent, 41 per cent and 30 per cent respectively. Of the sample households, 34.7 per cent opined that they had obtained the remunerative price when their produce was sold to the mixed category of GCC plus regulated market and here Warangal had a higher percentage over the other two districts with 52 per cent, where as Khammam and Adilabad have 31 per cent and 21 per cent respectively. But the regulated market alone accounts only for 7.3 per cent of the total sample households, though Adilabad had 17 per cent. Hence the contribution of regulated market for getting the remunerative price in Warangal and Khammam was observed to be marginal.

Table 20
Region-Wise Sample Households' Opinion about getting Remunerative Price when Produce Sold to the Agency

	Region			
Agency Particulars	*Khammam*	*Warangal*	*Adilabad*	*Row Total*
Not Getting(1)	41(35.0) (41.0)	30(25.6) (30.0)	46(39.3) (46.0)	117 (39.0)
GCC(2)	18(42.9) (18.0)	13(31.0) (13.0)	11(26.2)) (11.0)	42 (14.0)
Regulated Market(3)	1(4.5) (1.0)	4(18.2) (4.0)	17(77.3) (17.0)	22 (7.3)
Two Plus Three	31(29.8) (31.0)	52(50.0) (52.0)	21(20.2) (21.0)	104 (34.7)
Two Plus Three Plus Showkari	1(33.3) (1.0)	--	2(66.7) (2.0)	3 (1.0)
Three Plus Showkari+Shandy	2(100.0) (2.0)	--	--	2 (0.7)
Two Plus Three Plus Showkari+ Shandy	2(100.0) (1.0)	--	--	2 (0.7)
Two Plus Three Plus Showari+ Shandy+Others	4(50.0) (4.0)	1(12.5) (1.0)	3(37.5) (3.0)	8 (2.7)
Column Total	100 (33.3)	100 (33.3)	100 (33.3)	300 (100.0)

Chi-square	Value	DF	Significance
Pearson	51.2126	14	0.0000
Likelihood Ratio	52.8487	14	0.0000
Mantel-Haenszel Test for Linear Association	1.8713 r = 0.079	1	0.1713

Contd.

Statistic	Value	Approximate Significance
Phi	0.4131	0.0000 *1
Cramer's V	0.4131	0.0000 *1

* 1 Pearson Chi-square probability

From the above analysis it can be inferred that 61 per cent of the sample households had expressed their satisfaction over the price paid by the different marketing agencies in the study area and this had been in view of the obtained prices for both MFP and AP. But, while segregating the prices of MFP and AP, the above finding is contrary to the observation[11] made by the researcher during his field visit.

Table 21
Region-Wise Distribution of Sample Households As Per Middle Men Charges Incurred While Selling the Produce

	Region			
Details of Charges Incurred	*Khammam*	*Warangal*	*Adilabad*	*Row Total*
Not Applicable	15(48.4)	2(6.5)	14(45.2)	31
	(15.0)	(2.0)	(14.0)	(10.3)
Commission Charges	3(14.3)	18(85.7)	--	21
	(3.0)	(18.0)		(7.0)
Others	57(85.1)	4(6.0)	6(9.0)	67
	(57.0)	(4.0)	(6.0)	(22.3)
Loading & Unloading	2(100.0)	--	--	2
+Commission Charges	(2.0)			(0.7)
Commission Charges	23(17.0)	68(50.4)	44(32.6)	135
+Others	(23.0)	(68.0)	(44.0)	(45.0)
Commission Charges	--	4(10.3)	35(89.7)	39
+Charities in Market+Others		(4.0)	(35.0)	(13.0)
Commission Charges	--	4(80.0)	1(20.0)	5
+Charities in Market		(4.0)	(1.0)	(1.7)
Column	100	100	100	300
Total	(33.3)	(33.3)	(33.3)	(100.0)

Chi-square	Value	DF	Significance
Pearson	205.7012	12	0.0000
Likelihood Ratio	212.8866	12	0.0000
Mantel-Haenszel Test for Linear Association	27.8690	1	0.0000
	r = 0.305		

Contd.

Statistic	Value	Approximate Significance
Phi	0.8280	0.0000 *1
Cramer's V	0.8280	0.0000 *1

* 1 Pearson Chi-square probability

Table -21 depicts the region-wise distribution of the sample households as per the middlemen charges incurred while selling the agricultural produce by the households. The Table reveals that 89.7 per cent of the households had faced various problems while selling their agricultural produce to the informal marketing agencies in the study area. Among the three study areas in Warangal almost all the households (98 per cent) paid various charges involved in marketing at various stages while these percentages for Adilabad and Khammam are 86 and 85 respectively. Further, the data reveals that a majority of the sample had to incur the commission charges and others[12] and it had been the highest in Warangal with 68 per cent followed by Adilabad and Khammam with 44 per cent and 23 per cent respectively. A majority of the sample households, 57 per cent had to incur other charges involved in the marketing of the agricultural produce. In Adilabad district 35 per cent of the households had to incur the charges of the mixed category, i.e., commission charges plus charities in market plus others. All the estimated tests had also been found to be statistically significant.

The region-wise sample households' problems while purchasing and selling the produce at the marketing place in general (either at the shandies or regulated market yards in the study area) had been shown in Table -22.

All the problems of the sample households had been broadly categorized into the three basic problems. They are: administrative problems, trade related problems, and the socio-lingual-cultural problems. The set of problems like incorrect weights and measures, corruption, absence of shelters, inadequate drinking water facilities and the inadequate market area were included under the *'Administrative Problems'*. Another set of problems like lower prices, cheating or illegal activities of middlemen, limited variety and the inferior quality of goods were included in the second category of *'Trade related problems'*; and finally another set of problems like transportation, language, illiteracy, and inadequate communication facilities were included under the *'Socio-lingual-cultural problems'*.

Table 22
Region-Wise Sample Households' Problems While Purchasing and Selling the Produce

	Region			
Problems	*Khammam*	*Warangal*	*Adilabad*	*Row Total*
Not Applicable	13(44.8) (13.0)	6(20.7) (6.0)	10(34.5) (10.0)	29 (9.7)
Administrative Problems(1)	1(20.0) (1.0)	1(20.0) (1.0)	3(60.0) (3.0)	5 (1.7)
Trade Related Problems(2)	9(20.5) (9.0)	11(25.0) (11.0)	24(54.5) (24.0)	44 (14.7)
Socio-lingual cultural problems(3)	1(33.3) (1.0)	–	2(66.7) (2.0)	3 (1.0)
One Plus Two	22(35.5) (22.0)	14(22.6) (14.0)	26(41.9) (26.0)	62 (20.7)
One Plus Three	4(57.1) (4.0)	3(42.9) (3.0)	–	7 (2.3)
Two Plus three	12(30.0) (12.0)	14(35.0) (14.0)	14(35.0) (14.0)	40 (13.3)
One Plus Two Plus Three	38(34.5) (38.0)	51(46.4) (51.0)	21(19.1) (21.0)	110 (36.7)
Column Total	100 (33.3)	100 (33.3)	100 (33.3)	300 (100.0)

Chi-square	Value	DF	Significance
Pearson	35.0698	14	0.0014
Likelihood Ratio	38.2023	14	0.0004
Mantel-Haenszel Test for Linear Association	5.0255 r = 0.129	1	0.0249

Statistic	Value	Approximate Significance
Phi	0.3419	0.0014 *1
Cramer's V	0.3419	0.0014 *1

* 1 Pearson Chi-square probability

From the Table, it had been observed that 36.7 per cent of the households reported that they had all the three problems followed by the mixed category of administrative problems plus trade related problems and exclusively trade related problems with 20.7 per cent and 14.7 per cent respectively. Further even among the three study areas, Warangal had the highest (51) per cent of the sample households who had expressed that they had suffered all the three problems followed by Khammam and Adilabad with 38 per cent and 21 per cent respectively. In Adilabad, a relatively high (26) per cent of the households opined that they had both the problems (administrative problems plus trade related problems) simultaneously followed by Khammam and Warangal with 22 per cent and 14 per cent respectively. Of the sample households 24 per cent in Adilabad reported that they had only the trade related problems followed by Warangal and Khammam with 11 per cent and nine per cent respectively. The chi-square and other chi-square based measures and other related statistics were also found to be statistically significant.

In marketing a product, price information has a crucial role. The source of information in tribal villages is often the village merchant as shown in Table-23. Sometimes, others[13] like big farmers, shandy inspectors also provide information. The source of information about prices is the merchant prominently for the tribals in Khammam district as 71.3 per cent of the tribals receive information from him. In other districts this percentage is low for tribals as well as non-tribals, though the percentage is as low as five per cent for non-tribals in Adilabad district. *'Others'* providing information are an important source for tribals as well as non-tribals in Warangal and Adilabad, though percentage for non-tribals is relatively higher at Adilabad than in other districts, while for tribals it is relatively higher at Warangal than others. The Chi-square values for pearson and likelihood are statistically significant even at one per cent level in Khammam, while they are significant at 10 per cent level in Adilabad. This observation holds good in the same manner in the case of Phi and Cramer's V statistic in the two districts.

Table 23
Sources of Information about the Prices Group-Wise and Region-Wise

Sources of Information	*Region*								
	Khammam			*Warangal*			*Adilabad*		
	Tribal	*Non-tribal*	*Row Total*	*Tribal*	*Non-tribal*	*Row Total*	*Tribal*	*Non-tribal*	*Row Total*
Not Applicable	–	4 (100.0) (20.0)	4 (4.0)	–	–	–	2 (50.0) (2.5)	2 (50.0) (10.0)	4 (4.0)
Merchant/Village Merchant	57 (90.5) (71.3)	6 (9.5) (30.0)	63 (63.0)	12 (70.6) (15.0)	5 (29.4) (25.0)	17 (17.0)	18 (94.7) (22.5)	1 (5.3) (5.0)	19 (19.0)
Others	23 (69.7) (28.8)	10 (30.3) (50.0)	33 (33.0)	68 (81.9) (85.0)	15 (18.1) (75.0)	83 (83.0)	60 (77.9) (75.0)	17 (22.1)(85.0)	77 (77.0)
Column Total	80 (80.0)	20 (20.0)	100 (100.0)	80 (80.0)	20 (20.0)	100 (100.0)	80 (80.0)	20 (20.0)	100 (100.0)

Khammam

Chi-Square	Value	DF	Significance
Pearson	22.5108	2	0.0000
Likelihood Ratio	19.9694	2	0.0000
M-H Test for Linear Association	0.0086	1	0.9258

r = 0.009

Statistic	Value	Approximate significance	
Phi	0.4744	0.0000	*1
Cramer's V	0.4744	0.0000	*1

*1 Pearson Chi-Square Probability

Warangal

Chi-Square	Value	DF	Signifi-cance
Pearson	1.1339	1	0.2869
Likelihood Ratio	1.0503	1	0.3054
M-H Test for Linear Association	1.1226	1	0.2893

r = 0.106

Statistic	Value	Approximate significance	
Phi	0.1064	0.2869	*1
Cramer's V	0.1064	0.2869	*1

*1 Pearson Chi-Square Probability

Adilabad

Chi-Square	Value	DF	Signifi-cance
Pearson	5.0367	2	0.0805
Likelihood Ratio	5.4045	2	0.0670
M-H Test for Linear Association	0.3573	1	0.8500

r = 0.018

Statistic	Value	Approximate significance	
Phi	0.2244	0.0805	*1
Cramer's V	0.2244	0.0805	*1

*1 Pearson Chi-Square Probability

Table-24 deals with the region-wise sample households' knowledge about the type of concessions and other services rendered by GCC. Here, it is to be noted that the sample of non-tribal households and the sample of tribal households who were ignorant of the services of the Corporation are included in the 'Not Applicable' category. The Table reveals that 76.7 per cent of the sample tribal households had the knowledge about almost all the types of concessions and services provided by the Corporation. The region-wise breakup shows that this per cent had been the highest in Adilabad followed by Warangal and Khammam with 80 per cent, 79 per cent and 71 per cent respectively. Therefore, atleast it can be said that the tribal households had the awareness of the services provided by the Corporation even if they are not availing them to the extent possible due to the variety of reasons.

Table 24
Sample Households' Knowledge About the Type of Concessions and Other Services Rendered by the GCC

	Region			
Details of Concessions & Services	*Khammam*	*Warangal*	*Adilabad*	*Row Total*
Not Applicable	26(38.8) (26.0)	21(31.3) (21.0)	20(29.9) (20.0)	67 (22.3)
One*	2(100.0) (2.0)	–	–	2 (0.7)
Two**	1(100.0) (1.0)	–	–	1 (0.3)
Three***	71(30.9) (71.0)	79(34.3) (79.0)	80(34.8) (80.0)	230 (76.7)
Column Total	100 (33.3)	100 (33.3)	100 (33.3)	300 (100.0)

* Tools, implements and consumption loans for Gum pickers

** One Plus Supply of D.R.s.

*** One Plus Crop Loans & Supply of D.R.s.

Of the total sample households in the study area as Table-25 shows only 26.7 per cent of the sample tribal households had received the services provided by the

Corporation and this had been the highest in Adilabad with 42 per cent followed by Khammam and Warangal with 29 per cent and nine per cent respectively. The remaining 51 per cent did not receive the Corporation's services. Of these the highest had been in Warangal with 70 per cent followed by Khammam and Adilabad with 45 and 38 per cent respectively. Hence the activities of the Corporation were more intensive in Adilabad than in the two other districts in the study area, though the Corporation had not rendered its services to all the needy and poor tribal households in the study area.

Table 25
Whether Households' Received or Not Received the Services Provided by GCC

	Region			
Details	*Khammam*	*Warangal*	*Adilabad*	*Row Total*
Not Applicable	26(38.8)	21(31.3)	20(29.9)	67
	(26.0)	(21.0)	(20.0)	(22.3)
Received	29(36.3)	9(11.3)	42(52.5)	80
	(29.0)	(9.0)	(42.0)	(26.7)
Not Received	45(29.4)	70(45.8)	38(24.8)	153
	(45.0)	(70.0)	(38.0)	(51.0)
Column	100	100	100	300
Total	(33.3)	(33.3)	(33.3)	(100.0)

As a corollary to the above table, Table -26 deals with the region-wise list of the Corporation's services received by the sample households. Among the sample tribal households those who had received the services, 15 per cent had received most of its services, where in Adilabad had the preponderant position, but it is relatively a lesser (3%) per cent in Warangal. Therefore, from the above analysis it can be inferred that the Corporation had not been rendering its services to the full satisfaction of tribal households. During the field investigation, it had been observed that the organisational set-up of the Corporation is devoid of the tribals' participation and this sort of practice in the Corporation had created a debilitating climate in the functioning of the Corporation.

The chi-square and other chi-square based measures were found to be statistically significant, which signifies the inter-dependability of the variables in the Table and a similar finding had also been confirmed by the correlation co-efficient (r=0.438).

Table 26
List of the GCC'S Services Received By the Sample Households

	Region			
Details	*Khammam*	*Warangal*	*Adilabad*	*Row Total*
Not Applicable	71(32.3) (71.0)	91(41.4) (91.0)	58(26.3) (58.0)	220 (73.3)
One*(1)	27(100.0) (27.0)	--	--	27 (9.0)
Crop Loan(2)	2(28.6) (2.0)	5(71.4) (5.0)	--	7 (2.3)
Supply of D.Rs (3)	--	1(100.0) (1.0)	--	1 (0.3)
One Plus Two Plus Three	-- (3.0)	3(6.7) (42.0)	42(93.3)	45 (15.0)
Column Total	100 (33.3)	100 (33.3)	100 (33.3)	300 (100.0)

Chi-square	Value	DF	Significance
Pearson	141.6285	8	0.0000
Likelihood Ratio	152.7467	8	0.0000
Mantel-Haenszel Test for Linear Association	57.4522	1	0.0000
	r = 0.438		

Statistic	Value	Approximate Significance
Phi	0.6870	0.0000 *1
Cramer's V	0.6870	0.0000 *1

* 1 Pearson Chi-square probability

* Tools, implements and consumption loans for Gum pickers

A variety of reasons had been attributed by the sample households for not receiving the concessions and the services of the Corporation in general and the loans in particular as shown in Table -27. The sample tribal households who had expressed the reasons for not receiving the services were either that they were not in need of any assistance or lack of time due to other occupations or because of old age or time loss is high at the Corporation or lack of land or prevalence of single window system, and cumbersome procedures. Among all these reasons, 15.3% of the tribal households expressed the prevalence of single window system as the prime reason and its percentage had been the highest in Warangal with 34 per cent followed by six per cent each in Adilabad and Khammam. By and large, the reasons for not receiving the services of the Corporation are variegated in nature. Further, the pearson chi-square, likelihood ratio chi-square, phi and Carmer's V were found to be statistically significant except for Mantel-Haenszel test for linear association.

Table 27
Reasons for not Receiving the GCC'S Services by the Sample Households Region-Wise

	Region			
Reasons	*Khammam*	*Warangal*	*Adilabad*	*Row Total*
Not Applicable	55(37.4) (55.0)	30(20.4) (30.0)	62(42.2) (62.0)	147 (49.0)
Not in Need of Any assistance(1)	4(22.2) (4.0)	9(50.0) (9.0)	5(27.8) (5.0)	18 (6.0)
Lack of Time Due to Other Occupations(2)	22(66.7) (22.0)	8(24.2) (8.0)	3(9.1) (3.0)	33 (11.0)
Because of Old Age(3)	1(100.0) (1.0)	–	–	1 (0.3)
Time Loss is High(4)	1(4.0) (1.0)	10(40.0) (10.0)	14(56.0) (14.0)	25 (8.3)
Lack of Land(5)	1(12.5) (1.0)	2(25.0) (2.0)	5(62.5) (5.0)	8 (2.7)
Prevalence of Single Window System(6)	6(13.0 (6.0)	34(73.9) (34.0)	6(13.0) (6.0)	46 (15.3)
Cumbersome Procedures(7)	1(16.7) (1.0)	–	5(83.3) (5.0)	6 (2.0)
Two Plus Six	9(56.3) (9.0)	7(43.7) (7.0)	–	16 (5.3)
Column Total	100 (33.3)	100 (33.3)	100 (33.3)	300 (100.0)

Chi-square	Value	DF	Significance
Pearson	94.1738	16	0.0000
Likelihood Ratio	98.3537	16	0.0000
Mantel-Haenszel Test for Linear Association	0.0106	1	0.9179

r = 0.005

As shown in Table -28, of the total sample households in the study area, 64.7 offered suggestions and the remaining 35.3 per cent of the total sample households did not offer any suggestion for the better functioning of the existing marketing system. It reveals that the sample households who had offered their suggestions had been relatively higher in Adilabad followed by Warangal and Khammam, the respective percentages being 68, 67 and 59. The sample households had suggested certain steps to be taken for the effective functioning and strengthening of the prevalent marketing system in the tribal areas. They are: separate educational schemes had to be taken-up for the tribals to inculcate the knowledge about the functioning of the marketing system; assessment of exact potential of MFP availability and notification of the commercial items; storage facilities to be created for the products grown in tribal areas; mobile supply of DRs and mobile vigilance staff; provide adequate training methods and practices as in relation to the MFP; establishment of new locations for market centres; creation of timely transportation in the tribal areas; and steps should also be taken against excessive driages.

Table 28
Sample Households' Suggestions for Better Functioning of the Marketing System Region-Wise

	Region			
Suggestions	*Khammam*	*Warangal*	*Adilabad*	*Row Total*
Not Suggested any measures	41(38.7) (41.0)	33(31.1) (33.0)	32(30.2) (32.0)	106 (35.3)
Separate Educational schemes(1)	15(23.4) (15.0)	22(34.4) (22.0)	27(42.2) (27.0)	64 (21.3)
Two*(2)	10(35.7) (10.0)	9(32.1) (9.0)	9(32.1) (9.0)	28 (9.3)
Storage Facilities (3)	10(26.30) (10.0)	14(36.8) (14.0)	14(36.8) (14.0)	38 (12.7)
Four**	18(38.3) (18.0)	11(23.4) (11.0)	18(38.3) (18.0)	47 (15.7)
Five***(5)	3(33.3) (3.0)	6(66.7) (6.0)	–	9 (3.0)
New Location of Market Centres(6)	3(75.0) (3.0)	1(25.0) (1.0)	–	4 (1.3)

Contd.

Timely Transport (7)	-	1(100.0) (1.0)	-	1 (0.3)
Steps against Excessive Driages (8)	-	2(100.0) (2.0)	-	2 (0.7)
Three Plus Six	-	1(100.0) (1.0)	-	1 (0.3)
Column Total	100 (33.3)	100 (33.3)	100 (33.3)	300 (100.0)

* Assessment of exact potential of MFP availability and notify the commercial items.

** Mobile supply of D.R.s & Mobile vigilance staff

*** Provide adequate training methods and practices as in relation to MFP

Table 29
Sample Households' Suggestions for Further Improvement of GCC in All Respects (Credit & Marketing)

	Region			
Suggestions	*Khammam*	*Warangal*	*Adilabad*	*Row Total*
1	2	3	4	5
Not Suggested any measures	22(27.5) (22.0)	27(33.8) (27.0)	31(38.8) (31.0)	80 (26.7)
A	7(30.4) (7.0)	9(39.1) (9.0)	7(30.4) (7.0)	23 (7.7)
B	11(26.8) (11.0)	17(41.5) (17.0)	13(31.7) (13.0)	41 (13.7)
C	5(22.7) (5.0)	7(31.8) (7.0)	10(45.5) (10.0)	22 (7.3)
D	10(33.3 (10.0)	6(20.0) (6.0))	14(46.7) (14.0)	30 (10.0)
E	7(35.0) (7.0)	7(35.0) (7.0)	6(30.0) (6.0)	20 (6.7)
F	5(50.0) (5.0)	5(50.0) (5.0)	-	10 (3.3)
G	2(14.3) (2.0)	-	12(85.7) (12.0)	14 (4.7)
A + B	5(50.0) (5.0)	4(40.0) (4.0)	1(10.0) (1.0)	10 (3.3)
A + C	1(100.0) (1.0)	-	-	1 (0.3)
A + D	4(23.5) (4.0)	9(52.9) (9.0)	4(23.5) (4.0)	17 (5.7)
A + E	2(66.7) (2.0)	-	1(33.3) (1.0)	3 (1.0)
A + F	2(100.0) (2.0)	-	-	2 (0.7)

Contd.

	Region			
Suggestions	*Khammam*	*Warangal*	*Adilabad*	*Row Total*
1	2	3	4	5
B + C	4(100.0)	–	–	4
	(4.0)			(1.3)
B + D	3(75.0)	1(25.0)	–	4
	(3.0)	(1.0)		(1.3)
B + F	2(50.0)	2(50.0)	–	4
	(2.0)	(2.0)		(1.3)
C + D	1(100.0)	–	–	1
	(1.0)			(0.3)
C + E	1(100.0)	–	–	1
	(1.0)			(0.3)
D + E	2(50.0)	2(50.0)	–	4
	(2.0)	(2.0)		(1.3)
D + F	–	2(100.0)	–	2
		(2.0)		(0.7)
E + F	–	1(100.0)	–	1
	(1.0)			(0.3)
A + N	1(100.0)	–	–	1
	(1.0)			(0.3)
E + N	–	1(100.0)	–	1
	(1.0)			(0.3)
A + C + D	1(50.0)	–	1(50.0)	2
	(1.0)		(1.0)	(0.7)
B + C + D	2(100.0)	–	–	2
	(2.0)			(0.7)
Column Total	100 (33.3)	100 (33.3)	100 (33.3)	300 (100.0)

Chi-square	Value	DF	Significance
Pearson	79.0214	48	0.0031
Likelihood Ratio	91.9153	48	0.0001
Mantel-Haenszel Test for Linear Association	13.0369	1	0.0003
	r = 0.208		

A = Relax the Stringent Conditions and increase the loan amount
B = Increase MFP prices and decrease the D.Rs prices
C = Purchase of Agricultural Produce alongwith MFP
D = Timely supply of inputs - Land, Water, Credit and Marketing Facilities should be provided
E = Establishment of D.R. Depots In each village
F = No Purchase of MFP from Non-tribals
G = Provide adequate training methods and practices as in relation to MFP
N = Patta rights for new lands are to be provided

Table-29 depicts the region-wise sample households' suggestions for further improvement of the GCC in all respects especially in view of the twin objectives of credit and marketing. From the Table, it can be seen that 73.3 per cent of the sample tribals had suggested certain remedial measures for the strengthening of the GCC and this per cent had been the highest in Khammam with 78 per cent followed by Warangal and Adilabad with 73 per cent and 68 per cent respectively. They had suggested the following measures. They are: relaxation of the stringent conditions and an increase in the loan amount; enhancement of MFP prices and reduction of DRs prices; purchase of agricultural produce along with the MFP; timely supply of all the inputs– land, water, credit and marketing facilities; establishment of D.R. depots in each village; no purchase of MFP from non-tribals; sanctioning the patta rights for newly cultivated lands; and finally providing the adequate training methods and practices in relation to the extraction and tapping of the minor forest produce.

Chi-square and other chi-square based measures were found to be statistically significant.

SUMMING UP

The overall marketing pattern prevalent in the study area, suggests the emergence of two broad channels of tribal markets. One is the institutional one and the other is the non-institutional marketing agencies. The existence of periodical markets reflects the marketing pattern in tribal areas. The sample tribal households visit the periodic markets for purchasing the domestic requirements and selling their produce. Some of the sample tribals visit the shandy on social matters like settling the matrimonial alliances and the disputes as well. The frequency of visits to the shandy points in a month reflect the households' role as a seller and as a buyer, which in turn reflects the business transactions of the sample tribal households in the study area. Here most of them had paid their visit to the shandy points for selling their minor forest produce and inturn they make their purchases of the essential commodities like rice, oil, kerosene, pulses, sugar, etc. A variety of weights and measures were observed to be in use, apart from selling and buying through the approximation in the shandy point. The tribals as buyers are being cheated and deceived by the itinerant traders in the shandy points by wrong weighment.

The credit-cum-procurement assistants appointed by the Corporation act as catalysts while informing the MFP prices to the tribals and procuring the MFP and some times even agricultural produce from them also on behalf of the Corporation. Thus, they (CCPAs) also act as liaison between their employer and the tribal households. It had been observed that the problems like under-weighment, excessive driages, under rating the quality are the common grouses against CCPAs in the study area and it had also been observed that these problems are not only completely associated with shandy inspector alone but even with the weighing boys or measurers.

An overwhelming majority, 71 per cent of sample tribal households are engaged in the collection of minor forest produce. While marketing the MFP two channels are clearly visible. One is the GCC and the other is non-institutional agencies like private traders, merchants, money-lenders and needy consumers in the shandy points. It had been observed that a smaller quantity of MFP collected had been used for the consumption purposes. The consumable MFP items are Mohwa-flower, Mohwa-seed and wildbrooms as they are quite useful for the daily consumption of the tribals and they are unable to fetch high returns due to the low procurement prices. Thus, it had been observed that the MFP pickers sell the entire collection of gum, nuxvomica, pungam-seeds, myrobalans, cleaning nuts, while other items like wild-brooms, mohwa flower and seed, chiranji, honey, tamarind, and K.T. bundles, that are used for domestic consumption.

During the field investigation, it had been observed that in the case of certain items, the traditional marketing methods are still prevalent in the study villages especially in the case of wild-brooms and tamarind seed. So, it can be inferred that the system of barter is still prevailing in the tribal areas to a certain extent. But in the case of other items, they first convert their commodities into cash in order to make necessary purchases.

It had also been observed that almost all the sample tribal households are selling the items like wild-brooms, honey and K.T. bundles in open market to get higher prices than the prices offered by the Corporation. So, there is a need to enhance the prices of these MFP items by the Corporation to induce the tribals to sell their produce to GCC only and the same opinion was also expressed by the surveyed tribal households.

While selling the agricultural produce, a majority of the sample households had not preferred to sell it to the Corporation due to lower agricultural prices, intimacy with the private traders and village merchants and also due to the produce not being bought by the Corporation. But during the field investigation, it had been observed that the Corporation in Adilabad district entered into the domain of cotton procurement and hence purchased the cotton produced by tribals.

It had been observed that the private traders and merchants played a predominant role while purchasing the agricultural produce from the sample households in the study area due to the linkages of credit with product markets. Therefore, most of the households had preferred to sell their produce soon after harvesting.

The tribals sell their produce to the Corporation and in turn purchase their domestic requirements like rice, kerosene, matches, oils, controlled cloth, and pulses, from the D.R. depots of the Corporation. It had also been observed that some of the sample tribal households were sceptical about the quality of the commodities supplied by the Corporation due to the variety of reasons like low quality, higher prices, closure of store very often, heavy loss of time at the depots during the busy agricultural season and supplying the insufficient quantity had been claimed to be the prime reasons.

It had also been observed that the salesmen in the D.R. depots will not allow them to buy the smaller quantities of the commodities like 25 grams, 50 grams and even 100 grams and even some times in particular the rice will also be of very poor quality. By and large, despite its weaknesses in some of the areas, this line of activity of the Corporation is considered to be successful as it caters to the needs of the tribals on behalf of the channel of Civil Supplies through its D.R. depots. Hence almost all the consumable articles are being supplied at the subsidised rates.

Albeit, no household preferred to make their purchases exclusively from single source and their purchases depend on the availability of the items from three sources namely the Corporation, village showkaries and private merchants and inturn reflect their needs from time to time. A variety of reasons like assured marketing, better and graded price, perfect weighing and measurement, and being free from malpractices were responsible for the sample tribal households to make their purchases from the D.R. depots of the Corporation for meeting their day-to-day requirements. Still, some of the sample tribal households had also made their purchases from the private merchants and village showkaries. A variety of reasons like, better quality of the commodities, availability of multiple variety of items and non-availability of the item from the Corporation, longer acquaintance with the village showkaries or the private merchants, supplying the goods on the basis of credit, and the time loss being high in the queue at the D.R. depots of the Corporation during the busy seasonal employment activities etc., made some of the sample tribal households to make their purchases from the village merchants. By and large, a relatively higher per cent of sample tribals opined that the commodities bought from the village showkari had a better quality when compared with the items bought from the D.R. depots of the Corporation.

A majority, 61 per cent of the sample households expressed their satisfaction over the price paid by the different marketing agencies in the study area and this had been inview of the obtained prices of both MFP and AP. Even though, it had been observed that 36.7 per cent of the households reported that they had all the three problems, viz., administrative, trade related and the socio-lingual-cultural problems.

It had been observed that transportation facilities to the shandies as well as the regulated market yards are inadequate and the communication facilities are also insufficient. Further,it had also been observed that the shandy day in any one of the researcher's study areas posed the problem of high congestion as it is impossible to move in and around freely in the shandy area owing to the larger number of transactors with their respective goods both for buying and selling. Therefore, the researcher had felt that these shandy points are known for the *'hub of different cultural zones and centres'* from an ignorant Adivasi to a deceitful modern man in plain areas who used the shandy points on a specific day.

Further, it had been observed that a majority 76.7 per cent of the sample tribal households are aware of the Corporation's services and concessions that had been provided for the betterment of themselves. In this regard, it had also been surmised that the activities of the Corporation are more intensive in Adilabad than in the two other districts in the study area, though the Corporation had not rendered its services to all the needy and poor tribal households due to the organisational loopholes of the Corporation.

During the field investigation, it had been observed that the organisational set-up of the Corporation is devoid of the tribals' participation and this sort of practice in the Corporation had created a debilitating climate in the functioning of the Corporation in achieving its twin objectives of providing credit as well as marketing facilities. The reasons for not receiving the services are: not in need of any assistance; lack of time due to other occupations; because of old age; time loss is high at the Corporation; lack of land; prevalence of single window system; and cumbersome procedures.

The sample households had suggested certain steps to be taken for the effective functioning and strengthening of the existing marketing system in the tribal areas. They are as follows: separate educational schemes had to be taken-up for the tribals to inculcate the knowledge about the functioning of the marketing system; an assessment of exact potential of MFP availability and notification of the commercial items; storage facilities to be created for the products grown in tribal areas;mobile supply of DRs and mobile vigilance staff; provision of adequate training methods and practices as in relation to the MFP; establishment of new locations for market centres; creation of timely transportation facilities in the tribal areas; and steps should also be taken against excessive driages. Thus, the sample tribal households in the study area had felt that if the aforesaid steps are considered, the marketing system may become more viable in the tribal areas and accessible to the needy people in the area.

It had also been observed that an overwhelming majority (73.3 per cent) of the sample tribals had also suggested certain remedial measures for strengthening the GCC in achieving its twin objective of credit and marketing. They are: relaxation of stringent conditions and an enhancement in the loan amount; a rise in MFP prices and a reduction of DRs prices; purchase of agricultural produce along with the MFP; timely supply of all the inputs - land, water, credit and marketing facilities; establishment of D.R. depots in each village; no purchase of MFP from non-tribals; sanctioning the patta rights for newly cultivated lands; and finally providing adequate training methods and practices in relation to the extraction and tapping of the minor forest produce.

Finally from the preceding analysis, it had been observed that in the absence of organised, institutional and regulated markets in the tribal areas, the tribals are deprived of enjoying the fruits of a fair pricing system. Often the absence of organised marketing system leads to the emergence of a class of petty traders taking an advantage of the helpless situation of the tribals leading to their exploitation. If the State takes a serious view of the situation and establishes the regulated market yards for the betterment of the tribals at the vicinity of their work places and strengthens the existing shandy points by eliminating the exploitative mechanisms by strengthening the existing institutional marketing facilities, then the tribal households would also get a better and remunerative prices for their produce and reap the benefits out of the marketing mechanism.

NOTES & REFERENCES

1. Redfield, Robert, (1956), 'How Society Operates'? in Shapiro, Harry (Ed.), *Man, Culture and Society*, Oxford University Press, New York, p.354.
2. The peculiarity of the Shandy is that, the place of transacting business is new to both the sellers and the buyers of different products. In a shandy, the people congregate at a fixed common place, once during a week and the transactions at the shandy last for a couple of hours. The most strange feature of the shandy is that there are no fixed stalls and nobody is seen in the vicinity once the shandy is over for the day. For further details see, Murali Krishna Rao, I., *Marketing in Tribal Economy*, Inter-India Publications, New Delhi, 1988, pp.73-85.
3. For the detailed discussion also see infra Chapter-4.
4. The difficulties from physical environment arise from the niggardliness of nature, whereas the difficulties from the social environment are visualised more with the entry of non-tribal traders, money-lenders, forest and excise officials.
5. The former covers the co-operatives and the Girijan Co-operative Corporation; and the latter is associated with the private traders, money-lenders, petty traders, middlemen and finally the needy consumers in and around the villages or at the shandy points.
6. But this contradicts the researcher's observation during his field visits to the three shandy points in the study area where the tribals as buyers were being cheated and deceived by the itinerant traders in the shandy points under the guise of using standard weights and measures as it is due to fact that tribals were not able to identify them and this observation was proved by some of the case studies. For further details also see infra Chapter-IX.
7. During the field investigation, it had also been observed that these problems are not only completely associated with the Shandy Inspector, but are also associated with the weighing boys or measurers who took an active part and are supposed to act at the behest of Shandy Inspectors' whims and fancies.
8. During the field investigation, the researcher had observed that gum is an important MFP item fetching the sample tribals a handsome amount of income and this percentage is relatively higher in Khammam than either in Adilabad or in Warangal. The next in importance is nux-vomica, pungam-seed, myrobalans,

cleaning nuts, etc. Further, it had also been observed that the sample tribal households sell their entire collection of gum, nux-vomica, pungam-seeds, myrobalans, cleaning-nuts.

9. It includes the private traders, village showkaries/ merchants, and produce sold at the regulated market yards and the shandy points.

10. During the field investigation, it had also been observed that the salesmen in the D.R. depots will not allow them to buy the smaller quantities of the commodities like 25 grams, 50 grams and even 100 grams and even some times in particular the rice quality will also be very poor indeed. The fact had also been proved by some of the case studies presented in the *Chapter-IX*.

11. While looking at the received price of MFP alone, almost all the households are satisfied as most of them had sold their produce to the Corporation alone. But in the case of the marketing prices of agricultural produce, the reverse tendency had been observed. Their agricultural produce didn't obtain the remunerative price in general and non-institutional marketing agencies (private traders/ merchants) in particular and this had been due to the fact that the private traders (showkars) extend the credit to the households to raise the crops and at the same time they enforce a binding over the farmers to sell their agricultural produce to him only or to re-pay the loan in terms of kind along with the *vaddi or pechhulu* (interest). Furhter, in this connection it had also been observed that the tribals had to sell the produce after the harvest at a certain pre-determined price which was agreed upon at the time of taking the loan. Therefore, this price will be invariably much lower than the price that prevails in the market. Thus, it can be concluded that the main agents of exploitation in the study area are the *'private traders'* and the *'non-tribal merchants'*.

12. Other charges include the Gullavali, Hamali, Dadvai, driages under the name of baggage and also charges under the name of Kanta.

13. It also includes the Radio and other mass-media in the case of sample non-tribal medium and big farmers in the study area and they are the sources even for some of the big farmers among the tribals in the study area.

9

CASE STUDIES

The views and opinions of the tribal and non-tribal farmers in the study villages expressed during interviews are presented in this Chapter in the form of case studies. The methodology adopted here is that the opinions have been elicited through personal interviews. In all, ten cases have been presented in this chapter. These cases are designated here as *A, B,C,D,E,F,G,H,I* and *J* for the sake of anonymity. Among these, *A,B,C,D* are from Khammam District, *E,F,G,H* are from Warangal District and *I,J* are from Adilabad District.

CASE – I

Mr. *'A'* is a Koya Tribal big farmer and hails from Ankampallem village, Dammapet Mandal of Khammam district. Presently, he is working as a General Secretary of the Village Tribal Development Association (VTDA).

According to him, earlier the tribals have been growing only subsistance crops like maize, jowar, konda jonna[1] in the village. But now the attention had been shifted to other commercial crops especially cashewnuts. The availability of gum and addaleaves were in plenty earlier and now their collection had decimalised.

Most of the households in this area have been growing cashewnuts and in times of good yield, they earn an income. Both tribal and non-tribal farmers lease out their cashewnut crop. However, these crops are not leased-in by the local non-tribal farmers. It is the farmers from coastal Andhra region are obtaining income ranging between Rs.20,000/- to Rs. 30,000/-. by lease in the crops. This is the on going practice and in which those who lease-in even advance loans to the farmers on the promise that they would lease their crops only to them for the coming years too. However, no rate of interest is charged on such loans and therefore can be termed as *'Interest Free Loans'*. These loans range from Rs.10,000/- to Rs. 60,000/-.

He possesses 20 acres of land, of which four and seven acres of land have been allotted to the crops like cashewnuts and Paddy respectively and he gets an income to the tune of Rs.5,000/- and Rs.35,000/- from these crops respectively. As the cashewnut crop had been planted just 6 years back the yield rate has not been much. Therefore, he has been realising very meagre income from it. However, he anticipates that he would be getting double the present amount in near future. He has been taking 'crop loan' to the extent of Rs.4,000/- regularly from GCC during sowing season and repaying the amount soon after harvesting in the form of kind and the remaining produce is sold in the regulated market in Dammapet. He also hires labourers during busy and heavy agricultural season, depending on the nature of agricultural activity. According to him, the wages vary from Rs.20/- to Rs. 25/- and from Rs. 10/- to Rs. 15/- in the case of male and female labourers respectively. However, these rates are subject to the nature of their work.

He is aware of the Credit cum Procurement Assistants (CCPAS) who have been educating the tribals about process of tapping the gum and the application of fertilizers and pesticides. They also supply cash to the tribals under the crop loans. Inspite of such types of institutional flow of inputs, the farmers also approach the private dealers in Dammapet for more inputs needed for their agriculture.

The role of middle men in the village had declined in the recent past. Regarding the sale of the produce some times, the private traders come to the village and purchase it. Alternatively some of the households in the village together engage a lorry and take the grain to the market. In this case transport charges at the rate of Rs.5/- per quintal has to be borne by them.

Mr. 'A' stated that with the displayed prices on the notice board by the concerned authorities, farmers will be able to predict the prices. But the expected prices will not be realised in the market. For instance, if the households visit the market with the anticipated price of redgram at Rs.1,000/- per quintal, they will not realise the same price, but will get only Rs.800/- per quintal. Therefore, some times a wide gap prevails between the expected price and the realised price. Albeit, they are forced to sell the produce there itself. The same will be applied to all the crops. The prices will go down in the harvesting season for all crops and most of the farmers in general wish to sell the produce soon after the harvesting in order to purchase immediate necessities and to redeem the earlier debts that have been taken at the time of busy sowing season. Further, the traders never go for deferred payments.

The degree of exploitation by money-lenders was of a higher order. Money lenders normally offer petty loans for festivals, marriages and for purchase of clothes and collect at least three times of the original amount. Exploiting the situation, they used to grab the tribal lands prior to the implementation of 1 of 70 Act and other protective legislative acts. Besides, the loanee also used to give the money 'either in the form of a cow or a she buffallo' under the guise of 'Merumanam'[2] which was a common practice in this village.

His family members visit the shandy only for purchase of essential commodities such as sweet oil, onions, salt, pulses, turmeric, chillies, and vegetables. They also approach either the village showkari or GCC's D.R. depot in the village, when they are in need of other commodities. Moreover, his family members do not engage themselves in the collection of minor forest produce.

The household purchases the available commodities like sugar, rice, from the store and in the case of items like redgram, greengram, kerosene, etc., which are not available in the store they obtain them from small kirana shops in the village. He stated that the quality of the items bought from both these sources are good. As the D.R. depots do not supply the required quantities of necessities the tribals have to depend on the local shops even if they charged higher prices[3]. As the daily earnings will be a meagre one at Rs.10/- to Rs.15/-, there will be a greater demand for broken rice.

According to Mr. 'A' the institutions like GCC, ITDA have been working a little more actively than earlier times in the tribal areas. In this process the earlier discontinued 'crop loaning system' or 'S.A.O. loaning system' had again been introduced. At present, these institutions have been coming forward to supply the motors, pumpsets, goats, bullocks and other assets, and other crop loans for the development of the tribal households. Under the scheme of 'Jeevandhara' some of the wells have also been sanctioned in the village.

The tribals have been aware and making use of these institutional services and facilities in the recent years but earlier the tribals were not aware of their existence. If at all they had some knowledge about these institutions, it was some sort of lackadaisical attitude because they thought that these institutions never come forward to provide any services and facilities for their development.

Mr. 'A' stated that ITDA officials supplied cashewnut saplings and even they had also supplied the water for a period of one year for the sustenance of the crop to the tribal farmers in the area. The MPP and Mr. 'A' work as facilitators by giving oral certifications to those who are sanctioned loans.

Due to the interest free loan facility, the dependence of the farmers on the showkaries has been marginalised. The GCC has been extending its loaning operations in the recent years. Now-a-days, the day to day expenditure has also been increasing along with increasing incomes. Besides, the yield rate per acre has also been increasing due to the loaning operations of GCC.

CASE – II

Mrs. *'B'* is a Koya tribal woman belonging to Ankampallem village in Dammapet mandal of Khammam district. Presently, she is the president of 'Gum Pickers Association' (GPA) in this village.

She has no other loans except the consumption loan to the tune of Rs.500/- that was given by GCC. Of this amount Rs. 150/- was repaid and the remaining is outstanding.

Regarding the market for final products she expressed her opinion that the present situation is a changed one. Prior to the setting up of GCC, the tribals used to depend on the middlemen for the sale of their minor forest produce. They also used to be exploited by way of lower payments for their products than the market price[4]. After the GCC has been set up, they have not only started purchasing the MFP especially in the case of gum but also began imparting training to the local tribals regarding improved ways of tapping gum. She felt that the CCP Assistants present at the GCC are also very helpful to the tribals in the sale of MFP. The CCPAs increase the awareness of the tribals regarding differential pricing according to the quality of the products[5]. She did not reveal the exact price paid for the product 'Gum' but also stated that they would earn to the tune of Rs.30/- per day in case of greater availability of Gum and Rs.20/- under normal availability. The gum collection activity usually takes place round the year except in the rainy season. Besides gum, other minor forest products also would be available but in very marginal amounts.

Local shandies still play an important role in purchase and sale of products needed by the tribals. Exploitation practices regarding sale and purchase of products still prevail. Those who are aware of weights and measures are not susceptible to deception, but the innocent ones will fall prey to the deceptive practices in the local shandies. Inspite of such conditions almost all the households prefer the shandies for their transactions because of the availability of most of the commodities they use. Mrs. 'B' felt that during the course of time the rate of increase in incomes is easier than the rate of increase in expenditures. In order to adjust for the increased needs, she spreads her income over a number of commodities[6] that she needs resulting in very low quality of each good.

According to her, the role of money-lenders has declined in the last 15 years. She however stated that for the people of their close acquaintance, the money-lenders do not charge high rate of interest but for strangers or unknown persons the rate of interest is still very high. She felt that the credit needs of the local tribals could not be adequately fulfilled by the GCC or ITDA because of their stringent bureaucratic lending procedures. Even in the case of a sanctioned loan a major portion of it has to be given to the middlemen involved at various stages.

When asked about the usefulness of the GCC store, she stated that all the items that they need will neither be available nor will be in sufficient quantities[7]. She felt that eventhough the prices of the commodities are high in kirana shops, the quality would be good[8]. Another reason why she prefers purchases from showkari instead of GCC is that people like her do not have enough cash at hand to pay at one instance at the GCC, whereas they can obtain any good (usually durables) on instalment basis from kirana shop. She also felt that the quality of durable goods like clothing at GCC store is inferior and also the availability is most irregular and insufficient at GCC.

CASE – III

Mr. 'C' is a Koya tribal marginal farmer from the Chillagumpa hamlet of Patwarigudem village, Dammapet mandal of Khammam district. Besides looking after his own agriculture, he hires out his labour for agricultural works and also engages himself in the collection of MFP. Earlier he had taken Rs.1,600/- as loan from Land Mortgage Bank for the development of agriculture. Though the amount had been diverted towards the consumption expenditure, he repaid the entire amount. Therefore, at present he has no debts. Earlier he worked as attached labourer for a period of 16 years in his own village under a showkari named Bhushanam. He was given jowar weighing four, 'Manukalu'[9] and nothing else.

Regarding the agricultural inputs like seeds Mr. 'C' stated that because the institutional support from GCC and ITDA will not be timely, the farmers have to depend on private persons who possess seeds. The other alternative is obtaining the seeds under the practice of Nagulu[10].

Mr. 'C' stated that if the households in their hamlet are in need of cash in emergency situations, they approach the village showkari and make an agreement with him that the crop would be sold to him. In this process the showkaries also charge very high rates of interest ranging from 60 to 120 per cent. The local tribal people feel it difficult to obtain any agricultural input or cash loans from institutional sources. Since non-institutional support (local showkaries) has been present from decades, they feel more proximity towards them due to their easy accessibility. Therefore, even if the interest rate is too high they approach the showkaries for most of their needs.

He and his family members visit the shandy for sale of Minor Forest Produce such as cleaningnuts, nuxvomica, and in turn purchase their domestic requirements. He is neither aware of the price nor of the quality of the goods and therefore he purchases the items as sold to him. Moreover, he lacks knowledge with regard to the use of weights and measures in the shandy. With some bitterness towards the exploitative practices of the money-lenders, local village showkaries and petty merchants in the shandies, he remarked that had people like him knew about their trade practices, they also would have done the same and led a comfortable life like them. His earnings range from Rs.20/- to Rs. 30/- per day by way of toddy-tapping.

He stated that he is not aware of GCC and for that matter of any institutional agencies. His family members have not been taking any item from the store due to the possession of 'Red Ration Card'[11].

Because of his ignorance about the existence and functioning of GCC or ITDA, he is not in receipt of any loan. However, he feels that if some financial help is done to him he could develop his agriculture.

Though prices are very much high, he is forced to depend on the village showkaries/shops due to not getting daily requirements from the store.

Institutions like GCC/ITDA have been rendering services to the adjacent villages but not to this village and ITDA had not distributed any cashewnut saplings in this village. In recent years, the households have been struggling hard to lead their lives even at subsistence level due to the felling of trees and declining yield rates for some of the crops grown.

CASE – IV

Mr. *'D'* a non-tribal belonging to Velma caste, hails from a landlord family. He belongs to Patwarigudem village in Dammapet mandal of Khammam district. He is called as 'Dora' in the village. He received education upto 4th form. Agriculture is his primary occupation and he does not have any other occupation either in the village or outside the village.

Only one tribal household was living in the village whose name goes by *'Pattado'* at the time of his grand-father's settlement in the village and gradually an influx of the non-tribals had begun and settled in this village. At present no information is available about the first tribal household in the village which had disappeared. Presently, this village is a non-tribal village having S.C., B.C., and O.C., households. But all the hamlets adjacent to this village are inhabited by tribals. The 1 of 70 Act is also not applicable to this village due to the recognition of this village as non-tribal by the officials. Even if most of the households belonged to non-tribals in the adjacent village just away from 3 to 4 Kms, the Act applies to them. The land transactions are prevented in the tribal areas due to the prevalence of the Act. The market value of land in the case of wet and dry is Rs.17,000/- and Rs.25,000/- per acre respectively and the reason for this low land value, according to him was the existence of 1 of 70 Act even in the adjacent areas.

Instead of employing the attached labourers, he has been hiring-in the casual labourers during the busy agricultural season. This practice is due to the reluctance of most of the labourers to work as attached labourers. The reluctance is because they can obtain higher incomes working as casual labour than as attached labour. Even in a few cases of attached labour there is a lot of friction between the employer and labourer regarding the labour turned out by the latter. There are instances where the attached labour even went to the extent of complaining against the landlord to the Labour Officer. Due to these risky conditions, Mr. 'D' has been hiring-in the daily labourers. According to him, wage rates are different for male and female labour and also vary in accordance with the nature of work that one performs. The present wage rate is Rs.25/- and Rs.15/- for male and female labourers respectively.

Mr. 'D' stated that changes in the cropping pattern and in the living standards have been taking place at rapid strides. There are about 20-30 borewells dug by the ICDS. This has paved the way for extensive cultivation of commercial crops, and plantations like cashewnut and mango orchards. As a result, both incomes and expenditure have been increasing. Leasing is a common practice in the case of these plantations and the leasing rate is determined according to the anticipated yield in the ensuing year based on the realised yield during the current year. Depending upon the yield, normally leaser takes the advance from the leasee to the extent of Rs.4,000/- per acre during the season or alternatively the leasee gives the advance to the leaser.

Regarding the sale of produce, Mr. 'D' stated that usually big farmers like him retain some produce for their own consumption purpose and sell away the rest to the traders who come into the village for purchase of grain. If they are in need of money they sell out the whole produce and purchase again as and when required. Another alternative practice is to lease-out their cashewnut crop to those who advance the required amount to them. At the time of interview with Mr. 'D', he has taken Rs.60,000/- from the leasee and promised to lease-out the crop for the coming three years. His need was two fold: performing marriage of his daughter and construction of pucca house.

In this village no one directly goes to the market but showkari comes to the village and purchases the produce. Some times farmers are willing to dispose-off the produce even if prices are very low depending upon their personal needs.

In such case the traders deduct Rs. 10/- per quintal for transportation purpose in addition to the other charges- Hamali, Dadvai and Gullavali. Mr. 'D' said that he also visits the regulated markets now and then which have inadequate facilities.

Regarding their knowledge of the prices of the produce he mentioned that he either knows by enquiring the other farmers, or through the traders coming to the village or through the radio. If the farmers feel that the margin between price offered by traders in the village and the market price is too wide, then some of the farmers come together and take their produce to the regulated market either at Sathupally or Dammapet. Even then due to price fluctuations he said that they would not get the expected price. He also commented that they would not even get the minimum or support price announced by the government.

But the general trend is that the prices of the produce in open market have been increasing at faster rate soon after the disposal of the farmer's entire produce. Even in the regulated markets farmers wish to offer the grain for those who are ready to pay a little more than other Adti and Commission Agents. But there is no conditionality to dispose off the produce only for known persons. Still, usual practice is that every farmer or group of farmers in a particular village normally dispose-off their produce to a particular Adti and Commission Agent and perhaps this might be due to non-economic factors even in the marketing of the produce. Besides these non-economic factors, if the farmer has multiple transactions with a particular trader he gives away his produce to the trader even if the price is lower than the market price. The above process of marketing leads to the conclusion that there is an interlinkage between input and output marketing in the area.

Thus, it can be inferred from the above analysis that the farmer is the worst sufferer of the unpredictable price fluctuations in the market and traders have also been constantly making their efforts to fool the farmers. Alternatively if the farmers did not want to dispose off their produce immediately, sufficient godown or storage facilities do not exist. Those markets which have these facilities being far away from the present village are inaccessible and expensive for the farmers. Mr. 'D' lamented that the marketing aspect had been ignored and there were no *"Farmers' Committee"* to represent the matter to the government.

According to him, the rate of exploitation in the process of marketing had declined to some extent, eventhough at present some of the money-lenders are still charging exorbitant interest rates.

Earlier forms of exploitation were explicit without any discrimination between tribals and non-tribals. The traders used to manipulate the methods of marketing in a very subtle manner. Whenever the tribals or non-tribals approach the traders for sale of their produce, the latter would measure the produce with a bigger than normal size measure which they very subtly denoted as *'measure of the older girl'*[12]. When the people go for purchase of produce, then a smaller than normal size measure would be used in order to underweigh the produce which was denoted as *'measure of the younger girl'*.

In addition to the above practice, the showkaries used to make their men to fill one hundred and twenty (120) manukalu in each bag by using big bags instead of normal bag containing hundred manukalu. But now such type of the exploitative conditions no more exist.

He also feels that the prevalence of 1 of 70 Act in the tribal areas is good and if at all this Act is abolished, again the tribals would come forward to sell off their lands to the non-tribals in the villages. The amount that they would receive would be spent for conspicious consumption purposes and they would remain as landless farmers. Therefore, he vehemently supported the existence of 1 of 70 Act in the tribal areas.

CASE – V

Mr. *'E'* is a Koya tribal big farmer, who hails from Rangapur village, Tadvai mandal of Warangal district. He was the Sarpanch of the village from 1975 to 1987 and since then he has been working as President of VTDA.

He stated that most of the households in this village eke out their livelihood from agriculture which is their main occupation. He has saved nearly Rs. One lakh in both L.I.C. and Peerless Scheme. Mr. 'E's family also depend on agriculture and do not go for the collection of minor forest produce. However, most of the households in this village have also been actively engaging themselves in the collection of minor forest produce like wild/hill brooms, cleaning nuts, nuxvomica, mohwa flower and seed, and rella bark. He is in possession of 18 acres of land, in which crops like Paddy, Groundnut and Mirchi are cultivated.

According to him, there is no land leasing in this village, but if one wishes to do, the leasing rate is either 10 bags of paddy or Rs. 1,200/- per acre. Now-a-days the prices of inputs like chemical fertilizers have been increasing to the maximum extent but there is no rise in the price in the case of farmers' produce. Therefore, it is good for the farmers, when the produce is marketed with "*support prices*".

When he was a market director he formed a committee to fight against the lower prices of the produce. He felt that 'farmers can only afford to meet the ever increasing prices of chemical fertilizers, pesticides, seeds and other related inputs for agriculture only when they realise 'Supporting Prices' for their produce. But the efforts put by the committees were invain.

According to him, the households in the village have been growing only single crop in a year. Earlier the arable land had been devoted to the crops like - horsegram, nallajama, hilljowar, korra, bajra and linseed. But now, it has been shifted to the crops like paddy, groundnut, mirchi and farmers have also learnt methods to increase the productivity of the commercial crops with the application of chemical fertilizers. Even in the earlier times paddy crop was grown by the tribal farmers but by the usual method of transplantation[13]. Earlier, they simply used to spread over the seeds here and there in the land which does not yield much and gives more scope for weeding.

Mr. 'E' related that they had fought with the TRIFED General Manager for lowering the prices of fertilizers and pesticides. The farmers felt that the prices of these inputs are growing at a faster rate but the remuneration for the agricultural produce is not rising at the same rate. The reply that they got was to reduce the quantity of application of fertilisers and to depend more on organic mannures. To Mr. 'E' this piece of advice was felt like going a step backwards.

He is well aware of the facilities that are being provided by GCC for the cause of tribal betterment. It has also been extending the *'crop loan'* facility in both kind[14] and cash forms to the tribal households. But he has not taken any amount either from GCC or from any other institutional sources because he was not in need of them.

According to him, the farmers in an emergency situation take loans from a particular merchant and repay it by selling the produce to him. However, the rate of interest would be around 36 per cent.

He stated that while selling the forest produce, shandy inspector now called as Credit-Cum-Procurement Assistant (CCPA) normally underweighs the quantity with the help of weighing boy, who acts at the behest of CCPA. However, CCPA's comment was that the tribals market Kuccha[15] produce, therefore, it has to be underweighed so that it will be upto the mark while marketing to the GCC.

Mr. 'E' was asked to comment on the complaints made by shandy inspectors against the tribals, that they increase the forest produce by adulterating it or increase the weight of the gum by wetting it. However he stated that no tribal would normally adulterate their products but in the case of gum they would wet it or even adulterate and enlarge its quantity. However, the shandy inspectors deliberately do not distinguish between the different grades or qualities of gum, and would offer lower price for higher grades of gum. But while transferring the same produce to the godown they would label it as grade-I product. As a result the CCPAs would receive higher price for the product but would in turn pay lesser price to the tribals under the pretext of its lower quality, thereby increasing their profit margin.

Added to this, the shandy inspectors resort to malpractices like deducting larger quantitites of the produce towards driages particularly in the case of gum, tamarind, etc. He felt that this type of practice is illegitimate. According to him, the *'barter system'* is still in vogue but not in its earlier form. In the earlier form of barter system physical exchange of goods was taking place without any unit of measurement involved in it. The present barter system includes some unit of measurement between the exchange of goods.

Regarding marketing of the produce, he stated that normally all the farmers in the village prefer to visit regulated market at Warangal. Merchants normally pay for half of the produce marketed immediately and remaining amount will be paid after a period of two to four weeks.

He stated that despite the many difficulties[16] present in the market yard, the farmers have to dispose it off and they never prefer to bring back the produce because of absence of any alternative to dispose it. Adti and Commission Agents in the market deduct some amount in the name of marketing expenditure under different heads like Hamali, Dadvai, Transport, etc. Besides they also deduct Rs.3/- per every Rs. 100/- as Commission charges. But in the case of Mirchi they have been deducting Rs.6/- per every Rs. 100/-. He also stated that if any one questioned all these practices they simply refuse to purchase the commodity saying that the quality of commodity is not good. Inspite of adverse marketing conditions, there is no alternative for the farmers but to sell their produce in the regulated markets.

While he sells his produce at Warangal market yard, he purchases some of the essential items like sugar, kerosene, and pulses etc., from the D.R. depot located in the village. He stated that the quality of goods in GCC is also good, but they do not provide all the required commodities for the households. Though toilet soaps under the brand Girijan i.e., *'KUTEER'* are available in these depots, the tribals are not inclined to use them due to the availability of different brands in other shops.

Normally the prices are low in the GCC's D.R. depot when compared to the open market prices. But in the case of some commodities like onions as the GCC purchases them in bulk quantity, and stores the stock in the Godown at a particular point of time, the sale price may be even higher than in the open market. This higher price in the GCC depots is due to the fact that the GCC may have purchased when the rate was high. Similarly, is the case with Palmoil-the cost of one kilo in D.R. Depots being Rs.33/-, but the same is available at Rs. 25/- in the open market. Because of these price margins, Mr. 'E' stated that most of them wished to make purchases at the local shops rather than in the GCC's D.R. depots. However, he felt that if GCC would sell its produce keeping in view the open market prices, it would be better. Otherwise, people normally get a feeling that D.R. depots would always sell their produce at higher prices than others in the open market operations.

Regarding purchases, almost all the households in the village visit Katapur shandy on every sunday. But Mr. 'E' does not visit the shandy because he purchases most of the required items in the village itself. Sometimes some of the essential commodities - oil, soaps, tobacco, beedies, etc., required for domestic needs will be purchased either from Warangal or from Eturnagaram or from Pasra.

He felt that the quality of the commodities obtained from showkaries are relatively better than the commodities obtained from D.R. depots as they pay much attention towards the quality and they also purchase only smaller quantities from the nearest wholesale market. But in the case of GCC, the situation is reversed owing to the storage of bulk quantities for longer times due to which the quality of commodities get spoiled.

D.R. depot was established in this village in 1976. This village was also a shandy point. The importance of the shandy point had declined because of the introduction of card system and the establishment of D.R. depots in most of the adjacent villages too.

Prior to the introduction of card system tribal people from far off places in Khammam and Warangal districts also used to visit this shandy for making transactions. However, after cards for essential supplies were issued people started making purchases in their respective villages or nearby towns. The establishment of D.R. depots in most of these villages also reduced the importance of this local market. Consequently, the shandy point had also been rooted out from this village.

He stated that neither GCC nor ITDA helped them while knowing the modern practices of rice cultivation. But since 1980's the scenario has changed and the ITDA agricultural officers and the GCC[17] agricultural assistants began imparting knowledge about these practices.

Agencies like, TRICOR/ITDA have been offering the crop loans in addition to the GCC. Under the crop loaning system, they have been giving seeds in the form of subsidies. Banks are also extending loaning facility to the needy and credit-worthy farmers. However, the farmers are not able to make use of the facility because of its distant location. Moreover, the tribal households in the village are not willing to approach the non-tribals for loans. Because the earlier experiences show that in the name of repayment of loans, the non-tribals grabbed the properties of the tribal households. Earlier, the role of money-lenders was very high but now it had declined. He stated that earlier one would obtain the loan only under the practice of Nagu[18]. Earlier the yield rate per acre was very low owing to the prevalence of the method of 'KARADA' where in the moneylenders used to charge one rupee per Kuncham[19]. Thus, when the households were not able to repay their loans the debt burden would be high due to compound interest rate. As a result, most of the lands ranging between one or two acres with some irrigation facilities have been grabbed by the showkaries in which process the tribals were left alienated from their lands. This had happened in the adjacent tribal villages. However, there were no cases of tribal land alienation because of absence of non-tribal households in the village.

The gum picking activity declined to a great extent because of extinction of gum trees. The reason for the extinction had been due to the unscientific methods of gum tapping and also felling of these trees. According to Mr. 'E' both the tribals and the GCC are responsible for such extinction. However, as an eyewash, the MFP consultants and divisional managers started imparting training to the tribals about the scientific methods of gum tapping.

He stated that no direct barter transactions have been taking place between the parties as in the earlier case in the tribal areas. According to the modified barter system, the price of each good is determined depending upon its value and now this practice coordinates the entire barter system in the tribal areas.

CASE – VI

Mr. *'F'* is a Koya tribal farmer, belonging to Pambapur village, Tadvai mandal of Warangal District. He is 28 years old and received education upto 10th class. He had to discontinue his studies due to the poor economic conditions and due to the sudden demise of his father. Presently, he is the President of local Telugu Desam Party in the village.

He stated that in his childhood most of the households had poor economic background. Only if one could obtained of any gum in a day, he used to get one square meal a day. Earlier, most of the households in the village used to collect the forest produce - cleaning nuts and nuxvomica. In the olden days there was no irrigation facility but now a project has been sanctioned and was completed just 4 years back. This has resulted in diverting the tribals' attention towards the agricultural activities which has improved their living conditions over the past. The changes have also been taking place in all respects - customs and habits, food and clothing due to the farmers' increasing attention towards agriculture.

Regarding the role of money-lenders in the village, earlier they used to charge Rs.5/- per month per Rs. 100/- or 60 per cent per annum as interest rate. But now banks are coming forward to extend the loaning facility in the vicinity of the tribal village itself. Therefore, the role of money-lenders had declined when compared to earlier days. Now, they charge 36 per cent rate of interest instead of 60 per cent in some of the cases.

However, while selling the forest produce in the shandy or stores, he feels that there is not much exploitation. Under normal circumstances, shandy inspector purchases the produce and pays the price according to the Government's published price, which is to be displayed on the notice board in the shandy Inspector's room. The Shandy Inspector informed Mr. F that generally the prices paid by him for the forest products are genuine and there are cases when sellers of MFP were not satisfied by prices paid to them, but still they rely on shandy inspector for selling their produce. If any tribal comes to know that he was paid lesser amount than what he should have got, then being in an intoxicated mood, he demands an explanation from the shandy Inspector. However, Mr 'F' feels that the present situation is a slightly changed one than earlier, wherein the form and extent of exploitation had declined to some extent.

He and his family members visit shandy on every Sunday for selling the produce and purchase daily requirements. He said that some form of exploitation is still prevailing in the shandy point which is not explicit and identifiable by the tribals of the village. Further, the exploitation is likely to increase if the shandy point grows on a massive scale and then it becomes very much visible.

He is well aware of the existence and services of GCC and ITDA. He stated that the institutions like GCC and ITDA have been rendering services for the betterment of the tribals to some extent. Presently, they have been providing the services such as irrigation, power supply facilities and crop loans in the village. So far ten (10) horse power (h.p.) capacity motors have been sanctioned by them.

CASE – VII

Mr. *'G'* is a Koya tribal farmer who hails from Narsapur village, Tadvai mandal of Warangal district. He is 35 years old and is educated upto primary level. He is the Sarpanch of the village since 1983.

Since 1986 most of the households in the village have been getting financial assistance under different schemes of D.R.D.A. programmes like - Bullock-carts, Motors, Sheep and She-buffaloes. With the help of these loans, most of the households in the village have developed economically to some extent. However, those who have diverted the amount of loans for non-economic purposes have not improved their living standards.

When the Canara Bank was located in Katapur village it was of great help to the farmers. As it had been shifted from Katapur to Pasra because of some disturbances in the area, the woes of the farmers have increased. As it is far away from the village, even obtaining the sanctioned loan is becoming a difficult task for the farmers. He stated that earlier (when it was in Katapur), he used to get loan amounts very often from the bank in order to meet the labour charges. But in the present circumstances an entire day will be wasted to make any transactions with the bank.

Regarding the role of money-lenders in the village he commented that they kept the entire village under their control through their credit operations with exorbitant interest payments[20] and extracted all the produce and ruined the economic position of the tribal households in the village. But now their role had declined to a large extent in the village due to the existence of financial institutions with their extensive lending operations. Despite the presence of these institutions, the money-lenders have been continuing their lending operations at a lower rate of interest.

As banks do not provide assistance as and when the tribals need, their dependence on either showkaries or money-lenders is still high. They take advances from the latter on the conditions of disposing off the produce at a lower than market rate[21]. Under the guise of indebtedness the whole yield of the tribals is taken away at a cheap price.

Changes have also been taking place in the field of agriculture. Earlier the productivity of grains like horse-gram was very low. However, since 1986-1987 coarse grains are not being grown. Since then the tribal households have been paying much attention towards growing groundnut crop. Presently, the yield rate of this crop is about 20 to 30 bags per acre. If more fertilizers and pesticides were applied the yield rate per acre would even rise to 30 bags. By and large, each household who have grown this crop is likely to obtain an income ranging between Rs.7,000/- to Rs.8,000/- per acre. Most of the households in the village have been economically rising due to this crop alone. With the right application of good seed, fertilizers and pesticides and hard work, the yield rate of paddy crop also would be of 30 bags per acre.

Normally, most of the households in the village dispose off the produce to one Shankar Reddy, an Adti and Commission Agent in the Warangal regulated market. Regarding the difficulties during marketing he felt that the clerks, hamalies and persons who weigh the produce are more prone towards malpractices. These people survive at the cost of the farmers. As a way out of this grave problem, Mr. 'G' suggested that it would be ideal if a *'Farmers' Committee'* was formed to deal with the issues faced by the farmers. However, as the awareness towards the problem is marginal, collective action did not take place. He felt that if *Gram Committees* were formed they could actively pursue the problems.

He and his family members visit the shandy regularly. Commenting on the malpractices going on in the local shandies Mr. 'G' felt that the market conditions are generally adverse to the buyer and conducive to the seller to earn profits. This is because of the vulnerability of the tribals for deception. Recalling the history of the setting up of the village shandy, he said that sellers of old clothes were the first ones who used to visit the village once in a week. Later vendors of other goods like vegetables, salt, provisions, dry fish also started getting their products to the sale point. Thus the shandy point at Katapur had been functioning. However, Mr. 'G' felt that exploitation of tribals as buyers takes place in the shandy. This is usually in the form of the difference in the methods of sale between the 'Labbi Shets' and the petty traders in the shandy. The former usually sell the products by using scales but the latter put the goods in a heap and sell each heap at Rs.2/-. Though it appears to be cheap, the quality is worse. Still the tribal buyer usually prefers to purchase from the traders because they will be lured by the quantity and low price of the goods.

The quantity and collection of minor forest produce had declined to a greater extent due to the unscientific extraction or tapping of the forest produce. However, with the efforts of the GCC the tribals came to know of the scientific methods of extraction of MFP particularly in the case of Gum.

Similar to the feelings of Mr. 'F', Mr. 'G' felt that these efforts would have been of great use if they were imparted about ten years ago. He apprehended that even the collection activity of cleaning nuts, nuxvomica will cease to exist in near future because of rapid decline of forest cover.

In the recent years, the prices of forest products like gum, cleaning nuts, nuxvomica have increased. With the increased prices of MFP, the tribal households have also been obtaining more incomes than earlier. He recollected that when he was collecting the gum, a kilo of gum fetched only Rs.5/- but now it fetches around Rs.40/-. On the whole, he felt that changes have been taking place to some extent since the establishment of GCC in the tribal areas.

In view of the decline of tapsi trees in the forest, he opined that the tapsi plantation has to be taken up on a massive scale as in the case of teak plantation. If this takes place, there may be a scope for the tribals even to get incomes in the near future atleast after a period of ten years.

CASE – VIII

Mr. *'H'* is a backward caste non-tribal, who belongs to Katapur village, Tadvai mandal of Warangal district. Previously, he worked as a first salesman in the GCC in this area and latter was suspended from his duty as salesman. Since then he has been working as R.M.P. Doctor in the village.

When he was working as salesman in this area, the present GCC was called as 'Andhra Pradesh Scheduled Tribes Co-operative Finance and Development Corporation' (APSTCFDC), its head-quarters at Visakhapatnam. Agricultural Co-operative Marketing Societies (ACMS) were under the corporation's jurisdiction and it was looking after their varied functions in different regions and used to distribute the essential commodities like Rice, Sugar, Wheat, etc., through

ACMS to all the tribal and non-tribal households. Then there were only three ACMS in this region, viz., Eturnagarm, Chalpalk and Narlapur. He stated that he worked in Eturnagaram prior to the formation of ACMS in Katapur and there he was incharge of the sale and purchase transactions of the forest produce and the distribution of daily requirements as well.

In the year 1976, the then APSTCFDC was re-named as GCC under the Chairmanship of the then Managing Director Shri *Chandra Mouli*, Mr. 'H' was working for a monthly salary of Rs.80/-. In addition to the salary, he used to obtain Rs. 137/- or two per cent as commission over Rs.3,000/- worth of sales. Since 1969 he has been working in this village. Relating the beginnings of Gum extraction and sale, he told that it was only in Adilabad that Gum Karaya was extracted. However, there was no shandy point for the sale of gum. The process of gum extraction in this village has started in a peculiar way. Once thunder struck a tapsi (gum) tree and it fell down. After few days gum started oozing out of it which was collected by a tribal elder *Mukkati Achaiah.* He happened to approach Mr. 'H' and both of them took the produce to the General Manager who asked his men to purchase it at the rate of Rs.1/- per kilo. Later the gum trees were identified and the tribals began extraction of gum. In those days near famine conditions prevailed and the tribals had great difficulty to procure enough food and clothing. Under such conditions, Mr. 'H' stated that he started a shandy point in Rangapur village. He used to purchase forest produce like gum, K.T. bundles, R.S. roots, horns of animals, tamarind, mohwa-flower, mohwa-seed and other such items. He stated that the MFP procured on one shandy day, usually saturday, was ranging between 10 to 15 lorry loads. As the forest produce nuxvomica was abundantly procured it was also carried by Mr. 'H' and others when adequate number of lorries were not available. Atleast 140 lorry loads of Nuxvomica was purchased by GCC and in turn it also called for tenders for its sale. At that time the *'Biological Evans Company'* was the purchasing agent for the product.

Mr. 'H' stated that they made some attempts to develop the tribals in all respects especially socially and economically. Besides purchase of MFP, they used to sanction loans of Rs.50 lakh worth. to the tribals. In this area Rs. 25 lakhs from revolving fund and another Rs. 25 lakhs from R.B.I. were distributed in the form of loans to the tribals. They were also sanctioned agricultural loans. Some of the loans given to the tribals under revolving fund were waived, while some of the loans had been recovered. After a period of five years (Mr.'H') was transferred to Buttaigudem and again he started a shandy point there. On the whole, he stated that he has started and developed many shandy points in different areas and he took care that the tribals actively participated in the shandies' transactions.

While researcher was interviewing Mr. 'H', the present CCPA Sri Meghya Naik intervened in the discussion and explained the GCC's loaning operations in the area with his field experience in the following manner:

"The GCC loaning operations had continued upto 1975-1978 but later the loan recovery was not at desired level and meanwhile the loans that were given to the tribals were waived off. Besides, different schemes were also abolished due to the poor rate of recovery. Moreover, the department had also suffered from paucity of funds. Consequently, GCC had discontinued its loaning operations. And now, the loaning operations of the institution have been revived since 1991, despite poor recovery of loans. Even in this areas also the recovery is not at desired level".

Barter system prevailed in the shandy points till late sixties and the early seventies. One kilo of gum was exchanged for one kilo of rice. At that time price of one kilogram of gum was also equivalent to that of a kilo of rice. But after mid-seventies these conditions ceased to exist.

According to him, these shandies were developed only for the minor forest produce. Prior to these shandies, the households from each and every village - Alligudem, Bollepalli, Sarvapuram, Busapuram, Narsapuram used to approach the depots to sell their produce. Keeping the distance in view, more D.R. depots were started in the nearby villages.

Inspite of the big size of the Rangapur shandy its importance had declined due to the establishment of a shandy point at Gollagudem village under the supervision of Khammam district Divisional Office of GCC. As this is adjacent to the Rangapur village, most of the households used to visit the Gollagudem shandy point instead of Rangapur shandy. Therefore, the inflow into the former had declined. Meanwhile another shandy point at Katapur village in the Warangal district was also started. As the shandy day is on every sunday tribals from the adjacent villages used to attend the shandy for selling their products and purchase their day-to-day requirements from the D.R. depots in the shandy. The shandy Inspector comes once in a week, purchases the forest produce from the tribals and in turn makes payments to them. With the amount obtained for their products, the tribals purchase some of the items like pulses, salt, kerosene, rice, sugar, etc., from the GCC's sales depot located at the shandy point. The price here is less when compared to the shops outside the shandy point. He stated that tribals have to pay more if they made purchases from petty traders in the shandy. For instance: at the petty trader one kilo of sugar is sold at Rs.14/- to Rs.15/-, but the same would be sold at Rs.8.50/- in GCC sales depot. Therefore, the tribals generally preferred to purchase from the D.R. depots located in the shandy point.

According to him, GCC through its D.R. depots is catering to the needs of the tribals both in buying the produce from them and selling goods to them. However, certain difficulties also arose in the functioning of D.R. depots. Any way by all means the role of intermediaries or middlemen had declined to a large extent especially in the case of purchase of the forest produce. If any middleman offered to purchase the forest produce, they simply reject his offer and would say that they would like to give it to the shandy inspector instead. This change in attitude is due to the fact that for Grade-I gum the GCC is offering Rs.80/- per kilo, whereas the traders only offer Rs.20/- for the same.

Prior to the establishment of GCC/D.R. depots a container of nuxvomica used to be purchased at the rate of Rs.2.50/-

paise but now the same produce is purchased in terms of kilograms and GCC offers Rs.10/- per one kilo. Therefore, tribals have reached a stage where they can simply reject the middlemen. This is an indication of their awareness towards the illegal activities of middlemen and also about the different prices offered by both GCC and middlemen. If the actual price of a kilo gum is Rs.1/- the intermediaries used to purchase the Gum from the ignorant tribals at the rate of 0.50 paise or 0.75 paise per kilo and in turn again dispose it off at the rate of one rupee to GCC. But right now, the tribals have been selling their produce to the Shandy Inspector and they have been purchasing their requirements at sales/D.R. depots. Recently, card system had also been introduced for gum pickers.

Further, the GCC officials have been making efforts along similar lines to develop even the tribals' agriculture. Earlier if a tribal household obtained a fertilizer bag from GCC or other institutions, he used to dispose it off and squander with it. But now, if one is sanctioned a loan, a part of it is given in the form of kind, and it is monitored by a liaison worker of GCC. The liaison worker sees that it is used or applied only in his land. They also visit the villages for recovery of the loan. Soon after recovery of the loan the tribal will be again given a loan. Therefore, tribal agriculture has also been developing with the assistance offered by GCC. According to him, GCC has been playing a positive role since its inception in improving the socio-economic conditions and instilling the psychological confidence among the tribals.

He firmly stated that in most of the aspects such as life styles, customs, habits and dressing pattern. Changes have been taking place just due to the establishment of GCC. While he was saying this, he explained the grim situation that had been there prior to the establishment of GCC in the following manner:

"Almost all the tribal households in this area used to borrow money for Nagulu from some private persons or showkaries, who used to charge exorbitant interest rates. Therefore, whatever the yield that the tribals obtained from the land normally was sufficient only for payment of the interest and the tribals were unable to repay the principal amount. After a period of three or four years, the showkaries used to *'GIRAFTHAR'* (takeover) the lands of the indebted tribals. According to Mr. 'H' it is - Perkas, Showkaries and Muslims who had mostly grabbed the tribal lands. He emphatically stated that Katapur is totally inhabited by non-tribals who exploit the tribals living in and around Katapur.

According to Mr. 'H', the GCC should pay compensation to the tribal household who have been actively engaging in the collection of minor forest produce. This has to be done in order to encounter certain unforeseen incidents in the forests while collecting the forest products. And here again CCPA intervened in the discussion and said that they had been deducting Rs.2/- per kilo of gum under the name of 'contribution to common fund' for meeting unforeseen incidents from gum pickers who possessed a *'gum picking card'*. Besides, the CCPA had also taken active participation in the discussion regarding the 'required quota' and about the 'prices' that have been prevailing in the D.R.depots. The CCPA stated that normally GCC did not offer enough quota of rice for the tribals due to the dependency of GCC on the civil supplies for obtaining the rice. Therefore, within the limitations, GCC is also not able to provide required and enough quota to the tribal households. As per the prices, normally, showkari sells his produce as per the market prices and moreover he takes into account the price fluctuations in the open market operations. But the GCC will not take into account the day to day price fluctuations in the open market operations and sells the goods as per the determined price. Once price is fixed, it is very difficult to either lower or hike the prices of the products. Therefore, it is impossible to sell the daily requirements as per market rates.Thus when the prices of GCC items are compared with the outside prices or open market prices, there are two possibilities: either the price may be lower or the price may be higher.

The changes in cropping pattern are attributed to the GCC and ITDA. Earlier the people used to grow the crops like horse-gram, Paddy but now in addition to Paddy, they have also been growing groundnut. Irrigation facilities, digging of Kuntas, supplying better quality of seeds and fertilizers also paved the way for changing the earlier cropping pattern. In terms of development of tribals it can be said that both improved agriculture and the GCC have helped them in an equal measure.

Talking about the ways to improve the shandy points, he stated that steps should be taken to increase the quantity and availability of MFP to widen the scope of the shandies. With the help of social forestry, tapsi plantation should be taken up as in the case of teak plantation. Though it is a long-term process, it could yield desired or anticipated results atleast after 10 years. Besides, undertaking of tapsi plantation, the establishment of bee-keeping plants should also be undertaken, which is also helpful to the tribal households in generating incomes. In this direction GCC established a bee-keeping plant at Eturnagaram but it had failed due to lack of adequate training facilities to the tribals.

CASE – IX

Mr. *'I'* is an Andh tribal teacher, belonging to Anji Village, Indravelli mandal of Adilabad district. He is 20 years old. He was recruited as a teacher about 4 months back in the primary school of his village. Prior to this occupation, he was engaged in agriculture. Presently, his father is looking after the agriculture.

He said that the GCC officials have been giving loans to the tribal households but based on some selection criteria. The tribals are dissatisfied because the GCC is unable to cover the entire number of tribal households in the village. Even for getting loans from the institution they had to make hectic efforts for many days.

He stated that despite the presence of institutional loans, still the money-lenders have been making attempts to have their sway over the village due to the inadequate and meagre amounts that have been offered under the scheme of crop loans. Therefore, again the tribals inevitably had to approach and obtain loans either from showkaries or from some of the big landlords or from other known persons in the village even at higher interest rates. Earlier they (lenders) used to charge cent-per-cent interest rate but now they have been charging fifty per cent interest rate due to the loaning operations of GCC and ITDA in the recent years but not due to any concern towards the tribals.

Regarding the minor forest produce, most of the households have been collecting the mohwa flower, mohwa seeds, beedi leaves. Mohwa flower and mohwa seed are used for self consumption. Almost all the households who have been collecting the forest products, have also been selling to GCC. However, a few of them have also been selling to private traders. This is due to the lower prices offered for some of the products by GCC when compared to the private traders. The availability of forest products had declined due to the illegal cutting of the trees. Besides, earlier GCC has not given any sort of training either in the case of process of extraction of MFP or in the case of agriculture. He said that they were not aware of the training programmes that would be imparted by the GCC.

Almost all the households in the village visit the Indravelli Shandy on every Monday for obtaining the daily requirements and his family is not an exception to this. According to him, exploitation is common which can be in the form of underweighment and higher prices for the commodities.

Normally, the households obtain sugar, kerosene, palm-oil and rice, from GCC store. They have also been taking some of the items even from outside showkaries due to the inadequate supply of essentials by D.R.depots. GCC through its D.R. depots will not provide all the required items. This is due to the fact that supplying of 20 Kgs rice per month is not adequate for one household and therefore, it is quite but natural to depend on the showkaries for the daily requirements even if price is high. In general, households feel that the quality of the products in GCC is equally good even with a lesser price. But the quality is not good for all the times. The quality of rice in some of the bags is good and in some other bags is not equally good. But even if showkari offers a kilo rice at the rate of Rs.7/- or at a higher rate, the quality is very good when compared to the quality of GCC's D.R. depots.

CASE – X

Mr. 'J' is a backward caste non-tribal and progressive farmer in the village. He belongs to Indravelli village, Indravelli mandal of Adilabad district. He is 55 years old. His birth place is this village but he stated that his father had migrated to this village from Maharashtra. He has been living in the village with agriculture as a primary occupation and has no other subsidiary occupations to perform.

Ground water is the primary source of irrigation in this area. Land leasing is on a high scale and even here most of the households are willing to give their lands for lease but correspondingly the households are not willing to take the lands for lease due to higher investment cost. Therefore, even if they take the lands for lease, there may be a scope to have losses instead of profits. Therefore, every one is cultivating his own lands instead of leasing-out the lands. Albeit, some of the households who have irrigation facilities on their land and are unable to cultivate, have been coming forward to give the land for leasing.

The leasing rate per acre varies between Rs.500/- to Rs.1,500/-. This rate is subject to availability of the irrigation facilities and the nature of land. There is no remarkable change in the cropping pattern. Most of the farmers have been growing crops like cotton, jowar, paddy, redgram, blackgram. But there is a difference. Earlier farmers used to apply the traditional or local variety of seeds and now they have been using HYV seeds.

Regarding agriculture, he stated that they used to sow the traditional varieties of seeds or 'home made seeds' and there was no application of fertilizers and pesticides but only organic mannure or compost. But now, the households have been making use of all available HYV seeds, fertilizers and pesticides to a greater extent. Therefore, to that extent yield rates have also been increasing. Despite, the farmers both tribal as well as non-tribals are not even getting back the investment that they incurred on agriculture due to the increased prices of agricultural inputs. Another important factor is that the terms of trade are adverse to the farmers, that is they pay high prices at the time of purchases but receive low prices at the time of selling the produce due to the lack of support prices in the market.

Earlier the yield rate of Jowar was 2 quintals per acre but now if the crop is not susceptible to any pests and other diseases, the yield rate per acre would be about 10 quintals per acre. The yield rates of different crops have also increased. Similarly in the case of cotton, earlier if one had sown the cotton in a 5 acres piece he used to obtain about 2 to 3 quintals. But at present if one sows it in the same 5 acres of land, the yield is equivalent to 20 quintals. Therefore, the average rate of cotton yield per acre is about 4 quintals even without incurring any investment on it. If one cultivates the land with timely application of fertilizers, pesticides and also having assured well irrigation, then the yield rate per acre would be between 10 to 15 quintals.

In the recent years banks have also been coming forward to extend loans for the households in these villages. Sometimes, getting loans from the institutional sources is becoming difficult due to the non-payment of earlier loans. In addition to the waiver of some of the loans in Co-operative Societies, on an average the debt amount ranges between Rs.5,000 to Rs.10,000. Therefore, such loanees will not get the loan again. The Andhra Bank, Saraswathi Grameena Bank, Co-operative Banks have been coming forward to extend the credit facilities in this area, but the farmers have to obtain a *'No Due Certificate'* due to the prevalence of *"Single Window System"* which means the farmers have to obtain the loans from any one of the institutions but not from all.

At present, the role of money-lenders had declined to some extent. Earlier they used to charge Rs.10/- per month as a interest rate for Rs.100/-. But now money-lenders have been charging different interest rates ranging from Rs.3/-, to Rs.5/- depending upon the nature of need. Therefore, still he exploits the need of the peasants. Earlier, their exploitation was of a higher order and for this, Mr. 'J' cited an example: in earlier days if one takes a loan to the tune of Rs.100/- at the time of re-payment the money-lenders used to collect Rs.300/- per annum including the principal amount.

As per the marketing of cotton, some of the households have been selling their produce to the CCI and relatively a larger proportion of the households have also been selling to the private merchants. If the price offered by CCI is higher than the price offered by private merchants, naturally households prefer to sell it to CCI and Vice-versa. Here most of the farmers both tribal and non-tribal visit the regulated market for selling their agricultural produce and also most of the households prefer to sell the produce soon-after harvesting due to financial difficulties. The condition of the farmer is so pathetic that the labour charges for harvesting the crop on the harvest day also have to be met from the immediate sale of the produce to local showkaries.

While selling the produce, farmers invariably have to face many difficulties viz., lower prices, hamali, dadvai, driages and deduction of grain in the name of Kanta. No attention is being paid by the government or others towards these problems. In such conditions, even if one wishes to sell the produce to GCC, it also does not offer remunerative price, that is if the market price of a quintal of cotton is Rs.1,200/- the GCC offers to pay only Rs.1000/-. Normally, the showkari expects that the whole produce has to be sold to him. If the farmer gives some part of the produce to GCC and other part to the showkari, and if the latter comes to know of it, then he alienates the farmers by not giving any loans when the farmers are in an urgent need. Besides he will be reluctant even to supply the seeds as and when farmers require.

Mr. 'J' also supported the existence of 1 of 70 Act in the tribal areas. Most of the households have been eking out their livelihood from agriculture due to lack of industries in the area. Therefore, in order to develop the farmers economically 'support prices' are essential. Moreover, the lands here are very fertile but lack irrigation facilities. Therefore, in addition to support prices, irrigation facilities also have to be provided for the betterment of the farmers. Further, the prices of agricultural products should also be increased corresponding to the enhanced prices of other agricultural inputs needed for the farmers. For instance: the previous cost of bag of Urea was of Rs.60/- but now it increased to Rs.300/- and similarly in the case of D.A.P., a bag costed Rs.110/- but now it increased to Rs.420/-. But on the same lines, the prices of agricultural produce like cotton have not increased. It increased from Rs.500/- per quintal to Rs.1,000/-. The farmers agitated in the form of strikes, dharnas, jail bharos but all the efforts were invain indeed. Therefore, Mr. 'J' felt that the government has to declare the *'Minimum Support Price'* for cotton at Rs.2,500 per quintal and if this is done, there is a scope for the price in the open market to be increased. Even if the open market price does not rise then the farmers would sell atleast to the government.

At present, the farmers have been selling a kilogram of cotton for Rs.10/- and inturn the producers of cloth sell cloth worth one Kg. of cotton at Rs.80/-. Thus there is a glaring gap between the price of input and output. Keeping the above fact inview Mr. 'J' felt that the government should fix the price of a kilo cotton atleast between Rs.50/- to Rs.60/- and only then would it be beneficial for the farmers. Once, the economic position of the farmers is bettered, trickle down effect acts and the labour also would be paid in a better manner. Thus, it indirectly paves the way for the improvement of the economic conditions of the agricultural labourers.

The price policy should be such that the prices fixed or formulated by the Government should not become burdensome on the part of the farmers even though they are not remunerative. In such conditions atleast the farmers would have an opportunity to lead their lives on a *'no profit, no loss'* basis. If not both the tribal and non-tribal farmers have to face deplorable or despicable situation in the coming years.

Tribal households in this area also engage in collection of MFP. But in the recent years, the availability of minor forest products had declined due to the decline of forests. The decline of forests were also due to the cutting of trees in order to bring more land for cultivation. Besides, if there were trees on cultivable land the farmers eliminated them as they feel that the yield will not be high due to the shade of the trees. This also caused for the decline of forests in the region.

He stated his experience in this area, that about 15 years back, the tribals were even not aware of how to wear the clothing. If tribals wish to sell in the market, they used to come to the market with some measure and in turn we used to say that the produce brought by you is equivalent to four manukalu, which are equivalent to twenty serulu[22]. Then only they used to sell their produce in the market. But right now the situation is reversed because they are aware of the quantity of produce they bring to the market, and inturn they are also aware of the amount that they would obtain while selling their goods in the market. Keeping all these things inview, Mr. 'J' stated that changes have been coming slowly among the tribals due to the introduction of different Governmental Schemes for the betterment of the tribals. Besides, the number of educated youth among the tribes had also been increasing steadily and if all the educated youth obtain jobs, it paves the way for their further development.

SUMMING UP

From the above analysis the researcher could draw the following inferences. They are:

(i) A transformation process is slowly taking place in the tribal areas in almost all the spheres of life. The transformation process has its own merits and demerits. Due to the *'culture-contacts'* with the outer world, the tribals are more prone to exploitation, more so due to the penetration of commercial and market economy, which is inextricably intertwined with the internal circulation of monetary relations. A contradictory process is also taking place where tribals are becoming more aware of their rights. Hence, the positive sided transformation outweighs the negative sided transformation due to the fact that the tribal households have been learning so many modern methods of agricultural practices and its other related activities and in the meanwhile, they have been paying much attention to the commercial crops and plantation instead of going for mere subsistence and food crops. Therefore, at present they have been realizing more yield rate per acre as well as more incomes than earlier. This was clearly evident in the researcher's study villages.

(ii) Most of the tribal households of the study area have been making attempts to engage themselves in the collection of minor forest produce but its availability is at a lower level. Therefore, the dependence on it for livelihood has been on the verge of decline and in turn they are likely to become as either agricultural labourers or as poor and landless peasants. In the light of this, 'Podu' cultivation has been taking place extensively in some of the inaccessible and interior tribal areas, where thick forest vegetation had been prevailing.

(iii) Despite some of the fraudulent practices of GCC and ITDA, they have also been rendering yeoman services for the betterment of tribal households while creating the physical assets on behalf of the 'loaning system' and also providing daily requirements through D.R. depots. Besides, as GCC acts as a monopsonist in the sphere of marketing, it is actively involved in the marketing process in the tribal areas while purchasing the minor forest produce that had been collected by the tribals. Here, it is also viewed that the GCC should take stern steps to purchase the agricultural produce along with the purchase of minor forest produce at reasonable prices. Even in the recent years, these institutions have also been contributing for the transformation process that had been taking place in the tribal areas to some extent.

(iv) The role of money-lenders had also declined due to the active involvement of the various financial institutions in the tribal areas with their loaning operations and on the other side the inter-linkages between the product and credit markets are apparent and these linkages will lead to the exploitative relations under the guise of subtle and explicit methods of charging higher interest rates from tribals. It is also to be stated that the exploitation rate had been rampant on the part of snobbery consumable goods at the vicinity of petty traders in the shandy points. Therefore, the shandy points in the tribal areas have become the hub of economic and trade centres for exploitation by way of deceitful selling of the goods and other articles required for the households in the area. Thus, these shandy points have become, in due course of time, *Paradises for middlemen* as the *rate and speed of exploitation of ignorant tribals* is much higher than found in any other market. By and large, one has to surmise that the transformation process has been taking place at a slower pace in the tribal areas.

NOTES

1. Local name of the crop.
2. The word 'Merumanam' is a idiomatic expression in Telugu language which implies giving gifts with an affection or with cherished love.
3. The local shop-keepers charge exorbitant rates i.e., rice at Rs.7/- to Rs.8/- per kilogram and broken rice at Rs.5/- per kilogram.
4. For instance, if one brings the gum for selling, middlemen used to offer only either Rs.12/- or Rs.13/-, but the market rate could be of Rs. 20/-.
5. For instance, the CCPA has been telling about the prices of different types of gum products - Rs.80/- for grade-I, Rs.58/- for grade-II, Rs.26/- for grade-III.
6. The Spending pattern had been illustrated in the following manner: Rs.5/- for oil, Rs.2/- for dry fish, Rs.10/- for vegetables and if one wishes to have wet fish, one has to spend another Rs.20/- etc. Therefore, the spending pattern represents their *'habit persistence'*.
7. For instance, every family has been getting 20 Kgs of rice per month on the basis of ration card. But this quantity is not enough

to feed the entire family because each family consumes atleast from 1.5 Kg. to 2 Kg. rice per day.

8. For example, if one gets a 1 Kg. rice for Rs.3.50/- from the store but the same from showkari is Rs.6.50/-.
9. Four Manukulu are equivalent to one 'Kuncham'. In some of the areas it is equivalent to 10 Kgs, 12 Kgs, 14 Kgs & 16 Kgs. In this village it is equal to 16 Kgs.
10. This is a traditional practice in the village economy in general and tribal economy in particular to obtain the seeds or loans in the form of kind or cash. In this village most of the farmers obtain the seeds under the practice of 'Nagulu' that is if one gets one kuncham of seeds at the time of sowing he has to repay two kunchams at the time of harvesting.
11. Those who are issued with the red coloured ration cards are not eligible for obtaining rice from the GCC store.
12. Bigger measure is called as 'Pedda Ammayi Manuka' and smaller measure as 'Chinna Ammayi Manuka'. Manuka is the traditional weighing measurement.
13. This method gives scope for more yield rate per acre and less weeding activity.
14. In the form of kind loans, GCC or other financial institutions have been supplying the inputs required for the farmers-seeds, fertilizers, and pesticides.
15. Not polished or not refined.
16. Difficulties like price fluctuations, lack of storage facilities, no proper knowledge about prices are faced by the farmers at the time of marketing the produce.
17. Since the GCC's head office has been shifted from Warangal to Eturnagaram, it began rendering services to the tribals.
18. Infra p. 324.
19. 'Kuncham' is the traditional measurement to weigh the produce in the village economy and still this measurement is in vogue.
20. Some times they used to collect 100 per cent interest from the tribal households.
21. Usually Paddy will be given off at Rs.150/- per bag, whereas the open market price will be between Rs.250/-, to Rs.300/-.
22. One seru is equal to nearly one and half kilograme.

10

SUMMARY AND CONCLUSIONS

In the light of the analysis contained in the preceding chapters, this last and final chapter presents the overall conclusions of the study as they had been discussed in lieu of the backdrop of the entire debate in the earlier chapters.

In the *first introductory chapter*, besides a brief analysis of the topic chosen for study, the methodology adopted in this study had been presented. The taxonomy of markets includes many distinctions such as perfect, imperfect markets; regulated and unregulated markets; organised and unorganised markets; formal and informal markets. But markets operating in indigenous communities are not specifically distinguished, though they may be loosely called as imperfect market, unregulated market or unorganised market. These words may not connote the essence of markets that operate in indigenous communities. In a sense, they are imperfect, unregulated and also unorganised.

Thus, markets operating in indigenous communities, especially in tribal economies, can be labelled as indigenous markets as they blend contractual systems with personalised relations. These markets can be considered as imperfect, unregulated, unorganised, and informal in nature. Since no specific term had been used in the literature to explain all these connotations of the markets in tribal areas, an attempt is made here to designate them as *'Indigenous Markets'*, where they are simultaneously imperfect, unregulated, unorganised, and informal-all rolled into one. These markets contain various types of imperfections either in product markets or in factor markets, and governmental intervention is minimum and their unorganised nature often gives scope for a lot of exploitation. As contracts are informal in these markets, and as also the stability of these contracts is endangered by outside market forces, they do not have a continuity and this gives rise to the indigenous nature of the markets.

In the tribal areas of Andhra Pradesh, there is only one institutional marketing channel that is operating with Governmental support namely, Girijan Cooperative Corporation. Though this is institutionalised in nature, a few studies on the functioning of GCC had highlighted the leakages in its functioning and at times its unsystematic way of conducting marketing transactions. Since it is monopolistic in nature, especially as far as the purchase of minor forest produce is concerned from the tribals, all the attendant evils of monopoly had surfaced at times in the functioning of this organisation. The other market forms, though may follow the marketing principle, cannot be strictly called as regular markets and their irregularity coupled with the prescribed nature of transactions is a crucial feature of the indigenous markets. In order to capture these marketing transactions and marketing principles involved in the indigenous markets operating in the tribal areas, it had been felt that there is a need to study such relations that define the development process in those areas. Hence this study had been undertaken. As indigenous markets still flourish among indigenous communities, the study had been undertaken in the tribal areas of Andhra Pradesh, a state which has a concentration of tribal areas among different states in India next only to Madhya Pradesh.

As against this background, the present research work has been devised to study the following objectives.

The *objectives* of the study are:

(1) to analyse the interlinkages between the credit and product markets in the tribal areas with a view to examine the role of markets in the tribal economy;

(2) to describe the institutional and non-institutional marketing channels in the tribal areas;
(3) to examine the functioning of Girijan Cooperative Corporation, an institutional marketing system in providing marketing facilities for the products grown in tribal areas;
(4) to find out the factors that influence marketable surplus and marketed surplus of the products in tribal areas;
(5) to examine the accessibility of formal and informal credit institutions in the tribal areas;
(6) to analyse the impact of infrastructural facilities on indigenous markets.

The *hypotheses* of the study are as follows:

(1) The barter system in the tribal areas is slowly being replaced by a monetised economy, albeit slowly, and this is leading to the tardy growth of rural organised markets in tribal areas;
(2) While the markets are slowly developing for commodities as well as the inputs, the interlinkages between the factor markets, of which credit market has prominence, and product markets are still quite strong in tribal areas which is mainly due to the migration of non-tribals, with an adverse affect on the tribals;
(3) Monetisation of transactions in tribal areas is leading to changes in cropping pattern in such a manner that the tribals are also generating marketable surplus of agricultural produce with the benefits more in favour of non-tribals;
(4) The monopoly of GCC is leading to the decline of the imperfections in the unorganised markets.

The *methodology* adopted for the study had been mentioned hereunder:

The *research design* adopted for the study is for examining the functioning of indigenous markets as in relation to the institutional and non-institutional marketing process in the tribal areas. For this, the research design adopted in the study is an analytical one where both data from primary as well as secondary sources had been collected.

A *nested random sampling frame* had been adopted while selecting the sample households in the study area. At the first stage, three districts in Andhra Pradesh, representing the three different tribal concentrations of the state had been chosen. Among these three districts Khammam is popularly known for Hill Reddies, Warangal is known for Koyas and Adilabad is prominent for Gonds. At the second stage from each of these districts, the area under one divisional office of GCC had also been chosen. At the third stage from each divisional office, the area under one branch office had been chosen. The coverage had been such that at least one mandal and one Shandy point had also been selected, where the marketing centre is available. At the fourth stage, two and in some cases three villages from each mandal have been chosen at random, where they are located within a radius of 20 Kms. from the Shandy points. Finally, at the fifth stage, from each one of these villages, forty tribal households, and ten non-tribal households have been selected at random. Thus, altogether 240 tribal households have been drawn for the sample from the different tribal groups like Hill Reddies, Koyas, Gonds, Kolams, Pardhans, Andhs and further, 60 non-tribal households have also been drawn for the sample from different categories - SCs, BCs and OCs. Therefore, on the whole 300 households have been selected for the study from the two different strata - tribals and non-tribals.

In the sample design, further it is to be noted that one branch office out of five in Khammam; one branch office out of four each in Warangal and Adilabad had been selected for the present study. While selecting the jurisdiction under these branches, the number of shandy points under each branch, the procurement made by the branches during the last four and five years and the distance criteria from the shandy point were also taken into account in order to assess the functioning of GCC in the sample villages in the realm of tribal development especially as in relation to its credit and marketing objectives. Among branches of GCC, Eturnagaram branch in Warangal division, Dammapet branch in the Palwancha division and the Utnoor branch in the Utnoor division had been chosen. The rationale underlying the choice of these branches had been ascribed to the highest procurement than all other branches in the concerned divisional offices. By and large, three villages from the Tadvai Mandal of Eturnagaram branch in Warangal, two villages from the Dammapet Mandal of Dammapet branch in Khammam and finally three villages from the Indravelli mandal of Utnoor branch in Adilabad have been selected for the present study. Thus altogether it became a study of eight village.

The *data* for the study had been collected from the *primary as well as secondary sources.* The primary data have been collected through administering a structured questionnaire and also by interviews conditioning with the designed sample households to obtain the required information. To obtain the necessary information from the sample households, different types of interview schedules were prepared and also administered to the designed sample respondents and served to the key persons and for the collection of primary data. Besides, the researcher had also conducted personal interviews. On *'modus operandi'* of different marketing channels in the villages. Discussions were also held with private traders, money-lenders, shandy inspectors (credit-cum-procurement assistants), branch managers, measurers, weighing boys and other officials whose involvement is greater on the part of marketing. Discussions were conducted with the old and enlightened people and the concerned village patwaries and the respective village sarpanches in order to elicit the information.

In addition to the primary data, the articles published in various journals and the various books also published in this area of specialisation besides govt. reports and research studies by academicians had been referred.

The field investigation had been taken-up during the 1994-95 and the data relate to the 1993-94 reference year. Further, the field work had also been carried out at two terminal periods in a year. Altogether, six months had been utilised for the field investigation.

The *tools used* for processing the data are two-way and three-way cross-breaks. To find out the inter-dependability and the strength of the association between the variables used in the analysis and also to find out the relationships between the parameters used in the analysis, statistical techniques like chi-square and other measures based on chi-square, Karl Pearson correlation co-efficient, analysis of variance, multiple regression analysis, logistic regression analysis and the discriminant analysis had been utilised.

In the *second chapter* an attempt had been made to review the existing literature on indigenous markets to grapple with the intricacies of the problem chosen. The studies on the specific problem had been grouped into three broad categories. They are: i. research works on tribal economy as a backdrop for the marketing structure; ii. tribal markets (periodic markets); and iii. the research works done on interlinkages among factor markets.

The first comprehensive review of the tribal scene was conducted by the scheduled areas and scheduled tribes *(Dhebar)* Commission in 1961. The performance in respect of tribal development was again reviewed by a committee under the Chairmanship of *Shilu AO* in 1968. The task force on *'Development of Tribal Areas'* was constituted by the planning commission on the eve of the Fifth Five Year Plan. Most of these reports spot out the problem, as of tribal development and not that of developing the region inhabited by tribals. However, most of the reports are directed to highlight the problems of tribal society and the apparent lacunae in the programme initiated by various State Governments.

The entire literature on tribal economy in general reveals that most of the scholastic works have viewed the problem from macro perspective rather than from a micro perspective. In view of all the limitations, the linkages of tribal economy with the outside market economy have been highlighted. However, certain studies had been undertaken on marketing problems in tribal areas.

While the geographers' studies on the origin of shandies and periodic marketing system emphasised the spatio-temporal aspects of these markets, the anthropologists analysed the ethnic origin and the culture of the people participating in the periodic market activities. Thus, the literature on the role of shandies in the tribal economy is too limited and incomprehensive.

The deficiencies of indigenous rural marketing literature can be mentioned as follows:

(i) in terms of participants, it almost ignores the majority of rural population, the rural poor;

(ii) in terms of products, it concentrates on tangible and ignores some of the basic need satisfying 'products' like health, education, drinking water, housing and other products like transportation, labour, land, and money. Even in tangibles, the focus seems to be exclusively on economic goods.

Almost all the studies on the role of shandies in the tribal economy have highlighted the exploitation that takes place in these markets and how actively the business is transacted. But, they failed to examine as to how the periodic markets contribute to improve the standard of living of the rural people, especially downtrodden like tribals. Besides, all the studies under review touched upon the geographical and anthropological aspects only and hardly made an attempt to focus on the commercial and trading activities such as the nature of weights and measures used, mode of exchange and volume of trade, Albeit, only a few of them are related to rural markets. The interlinkages among different markets, that is land, labour and credit markets had not been analysed.

As regards the studies on interlinkages, most of them had analysed the existence of interlocking *perse,* and they do find these associated with very different production and accumulation conditions. The overall evidence is consistent with the view that certain aspects of such relationships change systematically with the penetration of capitalism, eventhough the outward form of interlocking may appear to be similar. Moreover, all the studies that had been conducted so far on the interlinkages of markets primarily concentrated on plain and non-tribal areas in different parts of the country. But no serious attempt had been made to examine the nature of interlinkages in the tribal areas. Hence this study has the objective of throwing some light on this aspect.

The *third chapter* traces the historical background of the tribal markets. The successive passage of human civilisation through the hunting, pastoral and agricultural stages went on increasing the division of labour and specialisation in production. This led to the output of a particular product of a man, far exceeding his own requirements. As he produced only a particular item, he had to supply himself with many other goods and services, essential to sustain his life. This was the beginning of marketing in economic process. The growth of urbanization also enhanced the importance of marketing because agricultural commodities had to be moved on to urban areas for the consumption of the people residing there. The Industrial Revolution further accentuated the importance of marketing, necessitating movement of agricultural raw materials from field to factory and manufactured goods from factories to consuming centres, including rural areas. Thus, the development of marketing has an evolutionary character and did not appear on the economic scene accidentally.

Rural markets are significant from social, economic and ethnic points of view and so the rural life tends to revolve around them. The rural markets in the country have been transformed due to the growing monetisation and new modes in techniques of exchange. High risks and low-profit margin - these were the two conditions of Indian trade in rural areas during the colonial and pre-colonial period which has gradually developed after the second world war period. The growing awareness of the importance of cost-benefit ratios on the part of the rural producers and state intervention in farm and non-farm trade has resulted in several sophisticated changes.They are: regulation of trade, government procurement, price support, speculation control, backward and forward linkages and extensive producer oriented approach. The major outcome of the change of the rural market structure was regulation of agricultural markets, which has eliminated the influence of middlemen to some extent.

The first attempt to regulate agricultural markets in India was made in 1897. An Act passed in that year authorised the then British Resident in Hyderabad assigned District to declare any place within his jurisdiction a market for sale and purchase of agricultural produce and to constitute a Committee to supervise and regulate the markets. The Law did help to improve the buying and selling of cotton, but in practice the Law was applied only to cotton, and it did not include grain.

The Royal Commission on Agriculture, reporting in 1928, urged that all provinces should establish regulated markets to help orderly marketing of all agricultural produce. Hyderabad, Central Provinces and Madras promptly acted on the Commission's recommendations and passed appropriate legislation. Similar directions and steps had also been taken to regulate the marketing systems and its evil machinations of the moneylender-cum-trader in tribal areas and the commission recommended the setting-up of an institutional agency, sponsored by the state, to put an end to exploitation. Therefore, in order to eliminate the abysmal process of exploitation and to free the tribals from the private traders and to ensure reasonable price to the MFP, the State Government had set-up the Andhra Pradesh Scheduled Tribes Finance and Development Corporation in 1956, as recommended by the Malayappan committee. This institution with its headquarters at Visakhapatnam started functioning from 1957 and in 1970, it has been renamed as *'The Girijan Co-operative Corporation'*. Keeping in view this background, the entire gamut of marketing relations under this sort of institutional set-up had been undertaken in the next chapter.

The *fourth chapter* makes an attempt to examine the genesis of Girijan Co-operative Corporation (GCC) of Andhra Pradesh and its marketing performance had been analysed in view of the overall question of tribal development. The main marketing activities of GCC can be identified as purchase of Minor Forest Produce (MFP) and Agricultural Produce (AP) and sale of domestic requirements to the tribals at fair prices. The main objectives of GCC are:

(i) to purchase MFP on outright monopoly basis from the tribal by paying them fair price;

(ii) to supply all daily requirements to the tribals through daily requirement depots at cheaper rates;

(iii) to meet their credit requirements for agricultural development;

(iv) to diversify the earning of the tribals and to supplement their income, the GCC is running some industrial units; and finally

(v) to take-up welfare schemes for the economic uplift of the tribals.

It is to be stated that, though the Girijan Co-operative Corporation has been making all out efforts by implementing its marketing policies that relatively benefit the economic lot of the tribals, certain deficiencies have also emerged out of its performance over the years. They are:

(1) The expenditure pattern of the GCC on establishment and the maintenance cost had exhibited an upward trend;

(2) Statutory monopoly rights over the collection of MFP has in a way led to the adoption of a price mechanism that offered low and unremunerative prices to the produce collected by the tribes; where only a few intermediary functionaries were benefited;

(3) An official appointed by the corporation and a few staff of the Depot have symbolised a centralised authority and tribal communities do not have a say in the fixation of the price to the produce collected. Hence the cooperation principle is missing in GCC's affairs;

(4) The efforts towards the periodical assessment of the purchase price to the produce collected by the tribals many a times is done arbitrarily. Although a few elite are incorporated in bodies at the apex level participation of tribals in price fixation is almost nil;

(5) In the operations of GCC, the whole process of marketing by the state agency is a sort of unilateral one leading to unequal exchange relations.

(6) Inspite of substantial revenue to the GCC, tribals get only a meagre share of their revenue in the form of prices alone rather than a price component and dividend component even though this Corporation is organised along coopertive lines.

The steps to be taken for a better functioning of GCC are:

(i) GCC should take necessary measures to ensure the remunerative procurement price to MFP items. It should also take necessary efforts to streamline the organisational aspects of it on a rational basis for effective and useful services to the tribals;

(ii) The Government should take necessary steps to curb the wide variation between the purchase price and sale price and it should also offer higher purchase prices for the produce, as sometimes the price offered by the GCC is lesser than the price offered by private merchants.

(iii) Measures should be taken both by the forest department and GCC to assess the exact potential of MFP and to maximise the MFP collection in a more scientific and systematic way tribals should be trained;

(iv) Mobile vigilance staff should be appointed to check the malpractices in the Shandy points and marketing centres;

(v) New location of market centres and other Shandy points should be given preference where these centres do not exist;

(vi) GCC should curtail its overhead expenses and should also take necessary measures to prevent the fraudulent practices adopted by the field staff;

(vii) GCC has to provide better infrastructural facilities like construction of sheds, provision of drinking water and sanitation facilities in tribal villages as a policy matter;

(viii) Steps should be taken to establish the local market committees in each tribal village to ensure a sense of accountability in the functioning of D.R. depots;

(ix) Illicit gem trade is ignored by the state and there should be a serious thinking over it by the state agencies operating in this region.

Though the Government's policy is mainly oriented towards the development of tribal economy through institutional support, it could not make much headway in achieving its objective.

The *Fifth chapter* throws light on some of the salient features of the study area and the socio-economic profile of the sample households All the three districts Viz. Khammam, Warangal and Adilabad have relatively higher percentage of tribals in the total population as per 1991 Census.. In Khammam district the scheduled tribes form 25.22 per cent of the total population, their number is 5.58 lakhs. In Warangal district, their percentage is 13.7 per cent of the total population, while their number is 3.8 lakhs. In Adilabad district, the tribals form 17.04 per cent of the total population, but their number is 3.54 lakhs. In this respect, Khammam has a higher concentration of tribals either in terms of its percentage or its number than Warangal and Adilabad.

Khammam district has a preponderant position over the two other study areas in the case of indicators such as percentage of forest area to total geographical area, percentage of irrigated area to total area and in the case of the scheduled tribes population in the district. Warangal district in the study area dominates over the other two study areas in regard to aspects like percentage of workers, percentage of cultivators and cropping intensity. Adilabad district is in a better position than other areas in the case of percentage of non-workers, percentage of cultivated area to total geographical area, percentage of cropped area to geographical area, and percentage of scheduled castes population. only nine per cent of irrigated area to the total cropped area is in this district and further the cropping intensity is also less; percentage of literacy is also very low and moreover, the percentage of non-workers is the highest. A similar tendency had also been observed even in the case of respective sample mandals and in the case of sample villages leading to the inference that Adilabad is less developed than the other two districts.

Apart from the districts chosen, one mandal each had been selected from these three districts. The percentage of scheduled tribes population is 44.92 in Dammapet mandal of Khammam district, 46.80 in Tadvai mandal of Warangal district and 57.90 in Indravelli Mandal of Adilabad district. Thus, all the Mandals have about 45 per cent of their population as tribals. The forest area is 41.26 per cent, 86.40 per cent and 42.46 per cent of the total geographical area in Dammapet, Tadvai and Indravelli respectively. Thus, Tadvai mandal has a higher proportion of geographical area under forests than the other two mandals. Agricultural labourers as a percentage of the total population is 22.75 per cent, 20.90 per cent and 20.20 per cent in Dammapet, Tadvai and Indravelli mandals signifying that they are predominantly tribal populated areas and one-fifth of the population belongs to the category of agricultural labourers. This signifies the growth of agricultural production in these areas.

The availability of general infrastructural facilities will also have an important bearing on the path of the development of any region. Out of the eight sample villages, only three villages possessed pucca approach roads and most of the villages have schooling facility and were electrified. It is evident that most of the households in the villages have been slowly paying attention towards the growing of commercial crops like cashewnuts, groundnut, cotton, mirchi and tobacoo. Most of the villages are far away from the major town in the district and even some of the villages too are far away even from the mandal headquarters. By and large, the villages do not have satisfactory infrastructural facilities and this limits physical access to formal markets for all farmers, especially the tribals.

The socio-economic analysis of the sample tribal and non-tribal households reveals that most of the decision makers in the sample households in the study area are aged less than 40 years which can be considered as the *'effective working group'*. Their involvement in the collection of MFP and pursuit of the agricultural activities is active and effective displaying greater dynamism, which can be a causal factor for the significant relationship between the effective age group and performing one's own occupation. The region-wise and tribal and non-tribal group-wise configuration with regard to the primary occupation lends support to generally held hypothesis that most of the village economies in tribal areas are undergoing a slow transition from forest-based economies to agriculturally oriented economies. The subsidiary occupations in the sample villages contribute substantially to the earnings of a few tribals. For instance less than five per cent of the total tribal population has no subsidiary occupation in all the districts and the maximum of five per cent can be seen in Adilabad. Tribals tend to depend on the collection of MFP only as subsidiary occupation during the off-season. The rate of illiteracy is more prevalent in the case of sample tribal households than the non-tribal sample households which in turn reflects tribals' socio-economic status.

The region-wise, and tribal and non-tribal group-wise distribution of the size of operational holdings reveals that the sample tribal households preponderate over the sample non-tribal households in the case of the small and marginal farmers and the reverse is held true in the case of the medium and big farmers.

The small and marginal farmers are more in Warangal followed by Khammam and Adilabad with 55 per cent, 53 per cent and the 36 per cent respectively. Further, sample villages in Adilabad do not possess public irrigation system and most of the land is rainfed. But sample villages in Warangal are in an advantageous position in accordance with the type of irrigation system when compared with the Khammam district.

Uneven distribution of agricultural incomes exhibiting greater inequalities is evident among the sample tribal and non-tribal households. These inequalities are more stark among the tribals than among non-tribals. Likewise, these inequalities are more in Khammam and Adilabad than in Warangal. One reason could be that the migrant non-tribals in Warangal are also income earning peasants. The MFP incomes of the sample households reveal that among the three districts, Warangal had a dominant position over the other two districts in the study area. The agricultural wage labour incomes didn't contribute substantially to the total earnings of the tribal households. The non-casual labour incomes in the study area reveal that Khammam district is able to absorb more labour than the rest of the districts in the study area. But a comparison of tribals shows the percentage is higher at Adilabad than in the other two districts.

The total incomes and expenditures of the sample tribal and non-tribal households also demonstrate that total incomes and expenditures of sample non-tribal households are on the higher side than the incomes and expenditures of the sample tribal households besides their uneven distribution. This pattern reveals that wherever the incomes generated are relatively high, the expenditures are also relatively high.

The *sixth chapter* examined the nature of interlinkages of credit with input and product markets. Among all the sample households, whether it is borrowers from exclusively institutional sources or exclusively from non-institutional sources the percentage is relatively higher for tribals than non-tribals, but for borrowers from both the sources, it is higher for non-tribals than tribals. This clearly shows the growing institutionalisation of credit in tribal areas and the existence of linked transactions among the sub-sample borrowers demonstrates the nexus between the credit and product markets. Among the borrower households the data confirms the hypothesis that the non-tribals are in an advantageous position than the tribals. This indicates the accessibility of loans from the institutional and non-institutional credit agencies for them in the study area. The data further reveals that the sample tribal borrowers who obtained the loans from the institutional sources are relatively higher in number than the sample non-tribal borrowers due to the operations of the institutions like ITDA and GCC created for the upliftment of the tribals. Most of the borrowers obtained the loans for agricultural inputs and loans related to the land development activities and other purposes like marriages and ceremonies. But a majority of the borrowers had diverted their loan amount for other than the purported purpose, that is from productive purposes to the unproductive purposes like conspicuous consumption.

The entire logit model analysis supports the argument that by merely having the formal lending agencies in the tribal, areas do not guarantee and protect the interests of the tribal households as well as the small and marginal non-tribal peasants in the tribal areas. The larger farmers' grip over the formal credit agencies had not diminished in the study area. The asset based lending policies adopted and practiced by the formal lending agencies buttress their hold in the villages. Low literacy level, lower caste status, lower incomes, small size of operated land holding, higher family size, and higher worker-dependent ratio adversely affect the small, marginal, poor and tribal farmers of the sample households while getting the loans from the formal lending agencies. Despite establishing formal lending agencies in tribal areas, their hierarchical structure deter the small, poor and tribal farmers to obtain the loans from them.

In tribal areas, a variety of credit relations and transactions signify the relative importance of non-monetised transactions in tribal areas. In all the districts under consideration for the study, the prevalent mode of repayment is cash to cash form which is more prominent, despite the relative importance of it being more in Khammam than in the other two districts. Among other forms, cash to labour is not found to be prevalent, while cash to kind is relatively more important in Warangal and Adilabad. The other form which is of relevance is cash to cash and output in all the districts. Hence in all the districts there is a greater degree of monetisation of transactions, though Khammam ranks first followed by Warangal and Adilabad.

On the basis of the analysis of linked and non-linked transactions in the study area, it can be said that the group of borrowers with linked transactions when compared with the group of borrowers with non-linked transactions have a lower mean literacy status, higher mean family size, higher mean agricultural income, lower MFP income, lower mean income from agricultural wage labour, lower level of income with respect to incomes from non-agricultural labour, a relatively higher mean total expenditures, a higher proportion of mean male workers to total workers and a lesser worker-dependent ratio.

The logistic regression analysis and the discriminant function analysis had also been taken up to identify the specific household characteristics that made the borrowres to opt for either the linked or non-linked transactions.

Among various causative factors influencing linkages, some are exhibiting positive impact while others are exerting a negative impact. An improvement in literacy status of the respondents has an overall negative influence on linkages in the overall sample, but it has a positive influence in Khammam sub-sample and tribal sub-sample. Agricultural incomes and incomes from agricultural/wage labour have a positive influence on linkages. In the case of MFP incomes, it has a negative impact in the case of tribals, signifying that an increase in MFP income would weaken the linkage effect. The same finding had been observed in the case of incomes from non-casual labour. The total expenditure has a negative influence on the linkage variable, but for tribals it has a positive influence. Further, the influence is positive for proportion of male workers to total workers. The worker-dependent ratio has a negative impact on linkage variable in the case of tribals sub-sample. Hence, in the case of tribals, an improvement in certain variables like literacy status of the borrowers, agricultural incomes, incomes from agricultural labour, total expenditures and proportion of male workers to total workers, contrary to certain earlier hypotheses leads to an increase in linkages rather than reducing it. On the other hand, a rise in MFP incomes, incomes from non-casual labour and worker-dependent ratio would reduce these linkages.

In the case of the total sub-sample discriminant function, agricultural incomes, total expenditures, literacy status and worker-dependent ratio contributed in the same hierarchical order to the function and explain the households decision of opting for the linked transactions in the study area. In the case of Khammam sub-sample, the hierarchical order of the relative contribution to the function are agricultural incomes, incomes from non-casual labour, and M.F.P. incomes. In the case of Warangal sub-sample, the crucial variables for the discriminant function are agricultural incomes, worker-dependent ratio, incomes from agricultural/wage labour and finally the literacy status that have had the potential power to discriminate between the linked and non-linked borrowings of the sample households in the district. But in the case of Adilabad, MFP incomes and proportion of male workers to total workers significantly contributed to the discriminant function. Finally, in the case of sub-sample of tribals in the study area, the relative magnitude of the variables by the total distance measured to the discriminant function are agricultural incomes, incomes from agricultural/ wage labour, MFP incomes and proportion of male workers to total workers that have a significant bearing in regard to the households decisions opting for the linked transactions in the area.

The contribution of agricultural incomes variable to the function is relatively higher in the case of sub-sample of tribals followed by total sub-sample, Khammam sub-sample and the Warangal sub-sample with the percentage contribution of 52.30, 40.40, 39.70 and 33.80 respectively. The percentage contribution of the total expenditures to the function 32.50 can only be seen in the case of total sub-sample of the study area. The relative percentage contribution of the literacy status to the function was observed in the sub-sample of Warangal and the total sub-sample with 18.40 and 9.60 respectively. A similar finding had also been observed even in the case of worker-dependent ratio. Its relative percentage contribution is relatively higher in Warangal with 24.40 followed by the total sub-sample with 8.50. The relative percentage contribution of the incomes from non-casual labour to the discriminant function 34.00 can only be observed in the case of sub-sample of Khammam. Its percentage contribution of MFP incomes to the function was the highest in Adilabad followed by Khammam and the sub-sample of tribals with 62.35, 26.00 and 15.70 respectively. The relative percentage contribution of agricultural/wage labour incomes to the function is apparent in the sub-sample of Warangal followed by the sub-sample of tribals with 23.40 and 21.25 respectively. Finally, the relative percentage contribution of proportion of male workers to total workers to the discriminant function can only be seen in the case of sub-sample of Adilabad followed by the sub-sample of tribals with 37.65 and 10.75. Though these variables reflect the regional diversity these variables have the potential power in discriminating the linked borrowers and others in the researchers' study area with in the sub-sample strata.

In the *seventh chapter* the factors that contribute to the variation in the marketable and marketed surplus have been examined by the application of multiple regression analysis to understand the causal relationships.

The average family size for sample households is about six, though Adilabad has a relatively higher value than Khammam and Warangal. The family size among the non-tribal households is relatively higher than the tribal households in the study area which is in contrast to the usually held hypothesis that the tribals have large sized families than the non-tribal households. If tribal and non-tribal distinction in the case of land possession is taken into account, the mean value for tribals is 0.313 acres, while it is 0.867 acres for non-tribals.

The tribal and non-tribal differences also show that the amount taken by the non-tribals is three times more than the amount taken by the tribals. The mean value for the inter-linkages between the two parties, where one party is the lender of the loan and the other party is leasee shows that the commitment is on the relatively high side and this phenomena is more evident in the case of Khammam, which is considered as relatively developed than Adilabad, which is less developed. Likewise, the sub-sample of non-tribals have a greater commitment against loan than the sample tribal households in the study area.

The study also points out that the percentage of produce as marketable surplus is relatively higher than the percentage of produce as marketed surplus for all the three districts uniformly. Both these values are relatively higher in Khammam than in Adilabad and the differences also exist in the case of tribals and non-tribals. One observation is that the percentage of marketed surplus is higher than the percentage of marketable surplus in the case of tribals, indicating around 2.5 per cent of the produce as 'forced sales'.

In Khammam district there is a positive and strong relationship between (r=0.705) the total incomes of the sample households and the commitment against the loan. Like wise an inverse but strong relationship (r=0.746) exists between percentage of produce marketed and the percentage of produce consumed. A similar relationship had also been observed even in the case of percentage of marketable surplus and the percentage of produce consumed (-0.759). In Warangal district, there is a better linear relationship between the total incomes of the sample households and the amount spent on shandy/ marketing (r=0.764).

In the case of non-tribal sample households in the entire study area, there is a perfect inverse relationship between the percentage of marketable surplus and the percentage of produce consumed (r=0.789). A similar relationship had also been observed even in the case of percentage of produce marketed and the percentage of produce consumed (r=-0.731).

As far as the marketable surplus as regressand is concerned one will be able to surmise that regional, tribal and non-tribal differences are more persistent in the study area. Percentage of produce consumed variable as regressor is common in all the regression equations that has been found to be statistically significant. Total incomes variable has been found to be statistically significant in the total sample size, in Khammam sub-sample, in tribal and non-tribal sub-sample regression equations. Amount taken variable has been found to be statistically significant for the fitted regression equations for the total sample, for Adilabad district and for the sub-sample of tribal households. Percentage of area under commercial crops variable has been found to be statistically significant for the fitted regression equations for total sample and for Adilabad district. Percentage of MFP consumed variable had been found to be statistically significant only for the total sample and for the sub-sample of non-tribal households. Total amount spent on shandy/marketing variable has been found to be statistically significant only for the sub-sample of Warangal district's fitted regression equation. And finally, number of acres under double crop variable has been found to be statistically significant only for the sub-sample of Adilabad district's fitted regression equation.

Inferences pertaining to the marketed surplus reveal that only percentage of produce consumed variable is common for all the regression equations. Amount taken variable is found to be statistically significant only in the first, fourth and fifth regression equations, that refer to the total sample, Adilabad and tribal sample households respectively. Percentage of area under commercial crops variable is statistically significant in the first, fourth and fifth regression equations, which refer to the total sample, Adilabad and tribal sample households respectively. Total amount spent on shandy/marketing variable is statistically significant only in Warangal district. Number of acres under double crop variable is statistically significant in Adilabad district. Percentage of MFP consumed and Total incomes variables are statistically significant only in the case of non-tribal households' regression equation. Further, it is also to be noted that only the regressors like percentage of produce consumed, amount taken and percentage of area under commercial crops variables are statistically significant both in total sample and sub-sample of tribals' regression equations.

The *eighth chapter* had been devoted for examining the various facets involved in the indigenous marketing pattern in tribal areas based on the field findings and it also throws light on the *'modus operandi'* of the GCC. Further, it also incorporates the sample tribal households' suggestions and views in regard to the strengthening of the corporation and to make it function effectively and efficiently.

Two broad channels of tribal markets are the institutional one and the other is the non-institutional marketing agencies. The existence of periodical markets reflects the marketing pattern in tribal areas. The sample tribal households visit the periodic markets for purchasing the domestic requirements and selling their produce. Some of the sample tribals visit the shandy on social matters like settling the matrimonial alliances and the disputes as well. Most of the households had paid their visit to the shandy points for selling their minor forest produce and in this process they make their purchases of the essential commodities like rice, oil, kerosene, pulses, and sugar. A variety of weights and measures were observed to be in use, apart from selling and buying through the approxi-mation in the shandy point. The tribals as buyers as well as sellers are being cheated and deceived by the itinerant traders in the shandy points under the name of the standard weights and measures as they are not able to identify them.

The credit-cum-procurement assistants appointed by the Corporation act as catalysts while informing the prices to the tribals and procuring the minor forest produce and some times even agricultural produce from them also. Under-weighment, excessive driages, under rating the quality are the common grouses against CCPAs, and weighing boys. It had been mentioned by tribals, on one hand that CCPAs are resorting to an illegitimate practice of keeping away larger quantities of the produce towards driages particularly in the case of gum and tamarind, but on the other the CCPAs complained that the tribals are resorting to the malpractices like: increasing the weight of the produce, mixing foreign matter in the produce and wetting the gum and tamarind.

An overwhelming majority of sample tribal households are engaged in the collection of minor forest produce and sell it to GCC, except for one or two items which are sold to non-institutional agencies. It had been mentioned that out of MFP collected a smaller quantity had been used for the consumption purposes. Hence MFP pickers sell their entire collection of gum, nuxvomica, pungam-seeds, myrobalans, cleaning nuts. While other items like wild-brooms, mohwa flower and seed, chiranji, honey, tamarind, and K.T. bundles, are used for domestic consumption. One reason for using mohwa flower, seed and other items is that they have low procurement prices as well as use value for household consumption.

The traditional marketing methods are still prevalent in the study villages especially in the case of wild-brooms and tamarind seed. But in the case of other items, they first convert their commodities into cash in order to make necessary purchases. It had been mentioned that almost all the sample tribal households are selling items like wild-brooms, honey and K.T. bundles in open market to get higher prices as prices offered by the Corporation are low. So, the tribal households expressed their opinion that there is a need to enhance the prices of these MFP items by the Corporation to induce the tribals to sell their produce to GCC only.

While selling the agricultural produce, a majority of the sample households had preferred to sell it to the private traders and village merchants due to intimacy, but also due to the produce not being bought by the Corporation. But the Corporation in Adilabad district entered into the domain of cotton procurement and hence purchased the cotton produced by tribals. It had been mentioned that the private traders and merchants play a predominant role while purchasing the agricultural produce from the sample households in the study area due to the linkages of credit with product markets. Therefore, most of the households had preferred to sell their produce soon after harvesting.

The tribals sell their MFP to the Corporation and in turn purchase their domestic requirements like rice, kerosene, matches, oils, controlled cloth and pulses, from the D.R. depots of the Corporation. Some of the sample tribal households were sceptical about buying commodities supplied by the Corporation due to a variety of reasons like low quality, higher prices, closure of store very often, heavy loss of time at the depots during the busy agricultural season and also due to supplying insufficient quantity.

Salesmen in the D.R. depots will not allow tribals to buy smaller quantities of the commodities like 25 grams, 50 grams and even 100 grams and even some times in particular the rice will also be of very poor quality. Inspite of certain limitations, Corporation is considered to be somewhat successful as it caters to the needs of the tribals on behalf of the channel of Civil Supplies through its D.R. depots. Therefore, almost all the consumable articles are being supplied at subsidised rates.

Every household preferred to make their purchases from different sources and their purchases depend on the availability of the items from three sources namely the Corporation, village showkaries and private merchants and inturn reflect their needs from time to time. A variety of reasons like assured marketing, better and graded price, perfect weighing and measurement, and being free from malpractices are responsible for the sample tribal households to make their purchases from the D.R. Depots of the Corporation for meeting their day-to-day requirements. Due to other reasons like, availability of multiple variety of items and non-availability of the item from the Corporation, longer acquaintance with the village showkaries or the private merchants, better quality of the commodities supplying the goods on the basis of credit, and the time loss being high in the queue at the D.R. depots of the Corporation during the busy seasonal employment activities made some of the sample tribal households make their purchases from the village merchants.

A majority of the sample households expressed their satisfaction over the price paid by the different marketing agencies in the study area and this had been inview of the obtained prices of both MFP and AP. But, this finding is contrary to the observation made by the researcher during his field visits when the prices of MFP and AP are aggregated.

It had been observed that a considerable percentage of the households reported that they had administrative, trade related and the socio-lingual-cultural problems. It had also been observed that inadequate transport facilities and lack of proper communication facilities, besides congestion in the shandies had mentioned as the deficiencies of the present marketing system.

An overwhelming majority of the sample tribal households are aware of the Corporation's services and concessions that had been provided for the betterment of themselves. On the basis of evidence it had been surmised that the activities of the Corporation are more intensive in Adilabad than in the two other districts in the study area, though the Corporation had not rendered its services to all the needy and poor tribal households due to the organisational loopholes of the Corporation. One loophole is that the organisational set-up of the Corporation is devoid of any participation by the tribals. The reasons for not receiving the services are mentioned as either tribals not being in need of any assistance or being busy in other occupations or old age or time loss being high at the Corporation or lack of land as a surety or prevalence of single window system and cumbersome procedures.

The sample households had suggested certain steps like separate educational schemes for tribals, an assessment of the exact potential of MFP, creation of storage facilities, mobile supply of daily requirements, establishment of new market centres, more transport facilities and prevention of excessive driages. The implementation of above suggestions would give more scope for the elimination of exploitation at least within the orbit of the shandy points that had been there in the tribal areas.

An overwhelming majority (73.3 per cent) of the sample tribals had also suggested certain remedial measures for strengthening the GCC in achieving its twin objectives of credit and marketing. They are: i) relaxation of stringent conditions and an enhancement in the loan amount; ii) a rise in MFP prices and a reduction of DRs prices; iii) purchase of agricultural produce along with the MFP; iv) timely supply of all the inputs - land, water, credit and marketing facilities; v) establishment of D.R. Depots in each village; vi) no purchase of MFP from non-tribals; vii) sanctioning of the patta rights for newly cultivated lands; and viii) providing adequate training methods and practices for the extraction and tapping of the minor forest produce.

From the preceding analysis, it had been inferred that in

the absence of an organised, institutional and regulated markets in the tribal areas, the tribals are deprived from enjoying the fruits of unfettered rights and a fair pricing system and often it leads to the emergence of a class of petty traders taking an advantage of the helpless situation of the tribals leading to their exploitation. The State should take a serious view of the situation and should establish the regulated market for the betterment of the tribals at the vicinity of their work places and strengthen the existing shandy points by eliminating the exploitative mechanisms. Moreover by strengthening the existing institutional marketing facilities in all the tribal areas, the tribal households will not only get a better and remunerative prices for their produce but they can also be benefitted through the sharing of gains of the corporation.

The views and opinions of the tribal and non-tribal farmers in the form of case studies in the selected villages had been presented in the *ninth chapter*. In all ten cases have been presented in this chapter. These cases are named here as A,B,C,D,E,F,G,H,I and J for the sake of anonymity. Among these, ABCD are from Khammam district, EFGH are from Warangal and I,J are from Adilabad district. From an analysis of case studies presented in this chapter the researcher could draw the following inferences.

Firstly, a transformation process has been slowly taking place in the tribal areas in almost all walks of life. Due to the *'culture-contacts'* with the outer world, the tribals are more prone to exploitation and again it is also due to the penetration of commercial and market economy, which is inextricably interwoven with the internal circulation of monetary relations. As tribals are becoming more aware of their rights, the positive sided transformation outweighs the negative sided transformation. Tribal households have been learning so many modern methods of agricultural practices and its other related activities, and they have been paying more attention to the growing of commercial crops and plantation instead of growing mere subsistence and food crops. Therefore, at present they have been realizing more yield rate per acre as well as more incomes than what they obtained earlier.

Secondly, most of the tribal households have been making attempts to engage themselves in the collection of minor forest produce but its availability is diminishing at a very fast rate. Therefore, the dependence on it for livelihood has made their lives precarious and they are likely to become either agricultural labourers or as poor and marginal farmers. Hence 'Podu' cultivation has been still taking place extensively in some of the inaccessible and interior tribal areas.

Thirdly, GCC and ITDA have also been rendering yeoman services for the betterment of tribal households while creating the physical assets by providing loans and also providing daily requirements through D.R. depots though at times the employees adopt devious methods to deceive tribals. As GCC acts as a monopsonist in the sphere of marketing, it is actively involved in the tribal marketing process while purchasing the minor forest produce that had been collected by the tribals. Here, it is also viewed that the GCC should take stern steps to purchase the agricultural produce along with the purchase of minor forest produce at reasonable prices. In the recent years, these institutions have also been contributing for the transformation process that had been taking place in the tribal areas.

Fourthly, the role of money-lenders had declined due to the active involvement and extension of credit facilities by the various financial institutions in the tribal areas. The obverse of it is the inter-linkages between the product and credit markets. These linkages are leading to the exploitative relations under the guise of subtle and explicit methods of charging higher interest rates from tribals. The rate of exploitation had also been severe either in the credit market or product markets. Thus, these shandy points have become, in due course of time, *paradises for middlemen* as the *rate and speed of exploitation of ignorant tribals* is much higher than found in any other market.

By and large, one has to surmise that the transformation process is proceeding at a slower pace in the tribal areas. As evident from the above analysis, a slow process of transformation from self-sufficient, subsistence economies to a dependent, commercially-oriented economies is taking place in tribal areas. This process of transformation depends, to a larger extent, on the growth of institutionalised structures in all markets - whether input or final product markets in tribal economies. Albeit, this analysis brings out the importance and role of non-price factors in generating marketed surplus, as marketed surplus as a percentage of total product is a crucial indicator for capturing the process of transformation. As marketisation of these economies improves, these traditional societies are also drawn into the vortex of markets leading to manifold changes in the tribal areas, especially in introducing a materialistic culture that can spur the development process in these areas. While one should take cognizance of regional diversities, as adumbrated in this study, a dynamic process of transforming tribal economies has begun and the intervention of the government either in actively involving itself in marketing activity through GCC or institutionalising the credit structure had a positive impact on lessening the indigenity of the markets in tribal areas.

SELECT BIBLIOGRAPHY

BOOKS

Alm, S. Mazoor, E. Gormsen and M. Von Oppen (1985), *Agricultural Markets in the Semi-Arid Tropics*, ICRISAT, Patancheru, Andhra Pradesh.

Bakken, Henry, H (1953), *Theory of Markets and Marketing*, Mimir Publishers, Inc.

Bhaduri, Amit: (1986), *Economic Power, Organisational Form and the Commercialisation of Backward Agriculture*, Mimeo, Delhi.

Bardhan, Pranab, K (1986), *Land, labour and Rural Poverty- Essays in Development Economics*, Oxford University Press, New Delhi.

————(1989), (Ed.), *The Economic Theory of Agrarian Institutions*, Clarendon Press, New York.

————(1989), (Ed.), *Conversations Between Economists and Anthropologists: Methodological Issues in Measuring Economic Change in Rural India*, Oxford University Press, New Delhi.

Belshaw, Cyril, S (1965), *Traditional Exchange and Modern Markets*, Prentice-Hall, Inc., Englewood Cliffs, N.J. London.

Bhowmick, K.L. (Ed.) (1971), *Tribal India - A Profile in Indian Ethnology*, The World Press, Calcutta.

Bohannan, Paul (1963), *Social Anthropology*, Rineheart and Winston, Inc., New York.

Bohannan, Paul & George Dalton (Ed.) (1962), *Markets in Africa*, Evanston, North-Western University Press.

Bose, N.K. (1971), *Tribal Life in India*, National Book Trust, New Delhi.

Bromley, R.J. (1974), *Periodic Markets, Daily Markets and Fairs : A Bibliography*, Monash University Publications in Geography, Clayton, No.10.

Boulding, Kenneth (1941), *Economic Analysis,* Harper & Row Publishers, New York.

Chattopadhyaya, Kamaladevi (1978), *Tribalism in India,* Vikas Publishing House, New Delhi.

Dalton, George (1971), *Economic Anthropology and Development - Essays on Tribal and Peasant Economies,* Basic Books, Inc., Publishers, London.

Das Gupta, K.K. (1974), *A Tribal History of Ancient India,* Navabharat Publishers, Calcutta.

Das Gupta,K.K. (1978), *Research in Economic Anthropology– An Annual Compilation of Research,* Vol.I, jai Press, Inc., U.S.A.

————(1979), Vol. (2).

————(1980), Vol. (3).

Desai, B.M. et. al (1984), *Agrarian Power and Agricultural Productivity in South Asia,* Oxford University Press, Delhi.

Dubey, S.N. & Murdia, Ratna (Ed.) (1977), *Land Alienation and Restoration in Tribal Communities in India,* Himalaya Publishing House, Bombay.

————(1976), *Administration of Policy and Programmes for backward Classes in India,* Somaiya Publications, Bombay.

Dube, S.C (1977), *Tribal Heritage of India,* (4 Volumes), Vikas Publishing House, Pvt. Ltd., New Delhi.

Elwin, Verrier (1947), *Mariya and their Ghotal,* Oxford University Press, London.

Firth, Raymond (1966), *Malay Fishermen: Their Peasant Economy,* Archow Books, Hamden, Conn.

Ghatak, Subrata (1976), *Rural Money Markets in India,* The Macmillan Company of India Limited, Delhi.

Ghurye, G.S (1963), *The Scheduled Tribes,* Popular Prakashan, Bombay.

Good, Charles, M (1970), *Rural Markets and Trade in East Africa– A Study of the Functions and Development Exchange Institutions in Ankole, Uganda,* Research Paper No. 178, The University of Chicago, Dept. of Geography.

Gopal, Raja (1986), *Dynamics of Agricultural Marketing in Tribal India,* Rainbow Publications, Tamil Nadu.

————(1989), *Rural Marketing in India,* Renaissance Publishing House, Delhi.

————(1991), *Understanding Rural Marketing*, Daya Publishing House, Delhi.

————(1987), *Planning Agricultural Marketing in India*, Rainbow Publications, Tamil Nadu.

————(1988), *Marketing in Peasant Economy - History and Trends*, Manas Publications, Delhi.

Gupta, A.P (1975), *Marketing of Agricultural Produce in India*, Vora & Co., Publishers, Pvt., Ltd., Bombay.

Gupta Ranjit (Ed.) (1977), *Planning for Tribal Development*, Ankur Publishing House, New Delhi.

Haimendorf, C.V.F (1982), *Tribes of India - The Struggle for Survival*, Oxford University Press, Delhi.

————(1943), *Tribal Hyderabad* (Four Reports), H.E.H. Nizam Dominions, Hyderabad.

————(1945), *The Reddies of the Bison Hills - A Study in Acculturation*, Vol.II, the Aboriginal Tribes of Hyderabad, London.

————(1945), *Tribal Population of Hyderabad : Yesterday and Today*, Census of India, 1941, Vol.21, Hyderabad.

————(1945), *Progress and Problems of Aboriginal Rehabilitation in Adilabad District*, Hyderabad.

————(1948), *The Raj Gonds of Adilabad*, (Vol. III), London.

————(1979), *The Gonds of Andhra Pradesh, Tradition and Change in an Indian Tribe*, Delhi (Vikas).

Harriss, Barbara (1984), *Exchange Relations and Poverty in Dry Land Agriculture*, Concept Publishing Company, New Delhi.

————(1981), *Transitional Trade and Rural Development : The Nature and Role of Agricultural Trade in a South Indian District*, Vikas Publishing House, Pvt., Ltd., New Delhi.

Hasnain, Nadeem (1983), *Tribal India Today*, Harnam Publications, New Delhi.

Herskovits, Melville, J. (1965), *Economic Anthropology : The Economic Life of Primitive Peopls*, W.W. Norton and Company, INC, New York.

Hicks, J.R. (1969), *A Theory of Economic History*, Oxford University Press, London.

Holmes, Lowell, D (1971), *Anthropology: An Introduction*, The Ronald Press Company, New York.

Hooja Rakesh (1990), *Planning, Interlocked Markets and Rural Development*, Rawat Publications, Jaipur.

Hoyt, E.E (1926), *Primitive Trade: Its Psychology and Economics*, Trubner & Co., Ltd., London.

Hutton, Webster (1916), *Rent Ways: A Study in Early Law of Morality*, Macmillan, New York.

Jagannathan, N. Vijay (1987), *Informal Markets in Developing Countries*, Oxford University Press, Inc., New York.

Jay, Edward, J (1968), *Tribal Village of Middle India*, Anthropological Survey of India, Memoi, No.21.

Kabra, K.N (1983), *Dependence and Dominance : Political Economy of a Tribal Commodity*, Indian Institute of Public Administration, New Delhi.

Kacker Madhav (1982), *Marketing and Economic Development*, Deep and Deep Publications, New Delhi.

Kmenta, J: *Elements of Econometrics*, Macmillan, New York, 1971.

Kaynak, Erdener (1986), *Marketing and Economic Development*, Praeger Publishers, Westport, New York.

Krishna Murthy, T (1989), *Organisation and Working of Rural Markets in Telangana Region*, Unpublished Ph.D. Thesis, Dept. of Commerce, Kakatiya University, April.

Lele, Uma, J (1972), *Food Grain Marketing in India*, Cornell University Press, Ithaca.

Manohar, K. Murali, et. al. (Ed.) (1985), *Political Economy of Tribal Development*, IIPA Local Branch, Warangal.

Mamoria, C.B (1957), *Tribal Demography in India*, Kitab Mahal, Allahabad.

Mohapatro, P.C (1987), *Economic Development of Tribal India*, Ashish Publishing House, New Delhi.

Mahalingam, S. (1990), *Role of Co-operative Organisations in Developing Tribal Economy– A Study of LAMP Tribal Co-operatives*, Mittal Publications, New Delhi.

Majumdar, D.N (1944), *Races and Cultures of India*, Asia Publishing House, Bombay.

———(1950), *The Affairs of a Tribe : A Study in Tribal Dynamics, Universal Publishers* Lucknow.

Misra, Prasanna Bani (1976), *Socio-Economic Adjustment of Tribals - Case Study of Tripura Jhumias*, People's publishing House, New Delhi.

Nag, D.S: *Tribal Economy* (1958), *An Economic Study of the Baiga*, Bhartiya Adima Jati Seva Sangh, Kingsway, New Delhi.

Naik, T.B. & Bhourskar, K.M. (1964), *Tribal Economic Organisation and Market*, Trisul Research and Training Institute, Chindwarg, Madhya Pradesh.

Patel, M.L (1985), *Economic Dimension of Land Distribution of Tribal India*, Book Emporium, New Delhi.

———(1969), *Agro-Economic Survey of Tribal Mandla*, People's Publishing House, Pvt. Ltd., New Delhi.

———(1972), *Agro-Economic Problems of Tribal India*, Progress Publishers, Bhopal.

———(1974), *Changing Land Problems of Tribal India*, National Publishing House, New Delhi.

———(1984), *Planning Strategy for Tribal Development*, Inter-India Publications, New Delhi.

Punalekar, S.P (1980), *Weekly Markets in Tribal Areas*, Centre for Social Studies, Surat, Gujarat.

Polanyi, Karl (1957), *The Great Transformation*, Rinehart & Company, Inc., New York.

——— (1957), et. al. (Ed.): *Trade and Market in the Early Empires*, Free Press, Glencoe.

Radcliffe Brown, A.R (1952), *Structure and Function in Primitive Society*, Routledge & Kegan Paul, London.

Raghavaiah, V (1969), *Tribes of India*, Bharatiya Adima Jati Sevak Sangh, New Delhi.

———(1971), *Tribal Revolts*, Andhra Rashtra Adima Jati Sevak Sangh, Nellore.

Ramaiah, P. & Manohar, K. Murali (1992), *Tribal Indebtedness*, Himalaya Publishing House, Bombay.

Ramaiah, P (1981), *Tribal Economy of India - A Case Study of Koyas of Andhra Pradesh*, Light and Life Publishers, New Delhi.

———(1988), *Issues in Tribal Development*, Chugh Publications, Allahabad.

Rao, C. Siva Rama Krishna (1986), *Changing Agrarian Relations in India-A Case Study of A.P.*, Mamidipudi Venkatrangaiah Publishers, Hyderabad.

Rao, B. Janardhan (1987), *Land Alienation in Tribal Areas,* KASPA, Warangal.

Rao, I. Murali Krishna (1988), *Marketing in Tribal Economy - A Study with Special Reference to Shandies (Periodic Markets) in the Tribal Belt of Srikakulam District of Andhra Pradesh,* Inter-India Publications, New Delhi.

Rao, K. Mohan (1993), *Socio-Cultural Profile of Tribals of Andhra Pradesh,* TCR & TI, Tribal Welfare Department, Andhra Pradesh, Hyderabad.

Rao, S. Jagan Mohan (1984), *The Girijan Co-Operative Corporation and Tribal Development with Special Reference to Warangal District,* Unpublished Ph.d. Thesis, submitted to the Department of Economics, Kakatiya University, Warangal.

Roth Hans-Dieter (1983), *Indian Moneylenders at Work,* Manohar Publications, New Delhi.

Sarkar, S.S (1954), *The Aboriginal Races of India,* Bookland, Pvt. Ltd., Calcutta.

Sarap, Kailas (1991), *Interlinked Agrarian Markets Rural India,* Sage Publications, New Delhi.

Saxena, H.M (1988), *Rural Markets and Development - A Case Study of Rajasthan State,* Rawat Publications, Jaipur.

Saxena, R.P (1964), *The Tribal Economy in Central India,* Firma, K.L. Mukhoyadhyan, Calcutta.

Sikindar, Sujit (1990), *Economic Development of Tribal India,* Ashish Publishing House, New Delhi.

Singh, Bhupinder (1983), *Co-operatives in Tribal Areas,* (Occasional Paper-32), Ministry of Home Affairs, Government of India, New Delhi.

Sinha, D.P (1968), *Culture Change in an Inter-Tribal Market,* Asia Publishing House, New Delhi.

Sharma, B.D (1981), *Economic Development of Extremely Backward Tribal Regions,* (Occasional paper 8), Ministry of Home Affairs, Government of India, New Delhi.

————: *Administrative Aspects of Marketing in Tribal Areas*, (Occasional Papers- 14), Ministry of Home Affairs, Government of India, New Delhi.

————(1978), *Tribal Development: The Concept and the Frame*, Prachi Prakashan, New Delhi.

Somasekar, A (1983), *Economic Conditions of Tribals - A Case Study of Koyas of Godavari Valley*, Unpublished Ph.D. Thesis, Submitted to the Department of Economics, Osmania University, Hyderabad.

Srivastava, H.C. & M.K. Chaturvedi (1989), *Dependency and common Property Resources of Tribal and Rural Poor*, Commonwealth Publishers, New Delhi.

Subba Rao, K (1978), *Rice Marketing System and Compulsory Levies in Andhra Pradesh*, Allied Publishers, Pvt. Ltd., Bombay.

Sudhakar, Gopu (1992), *Public Policy and Development: A Study of Forest Policy and Tribal Development*, Unpublished Ph.D. Thesis, Submitted to the Department of Public Administration, Kakatiya University, Warangal.

Thakur, Devendra (1986), *Socio-Economic Development of Tribals in India*, Deep and Deep Publications, New Delhi.

Theil, H. (1971), *Principles of Econometrics*, Amsterdam, North-Holland.

Trivedi, H.V (1985), *Economic Development of Tribes in India*, Himanshu Publications, Udaipur.

Thurnwald, Richard (1965), *Economics in Primitive Communities*, (Anthropological Publications), Oxford University Press, New Delhi.

Vidyarthi, L.P. (1978), *Rise of Anthropology in India: The Tribal Dimensions*, (Vol. I & II), Concept Publishing Company, Delhi.

Vidyarthi, L.P.(Ed.) (1959), *Anthropology and Tribal Welfare in India*, Council of Social and Cultural Research, Bihar.

————(1963), *The Maler- A Case Study in Nature- Man Spirit Complex of a Hill Tribe in Bihar*, Book Land, Calcutta.

Von Pischke, J.D., Dale W. Adams (Ed.) Gordon Donald (1983), *Rural Financial Markets in Developing Countries*, The Johns Hopkins University Press, Baltimore, USA.

Waddell, L.A (1986), *The Tribes of the Brahmaputra Valley*, Logos Press, New Delhi.

Wanmali, Sudhir (1980), *Periodic Markets and Rural Development in India*, B.R. Publishing Corporation, New Delhi.

Young, P. & Schmid (1975), *Principles and Techniques of Social Studies*, Prentice Hall, India (New Delhi).

PAPERS

Aiyappan, A. (1965), 'Development of Tribal Areas', *Economic and Political Weekly*, Vol. XVII, No.24, June 12, pp.949-950.

Aiyasami, U., & H.B. Bohle (1981), 'Market Access as Constraint on Marginal and Small Farmers', *Economic and Political Weekly*, Vol.XVI, No.13, March 28, pp.A.29-A.36.

Balagopal, K. (1989), 'Pitting the Tribals against the Non-Tribal Poor', *Economic and Political Weekly*, Vol.XXIV, No.21, May 27, pp.1149-1154.

Basu, Kaushik (1988), 'Economic Theory in Development Economics-Methodology, Agrarian Structure and Rent Control Laws', *Economic and Political Weekly*, Vol.XXIII, Nos.45, 46 & 47 (Special Number), November, pp.2309-2312.

————(1986), 'Markets, Power and Social Norms', *Economic and Political Weekly*, Vol.XXI, No.43, October 25, pp.1893-1896.

Bardhan, P.K., & T.N. Srinivasan (1971), 'Crop Sharing Tenancy in Agriculture : A Theoretical and Empirical Analysis', *American Economic Review*, Vol.LXI, No.1, March, pp.48-64.

Bardhan, P., & Ashok Rudra (1985), 'The Domain of Rural Labour Markets- Results of a Survey in West Bengal, 1981-82' *Economic and Political Weekly*, Vol. XX, Nos. 51 & 52, December 21-28, pp.A.153 and A.154.

————(1978), 'Inter-linkage of Land, labour and Credit, Village Survey Data in East India, *Economic and Political Weekly*, Nos. 6 & 7, Vol. XIII, February, pp.367-384.

————(1980), 'Types of Labour Attachment in Agriculture : Results of a Survey in West Bengal, 1979', *Economic and Political Weekly*, Vol.XV, No. 35, August 30, pp.1477-1484.

Bardhan, Pranab & Ashok Rudra (1981), 'Terms and Conditions of Labour Contracts in Agriculture: Results of a Survey in West Bengal 1979', *Oxford Bulletin of Economics and Statistics*, Vol.43, No.1, February, pp.89-111.

Bardhan, K.: 'Rural Employment, Wages and Labour Markets in India- A Survey of Research' - I, II & III, *Economic and Political Weekly*, Vol.XII, Nos. 26,27 & 28, June 25, July 2 & 9, pp.A.34-A.48; 1062-1074 & 1101-1118.

———— (1989), 'Poverty, Growth and Rural Labour Markets in India', *Economic and Political Weekly*, Vol.XXIV, No.12, March 25, pp.A.21-A38.

Bardhan, K.P. (1980), 'Interlocking Factor Markets and Agrarian Development: A Review of Issues', *Oxford Economic Papers*, Vol.32, No.1, March, pp.82-88.

Balakrishnan Pulapre (1984), 'On the Significance of Interlinked Factor Markets in Agrarian Economies', *The Indian Economic Journal*, Vol.31, No.4, April-June, pp.62-72.

Bansod, R.G. (1977), 'Shandies or the Village Weekly Markets', *The Administrator*, Vol.XXII, No.1, Spring, pp.399-402.

Bohle, Hans-George (1981), 'Spatio-Temporal Decision Making in South Indian Weekly Markets : An Investigation into Consumer/ Trader Perceptions and Preferences', *National Geographical Journal of India*, Vol.XXVII, parts 1 & 2, March-June, pp.1-13.

Bhattacharya, N. (1977), 'Rural Marketing and the Poor', *Kurukshetra*, Vol. XXVI, No.1, October, pp.36-40.

Bhaduri, Amit (1973), 'A Study in Agricultural Backwardness under Semi-Feudalism', *The Economic Journal*, March, Vol.83, No.329, pp.120-137.

Bharadwaj, Krishna & Das, P.K. (1975), 'Tenurial Conditions and Mode of Exploitation- A Study of Some Villages in Orissa', *Economic and Political Weekly*, Vol.X, Nos.5, 6 & 7, February, pp.221-240.

Baboo Balgovind (1986), 'Economic Exchanges in a Tribal Village', *Man in India*, Vol.66, No.2, June, pp.151-165.

Bromley, R.J., Symanski, Richard (et. al.) (1975), 'The Rationale of Periodic Markets', *Annals of the Association of American Geographers*, Vol.65, No.4, December, pp.530-537.

Balakrishna Mandira Dutta (1978), 'Rural Marketing : Myth and Reality', *Economic and Political Weekly*, Vol.XIII, No.34, August 26, pp.M.75-M.80.

Bottomley, Anthony (1964), 'The Structure of Internal Rates in Underdeveloped Areas', *Journal of Farm Economics*, Vol.46, No.2, May.

Baker, David (1991), 'State Policy, the Market Economy and Tribal Decline: The Central Provinces, 1861-1920', *The Indian Economic and Social History Review*, Vol.XXVIII, No.4, October-December, pp.341-370.

Bell Clive & Srinivasan, T.N. (1989), 'Interlinked Transactions in Rural Markets: An Empirical Study of Andhra Pradesh, Bihar and Punjab', *oxford Bulletin of Economics and Statistics*, Vol.51, No.1, February, pp.73-83.

Bhowmik, Sharit Kumar (1988), 'Development Perspectives for Tribals', *Economic and Political Weekly*, Vol.XXIII, No.20, May 14, pp.1005-1007.

Bose, Pradip Kumar (1981), 'Stratification Among Tribals in Gujarat', *Economic and Political Weekly*, Vol.XVI, No.6, February 7, pp.191-196.

Caplan, Lionel (1991), 'From Tribe to Peasant? The Limbus & the Nepalese State', *The Journal of Peasant Studies*, Vol.18, No.2, January, pp.305-321.

Chakravarti, Ila & Verma Rekha (1991), 'Marketing of a Minor Forest Produce (MFP) in Tribal Sub-Plan (TSP) Area through Co-operatives in Rajasthan', *The Indian Journal of Economics*, Vol.LXXI, No.282, January, pp.311-320.

Chattopadhyaya, Gouranga & De Barun (1969), 'Problem of Tribal Integration to Urban Industrial Society', *Economic and Political Weekly*, Vol.IV, No.52, December 27, pp.1985-1994.

Chaudhuri, Mamata (1976), 'Ancient Indian Tribes and their Integration into the Hindu Society', *Journal of the Indian Anthropological Society*, vol.II, No.2, pp.125-145.

Chandra Ramesh (1973), 'Market in a Tribal Village - Its Socio-Economic Implications among the Bhils', *Vanyajati*, Vol.XXI, No.2, April, pp.52-59.

Chattopadhyaya, M., & Bhattacharyya, R. (1984), 'Land, Labour and Credit Relations in a Peasant Movement Belt', *Social Scientist*, Vol.12, No.3, March, pp.36-51.

Deshpande, C.D. (1941), 'Market Villages and Periodic Fairs of Bombay and Karnataka', *The Indian Geographical Journal*, Madras, Vol.XVI, No.4, October-December, p.327.

Dalton, George (1978), 'Economics and Anthroplogy: Developing and Primitive Economies- Is Economic Anthropology of Interest to

Economists?, *The American Economic Review*, Vol.68, No.2, May, pp.23-27.

Dhankar, G.H.(1991), 'Survey and Planning of Rural Markets', *Agricultural Marketing*, Vol.XXXIV, No.3, October-December, pp.34-39.

Eighmy, T.H. (1972), 'Rural Periodic Markets and the Extension of an Urban System: A Western Nigeria Example', *Economic Geography*, Vol.48, No.3, July, pp.299-315.

Fernandes, Walter (1993), 'Editorial on the Review of Indigenous People', *Social Action*, Vol.43, No.1, January-March, pp.iii-v.

Gangopadhyay Shubhashis & Kunal Sengupta (1986), 'Inter-linkages in Rural Markets', *Oxford Economic papers*, Vol.38, No.1, March, pp.112-121.

Geertz, Clifford (1978), 'The Bazaar Economy: Information and Search in Peasant Marketing', *The American Economic Review*, Vol.68, No.2, May, pp.28-32.

Guha, B.S. (1939), 'The Aboriginal Races of India', *Science and Culture*, Vol.IV, No.12, pp.677-683.

————(1951), 'The Indian Aborigines and their Administration', *Journal of the Asiatic Science*, Vol.17, No.1, pp.19-44.

Guha Ramachandra (1983), 'Forestry in British and Post-British India - A Historical Analysis', *Economic and Political Weekly*, Vol.XVIII, No.44, October 29, pp.1882-1896.

Gupta, M.D. (1991), 'Land Alienation among Tripura Tribals', *Economic and Political Weekly*, Vol.XXVI, No.36, September 7, pp.2113-2118.

Harriss, B., & Harriss, J.(1984), '"Generative" or "Parasitic" Urbanism?, Some Observations from the recent History of a South Indian Market Town', *The Journal of Development Studies*, Vol.20, No.3, April, pp.82-101.

Hill, Polly & Smith, R.H.T. (1972), 'The Spatial and Temporal Synchronization of Periodic Markets: Evidence from four Emirates in Northern Nigeria', *Economic Geography*, Vol.48, No.3, July, pp.345-355.

Ibarra, Mario (1993), 'Annotations for a Chronology of Indigenous Peoples in International Law', *Social Action*, Vol.3, No.1, January-March, pp.49-59.

Iqbal, Farrukh (1983), 'The Demands for Funds by Agricultural Households: Evidence from Rural India', *The Journal of Development Studies,* Vol.20, No.1, October, pp.68-86.

Jain, H.C., & Sarawgi, A.K. (1981), 'A Study on the Impact of Farm Credit on Farm Income - Production and Employment in Selected Tribal Areas of Madhya Pradesh', *Land Bank Journal,* Vol.XX, No1., pp.53-59.

———(1982), 'A Comparative Study into the Impact of Farm Credit provided by the Co-operative and Commercial Banks in Tribal Areas of Madhya Pradesh', *Co-operative Perspective,* Vol.17, No.1, pp.61-69.

Jana, M.M. (1978), 'Hierarchy of Market Centres in Lower Silabati Basin', *Geographical Review of India,* Vol.40, No.2, June, pp.164-174.

Jay, Edward (1974), 'A Comparison of Tribal and Peasant Villages in India', *Journal of the Indian Anthropological Society,* Vol.9, No.1, pp.39-69.

Jha, Mithileshwar (1988), 'Rural Marketing: Some Conceptual Issues', *Economic and Political Weekly,* Vol.XXIII, No.9, February 27, pp.M.8-M.16.

Khasnabis, Ratan & Chakravarty, Jyotiprakash (1982), 'Tenancy, Credit and Agrarian Backwardness - Results of a Field Survey', *Economic and Political Weekly,* Vol.XVII, No.13, March 27, pp.A.21-A.32.

Kulkarni, S.D. (1980), 'Problems of Tribal Development in Maharashtra', *Economic and Political Weekly,* Vol.XV, No.38, September 20, pp.1598-1600.

———(1977), 'Monoploly Trade in Tribal Areas and Its Politics in Maharashtra', *Economic and Political Weekly,* Vol.XII, No.51, December 17, pp.2085-2087.

———(1979), 'Class and Caste in a Tribal Movement', *Economic and Political Weekly,* Vol.XIV, Nos. 7 and 8, Annual Number, pp.465-468.

Kurien, C.T. (1987), 'State and Market in Economic Processes : Some Basic Issues', *Economic and Political Weekly,* Vol.XXII, Nos. 19, 20 and 21, Annual Number, May, pp.AN.21-AN.34.

Mahalingam, S. (1989), 'Tribal Groups and Market Development in India', *Journal of Rural Development,* Vol.8, No.2, pp.135-145.

———(1991), 'Institutional Finance for Marketing of Agricultural Produce of Tribals: Key Issues and Challenges', *Agricultural Marketing,* Vol.XXXIV, No.3, October-December, pp.18-24:

Mahendra Dev, S., M.H. Suryanarayana, & Kirit S. Parikh (1992), 'Rural Poverty in India: Incidence, Issues and Policies', *Asian Development Review,* Vol.10, No.1, January-June, pp.35-66.

Manohar, K. Murali & Ramaiah, P. (1982), 'Marketing through Girijan Co-operative Corporation', *Indian Journal of Marketing,* Vol.XII, No.7, March, pp.9-12.

Mckim, Wayne (1972), 'The Periodic Market System in North-Eastern Ghana', *Economic Geography,* Vol.48, No.3, July, pp.333-344.

Minz, Normal (1993), 'Cultural Identity of Tribals in India', *Social Action,* Vol.43, No.1, January-March, pp.32-40.

Mody, Ashoka (1982), 'Growth, Distribution and the Evaluation of Agricultural Markets - Some Hypotheses', *Economic and Political Weekly,* Vol.XVII, Nos. 1 and 2 January 2-9, pp.25-38.

Mohan, M. (1970), 'The Dynamic Concept of Marketing', *Economic and Political Weekly,* Vol.V, No.22, May 30, pp.M.59-M.64.

Mukhopadhyaya, Tarasish (1967), 'Ecology and Markets in Eastern Midnapur', *Man in India,* Vol.47, No.1, January-March, pp.61-73.

Nabi, Ijaz (1985), 'Rural Factor Market Imperfections and the Incidence of Tenancy in Agriculture', *Oxford Economic Papers,* Vol.37, No.2, June, pp.319-329.

Naidu, N.Y.(1972), 'Tribal Revolt in Parvatipuram Agency', *Economic and Political Weekly,* Vol.VII, No.48, November 25, pp.2337-2344.

Pathy Jaganath (1989), 'The Idea of Tribe and the Indian Scene', *Man in India,* Vol.69, No.4, December, pp.346-358.

Pathy Suguna (1993), 'Political Economy of the Ethnic Pepoles in India: Some Reflections', *Social Action,* Vol.43, No.1, January-March, pp.41-48.

Pawar, J.R. et. al. (1984), 'Pattern of Borrowing and Repayment of Loans of the Farms in the Tribal Sub-plan Areas of Western Maharashtra', *Tribal Research Bulletin,* Vol.VI, No.1, pp.10-12.

Perlin, Frank (1984), 'Growth of Money Economy and Some Questions of Transition in late pre-colonial India', *The Journal of Peasant Studies,* Vol.11, No.3, April, pp.96-107.

Prasad, Pradhan, H. (1973), 'Production Relations: Achilles', Heel of Indian Planning', *Economic and Political Weekly,* Vol.VIII, No.19, May 12, pp.869-872.

————(1974), 'Reactionary Role of Usurers' Capital in Rural India', *Economic and Political Weekly,* Vol.9, Special Number, August,, pp.1305-1308.

Radhakrishna, Meena (1989), 'From Tribal Community to Working Class Consciousness - Case of Yerukula Women', *Economic and Political Weekly,* Vol.XXIV, No.17, April 29, pp.WS.2-WS.6.

Rao, J.M. (1988), 'Fragmented Rural labour Markets', *The Journal of Peasant Studies,* Vol.15, No.2, January, pp.238-257.

————(1988), 'Interest Rates in Backward Agriculture', *Cambridge Journal of Economics,* Vol.4, No.2, January, pp.159-167.

Rao, V.M. (1974), 'Village Lease Markets for Agricultural Land - Some Approaches for Analysis', *Economic and Political Weekly,* Vol.IX, No.26, June 29, pp.A.55-A.62.

Roy Burman, J.J. (1990), 'A Need for Reappraisal of Minor Forest Produce Policies., *The Indian Journal of Social Work,* Vol.LI, No.4, October, pp.649-658.

Roy Burman, B.K.(1983), 'Transformation of Tribes and Analogous Social Formations', *Economic and Political Weekly* Vol.XVIII, No.27, July 2, pp.1172-1174.

————(1990), 'Land and Forest Rights', *Seminar,* (366), February, pp.25-29.

————(1992), 'Indigenous and Tribal Peoples, Global Hegemonies and Government of India', *Mainstream,* Vol.XXX, No.46, September 5, pp.31-35.

————(1989), 'Problems and Prospects of Tribal Development in North-East India', *Economic and Political Weekly,* Vol.XXIV, No.13, April 1, pp.693-697.

Reddy, N. Subba (1989), 'Sword of Damocles over Tribal People of Andhra Pradesh', *Economic and Political Weekly,* July 1, Vol.XXIV, No.20, pp.1442-1445.

Reddy, T. Prabhakar (1989), 'Tribal land Alienation in Andhra Pradesh', *Economic and Political Weekly,* Vol.XXIV, No.28, July 15, pp.1571-1573.

Reddy Narayana, M.V. (1992), 'Interlinkages of Credit with Factor and Product Markets- A Study in Andhra Pradesh', *Indian Journal of Agricultural Economics,* Vol.47, No.4, October-December, pp.618-630.

Sanders Douglas (1993), 'Indigenous Peoples on the International Stage', *Social Action,* Vol.43, No.1, January-March, pp.1-7.

Sarap, Kailas (1991), 'Collateral and Other Forms of Guarantee in Rural Credit Markets - Evidence from Eastern India', *Indian Economic Review,* Vol.XXVI, No.2, July-December, pp.167-188.

Sarap, Kailas (1991), 'Changing Contractual Arrangement in Agriculture Labour Market : Evidence from Orissa, *Economic and Political Weekly,* Vol.XXVI, No.52, December 28, pp.A.167-A.176.

Sen, Jyoti (1960), 'Missionary Activities in Chotanagpur', *Journal of Social Research,* Ranchi, Vol.3, No.2, pp.128-131.

Sengupta, Nirmal (1980), 'Class and Tribe in Jharkhand', *Economic and Political Weekly,* Vol.XV, No.14, April 5, pp.664- 671.

Shah, Ghanshyam (1979), 'Tribal Identity and Class Differentiations - A Case Study of the Chaudhri Tribe', *Economic and Political Weekly,* Vol.XIV, Nos. 7 and 8, (Annual Number), February, pp.459-464.

Singh, R.L., & Singh, Rana, P.B. (1977), 'Spatial and Structural Analysis of the Rural Market Network and its Relation to Society in an Indian Environment', *The National Geographical Journal of India,* Vol.XXIII, Parts 3 and 4, September-December, pp.151-159.

Singh, Shiw Mangal (1965), 'The Stability Theory of Rural Central Place Development', *National Geographical Journal of India,* Vol.II, pp.13-21.

Singh, K.S (1982), 'Transformation of Tribal Society- Integration Vs. Assimilation', *Economic & Political Weekly,* Vol.XVII, No.33, August 14, 1982, pp.1318-1325 & Vol.XVII, No.34, August 21, pp.1376-1384.

Sinha Surajit (1965), 'Tribe- Caste and Tribe- Peasant Continua in Central India', *Man in India,* Vol.45, No.1, January-March, pp.57-83.

————(1962), 'State Formation and Rajput Myth in Tribal Central India', *Man in India,* Vol.42, No.1, January-March, pp.35-80.

————(1951), 'The Weekly Market at Bannri– A Village in South Manbhum', *Geographical Review of India,* 13(4), p.20.

————(1958), 'Tribal Cultuers of Peninsular India as a Dimension of Little Tradition in the Study of Indian Civilisation: A

Preliminary Statement', *Journal of American Folklore*, vol.71, No.279, pp.504-518.

Skinner, G. William (1964-1965) 'Marketing and Social Structure for Rural China', *Journal of Asian Studies*, Vol.XXIV, pp.3-44, 195-228 and 263-299.

Srivastava, Ravi (1989), 'Interlinked Modes of Exploitation in Indian Agriculture During Transition: A Case Study', *The Journal of Peasant Studies*, Vol.16, No.4, July, pp.493-522.

Srivastava Pradeep (1992), 'Are Formal and Informal Credit Markets in India Interlinked?', *Economic and Political Weekly*, Vol.XXVII, No.41, October 10, pp.2241-2245.

Srinivasan, T.N (1979), 'Agricultural Backwardness under Semi-Feudalism- Comment', *The Economic Journal*, Vol.89, No.354, June, pp.416-419.

Stine, James, H. (1962), 'Temporal Aspects of Teritiary Production Elements in Korea', *Urban Systems and Economic Development*, Oregon, pp.68-88.

Tamaskar, B.G. (1978), 'Geographic Perspective on Periodic Marketing System and Network in the Chhattisgarh Plan', *Geographic Review of India*, Vol.40, No.1, March, pp.15-24.

————(1955), 'Patharia- A Study of the Settlement Pattern and Weekly Market', *Geographical Review of India*, Vol.XVII, No.4, December, pp.1-12.

Trivedi, Harshad, R.(1989), 'Nehru and Tribals', *The Indian Journal of Public Administraiton*, Vol.XXXV, No.2, April-June, pp.286-291.

————(1991), 'Planning and Tribal Development', *The Indian Journal of Public Administration*, Vol.XXXVII, No.2, April-June, pp.182-198.

Trenk, Martin (1990), 'The Rediscovery of the "Oriental Money-lenders"', *Economics*, Vol.41, pp.96-111.

Thusu, K.N. (1965), 'The Weekly Market at Leda- A Village in South-East Bastar', *Vanyajati*, Vol.XIII, No.4, October, pp.149-160.

Venugopal, C.N. (1967), 'Analysis of a Weekly Market', *The Indian Journal of Social Work*, Vol.XXVIII, No.3, October, pp.335-337.

REPORTS AND OTHER GOVERNMENT PUBLICATIONS

A Brief Report on *Shandies in Agency areas of Visakhaptnam District*, Undertaken by the Regional Centre, Paderu, January, 1986.

A brief notes on the activities of the GCC Ltd. Warangal Division, Palwancha Division and Utnoor Division.

Ayyappan Committee Report, 1948.

Census of India Reports and other related Census Abstracts of 1951, 1961, 1971, 1981 and 1991, Manager Publications, Government of India, New Delhi.

Committee of the House Report on *The Girijan Co-operative Corporation*, Andhra Pradesh Legislative Assembly, Government of Andhra Pradesh Publications, Hyderabad, 1976.

Executive Instructions to the Managers and other field staff of the GCC Ltd., Visakhapatnam, date 23-11-1977.

Facts and Figures, 1993, Issued by the Principal Chief Conservator of Forests, Andhra Pradesh, Hyderabad.

Handbooks of Statistics, Khammam, Warangal and Adilabad Districts, 1992-93.

ITDA, *Annual Action Plan*, 1987-88, Eturnagaram, Warangal.

Malayyapan Committee Report, 1952.

Mandal Gananka Darshinies of Dammapet, Tadvai and Indravelli Mandals, Published by the respective Chief Planning Officers of the concerned Districts, 1991-92.

Pratap, D.R.: Report on *A Study of the Andhra Pradesh Scheduled Tribes', Co-operative Finance and Development Corporation Ltd.*, TCR and TI, Hyderabad, 1968.

Raghava Rao, D.V. "Marketing of Produce and Indebtedness among Tribals"- Report on a Study in Chintalapalli Block, Visakhapatnam District, Agro-Economic Research Centre, Waltair, June 1973.

Royal Commission Report on *Agriculture in India*, 1928

Report on *Fairs, Markets and Produce Exchanges in India*, Published by Government of India, 1943.

Report of the Committee on *Setting-up of a National Level Federation of Tribal Development Co-operative Corporations* (TRIFED), Government of India, Ministry of Home Affairs, New Delhi, 1985.